Women and Work:
A Research and Policy Series

The Sage Series **Women and Work: A Research and Policy Series** brings together research, critical analysis, and proposals for change in a dynamic and developing field—the world of women and work. Cutting across traditional academic boundaries, the series approaches subjects from a multidisciplinary perspective. Historians, anthropologists, economists, sociologists, managers, psychologists, educators, policymakers, and legal scholars share insights and findings—giving readers access to a scattered literature in single, comprehensive volumes.

Women and Work examines differences among women—as well as differences between men and women—related to nationality, ethnicity, social class, and sexual preference. The Series explores demographic and legal trends, international and multinational comparisons, and theoretical and methodological developments.

Women in Management

Trends, Issues, and Challenges in Managerial Diversity

Edited by

Ellen A. Fagenson

Volume 4

Women and Work
A Research and Policy Series

ISSN 0882-0910

SAGE Publications
International Educational and Professional Publisher
Newbury Park   London   New Delhi

For information address:

SAGE Publications, Inc.
2455 Teller Road
Newbury Park, California 91320

SAGE Publications Ltd.
6 Bonhill Street
London EC2A 4PU
United Kingdom

SAGE Publications India Pvt. Ltd.
M-32 Market
Greater Kailash I
New Delhi 110 048 India

Printed in the United States of America

Library of Congress Cataloging-in-Publication Data

ISBN 0-8039-4592-2 (p)
ISBN 0-8039-4591-4 (c)
ISSN 0882-0910

93 94 95 96 97 10 9 8 7 6 5 4 3 2 1

Sage Production Editor: Astrid Virding

658.0082
Wom

Contents

Section V: Challenges

This book is dedicated to my mother, father, brother, husband, and Dorothy Reed, who have all contributed to this book by providing me with support, humor, encouragement, and inspiration. Without the unconditional love of Merlin, Casey, Suzie-Q, Mrs. Bojangles, and all the homeless cats I fostered while writing this book, it would not have been written.

Acknowledgments

I would like to thank the many individuals who helped in the review process of the chapters included in this book: the Editorial Review Board and the following ad hoc reviewers, Lotte Bailyn, Gerald Barrett, Radha Chaganti, Leonard Chusmir, Taylor Cox, Jennie Farley, Sara Freedman, Joy Schneer, and Lois Verbugge. A special thanks is sent to Laurie Larwood, Barbara Gutek, and Harry Briggs for their guidance and support and to Ann Stromberg for her thoughtful comments.

Also acknowledged are my mother, Sue Fagenson, Debbie Becker, Laurie Kaufman Amber, Sheila Kraft Budoff, Dorothy Reed, and Rosalie Zuckerman as professional-managerial women much admired.

Series Editors' Introduction

The **Women and Work** series is designed to serve as a stage. With the inaugural volume in 1985 and two subsequent volumes, the series has brought together research from a variety of disciplines focusing on women's paid and unpaid work experiences. The authors chosen were scholars representing current thinking in one of the many disciplines in which research on women and work is found. Many chapters summarize a significant stream of research while others present unusual perspectives or unique departures that deserve broader recognition.

The series is based on the notion that being multidisciplinary is essential to a deep understanding of the situation of working women. Progress will be made in the field of women and work to the extent that researchers in sociology and history can be understood by others in management and political science or psychology and anthropology. We made an effort as editors to ensure that the volumes we published included contributions from various disciplines, with the intent that, together, they would cross-fertilize the emerging new discipline of women and work. Thus Volume 1 included chapters representing economics, sociology, psychology, history, and education; Volume 2 contained a health symposium with contributions from medicine, public health, economics, and law; and the international issues symposium in

Volume 3 represented sociology, political science, anthropology, and psychology.

Research on women and work seems to be coming together rapidly. Ideas are widely shared and broadly understood across disciplines. The shared thinking has moved the field much more swiftly than any of us might have believed possible a decade ago. The phenomenon has also brought us a broader colleague base than any traditional discipline allowed and has in fact allowed our thinking to become more widely accepted in our parent disciplines.

This and the following volumes of the **Women and Work** series will maintain the commitment to publishing current and creative research in interdisciplinary volumes, but these volumes also represent a new departure in several ways. When we began, it was difficult to identify topics on women and work in which there was sufficient current research to support an entire volume. With the rapid growth of the field, however, there is now ample material to examine single topics in depth. Beginning with the current volume, most will have a guest volume editor and will be centered on a single topic of acknowledged interest and importance. The material for the volumes will represent thinking across the traditional disciplines—not from a single perspective. As before, we intend that the work will be insightful—both summative of research and provocative in its presentation of new thinking.

This volume, guest edited by Ellen Fagenson, is the first in the new format. Professor Fagenson, among the leading writers in the area of women in management, has focused the volume entirely on women in that field. The researchers whom she has carefully selected represent a cross section of the top researchers in the field and bring a wide variety of perspectives to bear on some of the most important questions facing our economic system.

The guest volume editors themselves may introduce innovations in format. Fagenson does this, for example, by including commentaries on scholars' chapters by others who are in a position to assess their relevance. She believes that the further understanding of the experiences of women in management requires everyone's contribution.

Management is well suited to be the topic for the first volume in our new format, as it is symbolic of the newly available opportunities for professional women over the past few decades. The history of women in management, in numbers as well as in importance, has been closely connected with the rhythm and health of the women's movement. That substantial progress has been made is easily seen. That there is much more progress needed and work to be done is indisputable. Women have moved up but have not reached the top. Women in management are doing important tasks but have not advanced to the top positions in anywhere near the numbers that their growing representation in the work force would suggest. Life-styles and workplace policies have adjusted somewhat toward accommodating women managers, but they have not produced a situation that most observers would label as equal for women and men. What are the implications of the changes? And what are the causes of the lack of change? What can, and what should, be done? These are the topics of the current volume.

Although managerial women may be seen to represent professional women in many ways, they certainly do not represent all women or even a major portion. Compared with those in the female work force as a whole, managerial women are generally well educated and middle class, most often white, and more likely to be fully employed. Successful women in management are also less likely to be married and they have smaller families. Future volumes will address the experiences of other groups of women workers.

—*Laurie Larwood*
Barbara A. Gutek
Ann Stromberg

SECTION I

Trends

1

Diversity in Management: Introduction and the Importance of Women in Management

ELLEN A. FAGENSON

In a cartoon featured in a popular magazine, a humorous yet poignant statement about the lives of women managers is made. The cartoon features a woman with her eyes closed sitting next to a podium as she is being introduced: "Our featured speaker is a woman who has done it all—challenging job, a wonderful family, PTA president, a prominent civic leader. Please applaud loudly to wake her up!" (Schwadron, 1991).

Consistent with an old Chinese proverbial curse, "May you have an interesting life," for better or worse, women managers today lead very *interesting*, busy, and challenging lives. Indeed, more women are landing jobs in the managerial ranks than ever before. Few, however, are obtaining positions of significant corporate power. When managerial women are on track to experience traditional definitions of success, they often encounter unique problems. How can they manage having a family and a satisfying career? How can they ensure that their experiences and concerns will be taken seriously, and given priority, and that each, individually, will be treated with respect by the male community? The authors in this book offer intriguing answers to these types of questions, shedding light on the *very* interesting lives of women managers.

Women managers' backgrounds, experiences, circumstances, and environments are multidimensional. Women managers function in the home and the workplace. This book examines their relationships with men in these two life domains. Women have made the ranks of management more diverse, but as a group they are not monolithic. We explore their racial and ethnic diversity and their treatment and experiences historically and internationally in search of significant patterns. The business world is not evenhanded in its treatment of men and women managers and we debate whether discrimination against women managers will ever cease. The book examines how women managers are faring in the legal system and whether the management experience has been a significant source of stress for them. We also consider whether traditional management philosophy and practice are optimal for women and evaluate whether women managers would be "better off" if organizations were restructured to incorporate a feminist philosophy and approach to management.

This book focuses on women managers' "triumphs and tribulations," their past and current time, and it ventures predictions about their futures. It chronicles the experiences of women managers and the impact they have had within and beyond the walls of organizations.

BACKGROUND

Women have become enduring figures in the workplace and in the management profession (Packer & Johnston, 1988; U.S. Department of Labor, 1991). Yet, as the statistics reveal, this has not always been the case (Fagenson & Jackson, in press). In 1900, when 19% of all women were working outside the home, women constituted 4.4% of the managerial work force. By 1950, women were 33.9% of the labor force and 13.6% of management professionals. In 1990, employed women constituted 45.6% of the labor force and, as of 1992, 41.5% of managers (U.S. Department of Labor, 1993). It is predicted that by the year 2000 the majority of new entrants into the labor force will be women and even more women will pursue management careers (Packer & Johnston, 1988). Thus women are becoming an increasing segment of the labor force as a whole and the management profession in particular.

While women's numbers in the management profession are on the rise, women are still largely clustered in lower and, to a lesser extent, middle-level management positions (U.S. Department of Labor, 1990a).

They have yet to make their mark in significant numbers in upper management levels, currently representing only 5% of senior executives (U.S. Department of Labor, 1991). Much attention has been given to women's struggle to crack through this proverbial "glass ceiling" and assume positions in the upper echelons of organizations. Yet, few significant inroads have been made. In fact, once conceived as the barrier that keeps women from high-level management positions, the glass ceiling is now recognized as existing at the middle levels of management (U.S. Department of Labor, 1991).

Nevertheless, women's membership in the management field has helped to bring new issues to the fore of this profession. Dual-career dilemmas, child-care concerns, and parental leaves have moved to center stage now that many women are employed and increasing numbers of them have become managers (Greenhaus, Bedian, & Mossholder, 1987; Gutek, Searle, & Klepa, 1991; Sekaran, 1986). Evidence suggesting that women managers have a transformational, democratic, and/or "web" rather than hierarchical style of leadership and more satisfied subordinates than men managers has raised questions about the appropriateness and effectiveness of a masculine military model of management in corporate settings (Bass, 1991; Eagly & Johnson, 1990; Lodan, 1985; Rosener, 1990). Documented cases of discrimination and sexual harassment of women managers have spearheaded organizational policies and legal reforms to help ensure that women are duly processed for promotions, pay, and partnerships (Morrison & Von Glinow, 1990; *Price Waterhouse v. Hopkins,* 1989). As more and more women have become managers, the dynamics of office interactions have changed; men are increasingly working with women as their peers, supervisors, and subordinates. Women managers have had an important impact on the nature of relationships at work and home and on the manner in which international business is conducted. They are helping to change the fabric of our society as we know it today. *Women in Management: Trends, Issues, and Challenges in Managerial Diversity* traces women managers' experiences using an interdisciplinary, broad-based analysis.

THEORETICAL FRAMEWORK

Since the 1970s, women managers' experiences and impact on the workplace have been the subject of much discussion, investigation, and theorizing (Powell, 1988). An approach often taken to the study of gender diversity in management is known as the "person-centered" or "gender-centered" approach (Horner, 1972; Riger & Galligan, 1980; Terborg, 1977). This framework argues that gender influences men and women's behaviors, attitudes, traits, and the like and encourages comparisons between women and men to evaluate the occurrence of gender-based differences. When gender differences are found, they are often attributed to differences in women's and men's biological heritage and/or their socialization patterns (Powell, 1988; Riger & Galligan, 1980).

While the gender-centered perspective has proven useful in the analysis of women managers' experiences, actions, and impact in organizations, it has been criticized for ignoring situational variables in organizations that may be orchestrating women's and men's movements, behaviors, attitudes, etc. (Fagenson, 1990a, 1990b; Kanter, 1977; Riger & Galligan, 1980). According to an alternative theory—that is, the situation or organization structure perspective—the perceptions, beliefs, and behaviors of men and women managers are a function of the different organizational structures they experience (Kanter, 1977). Women are typically few in number in the management ranks, are placed in positions with little job mobility and opportunity, and are vested with little organizational power as compared with men (Kanter, 1977; Mainiero, 1986). According to this perspective, any observable differences in the behavior, attitudes, traits, etc. of men and women managers are attributed to such structural and situational factors.

A third approach, the gender-organization-system (GOS) perspective, agrees with the basic tenets of both the theories presented above and makes two additional assumptions: (a) An individual and his or her organization cannot be understood separate from the society (culture) in which he or she works, and (b) when the individual, the organization, or the system in which they are embedded changes, the other components change as well. Systemic factors that can influence individuals and organizations include but are not limited to laws, policies, sex role stereotypes, expectations, ideologies, cultural values, and histories (Fagenson, 1990b; Martin, Harrison, & Dinnito, 1983). The GOS approach further suggests that the organizational context affects individuals' behaviors, experiences, and orientations. The organizational context includes such factors as corporate policies, history, ideology, and culture as well as the organization's structure. Thus the GOS model examines the status and experiences of women (and men) in organizations but also the organizational and societal system in which they function. Differences in men and women managers' behavior, attitudes, traits, etc. are attributed to individual, organizational, and/or systemic factors.

The GOS perspective was used as the organizing framework for the selection of topics in this book. It suggests the use of several levels of analysis (systemic, organizational, and individual) to explain the experiences, actions, and impact of women managers. While a number of topics could be investigated using this paradigm, not all can be covered in this one volume. Readers are urged to consult earlier volumes of **Women and Work** to supplement their study of women in management issues.

The GOS perspective was also used as an overarching guide by the book's authors in their approach to their individual topics. This was done to provide consistency across chapters and a broad-based analysis within each chapter while still allowing each to retain its own identity. Some of the chapters' subject matter lent itself to the application of this framework more than others and some authors supplemented this approach with other models.

AUDIENCE AND APPROACH

The book presents a summary and critical analysis of the key issues facing women managers today and suggests directions for their futures. The chapters in the book were written for academics and scholars in many disciplines and for managers and others employed in organizations. The literature reviews, critical analyses, and research agendas should be especially appealing to academics/scholars. Individuals who work for or with women managers, are women managers themselves, or share their lives with them should also find this book informative as it will provide a descriptive account of women managers' experiences, goals, and expectations and evaluate the demands placed upon them.

A cross-disciplinary approach is taken in this book. The authors contributing to this volume are experts in the fields of psychology, sociology, policy, law, economics, management, journalism, education, and history as well as gender studies. Thus the volume should appeal not only to individuals in management but to individuals in other disciplines as well.

Women managers are part of the female labor force and thus have issues in common with many other women workers, such as balancing job and family concerns, job-related stress, pay equity, and equal opportunity. They are, however, a relatively distinct group, and some of their experiences are particular to their field. This book addresses issues and experiences that are both common to all employed women and distinct for women managers.

THE SECTIONS, CHAPTERS, AND COMMENTARIES

The chapters are grouped into sections with overarching themes. The sections discuss timely and important issues for women in management. A commentary is presented at the end of each section following this first introductory section. The purpose of the commentaries is to highlight the most important elements of each chapter, determine common themes across chapters, and raise thought-provoking issues.

The second section of the book, "Historical and Global Issues," looks at the history of women managers and examines their status and experiences within an international context. The third section, "Individual and Organizational Issues," explores differences among women managers, their personal experiences, interactions with men in the workplace, and the interface between their family and organizational lives. The fourth section, "Future Directions and Systemic Issues," focuses on matters that transcend organizations and/or have the potential to transform organizations and the individuals in them. While each of these sections is followed by a commentary, the book concludes with the "Final Commentary," which discusses all of the chapters. It should be noted that the sections are "fluid." That is, material covered in one section may be relevant to material covered in other sections.

In the first chapter in the "Historical and Global Issues" section (Chapter 2), "In the Beginning: A History of Women in Management," historian Sara Alpern traces women's journey into management positions in the United States from colonial days until the 1980s. Alpern analyzes women's entry into the labor force and their specific contributions as businesswomen. The effects of sex role expectations, wars, women's networks, constitutional amendments, and laws on women's access to managerial positions are examined. The author pays particular attention to female entrepreneurs of the past two centuries who paved the way for business-minded women of today. The chapter concludes with a brief analysis of women's place in corporations from the 1960s through the 1980s.

In Chapter 3, "A Global Comparison of Women in Management: Women Managers in Their Homelands and as Expatriates," sociologists Ariane Berthoin Antal and Dafna Izraeli examine the status of women managers around the world. The chapter highlights the usefulness of a cross-national approach to studying the general situation of women managers. The authors compare women managers from several countries, paying particular attention to those of Western Europe, Israel, and Japan. A cross-cultural analysis is used to critique accepted assumptions about women's limited progress in management and to evaluate the major barriers they face. The authors highlight legislation and public policy, corporate programs, and interventions undertaken by international organizations to improve the status of women managers. The chapter also takes a close look at women as expatriate managers—managers assigned to foreign countries—in (mainly) U.S. multinational corporations. The authors offer a critique of reasons commonly given for the paucity of women expatriate managers and evaluate current predictions, which suggest that an increasing proportion of expatriate managers will be women. The chapter closes with a discussion of the role of international organizations in promoting change and highlights challenges for the research community.

Jennie Farley's comments on Chapters 2 and 3 complete the first section of the book. In her analysis of these chapters, labor relations professor Farley notes how women's opportunities expand in the business world during times of war and how opportunities are lacking when peace prevails. She identifies factors that predict women's emergence as business leaders and draws our attention to the similarity in arguments used (a) against sending women managers abroad and (b) to explain their failure to advance at home. She questions whether reforms advanced in the name of women managers are truly beneficial for them and whether we should hope, expect, or demand that women managers be "better" than their male counterparts.

Chapter 4, "Women of Color in Management: Toward an Inclusive Analysis," the first chapter in the "Individual and Organizational Issues" section, was written by Toni Denton, a professor of career and interdisciplinary studies, and management professors Ella Bell and Stella Nkomo. The chapter delineates the deficiencies in our knowledge about the experiences of women of color in management. The authors indicate that previous research about women managers has been based on individuals who are white and privileged, culminating in little being known about women of color in management. Three conceptual models—

intergroup theory, the bicultural model, and the women's life context model—are discussed. These frameworks suggest some ways in which women's race and ethnicity contribute to women managers' experiences. More specifically, relationships among women who share or differ in their cultural identity are addressed by intergroup theory; the bicultural model examines relationships between minority and dominant group cultures; and the major life domains of a woman's world are addressed in the woman's life context model. The authors also propose a multifaceted research agenda to rectify management sciences's almost exclusive focus on white women in management while generalizing to all women in management. The research agenda calls for an examination of the factors affecting women's personal and professional relationships within cultural groups, across cultural groups, and within the larger social context. The chapter advocates use of multiple disciplines, application of a broad range of research methods, generation of new theory, and exploration of contemporary forms of racism and sexism.

The health of women managers is an important concern for women managers, their families, and their organizations. In Chapter 5, "Stress and the Woman Manager: Sources, Health Outcomes, and Interventions," psychologists Lynn Offermann and Michele Armitage examine stress and its effect on the health of women managers. The authors consider three major sources of stress—stress generated from society at large, by organizations, and by the women themselves. The authors focus on factors involved in stress production and health outcomes that are either unique to women managers (e.g., tokenism) or that appear to express themselves differently for men and women managers (e.g., career-family interface). Three categories of intervention options designed to reduce stress are presented: systemic options (e.g., laws, community support), organizational options (e.g., training and development), and individual options (e.g., relaxation training, biofeedback). The authors conclude by proposing important issues for future research and application.

Chapter 6, "Dangerous Liaisons? A Review of Current Issues Concerning Male and Female Romantic Relationships in the Workplace," written by management scholar Lisa Mainiero, poses and answers the question: Should women enter into romantic relationships at work? In this chapter, Mainiero examines coworker suspicions and fears, the positive and negative outcomes of romantic relationships on work group morale, gender-related stereotypes concerning office romances, the impact of public knowledge on the liaison, the risks associated with being romantically involved, and potential legal entanglements. The stress and role conflicts that office romancers experience and the impact of the romance on the couple's productivity and their career advancement are also evaluated. Mainiero explores the perspectives of participants and observers. A model of the power dynamics in office romances is presented to explain why hierarchical romances generally are more negatively evaluated by coworkers than romances between peers. Mainiero concludes with suggestions for future research and management intervention strategies.

Clarence Darrow once said that "the first half of our life is ruined by our parents, the second half by our children." Chapter 7, "Personal Portrait: The Life-Style of the Woman Manager," written by management professors Saroj Parasuraman and Jeffrey Greenhaus, may prompt some readers to question whether we should also include "spouse and work" after "children" in Darrow's poignant and cynical observation! This chapter discusses women managers' experiences in the career and family domains and, unlike Darrow's analysis, paints a more even-handed picture of the lives of women managers. The authors begin with an examination of the impact of women managers' career experiences on their family lives. Research that compares managerial women's and men's career aspirations, interruptions, advancement opportunities as well as their salary levels, job attitudes, job performance, and job involvement is reviewed and critiqued. This is followed by a discussion of the impact of family experiences on women managers' careers. The authors review women versus men managers' marital and parental status, analyze spousal characteristics, and evaluate the structure of marital relationships with respect to income, career priority, gender role ideology, leisure, parenthood, housework, child care, and commuter marriages. Parasuraman and Greenhaus end the chapter with conclusions regarding alternative life-styles and propose and discuss a typology of managerial women consisting of the "career-primary," the "family-primary," and the "career-family" woman.

A commentary by Mary Anne Devanna, Director of Columbia University's Executive MBA program, rounds out the "Individual and Organizational Issues" section of the book. She critically draws the reader's attention to our tendency to zealously look for differences between men and women rather than noticing differences within each gender. Moreover, Devanna discusses how the values of society are enacted in organizations and examines the trade-offs that men and women must make to be successful in their careers and personal lives.

The final section of the book contains three chapters that focus on future directions and systemic issues influencing the status of women managers. In Chapter 8, "Point-Counterpoint: Discrimination Against Women in Management—Going, Going, Gone or Going But Never Gone?" two points of view are presented. The first position, argued by management professor Gregory Northcraft, contends that discrimination against women in management—described as overt or covert differential treatment based on gender—will disappear, and the other position, argued by psychologist and management professor Barbara Gutek, contends that discrimination will never disappear. The first argument is based on the managerial potential of women, the evolving norms and changing stereotypes in the workplace, and the principle that greater contact and familiarity with women managers breeds acceptance. Other promising trends toward the elimination of sex discrimination that are noted by Northcraft include increased sharing of parental responsibilities by men and women's efforts to help themselves through networking, mentoring, and running their own enterprises. Northcraft concludes by highlighting how women managers help organizations meet the bottom line.

In the second half of the chapter, Gutek presents several reasons why discrimination will never disappear. These include the salience of women's gender in a male-dominated profession, the unequal role responsibilities of women and men managers outside the workplace (e.g., family responsibilities), workplace factors that disadvantage women managers (e.g., job segregation, relocation, pay discrimination), and the limitations of legislative changes, as promising as they may seem (i.e., the associated cost factors and difficulty of implementation and enforcement). The chapter ends with Gutek and Northcraft finding some common ground.

Chapter 9, "The Legal and Political Realities for Women Managers: The Barriers, the Opportunities, and the Horizon Ahead," was written by Barbara Lee, attorney and professor of human resource management. In this chapter, Lee discusses how the courts and legislatures have responded to the concerns of women (and men) managers. Lee presents an overview of antidiscrimination laws often used to redress discrimination with particular attention paid to the 1991 Civil Rights Law. She also reviews the many barriers women face when they file legal claims, despite the protections offered by state and federal civil rights laws. The chapter includes a report of the outcomes of legal cases for women employees and managers and an analysis of their success rates. Lee also discusses recent U.S. Supreme Court decisions that have narrowed civil rights protections and analyzes their implications for women managers.

Chapter 9 also examines a series of gender-related problems that women managers may face and assesses how the courts and enforcement agencies have dealt with these problems. To this end, the chapter addresses fetal vulnerability policies, drawing our attention to the conflict between equal employment opportunity and the health of the unborn. Lee discusses the legality and practical implications of the controversial "mommy track" for all managers. She also outlines legal remedies for sexual harassment, sex discrimination, and romantic liaisons at work and analyzes women managers' disinclination to report these types of incidents when they occur. In addition, Lee comments on pending legislation. The chapter ends by questioning and evaluating the ability of corporations and legal and political systems to dismantle the barriers faced by women managers.

Chapter 10, "Feminist Practice in Organizations: Implications for Management," was written by sociologist Patricia Yancey Martin. The author submits that feminism, defined as a political orientation and practice that strives to improve the status of women, can reform corporate management. The author argues that women managers are devalued in a corporate context that is predominately masculine and gendered to women's detriment. Eight feminist practices are presented that Martin contends can be employed to enhance women's status and improve organizational effectiveness, that is, questioning corporate practices that are detrimental to women, using feminist practical reasoning, raising consciousness about women's experiences, promoting a sense of community and cooperation, advocating nurturance and caring, promoting democracy and participation, empowering subordinates, and striving for transformational outcomes. Martin concludes with an evaluation of the costs and benefits of feminist management for women, the corporation, and majority men.

Heidi Hartmann, an economist and policy analyst, comments on the chapters in this final section. She considers whether women managers have been duped into believing that things will be fair, that everything will work out, and that they can succeed in a man's world. She discusses how women managers can come to terms with unpleasant workplace realities as well as change them for women's betterment.

Chapter 11, "Final Commentary," was written by management professor Janice Jackson, and myself, Ellen Fagenson, management professor, psychologist, and the book's editor. In this final section, we highlight recurring themes in the book and critique and analyze the issues discussed by the other chapter authors. We explore emerging trends, evaluate unfounded assumptions, refute myths, highlight directions for future research, and present recommendations to improve the situation of women managers. Issues addressed in this chapter include the nonhomogeneity of women of color and white women, the pro-male bias in the medical research community, the importance of understanding women managers' behavior in a white male work and societal context, the devaluation of women and work performed by them, the careers and perceptions of women managers married to versus not married to men in their fields, the benefits of women's business ownership, the positive change in status that can occur for women managers working abroad, the advantages of "feminine" traits and managerial mothers, the impact of progressive and nonprogressive actions undertaken in organizations and in the legal sphere on women managers.

The purpose of this book is to enhance and expand our understanding of women in management in a meaningful way. It is expected that, after completing this book, the reader will have had many questions answered and even more raised. The stories of women managers are unfolding. Are their futures bright? Are they destined to lead "interesting" lives? The information contained in the chapters ahead will help the reader formulate answers to these intriguing questions.

REFERENCES

Bass, B. (1991, January-February). Debate: Is it time to stop talking about gender differences? *Harvard Business Review*, pp. 151-153.

Eagly, A., & Johnson, B. T. (1990). Gender and leadership style: A meta-analysis. *Psychological Bulletin, 108*, 233-256.

Fagenson, E. A. (1990a). Perceived masculine and feminine attributes examined as a function of individuals' sex and level in the organizational power hierarchy: A test of four theoretical perspectives. *Journal of Applied Psychology, 75*, 204-211.

Fagenson, E. A. (1990b). At the heart of women in management research: Theoretical and methodological approaches and their biases. *Journal of Business Ethics, 9*, 267-274.

Fagenson, E. A., & Jackson, J. J. (in press). The status of women managers in the United States. In N. Adler & D. Izraeli (Eds.), *Competitive frontiers: Women managers in a global economy*. Boston: Basil Blackwell.

Greenhaus, J. H., Bedian, A. G., & Mossholder, K. W. (1987). Work experiences, job performances and feelings of personal and family well being. *Journal of Vocational Behavior, 31*, 200-215.

Gutek, B. A., Searle, S., & Klepa, L. (1991). Rational vs. gender role explanations for work-family conflict. *Journal of Applied Psychology, 76*, 560-568.

Horner, M. (1972). Toward an understanding of achievement related conflicts in women. *Journal of Social Issues, 28,* 157-176.

Kanter, R. M. (1977). *Men and women of the corporation.* New York: Basic Books.

Kaplan, D. L., & Case, M. C. (1958). *Occupations trends in the United States, 1900-1950.* Washington, DC: Department of Commerce, Bureau of the Census.

Lodan, M. (1985). *Feminine leadership or how to succeed in business without being one of the boys.* New York: Times Books.

Mainiero, L. (1986). Coping with powerlessness: The relationship of gender and job dependency to empowerment strategy usage. *Administrative Science Quarterly, 31,* 633-653.

Martin, P. Y., Harrison, D., & Dinnito, D. (1983). Advancement for women in hierarchical organizations: A multi-level analysis for advancement and prospects. *Journal of Applied Behavioral Science, 19,* 19-33.

Morrison, A., & Von Glinow, M. A. (1990). Women and minorities in management. *American Psychologist, 45,* 200-208.

Packer, A., & Johnston, W. (1988). *Workforce 2000: Work and workers for the 21st century.* Indianapolis, IN: Hudson Institute.

Powell, G. (1988). *Women and men in management.* Newbury Park, CA: Sage.

Price Waterhouse v. Hopkins, 109 S.Ct. 1775 (1989).

Riger, P., & Galligan, S. (1980). Women in management: An exploration of competing paradigms. *American Psychologist, 35,* 902-910.

Rosener, J. (1990, November-December). Ways women lead. *Harvard Business Review,* pp. 119-125.

Schwadron, H. L. (1991, August). *Prevention Magazine,* p. 126.

Sekaran, U. (1986). *Dual-career families.* San Francisco: Jossey-Bass.

Terborg, J. (1977). Women in management: A research review. *Journal of Applied Psychology, 62,* 647-664.

U.S. Department of Labor, Bureau of Labor Statistics (1993, January). *Employment and earnings,* vol. 40 (1), pp. 171-173, 195. Washington, DC: Government Printing Office.

U.S. Department of Labor. (1990a). *Unpublished tabulations from the current population survey.* Washington, DC: Government Printing Office.

U.S. Department of Labor, Office of Information and Public Affairs. (1990b). *Women & work.* Washington, DC: Government Printing Office.

U.S. Department of Labor. (1991). *A report on the glass ceiling initiative.* Washington, DC: Government Printing Office.

SECTION II

Historical and Global Issues

2

In the Beginning: A History of Women in Management

SARA ALPERN

The August 1986, fiftieth anniversary, issue of Consumer Reports graphically illustrated a change in the business world: the increased presence of women. The issue highlighted good deals in women's as well as men's business suits compared with its premier issue in 1937, which evaluated men's suits only, and later that year, women's house dresses. Certainly, times have changed ("Good Gray Suit," 1986). According to 1990 data, women made up 58% of the civilian labor force and held 39% of management positions (see Tables 2.1 and 2.2).

The entrance of women into corporate America has a long history. This chapter will discuss the various historical, societal, personal, legal, and structural factors that have helped and hindered women in their access to the "managerial and professional specialty" positions as designated by the U.S. Bureau of the Census. Women's managerial skills are often hidden under different names over time. Women who demonstrated these skills have been called deputy husbands, she Merchants, women of business, businesswomen, proprietors, managers, entrepreneurs, settlement house workers, private secretaries, advertisers, governmental administrators, and

AUTHOR'S NOTE: The author would like to thank Carole Srole for her many helpful suggestions. She is also grateful to the Radcliffe Research Support Program and to Texas A&M University for grants to conduct her research.

executive women. Other women who worked as managers were hidden as well—but for a different reason. They worked as managers alongside their mates or fathers in small family businesses. Women's managerial roles can easily be hidden under a husband or father's work.

According to the *Oxford English Dictionary* (1989), a *manager* is "one whose office it is to manage a business establishment or a public institution." Management, as we think of it today, was established in the late nineteenth century when the development of bureaucracies in organizations required such specialization (Galambos & Pratt, 1988). Women's participation in management came even later because of assorted societal, personal, and structural factors.[1] Therefore, before discussing women's entry into managerial positions, it is helpful to review the general history of women in the work force. Furthermore, documenting women's involvement in business in general, especially as proprietors, provides some of the historical background that has led to an acceptance of women in management. The impact of major wars, industrialism, technology, education, legal decisions, governmental policies, the women's movement, and the experiences and accomplishments of pioneer women will be discussed in this chapter.

GENERAL HISTORY OF WOMEN AT WORK DURING PREINDUSTRIAL AMERICA

The colonists brought their belief system of appropriate sex roles for men and women to the new world of America. While a few women performed midwifery and other paid work outside of the household (Ulrich, 1991), most women raised the children and worked in the household-based economy, while the men worked in or around the home and engaged the public world. Yet, contrary to societal expectations, even in these early days, some women also took part in the public economic life. Businesswomen existed as proprietors of their businesses, whether as "she Merchants" or manufacturers (Dexter, 1931, pp. 56, 18). Often carrying out the work of a deceased husband or father, these women were even in professions considered untraditional for women, such as being blacksmiths or fish curers (Dexter, 1931, pp. 53,

48, 51). Historian William Chafe reported that women ran 40% of the taverns in Boston in 1690 (Chafe, 1977, p. 19). According to another scholar, there seemed to have been a fair acceptance of women "buying and selling, suing and being sued, acting as administrators and executors, and having power of attorney" (Dexter, 1931, p. 185). Women involved in these activities must have been widows, unmarried women, or women who had the foresight to obtain a prenuptial agreement before entering marriage, because, according to the British common law that bound them during those times, once a woman married, she became one with her husband. This meant she ceased to exist as a legal person; she could not sue or be sued, buy or sell property, or sign contracts. If she worked for wages, her money legally belonged to her husband (Norton, 1980, pp. 45-46).

One important source on the history of women, *Notable American Women* (James, James, & Boyer, 1971), documents the work of some Northern white colonial women who were proprietors. Margaret Hardenbrook Philipse (1659-1690), a colonial merchant and shipowner, carried on mercantile activities in her maiden name. Elizabeth Haddon Estaugh (1680-1762), a colonial proprietor who became known as the founder of Haddonfield, New Jersey, began her business career in the new world with her father's power of attorney. Once she married John Estaugh, her husband became the legal administrator of the Haddon lands. Because his work as a traveling minister often took him away from the estate, however, Elizabeth Estaugh continued to manage the Haddon lands during his frequent absences. Mary Spratt Provoost Alexander (1693-1760) was another Northern colonial businesswoman who shared a mercantile business with her first husband, Samuel Provoost, and, after his death, continued to expand that business and run it while remarried to a lawyer, James Alexander (James et al., 1971, pp. 61-62, 584-585, 35-36).

In contrast to these women with business acumen, most prerevolutionary women, who had limited educational opportunities in general, were often ignorant of financial matters. Historian Mary Beth Norton explained that, because of the common acceptance of the distinctions between the male public world and the female private world, the majority of women in this time period had little information about the economic status of their own families (Norton, 1980, pp. 7-8).

THE AMERICAN REVOLUTION AND
ITS AFTERMATH

Historian Laurel Thatcher Ulrich points out that generally during a husband's absence, the wife was expected to take over for him and become the "deputy husband" (Ulrich, 1983, pp. 35-50). This is particularly necessary during a war. As is typical in all wars, women's knowledge about economic matters grew a great deal during the American Revolution. With husbands away fighting, women were forced to master the public economic sphere as well as the private one. More women took over businesses and learned how to run them. Norton noted a significant change in the way the wife referred to that business in corresponding with the husband. As the war continued, she stopped referring to the business as " 'your business' " and began referring to " 'our business' " or " 'our crops' " (Norton, 1980, p. 222). One woman pursued a court case against her husband's wishes and explained to him: " 'I[f] it had been Left alone till your return their [sic] would have been nothing Left for us' " (Norton, 1980, p. 222). Another woman explained to her husband that she had become " 'quite a woman of business' " and hoped he would not consider himself " 'commander in chief of your own house' " upon his return to civilian life (Norton, 1980, pp. 223-224). Thus, for many women who developed confidence in their abilities during their domestic front war experiences, traditional male and female roles blurred. Furthermore, the postrevolutionary era fostered better education for women, even if only motivated by the need to train young boys with the ideals of the new republic (Norton, 1980, pp. 256-294). Women became educated for Republican Motherhood (Kerber, 1980/1986, pp. 190-200, 228).

The Cult of True Womanhood

While the aftermath of the Revolution opened up some educational possibilities for white middle- and upper-class women, it had a paradoxical effect of limiting what was considered appropriate behavior for them. As Norton argued: "In the prerevolutionary world, no one had bothered to define domesticity. . . . In the postrevolutionary world, the social significance of household and family was recognized, and simultaneously women began to be able to choose different ways of conducting their lives. As a direct result, a definition of domesticity was at last required" (Norton, 1980, p. 298). Historian Barbara Welter (1966) has described the pervasive set of beliefs surrounding white middle- and upper-class women of the early nineteenth century as "the cult of true womanhood." Gift books, religious tracts, etiquette books, and ladies' magazines urged women to become "true women." By cultivating the traits of purity, piety, domesticity, and submissiveness, women were promised the rewards of power and happiness. Women were to become ladies of leisure, status symbols, attesting to the success of their husbands.

This ideology of "the cult of true womanhood" and the ideal of the leisure class responded to the reality of the entrance of numbers of young white women and later immigrant women into the labor force as mill workers. Black free women had been working as domestic servants, and, in the South, black women worked alongside black men as slaves until the Thirteenth Amendment to the Constitution abolished slavery in 1865.

Elisabeth Dexter's study, *Career Women of America 1776-1840* (1950/ 1972), pointed to "the ideal of dignified leisure for women" in the nineteenth century, which created negative judgments of women working outside the home. She argued that nineteenth-century women found more strictures prohibiting their entrepreneurial spirit than had their predecessors in colonial years.[2] She also noted that, although women continued to enter business in increasing numbers as merchants or manufacturers, they were more often associated with products that were chiefly made for females (Dexter, 1950/1972, p. 225). Of those who ran businesses, most continued an already established family business started by a male relative (Dexter, 1950/1972, p. 156). There were exceptions, however, such as the unmarried Ann Bent (1768-1857), who apprenticed in a Boston shop that sold crockery and dry goods. At the age of 21, she opened her own shop in Boston and advertised goods imported from England (Dexter, 1950/1972, p. 164). There were women in charge of boarding houses, women tailors, and even a few women running the new mills. A Mrs. Ramage is credited with operating a cotton mill on James Island, near Charleston, South Carolina, in the late eighteenth century. Mrs. Pecker owned a Boston factory that made sail cloth during that same period (Dexter, 1950/1972, p. 200).

Most women associated with the mills, however, did not own them but rather worked in them for low wages. The century-long transition from household production of goods for family use to factory production broke down the labor process into simplified tasks and resulted in what historian Alice Kessler-Harris calls "a de-skilling process" for women (1982, p. 29). This process, the fact that women had always worked in the home without pay, and societal attitudes toward proper roles for women meant that women received lower wages than men for their labor outside of the home. Unpaid female labor and lower wages for employed females than for employed males would adversely affect the pay scale for future fields of women's employment, including managerial positions.

During the late 1830s and early 1840s, the number of employed women in general was still small. Kessler-Harris estimated that probably less than 5% of free married women worked outside of the home. In the 1840s, there was an increase in immigrants, who added to the labor force. Even with these additional workers, she estimated that only about 10% of all free women took jobs outside of their homes in 1840. Of those, about 70% worked as domestic servants; 25% worked in manufacturing; and the remainder found jobs in teaching, nursing, typesetting, and book binding (Kessler-Harris, 1982, pp. 29, 45-48). It must be noted that factory work in the early nineteenth century was restricted to white women since racial prejudice toward free black female workers excluded them from this work (Harley, 1978, pp. 7-8). Free black women worked mostly as washerwomen, cooks, seamstresses, and dressmakers (Kessler-Harris, 1982, p. 47). Gary N. Powell calculates that by 1870 only 13% of all women were in the wage labor force. (See Powell's table, reproduced in Table 2.1.) It should be noted that these are official numbers of women working outside of the home. We can not be certain of the numbers of women, especially married women, who continued to produce goods for profit at home.[3]

Threaded throughout the nineteenth century were conflicting belief systems of "proper" married white upper- and middle-class activities with the lives of working-class women and most immigrants and blacks. The belief systems reinforced the view that white married upper- and middle-class women remain in the home or do work deemed "appropriate," such as charity or religious organizational work outside of the home, while their less-well-off single sisters provided cheap labor for growing industrialism or for domestic services. While "the cult of true womanhood" beliefs kept many women out of the business world, these beliefs also justified women's entrance into certain careers, such as a few into medicine and many into teaching (Morantz-Sanchez, 1985; Sklar, 1973).

Nineteenth-century statistics mislead us to underestimate women's skills. As late as the turn of the twentieth century, statistics showed a labor force primarily populated by men. While 80% of men were in the labor force, only 19% of women were employed outside the home

Table 2.1 Labor Force Participation Rates

| | Percentage in the Labor Force | |
Year	Women	Men
1870	13	75
1880	15	79
1890	17	79
1900	19	80
1910	23	81
1920	21	78
1930	22	76
1940	25	79
1950	34	86
1960	38	83
1970	43	80
1980	52	77
1990	58	76
2000 (projected)	63	76
2005 (projected)	66	73

SOURCE: Table from *Women & Men in Management* (G. N. Powell, 1993, p. 19); Copyright 1993 by Sage. Reprinted by permission. Data from 1870-1940: U.S. Department of Commerce, Bureau of the Census, *Historical Statistics of the United States: Colonial Times to 1970* (Washington, DC: Government Printing Office, 1975), pp. 127-128, series D13; 1950-1980: U.S. Department of Labor, Bureau of Labor Statistics, *Handbook of Labor Statistics* (Washington, DC: Government Printing Office, 1989), pp. 25-30, table 5; 1990: U.S. Department of Labor, Bureau of Labor Statistics, *Employment and Earnings* 39, no. 1 (January 1992), p. 163, table 2; 2000 (projected): H. N. Fullerton, Jr., "New Labor Force Projections, Spanning 1988 to 2000," *Monthly Labor Review* 112, no. 11 (November 1989): p. 8, table 4; 2005 (projected): U.S. General Accounting Office, *The Changing Workforce: Demographic Issues Facing the Federal Government* (Washington, DC: General Accounting Office, 1992), p. 23.
NOTE: 1870-1930: data for persons 10 years old and over; 1940-1960: data for persons 14 years old and over; 1950-2005 (projected): data for persons 16 years old and over.

(Table 2.1). By 1900, some 41% of all nonwhite women were employed, but only 17% of white women worked, and most of these women were "from immigrant stock" (Chafe, 1977, p. 23). Statistics don't tell the whole story. It is important to note, that women who did voluntary work in benevolent societies gained valuable organizational skills that they would apply in later struggles to gain woman suffrage (see, e.g., Berg, 1978). College-educated black women also created and used separate black woman's clubs to support suffrage. Through woman's club work and educational reform, they also strove to restore dignity for their sex and race by working toward " 'race uplift' " and combating stereotyped views and racial discrimination (Perkins, 1988, p. 74; Terborg-Penn, 1978). Thus, women of various races and ethnicities who ran effective organizations developed skills that would be useful in managerial pursuits. These women would also become role models for future women who wanted to gain entrance into the field of management.

WOMEN IN BUSINESS AND MANAGEMENT DURING THE LATE NINETEENTH AND EARLY TWENTIETH CENTURIES

While most white upper- and middle-class women continued volunteering, the late nineteenth and early twentieth centuries witnessed the persistent entrance of women into various occupations. During the Civil War (1861-1865), many women worked in 20,000 aid societies, supplying food, clothing, and medicine to the soldiers on both sides. In the North these societies were led mostly by women and coordinated by the Sanitary Commission, while Southern women were involved in local societies (Evans, 1989, p. 114). Women also made inroads into office work during the labor shortage caused by the Civil War. With the manufacture and marketing of the typewriter in the 1870s, women continued to be recruited for office work, partly because the typewriter was a new machine and had no historical association with males (Davies, 1982, p. 170). It was the common use of the typewriter in the 1880s, however, that secured clerical jobs for them (Srole, 1987, p. 86). Women began to enter white-collar occupations, but a very small percentage of them worked as managers. Powell (1993) shows that, by 1900, 19% of white-collar workers were women. In managerial positions that year, however, only 4% were females. The actual percentage of women in managerial positions was .0024 of the total work force. (See Powell's table, reproduced in Table 2.2.) Again, while the statistics show a very small percentage of women working as managers, the actual number of women doing managerial work is underestimated because of different definitions given to male and female work (Aron, 1987).

Entrepreneurial Women

By definitions of these times, some women were classified as entrepreneurs by taking added advantage of the new technology of the typewriter. Mary Foot Seymour (1846-1893), who had taught herself

Table 2.2 Participation in White-Collar Occupations

Year	White-Collar Total	Nonfarm Executives Adminstrators and Managers	Professional and Technical	Clerical Workers	Sales Workers
Percentage of Total Labor Force					
1900	18	6	4	3	5
1910	21	6	5	5	5
1920	25	7	5	8	5
1930	29	7	7	9	6
1940	31	7	7	10	7
1950	36	9	8	12	7
1960	43	11	11	15	6
1970	48	11	14	17	6
1980	52	11	16	19	6
1990	58	13	—	—	—
1992	58	13	—	—	—
Percentage of Female Workers in Occupation					
1900	19	4	35	24	17
1910	24	6	41	35	22
1920	32	7	44	48	26
1930	33	8	45	52	24
1940	35	11	41	54	27
1950	40	14	40	62	34
1960	42	16	36	68	40
1970	47	16	39	75	43
1980	53	26	44	80	45
1990	56	39	—	—	—
1992	56	42	—	—	—

SOURCE: Table from *Women & Men in Management* (G. N. Powell, 1993, p. 21); Copyright 1993 by Sage. Reprinted by permission. Data from 1900-1950: U.S. Department of Commerce, Bureau of the Census, *Historical Statistics of the United States: Colonial Times to 1970* (Washington, DC: Government Printing Office, 1975), pp. 139-140, series D182-232; from 1960-1980: U.S. Department of Labor, Bureau of Labor Statistics, *Handbook of Labor Statistics* (Washington, DC: Government Printing Office, 1983), pp. 44-48, table 16; from 1990: U.S. Department of Labor, Bureau of Labor Statistics, *Employment and Earnings* 37, no. 2 (February 1990), p. 29, table A22; from 1992: U.S. Department of Labor, Bureau of Labor Statistics, *Employment and Earnings* 39, no. 5 (May 1992), p. 29, table A22.
NOTE: — indicates that 1990 and later data were not compatible with earlier data.

shorthand, established the Union School of Stenography in New York City in 1879. She also operated the Union Stenographic Company, where she employed 25 stenographers, and she opened an employment bureau, the Union Stenographic and Typewriting Association. In January 1889, she began publication of the *Business Woman's Journal*, which highlighted the work of successful women and included articles of interest to clerical workers and managers. She served as the president of the Mary F. Seymour Publishing Company, which published this journal. The company had all female officers. While a minority of women tried their fortune in business, those who did could serve as role models for women in the future. Indeed, Seymour actively assisted women in various ways from helping diverse women's groups to writing her own series, "Practical Hints to Stenographers and Type-Writers" (James et al., 1971, pp. 271-272). She also worked toward gaining woman suffrage, which had as a goal the empowerment of women by giving them a voice in political affairs.

Sarah Breedlove McWilliams Walker (1867-1919) served as a role model for black businesswomen. Better known as Madame C. J. Walker, she became a millionaire by marketing a hair straightening formula for black hair. A widow living in St. Louis, Missouri, she supported herself and her daughter for 18 years as a washerwoman. In 1905, she had a dream about and then created her successful formula and her "Walker method" of door-to-door demonstrations. President of the Madame C. J. Walker Manufacturing Company, which produced a complete line of cosmetics, she employed some 3,000 people, principally women. A philanthropist, she gave generously to her friend Mary McLeod Bethune's educational projects for black women and black youth. Thus, even though there were few women in entrepreneurial positions, those who succeeded shared their profits and sometimes were emulated by others. Following Madame Walker, Mrs. Annie M. Turnbo Malone created another product, a hair grower, which she called the "Poro System" (Davis, 1982, pp. 339-341; James et al., 1971, pp. 533-535).

The twentieth century witnessed an increase of women entering business, but not all at the proprietor level, and not without societal reminders to middle- and upper-class women that they should focus primary attention on their domestic lives. Thus some advice given to women entering business reinforced traditional roles in the home as well as success outside the home. William Drysdale's *Helps for Ambitious Girls,* published in 1900, emphasized that all of his advice for women entering the labor force should be understood to supplement their central concern with the home. "Whether at study or at work, home should be to her the centre of the earth" (Drysdale, 1900, p. iii). Thus, even when women were encouraged to consider a career in business, they were reminded that the home should remain their first priority. Drysdale determined that practically all "reputable businesses" were open to women in 1900, though he considered some occupations unsuitable for females. "You would not care to be a brakeman (shall we say brakewoman?) on a coal train, for instance, nor a digger with picks in a coal mine. But if you have sufficient business ability your sex will not prevent you from owning the railroad, or the coal mine, which is much better" (Drysdale, 1900, p. 496).

At the beginning of the twentieth century, growing numbers of white upper- and middle-class women took advantage of higher education. Women attended college in increasing numbers between 1870 and 1920. In 1870, women represented 21.0% of all college students, but female college students still represented a minuscule percentage of the total female college-age population; in that year, they constituted 0.7% of all 18- to 21-year-old women. In 1920, women represented some 47.3% of all college students, and college women represented 7.6% of the general female college-age population (Solomon, 1985, pp. 63, 64). The same pattern did not hold for black women. Scholar Linda M. Perkins points out that "by 1890 only 30 black women had earned baccalaureate degrees compared with more than 300 black men and 2,500 white women" (Perkins, 1988, pp. 77-78). In 1911, only 0.3% of the female student population was black. As historian Barbara Solomon concluded, "The black college woman was the exception of exceptions" (Solomon, 1985, p. 76). But, even among upper- and middle-class white women, the increase in college education did not similarly reflect a proportional increase of entry into the professions (Harris, 1978, pp. 103-104).

Social Settlement House Work

One new occupation did develop for women, that of social settlement house worker. Jane Addams founded the first settlement house, Hull House, in Chicago in 1889, replicating a model she had seen in England. She recruited a staff of talented women to live in the house and work among the city poor, providing them with various social services, including access to health care from visiting nurses. Hull House became a model for 412 other settlement houses that sprang up in the United States over the next two decades (Woods & Kennedy, 1911, p. vi). Settlement house workers not only provided tangible relief for city dwellers but also contributed statistical studies of factories and community sanitation needs as a means to lobby for legislation to improve life and work in the city.

The term businesswomen has typically excluded administrators and government workers, although these careers have required extensive managerial skills. Settlement house work is a case in point, since the work performed provided a training ground in managerial skills. Whether they were working in academia, city government, or lobbying city government, women exhibited managerial skills. Many women and some men conducted investigative studies and worked to facilitate better lives for the surrounding city poor. One of these women, Florence Kelley, Chief Factory Inspector for Illinois and General Secretary of the National Consumers' League, along with her coworker, Josephine Goldmark, was instrumental in gathering the facts for lawyer Louis D. Brandeis's successful arguing of the 1908 Supreme Court case *Muller v. Oregon* ([208 U.S. 412 (1908)] in Goldstein, 1989, pp. 20-22). Contending that excessive work hours had injurious effects on the health of women, this case legalized the establishment of maximum hours for women's employment in Oregon laundries.

Protective Labor Legislation

Muller v. Oregon, which set a precedent for protective labor legislation, was heralded as a reform because it used arguments that considered humane factors and because it temporarily toppled the prevalent laissez-faire attitude of noninterference with business. Supporting governmental restrictions on the number of hours women could work outside the home protected employed women (Flexner, 1975, pp. 214-221; Kessler-Harris, 1985, pp. 141-161). Years later, however, Brandeis's arguments that " 'women are fundamentally weaker than men in all that makes for endurance; in muscular strength, in nervous energy, in the power of persistent application and attention' " were discredited. His decision nevertheless was long used as a basis for protective legislation. Brandeis's argument against long hours for women during and after pregnancy because of the injurious effects on both mother and child is still accepted by many (quoted in Flexner, 1975, pp. 220-221). Yet, the perceived weakness of women and their inability to work overtime (often a requirement for a promotion) have taken their toll on women in the work force. A gender-based protective labor legislation system primarily aimed at industrial and sometimes saleswomen has had the long-term effects of preventing many women from advancing into management positions (see, e.g., Berch, 1982, pp. 46-

51) and has reinforced stereotyped views of women as inferior to men in the workplace.

About the same time as the *Muller* case, in 1911, women in New York founded the Intercollegiate Bureau of Occupations to assist women's entrance into occupations other than the field of teaching, which was by then overcrowded (Leaycraft & Bush, 1917, pp. 146-147). The bureau provided information to women and did studies on economic conditions and placement problems. The bureau sponsored many symposia to fulfill its original purpose: "to investigate and to do all in its power to develop opportunities for women and to increase their efficiency in occupations." The bureau stressed the increasing necessity of a college education for starting out in business (Leaycraft & Bush, 1917, pp. 149-150).

The recommendation of a college education for women entering business helps explain additional hurdles for black women to overcome to enter the field. It wasn't until the years 1950-1980 that college-educated black women entered diverse occupational fields. Yet, in the early 1980s, black women still lagged behind both white women and black men in managerial jobs (Noble, 1988, p. 101).

WORLD WAR I AND WOMAN SUFFRAGE

With the U.S. entrance into World War I, the Intercollegiate Bureau of Occupations participated in publicizing opportunities for wartime training.[4] During this war, some women did gain access to occupations that had been previously closed to them because of gender. Women in banking made some advances, managing departments, for example. Some black women were able to move into industrial jobs. But, as Kessler-Harris reminds us, "When the war ended, the entire structure slipped back down nearly, but not quite, to where it had started" (Kessler-Harris, 1982, p. 219). With the end of the war came other benefits, however. One was the creation of a permanent Women's Bureau in the federal government. Over the years, several women's organizations had urged Congress to create such a bureau. Formed in 1920, the Women's Bureau was to collect information that would be used to promote women's rights by shaping government policy. The bureau was to gain economic rights for women and to "promote the general status of all women" (Lemons, 1973, p. 31). The end of the war also added support for the vote, realized in August of 1920 with the ratification of the Nineteenth Amendment to the Constitution (Evans, 1989, pp. 164-172). Women getting the vote contributed to the break up of the woman suffrage coalition and separated out issues of economics from politics (Cott, 1987, pp. 117-142). Certainly, the war had given women some concrete benefits.

As historian William Chafe pointed out, U.S. participation in World War I helped women gain access to more training and more responsibilities in business. In the decade of the 1920s, a time when business exercised an inordinate amount of influence, the number of women employed in business increased by more than 100,000. Yet, Chafe cautioned that progress at the executive levels was far less dramatic (Chafe, 1972, pp. 89-91, 140-142). Banks, for instance, provided a new area for women as the Columbia Trust Company created the first women's department in 1919, appointing Virginia D. H. Furman manager. It was thought that women who had paychecks to deposit or investments to make would feel more comfortable dealing with a female bank officer. Other banks in New York followed Columbia Trust Company's lead, as did banks in other parts of the country, as they created women's departments of their own (Alpern, 1990). According to Chafe, women's particular entry as female specialists meant rarely an office higher than assistant cashier and lower status than males in banking (Chafe, 1972, p. 90). There were exceptions, however. In Tennessee, from 1919 to 1926, Mrs. F. J. Runyon was president of the First Woman's Bank, a bank managed entirely by women. A black woman, Maggie Lena Walker, served as president of St. Luke's Penny Savings Bank in Richmond, Virginia, from 1903 to 1930 (Alpern, 1990).

WOMEN IN BUSINESS AND MANAGEMENT
IN THE 1920s AND 1930s

Meanwhile, throughout the 1920s and 1930s, attention continued to be paid to the position of women in the field of business. In 1920, 21% of the labor force was female (Table 2.1). In 1920, 25% of the total labor force held white-collar jobs, with 7% doing managerial work. Women held 32% of the white-collar positions but only 7% of the managerial jobs. In 1920, 48% of clerical jobs were held by women (Table 2.2). Reflecting upon the possibilities for advancement in the 1920s, author

Elizabeth Sears argued that "the business woman now has come into her own" (Sears, n.d., p. 74). Irving T. Bush, President of the Bush Terminal Company, heaped praise on the potential of women in business, most particularly the potential of Henrita F. Ried, who was secretary of the Bush Terminal Company. Bush said that he had promoted Ried to secretary and assistant to the president because of ability, not because of gender (Bennett, 1920, pp. 64, 65, 98). Ried, as secretary and assistant to the president of the Bush Terminal Company, was in charge of the 30-story Bush Terminal Sales Building in Times Square, New York. She was "America's highest-salaried woman executive" in 1919. At one point, Bush said of Ried, " 'She has all the ability of a great executive, combined with the intuition of a woman' " (Ried, 1919, p. 4).

Ried illustrates the possibility of promotion for those few women who took the path to executive status by becoming private secretaries. The private secretary in its earliest manifestation in the late nineteenth and early twentieth centuries was clearly an executive position. When most private secretaries were male, the position of secretary could be seen as an "apprentice executive," with the secretary being promoted to an executive within the corporate structure. But, as with the general feminization of clerical work, women also began to dominate the secretarial positions. According to historian Margery Davies, by 1930, the secretary's "apprentice executive" possibilities had virtually disappeared (Davies, 1982, p. 167, 168). Ried was one of the early beneficiaries of true promotion to executive power via the secretarial path. A few years after her appointment as secretary, she continued that position while becoming vice president of all subsidiary companies of Bush Terminal Company. When her boss was interviewed about the place for women in business, he said that advertising and sales were the two most promising fields for women to enter (Bennett, 1920, p. 65).

Women in Advertising and Sales

Indeed, several vocational bureaus for women promoted advertising as a good field for women. As one study argued, it was a relatively young field in which "prejudice is less pronounced." Furthermore, it was assumed that women would know how to market a product to other women, who were now recognized as the major consumers. Estimating some 85% of buying in the United States was being done by women, the Philadelphia Bureau of Vocations argued: "With years of buying experience woman's viewpoint should be valuable" (Pyle, 1923, p. 40; see also *Advertising Opportunities for Women in Denver*, 1924).

In one book written especially for women in the 1920s, *To Women of the Business World* (1923), Edith Johnson suggested several careers for women in large enterprises, including selling life insurance, the income from which was limited in amount only by a woman's ability and her willingness to work. In 1923, Johnson optimistically concluded that women had just begun to pioneer the field of big business. "No one dares to predict what her achievements will be within the next half-century" (Johnson, 1923, pp. 241, 242, 243). *Girls Who Did* (Ferris & Moore, 1927, originally copyrighted by the Girl Scouts, Inc., in 1926) included stories about several women who had become successful in business. Minna Hall Carothers, past president of the New York League of Advertising Women and the Federation of Advertising Women's Clubs of the World, saw vast opportunities for women in the field of advertising (Ferris & Moore, 1927, p. 99). The first club for women in the field of advertising had been set up in 1912 as the League of Advertising Women of New York, later to become the Advertising Women of New York, Inc. In 1938, one of its founders, Christine Frederick (1883-1970), argued that the proof of women's importance in advertising came from the fact that women had been in advertising "almost from the very beginning of the profession." She traced the history to Matilda C. Weil, who created the M. C. Weil Advertising Agency in New York City in 1867. Frederick argued that, by the 1890s, at least a dozen women held executive positions in advertising, and she pointed to her contemporary businesswomen, whom she called "national advertisers": Rose B. Knox, Harriet Hubbard Ayer, Elizabeth Arden, and Helena Rubinstein. After recounting biography after biography of advertising women in the past, she encouraged her contemporaries to "make ourselves felt constructively, in keeping with those hardy pioneers of our sex, in advertising who had to deal with so many discouragements" (Frederick, 1938).

With the rise in popularity of movies and a growing beauty culture, cosmetics grew into an important industry (Banner, L. W., 1983, pp. 212-219; 278-280). One of those contemporaries, Elizabeth Arden, born Florence Nightingale Graham (1878?-1966), created a successful cosmetics business after opening her first shop in Washington, DC, in 1914, where she introduced the use of mascara and eye shadow. Her arch rival Helena Rubinstein (1870-1965) brought over an established salon business from Europe in 1915. By 1917, she had salons in several U.S. cities. Various movie stars helped her gain even more visibility. For example, she created movie star Theda Bara's vamp look. While Rubinstein's enormous success certainly could have encouraged future female entrepreneurs, her autobiography, *My Life for Beauty,* blaming her absorption with business for the breakup of her marriage, may have dissuaded other women considering careers in business (Sicherman & Green, 1980, pp. 32-33, 607-608). The belief system of putting family ahead of career or the dangers of not putting family ahead of career continued to adversely affect women's entrance into managerial positions in the twentieth century. Rubinstein's autobiography reflects the tension surrounding feminism as early as the end of the 1920s and the decline of support for career women in post-World War II America.

Edith Mae Cummings, whose 1929 book *Pots, Pans and Millions,* subtitled *A Study of Woman's Right to Be in Business, Her Proclivities and Capacity for Success,* looked toward woman's general progress in business. As she announced early in her book: "Success in business is no longer a matter of sex. . . . Business is a science; it can be learned." She cautioned women: "Do not pay any attention to published reports and surveys containing analyses to prove that women are failures in business" (Cummings, 1929, pp. 5, 99). She may have been referring to journalist Dorothy Dunbar Bromley's "Are Women a Success in Business?" published a year earlier, for it painted a less optimistic answer to the question and raised other questions about their ambitions and what men saw as women's glaring fault, "their highly personal attitude" (Bromley, 1928, p. 302).

Acknowledging women's success in selling female-related products or services seen specifically for women, such as interior decorating, establishing their own food production businesses, or manufacturing and selling cosmetics, Bromley said that only in advertising and selling had women begun to compete with men. In sales and advertising, she may have had in mind Dorothy Shaver (1897-1959), who, by 1925, had become director of interior decoration and fashion for a major department store. She, along with her sister, Elsie, had gained entrance to Lord & Taylor's Department Store in 1920, the year their distant cousin, Samuel W. Rayburn, became president of the store. He had agreed to sell "The Little Shavers" dolls at the store. After four years, Elsie became bored making the dolls, and Dorothy began her career at Lord & Taylor's in the comparison shopping bureau. Elected to the board of directors in 1927, she served as vice president in charge of advertising, publicity, and the bureau of fashion from 1931 to 1945. She promoted U.S. fashion designers and, among other innovations, created the first teenager's fashion department. (When elected president in 1945, she received a salary of $110,000, the largest salary of any woman in the country, although it was reported to be only one fourth as large as that of a man in a comparable position; Sicherman & Green, 1980, pp. 645-646.)

While Shaver never married, Bromley reported that the question universally asked whenever discussing a woman's ambition in business was this: How could a woman be married and have a career in business? Opinions among employers varied. Some, such as Samuel W. Rayburn, then president of Lord & Taylor's Department Store, insisted that big business must have some policy to enable the woman executive to marry and have children and keep her position as long as the woman kept informed about the business during her absence. As another employer concluded:

> Any discussion of women's success in business as compared with that of men, is a purely academic one, so long as big business requires them to live such unnatural one-sided lives, hedged about by all sorts of restrictions. Business heads must not only yield the point of allowing married women to continue working, but—if they really value the services of women—they must formulate some such plan as Mr. Rayburn has suggested, with the purpose of enabling women to be wives and mothers as well as business women. (Bromley, 1928, pp. 301, 307)

Attempts to find creative solutions for the married female executive would not be a priority in the 1930s, as the stock market crash of 1929 and the resulting Great Depression brought discrimination instead (see, e.g., Bird, 1966, p. 56). In fact, in the 1930s, corporate rules prevented many women from obtaining supervisory jobs. Historian D'Ann Campbell reported: "84 percent of the nation's insurance companies, 65 percent of the banks and 63 percent of public utilities had restrictive rules preventing married women from holding *any* jobs" (italics in original; Campbell, 1984, p. 110).

THE NEW DEAL'S "WOMEN'S NETWORK"

Contrary to these employment practices, President Franklin Delano Roosevelt, with the encouragement of his wife Eleanor, promoted the advancement of women into high-level government positions during his New Deal years. First Lady Eleanor Roosevelt became the informal head of what came to be called the "women's network," consisting of 28 women involved in government and politics, including the first female Cabinet member, Secretary of Labor Frances Perkins; Mary W. ("Molly") Dewson, director of the Women's Division of the Democratic National Committee; Mary Anderson, Chief of the Women's Bureau; and various administrators of the New Deal alphabet agencies. Black educational reformer Mary McLeod Bethune, head of the Office of Minority Affairs within the National Youth Administration, saw herself as representing her race rather than her gender; she was rarely mentioned in this network. While not designated as businesswomen, these women held high level government positions, administered policies, and served as supervisors. Bethune and members of this "women's network" truly can be considered managers in the public service arena. Yet, despite their influence and protest, they were unable to prevent the passage of Section 213 of the National Economy Act of 1932, which affected many more female workers. This stipulation prohibited both husband and wife from working for the federal government at the same time. The law did not specify that the wife should leave her job, but, between 1932 to 1937, some 1,600 female government employees were dismissed (Ware, 1981).

The 28 productive women in the "women's network" could serve as role models for future women who wanted to take on managerial positions in government or politics. However, the network remained a unique phenomenon, occurring during unusual times, with the support of a particularly experimental president. The network members did not consider themselves feminists and emphasized a commitment to social change without regard to sex. Because the members failed to train younger women to take their places when they retired, managerial positions for women were not institutionalized in government, let alone in the business world in general (Ware, 1981, pp. 116-131). Furthermore, the lack of societal support for women's advancement to high-level positions remained an important factor for the slow overall access to positions in management. One writer noted that, in 1931, women were still seen as usurpers in the business world and therefore could not start on an equal footing with men. They were handicapped by being female. He argued that, if woman's presence were taken for granted, there would be "no need of so much talk about her place in business and her prospects." He advised women to acquire a thorough knowledge of economics in order to succeed (Hirschfield, 1931, p. 299).

WOMEN IN MANAGEMENT
DURING WORLD WAR II

The above advice could bear fruit more easily at a time of economic demand for women workers. As during previous wars, America's participation in World War II created a receptivity toward women's employment and opened some executive positions to women. In 1943, Mary Anderson, Director of the Women's Bureau, claimed that opportunities beckoned professional women " 'in an unprecedented way' " (quoted in Chafe, 1972, p. 142). Although she overstated the case, some progress did occur as corporations and Wall Street recruited female specialists to replace men serving on the battlefront (Chafe, 1972, p. 141). Women became part of the "hidden army" employed in U.S. industry. Public attitudes toward women working outside of the home shifted as newspapers and magazines joined government efforts to depict employed women as heroines (Chafe, 1972, pp. 135-150; see also, Rupp, 1978).

According to William Chafe, World War II served as a watershed for employed women. In sheer numbers, within five years, more than 6 million women joined the labor force for a total of 18 million female workers. In addition, these workers were mostly married, over 35, and increasingly from the middle class. The war legitimized employment for women of various social, economic, and racial backgrounds (Chafe, 1976, pp. 15-18). During the war, many black women were able to leave domestic service and farm work for the better salaries of the industries (Chafe, 1972, p. 143).[5]

Banks that had discontinued their women's departments during the Depression, returning these responsibilities to men, offered women employment opportunities during the war. They hired women as cashiers, tellers, and loan officers. In fact, they hired so many women that feminization took place in banking, thereby reducing the salary and status of those positions. By 1950, half of all bank employees were female, while 15% of middle management and only 1% of senior positions were held by women (Campbell, 1984, pp. 218-219, 252, 110-111).

Campbell concluded that World War II provided a breakthrough in middle management for women. She found that women made up 11.7% of the managerial occupation in 1940. At the end of the war, in 1945, women in the managerial category had increased to 17.4%, but, just two years later, their number had decreased to 13.5% (Campbell, 1984, table 1). So, despite the breakthroughs during the war, changing attitudes regarding proper sex roles did not follow. According to Campbell, women students continued to avoid a managerial curriculum for many years to come (Campbell, 1984, p. 111).[6]

POSTWAR ATTITUDES TOWARD EMPLOYED WOMEN

After the war, receptivity to women entering management again declined. As William Chafe has stated, "If anything was more striking than the changes in the female labor force, it was the persistence of traditional attitudes toward woman's proper 'place,' " (Chafe, 1976, p. 19). A general postwar reaction against women in the workplace created a devastating impediment to women's entrance into management. Postwar popular culture and academic studies pushed women back from visible roles in business. A recent study of best-selling novels found a drastic shift away from positive views of entrepreneurial women in 1945 to a 1955 portrayal of career women as " 'selfish' " (Elizabeth Long's *The American Dream and the Popular Novel,* 1985, cited in May, 1988, p. 176). The influential book *Modern Women: The Lost Sex* (1947), by Marynia Farnham and Ferdinand Lundberg argued that women " 'would do well to recapture those functions in which they have demonstrated superior capacity. Those are, in general, the nurturing functions around the home.' " The authors warned women who chose " 'fields belonging to the male area of exploit or authority—law, mathematics, physics, business, industry and technology—government and socially minded organizations . . . that such pursuits are not generally desirable for women' " (quoted in Kessler-Harris, 1982, p. 297).

Fortune magazine, which had already made short shrift of executive women in business, giving them a poor prognosis as early as 1935, added to postwar negativity toward women executives with their 1946 poll results. "In response to a *Fortune* poll, 53% of the executives said that women handled people less well than men, and 65.9% asserted that females were less able to make decisions" ("Women in Business III," 1935, p. 81; see also Chafe, 1972, p. 185). Clearly, in the late 1940s and early 1950s, women found formidable barriers to advancement in careers in management.

Nonetheless, a grant from the National Federation of Business and Professional Women's Clubs to Margaret Cussler made possible a book encouraging female executives. Cussler published *The Woman Executive* in 1958. For her study, she defined *executive* as "someone having three or more people under her and earning more than $4,000 a year" (Cussler, 1958, p. xi). Although she tapped a wide range of professions, top echelon executives were underrepresented in her study of some 55 executives from the Boston and Washington, DC, areas. Cussler specifically challenged earlier findings of Lundberg and Farnham, insisting that the successful executives in her study handled the multiple roles of employment and family. Several women executives in her study attributed part of their success to finding a mentor. From her perspective in 1958, she looked back to 1908 and found that the most progress female executives had made was reflected at the lower executive levels. Yet, she looked forward to the next 50 years, hoping that women could "abandon some of the attitudes of inferiority and defensiveness that accompany discrimination" (Cussler, 1958, pp. xiv, 53, 17, 154, 153). Some of the defensiveness women felt came as a reaction to uncomplimentary media portrayals. For example, journalist Agnes E. Meyer lashed out against the business woman: "God protect us from the efficient, go-getter businesswoman whose feminine instincts have been completely sterilized" (Meyer, 1958, p. 345).

Predicting an attitudinal change that reflected the increasing numbers of women working outside of the home in the late 1950s, *Executive Careers for Women,* written between 1957 and 1961, presented quite a different view of business women. Frances Maule dedicated her book "TO YOU THE YOUNG WOMEN OF TODAY WHO HAVE SET YOUR SIGHTS ON A TOP JOB AND ARE DETERMINED NOT TO SETTLE FOR LESS" (Maule, 1957/1961, dedication page). According to Maule, most successful executive women in the late 1950s attributed their success to " 'hard work.' " While acknowledging some remaining prejudice against women in higher positions, she argued, "If you will fill up those gaps in the job equipment and discipline yourself to weed out the obstructive attitudes, nothing can prevent you from reaching the upper levels" (Maule, 1957/1961, pp. 227, 193, 236).

Maule was no doubt talking about exceptional women, for she was too optimistic for the times. Women would not gain substantive access to managerial positions until the 1970s. According to Powell's table (see Table 2.2), in 1950, 14% of managerial positions were held by women, while managerial positions made up 9% of the total labor force. In 1960, 16% of managers were females, with managers making up 11% of the total work force. In 1970, 16% of the managerial category were female, with a continued 11% of managers in the total work force. In 1980, 26% of the managerial positions were held by women, with managers representing 11% of the total work force (Table 2.2). In 1990, 39% of the managers were women while managers represented 13% of the total labor force.

IMPACT OF THE 1960s

Some of the reforms for women in the 1960s actually stemmed from 1940s' conflicts between women's interest groups that split off from the old suffrage coalition. For some 15 years, a struggle ensued between those who supported an Equal Rights Amendment and those women's activists who fought vigorously against it. The National Woman's Party (NWP) supported one; the coalition surrounding the Women's Bureau opposed it, seeking an equal pay act instead (Harrison, 1988). With a combination of motivations, Kennedy's presidency paid some attention to women's employment issues, and thus offered some hopes for women aspiring to careers in management. In 1961, the year Maule's book was published, and at the prodding of Esther Peterson, Assistant Secretary of Labor and Director of the Women's Bureau, President John F. Kennedy appointed a presidential Commission on the Status of Women, chaired by Eleanor Roosevelt (Woloch, 1984, p. 489). The commission issued its findings on the status of women in 1963, giving women's issues of wages and working conditions prominent political visibility. While the Commission defined as a goal putting an end to sex discrimination in employment, it also proposed goals that would enable women " 'to continue in their role as wives and mothers while making a maximum contribution to the world around them' " (quoted in Hartmann, 1989, p. 52), thereby reinforcing the primacy of women's family responsibilities.

This reinforcement of sex-role expectations would not have surprised Betty Friedan, who, in the same year—1963—published *The Feminine Mystique,* in which she argued that twentieth-century white women's identities were equated with their femininity. Friedan pointed out that post-World War II media and education had insisted that women's happiness was to be found in the roles of marriage and motherhood. At a time when advances in birth control techniques (including FDA approval of the Pill) and mechanization of domestic tasks freed women from the home, "the feminine mystique" encouraged women to stay there. Friedan argued that women were urged to sacrifice their identities for "femaleness" (Friedan, 1963).

Friedan's ideas reached a growing audience of articulate, college-educated women and appealed to many of the increasing numbers of women in the workplace. Friedan's call for women's self-determination resulted nationwide in the formation of consciousness-raising groups among mostly upper- and middle-class white women. Her ideas, combined with the principles of the civil rights movement, gave birth to the women's liberation movement in the United States.

Some of the same women who began the women's liberation movement had participated in the civil rights movement even earlier and had gained valuable organizational skills there (see Evans, 1980). The combination of a civil rights movement and a women's liberation movement gave rise to higher expectations for employed women, including women employed as managers.

It should be noted that Friedan's thesis applied primarily to white women. As Paula Giddings writes, "Not only were the problems of the White suburban housewife (who may have had Black domestic help) irrelevant to Black women, they were also alien to them" (Giddings, 1984, p. 299). While black women could not relate to Friedan's "feminine mystique," they also had suffered from a history of racial and sexual discrimination. They shared with white women living in times of protest that demanded that the government confront both sexual and racial discrimination in the United States.

Some of the resulting governmental legislation facilitated the attempts of women to advance in their occupations. As historian Cynthia Harrison points out, the Women's Bureau was able to push through the Equal Pay Act in 1963, thereby deflating forces pushing for the Equal Rights Amendment. Even though part of the motivation for the act was to defeat the ERA, and even though the Equal Pay Act had a narrow focus, this act did bring the federal government into the role of protecting women's rights to employment on the same basis as men (Harrison, 1988, 89-105). Then, in 1964, the Civil Rights Act passed; this Act included Title VII, prohibiting discrimination on the basis of sex as well as race, color, religion, and national origin. Executive Order 11375 forbade general contractors from discrimination against women (see, e.g., Kessler-Harris, 1982, pp. 314-315). By 1971, as a result of sex discrimination cases pressed by both state and federal equal opportunity commissions, some $30 million in back pay had been awarded (Banner, 1984, p. 261). From the late 1960s into the 1970s, the public focused on women's equality in employment and on access to places of authority.

WOMEN IN CORPORATIONS

In analyzing the U.S. labor force in 1977, however, Rosabeth Moss Kanter found continued sex segregation of occupations. From 1900 to 1970, each census year showed female workers concentrated in female occupations. In 1970, half of all women workers worked in 17 occupations, while half of the men were divided into 63 occupations. Between 1960 and 1969, the growth of women in the professional and technical group, in the skilled trades, and in the managers and officials categories was less than the overall growth of women's labor force participation, while growth in the clerical worker group was larger. Thus, while the work force was growing, women had not yet entered the more lucrative positions (Kanter, 1977, p. 16).

Still, as the female labor force grew, so too did analyses of women in the business world. In 1970, Letty Cottin Pogrebin, in her book *How To Make It in a Man's World*, pointed out male executives' complaints about female executives, such as the ever present remark: "Women are too damned emotional." But, when Pogrebin pointed out *Harvard Business Review*'s 1965 survey of *HBR* subscribers and members of various professional and trade groups, which found some 41% of the 1,000 executives queried had misgivings about female executives, she suspected another factor was holding women back. As one male executive put it: "I'll always view a woman executive as someone whose job could have gone to a man. Women can work for gratification, for fun or for a lark. Men work for a living" (Pogrebin, 1970, pp. 213, 216-217, 216). This "pin money" argument—that women only worked for luxury items—had been used over the decades and clearly did not hold up statistically in the past and certainly not in 1970, when 10.8% of all families in the United States had female heads of household with no spouse present (U.S. Department of Commerce, Bureau of the Census, 1987).

When Charlotte Decker Sutton and Kris K. Moore duplicated the 1965 *Harvard Business Review* survey in 1985 on 1,900 male and female executives, randomly selected from the 1982 *Standard and Poor's Register of Corporations, Directors and Executives* and 1982-1983 *Dun & Bradstreet Reference Book of Corporate Management,* they found some interesting changes. Using 1984 government statistics, they found some 33% of all managerial and administrative positions were held by women, whereas, in 1965, only 14% of those positions were held by females. Yet, despite the pressures of Title VII of the Civil Rights Act and affirmative action plans, attitudes still seemed to be a major stumbling block in the progress for executive women. More than half of the respondents did not think that women would ever be totally accepted in business.

In the 1980s, a decade of Reaganomics, women became part of the young upwardly mobile professional generation (Yuppies) and Sutton and Moore found the most significant change in attitudes toward women's aspirations in business. Half of the men and women surveyed in 1965 thought that women did not seek positions of authority. The 1985 answers showed that only 9% of the men and 4% of the women still held this view. The survey also assessed the degrees of comfort working under a woman. The percentage of executives who thought that women felt uncomfortable working under women increased, while fewer thought that men were uncomfortable working under women. In fact, the authors cited the unfavorable attitude of men working under women as having dropped from 41% in 1965 to 5% in 1985. As the authors pointed out, there is no way to determine if this represents an honest change of attitude or if this reflects the desire to answer with a currently acceptable social position. But, in several ways, men's attitudes seemed to have changed more than those of women.

The authors found a substantial change in the stereotype that women are too emotional to be good managers. In answer to the question, "Are women temperamentally unfit for management?" 51% of the male executives said yes, and 74% of the women said no in 1965, while, in 1985, 82% of the male executives and 95% of the female executives answered no to that question. With that as some good news, Sutton and Moore pointed to a less positive statistic, that of salary disparities. The median income category for men was $100,000 and over, while, for women, it was $30,001-$50,000. While 58% of women earned salaries of $50,000 and under, only 16% of men earned that amount. Female executives, when matched with males of similar experience, still showed considerably lower salaries than their male counterparts (Sutton & Moore, 1985, p. 3).

Time magazine reported the Sutton/Moore study but did not mention the salary discrepancies. Instead, the article featured the positive changes identified in the survey. "More and More, She's the Boss," proclaimed *Time*'s focus on executive women on the move (Castor, 1985). An economist was quoted as saying, " 'The growth of women in the work force is probably the single most important change that has ever taken place in the American labor market. Their arrival at high executive levels will be the major development for working women over the next

20 years.' " Yet, only Katherine Graham, chairperson of the board of the *Washington Post,* had made the list of chief executive officers of the *Fortune* 500 companies by 1985. Thomas Peters, coauthor of *In Search of Excellence,* pointed to barriers to the top jobs for females. He argued that it would be easier for a woman to become president of the United States than to head one of the " 'male bastions in corporate America' " (quoted in Castor, 1985, pp. 64-65).

SUMMARY AND CONCLUSIONS

While some see women managers hitting a glass ceiling that impedes their rise to the highest levels of management, others see women making great strides in closing the gap with male managers. Debate continues about the progress of women managers. *Fortune*'s July 1990 cover story asks, "Why Women *Still* Aren't Getting to the Top" (Fierman, 1990); the article details evidence of a glass ceiling. Of 4,012 people at the highest category, *Fortune* found only 19 women—less than one half of 1% (Fierman, 1990, p. 40). Judy B. Rosener paints a more optimistic view of women as corporate leaders by presenting her findings about how women lead in *Harvard Business Review*'s November-December 1990 article (Rosener, 1990). She describes an "interactive leadership" style shared by the women she interviewed; this style contrasts with the traditional "command-and-control" leadership style. While Rosener thinks more women manage by interactive leadership, she says that this leadership style is not confined to women. Still, she states that, when organizations value diversity in leadership styles, managers can lead using their individual strengths. This implies more leadership opportunities for female managers in the future.

Tracing the history of women in management is helpful as a background for understanding whatever the future holds for female managers. There has been a paucity of women in managerial positions from colonial times until at least the 1970s. To understand the slow pace of women's access to managerial positions, this chapter reviewed the general history of women's employment outside of the home. Yet caution must be applied when assessing the underrepresentation of women as managers since women's managerial skills are sometimes hidden under gender specific labels or under family names.

Women have always worked in the home, but that reality of unpaid work may have led to lower wages for women when they left the home to work for wages. Free black and white women were employed in domestic work, and both free and slave black women did agricultural work. When some white women began factory work, they encountered a "de-skilling" process that forced them to abandon the skills formerly required to create a complete product. Their work was reduced to a simple task, creating a small portion of the product. Furthermore, stereotyped assumptions followed women into the work force, such as the assumption that women worked for luxury items or "pin money." One of the significant impediments to women's employment, also involving women's specific lack of access to managerial positions, has been a persistent distinction between the private world of women and the public world of men.

The longevity of sex role expectations for white upper and middle-class women, which assumed that they should focus on the home while men worked in the public realm, undermined the possibility of permanent acceptance of women in the workplace, as well as in supervisory roles in that milieu. Thus, even during times when public attitudes supported the idea of women in the work force, such as during wars, the change was only temporary.

Sex-role expectations for white upper- and middle-class women of the early nineteenth century called for "true women" to stay in the home, serving as decorative status symbols for their husbands. Access to higher education motivated some of these women to seek managerial positions outside of the home. Black women, whose access to college education came much later than white women's, had an even more difficult time gaining access to managerial careers as they also faced racial discrimination in employment.

In the twentieth century, some women continued to confront sex-role expectations, which often placed them at home rather than in the business world. The pervasive assessment of women as females first rather than human beings first hindered women's progress in management throughout the years as women were viewed primarily as wives and mothers or potential wives and mothers. Gender-based protective labor legislation at the beginning of the twentieth century also impeded some women's progress.

Despite societal pressures against them, successful individual female proprietors and entrepreneurs as well as women who managed organizations in the public sector, such as settlement houses or in government, paved the way as role models for future women's entrance into the corporate world. Their work and their assessment of that work both helped and hindered the progress of future women in corporate America. During the New Deal, an extraordinary group of women, a "women's network," held high-level political and government positions, but the gains they made were not institutionalized.

Women did acquire managerial positions in several ways. Some women found managerial positions in fields that produced products for females or sold services usually associated with women. Women who found employment in a new field that had no previous association with males could achieve executive status. Thus the new field of office work created the position of private secretary, which originally offered the potential of "apprentice executive." This was no longer the case after 1930, when women dominated these positions and the occupation of private secretary suffered from feminization, with the resulting lower status and lower wages. The definitions of women's work have been problematic, often hiding managerial skills under gender-specific categories.

Each of our country's wars called women out of the home into the work force, including into managerial positions, but this call to employment was seen as a necessary but temporary war measure instead of an opportunity for permanent advancement for women. When each war ended, women were encouraged to return to the home. While some women entered the corporate world as managers at the beginning of the twentieth century, a major increase of women in that occupation has been taking place since 1970, following pressures from a women's movement and the implementation of federal antidiscrimination legislation.

This chapter has shown how structural barriers, institutional practices of discrimination, exclusionary laws, and attitudes regarding proper sex roles for upper- and middle-class white women have all had a negative impact on women's advancement into managerial positions. Along with antidiscrimination legislation, the presence of large numbers of women in the labor force, a substantive number of women holding managerial positions during times of peace, and the possibility of acceptance of a diversity of leadership styles may provide enough of a critical mass of people to change attitudes toward the permanent acceptance of women doing executive work and to break down the structural barriers that have held back many women managers over the years.

NOTES

1. This chapter does not include analysis of housewives who may well have managed considerable funds and people within the household (P. E. Tarlow, personal communication, July 4, 1990).

2. Just as Norton has questioned many of Dexter's conclusions about the eighteenth century, current scholars may challenge Dexter's analysis about women in the nineteenth century.

3. We know that farm women were increasing their productivity of items for sale. See Chapter 5 in Joan Jensen, *Loosening the Bonds: Mid-Atlantic Farm Women, 1750-1850*, New Haven, CT: Yale University Press, 1986.

4. This bureau disbanded after the war and was reconstituted as the Bureau of Vocational Information in 1919 (see "College Alumna's Work" and letter from Beatrice Doerschuk to Mrs. Richard Boerdonen, May 7, 1953, Inventory, Bureau of Vocational Information papers, Schlesinger Library, Cambridge, MA).

5. There is still controversy about the degree of net gains for women during the war years. See Alice Kessler-Harris, *Out to Work: A History of Wage-Earning Women in the United States*. New York, NY: Oxford University Press, 1982.

6. Showing a somewhat positive statistic, Campbell points out that, by the end of the 1940s, there was some support from female networking among the 150,000 members of the National Federation of Business and Professional Women, of whom 14% held managerial jobs (Campbell, 1984, p. 111).

REFERENCES

Advertising opportunities for women in Denver. (1924, May). Denver, CO: Collegiate Bureau of Occupations (Women's Educational and Industrial Union papers in Box 10, folder 10, Schlesinger Library, Cambridge, MA).

Alpern, S. (1990). Women in banking: Early years. In L. Schweikart (Ed.), *Encyclopedia of American business history and biography: Banking and finance, 1913-1989.* New York: Facts on File.

Alpern, S., & Baum, D. (1985). Female ballots: The impact of the Nineteenth Amendment. *Journal of Interdisciplinary History, 16*(1), 43-67.

Aron, C. S. (1987). *Ladies and gentlemen of the civil service: Middle-class workers in Victorian America.* New York: Oxford University Press.

Banner, L. W. (1983). *American beauty.* New York: Alfred A. Knopf.

Banner, L. W. (1984). *Women in modern America: A brief history* (2nd ed.). New York: Harcourt Brace Jovanovich.

Bennett, H. C. (1920, February). Women in business: Interview with Irving T. Bush. *The Green Book Magazine* (in Box 4, folder 59, Bureau of Information papers, Schlesinger Library, Cambridge, MA).

Berch, B. (1982). *The endless day: The political economy of women and work.* New York: Harcourt Brace Jovanovich.

Berg, B. J. (1978). *The remembered gate: Origins of American feminism, the woman and the city, 1800-1860.* New York: Oxford University Press.

Bird, C. (1966). *The invisible scar.* New York: Longman.

Bromley, D. D. (1928, February). Are women a success in business? *Harper Weekly, 156,* 299-307.

Campbell, D. (1984). *Women at war with America: Private lives in a patriotic era.* Cambridge, MA: Harvard University Press.

Castor, J. (1985, December 2). More and more, she's the boss. *Time,* pp. 64-65.

Chafe, W. H. (1972). *The American woman: Her changing social, economic, and political roles, 1920-1970.* New York: Oxford University Press.

Chafe, W. H. (1976). Looking backward in order to look forward. In J. M. Kreps (Ed.), *Women and the American economy.* Englewood Cliffs, NJ: Prentice-Hall.

Chafe, W. H. (1977). *Women and equality.* New York: Oxford University Press.

Cott, N. F. (1987). *The grounding of modern feminism.* New Haven, CT: Yale University Press.

Cummings, E. M. (1929). *Pots, pans, and millions.* Washington, DC: National School of Business Science for Women.

Cussler, M. (1958). *The woman executive.* New York: Harcourt, Brace.

Davies, M. W. (1982). *Woman's place is at the typewriter: Office work and office workers 1870-1930.* Philadelphia: Temple University Press.

Davis, M. W. (Ed.). (1982). *Contributions of black women to America* (Vol . 1). Columbia, SC: Kenday.

Dexter, E. A. (1931). *Colonial women of affairs: Women in business and the professions in America before 1776* (2nd ed.). Boston: Houghton Mifflin.

Dexter, E. A. (1972). *Career women of America: 1776-1840.* Clifton, NJ: Augustus M. Kelley. (Original work published 1950)

Drysdale, W. (1900). *Helps for ambitious girls.* New York: Thomas Y. Crowell.

Evans, S. M. (1980). *Personal politics.* New York: Vintage.

Evans, S. M. (1989). *Born for liberty: A history of women in America.* New York: Free Press.

Ferris, H. J., & Moore, V. (1927). *Girls who did.* New York: E. P. Dutton.

Fierman, J. (1990, July 30). Why women still don't hit the top. *Fortune, 122,* 40-62.

Flexner, E. (1975). *Century of struggle: The women's rights movement in the United States* (rev. ed.). Cambridge, MA: Harvard University Press.

Frederick, C. (1938, September). *The rise of advertising women* (Speech, Advertising Women of New York papers in Box 1, folder 3, Schlesinger Library, Cambridge, MA).

Friedan, B. (1963). *The feminine mystique.* New York: Dell.

Galambos, L., & Pratt, J. (1988). *The rise of the corporate commonwealth.* New York: Basic Books.

Giddings, P. (1984). *When and where I enter: The impact of black women on race and sex in America.* New York: William Morrow.

Goldstein, L. F. (1989). *The constitutional rights of women.* Madison, WI: University of Wisconsin Press.

Good gray suit. (1986, August 8). *Consumer Reports, 51,* 495, 496, 504-509.

Harley, S. (1978). Northern black female workers: Jacksonian era. In S. Harley & R. Ternborg-Penn (Eds.), *The Afro-American woman: Struggles and images,* pp. 5-16. Port Washington, NY: Kennikat.

Harley, S., & Terborg-Penn. (Eds.). (1978). *The Afro-American woman: Struggles and images.* Port Washington, NY: Kennikat.

Harris, B. J. (1978). *Beyond her sphere: Women and the professions in American history.* Westport, CT: Greenwood.

Harrison, C. H. (1988). *On account of sex: The politics of women's issues, 1945-1968.* Berkeley, CA: University of California Press.

Hartmann, S. M. (1989). *From margin to mainstream: American women and politics since 1960.* New York: Knopf.

Hirschfield, G. (1931, July). What should the business women know about economics? *The Independent Woman, 10.*

James, E. T., James, J. W., & Boyer, P. S. (Eds.). (1971). *Notable American women* (Vols. 1-3). Cambridge, MA: Harvard University Press.

Jensen, J. (1986). *Loosening the bonds: Mid-Atlantic farm women, 1750-1850.* New Haven, CT: Yale University Press.

Johnson, E. (1923). *To women of the business world.* Philadelphia: J. B. Lippincott.

Kanter, R. M. (1977). *Men and women of the corporation.* New York: Basic Books.

Kerber, L. K. (1980/1986). *Women of the republic: Intellect and ideology in revolutionary America.* New York: Norton.

Kessler-Harris, A. (1982). *Out to work: A history of wage-earning women in the United States.* New York: Oxford University Press.

Kessler-Harris, A. (1985). The debate over equality for women in the work place: Recognizing differences. In L. Larwood, A. H. Stromberg, & B. Gutek (Eds.), *Women and work* (Vol. 1, pp. 141-161). Beverly Hills, CA: Sage.

Leaycraft, J. S., & Bush, M. L. (1917, March). The college alumna's work. *Columbia University Quarterly*, pp. 145-156 (Bureau of Vocational Information papers in Box 1, folder 1, Schlesinger Library, Cambridge, MA).

Lemons, J. S. (1973). *The woman citizen: Social feminism in the 1920s.* Urbana: University of Illinois Press.

Maule, F. (1961). *Executive careers for women.* New York: Harper. (Original work published 1957)

May, E. T. (1988). *Homeward bound: American families in the cold war era.* New York: Basic Books.

Morantz-Sanchez, R. (1985). *Sympathy and science: Women physicians in American medicine.* New York: Oxford University Press.

Meyer, A. E. (1958). *Out of these roots.* Boston: Little, Brown.

Noble, J. (1988). The higher education of black women in the twentieth century. In J. M. Faragher & F. Howe (Eds.), *Women and higher education in American history.* New York: Norton.

Norton, M. B. (1980). *Liberty's daughters: The revolutionary experience of American women, 1750-1800.* Boston: Little, Brown.

Oxford English Dictionary (1989). (2nd ed.). Oxford, UK: Clarendon.

Perkins, L. M. (1988). The education of black women in the nineteenth century. In J. M. Faragher & F. Howe (Eds.), *Women and higher education in American history.* New York: Norton.

Pogrebin, L. C. (1970). *How to make it in a man's world.* Garden City, NY: Doubleday.

Powell, G. N. (1993). *Women & men in management* (2nd ed.). Newbury Park, CA: Sage.

Pyle, M. (1923). *Advertising: A field for women.* Philadelphia: Bureau of Occupations (Women's Educational and Industrial Union papers in Box 10, folder 109, Schlesinger Library, Cambridge, MA).

Ried, H. F. H. (1919, October). *Sizing yourself up* (Clipping in Box 28, folder 349, Bureau of Vocational Information papers, Schlesinger Library, Cambridge, MA).

Rosener, J. B. (1990, November/December). Ways women lead. *Harvard Business Review, 68,* 119-125.

Rubinstein, H. (1965). *My life for beauty.* London: Bodley Head.

Rupp, L. (1978). *Mobilizing women for war: German and American propaganda, 1936-1945.* Princeton, NJ: Princeton University Press.

Sears, E. (n.d., post-1920). Women's power in business. *The Green Book Magazine* (Bureau of Vocational Information papers in Box 4, folder 59, Schlesinger Library, Cambridge, MA).

Sicherman, B., & Green, C. (Eds.). (1980). *Notable American women: The modern period.* Cambridge, MA: Harvard University Press.

Sklar, K. K. (1973). *Catherine Beecher: A study in domesticity.* New Haven, CT: Yale University Press.

Solomon, B. M. (1985). *In the company of educated women.* New Haven, CT: Yale University Press.

Srole, C. (1987). A blessing to mankind, and especially to womankind: The typewriter and the feminization of clerical work, Boston, 1860-1920. In B. D. Wright (Ed.), *Women, work, and technology* (pp. 84-100). Ann Arbor, MI: University of Michigan Press.

Sutton, C. D., & Moore, K. K. (1985, September-October). Executive women: 20 years later. *Harvard Business Review, 12,* 1-12.

Terborg-Penn, R. (1978). Discrimination against Afro-American women in the woman's movement, 1830-1920. In S. Harley & R. Terborg-Penn (Eds.), *The Afro-American woman: Struggles and images* (pp. 17-27). Port Washington, NY: Kennikat.

Ulrich, L. T. (1983). *Good wives: Image and reality in northern New England, 1650—1750.* New York: Oxford University Press.

Ulrich, L. T. (1991). *A midwife's tale: The life of Martha Ballard, based on her diary, 1785-1812.* New York: Vintage.

U.S. Department of Commerce, Bureau of the Census. (1975). *Historical statistics of the United States: Colonial times to 1970.* Washington, DC: Government Printing Office.

U.S. Department of Commerce, Bureau of the Census. (1986). *Women in the American economy.* (Series P-23, No. 146). Washington DC: Government Printing Office.

U.S. Department of Commerce, Bureau of the Census. (1987). *Statistical abstract of the United States* (107 ed., Table 68). Washington, DC: Government Printing Office.

U.S. Department of Commerce, Bureau of the Census. (1989). *Statistical abstract of the United States.* Washington, DC: Government Printing Office.

U.S. Department of Labor, Bureau of Labor Statistics. (1983). *Handbook of labor statistics.* Washington, DC: Government Printing Office.

U.S. Department of Labor, Bureau of Labor Statistics. (1987, June). *Employment and earnings* (34, no. 6). Washington, DC: Government Printing Office.

U.S. Department of Labor, Bureau of Labor Statistics. (1989, December). *Facts on working women: Women in management* (no. 89-4). Washington DC: Government Printing Office.

Ware, S. (1981). *Beyond suffrage: Women in the New Deal.* Cambridge, MA: Harvard University Press.

Welter, B. (1966). The cult of true womanhood: 1820-1860. *American Quarterly, 17,* 151-174.

Women in business III: Executives. (1935, September). *Fortune,* p. 12.

Woloch, N. (1984). *Women and the American experience.* New York: Knopf.

Woods, R. A., & Kennedy, A. J. (Eds.). (1911). *Handbook of settlements.* Philadelphia, PA: Wm. F. Fell.

3

A Global Comparison of Women in Management: Women Managers in Their Homelands and as Expatriates

ARIANE BERTHOIN ANTAL
DAFNA N. IZRAELI

THE EMERGENCE OF AN ISSUE

Until the late 1970s, women managers were virtually invisible in most countries. As one writer observed laconically: "Statistics show that women represent one third of the world's workforce, do two-thirds of the world's working hours, but they earn only one tenth of the world's income and own one-hundredth of the world's goods . . . they hold less than one percent of the world's executive positions" (Ho, 1984, p. 7). The absence of women in positions of responsibility received almost no attention from the media, political parties, academics, or the business community, except in the United States and to a lesser extent in Canada and Great Britain. Elsewhere, it was a nonissue. Few of the large

AUTHORS' NOTE: The authors names are in alphabetical order. We extend our appreciation to Nancy Adler, Rhoda Blumberg, Valerie Hammond, Judy Lorber, Simcha Ronen, and Yoram Zeira for their helpful comments on earlier versions of parts of this chapter. We acknowledge the contribution of the editor, Ellen Fagenson, and four anonymous reviewers whose thoughtful reading and critique of this chapter in all its parts were very helpful and give our thanks to Kristina Vaillant for her invaluable assistance in collecting the international data.

companies hired women for senior positions or promoted women into them and fewer still indicated an interest in changing the situation, although the proportion of women among managers varied somewhat from country to country (see Table 3.1).

During the 1980s, the underrepresentation of women in positions of power emerged as a "problem." It became an item on the public agenda of industrialized countries—albeit not one of high priority. Adler and Izraeli (1988), in their overview of *Women in Management Worldwide*, outlined some of the forces contributing to the change.

- *Globalization:* The globalization of competition led to a greater emphasis on the need to develop a competitive edge, to encourage excellence, and therefore to maximize the human potential in the work force.
- *Skill shortage:* Demographic forecasts concerning the post-baby-boom squeeze—the "baby-bust" (Sullivan, 1986, p. 18)—were perceived by government, business, and social scientists as predicting a shortage of qualified (white) men for top-level jobs.
- *Labor force participation:* The increased participation of women in the labor force, and the visibility given to women's issues by the U.N. Decade for Women, contributed to the perception of women as an underused source of human capital.
- *Women's resources and commitment:* The active search on the part of women themselves for access to management positions and their continuing investment in education and training made it more difficult to overlook them in recruitment and promotion decisions.

In this chapter, we examine assumptions about the predictors of women's progress in management and review the major barriers and alternate routes from a primarily European perspective. We describe highlights in legislation and public policy and corporate programs. The role of multinational corporations, particularly in the promotion of opportunities for women as expatriate managers,[1] is explored. The reasons commonly given for "why so few" and the impact of uncertainties in the expatriate role on women's opportunities are reviewed, and current trends predicting an increase in women as expatriate managers are critically examined. This chapter emphasizes the fruitfulness of a cross-national approach for analyzing the issue of women in management. Wherever data permit, we suggest similarities and differences across countries, especially those of Western Europe and Japan and Israel, for which current data are more readily available and point to persisting gaps in our knowledge. The role of international organizations

text continued on page 56

Table 3.1 Women in the Labor Force and Women in Management: An International Overview for 1970 and 1987 (in percentages)

	Women in the Economically Active Population		Women in Administrative and Managerial Positions		Women in Middle Management	Women in Top Management
	1970	1987	1970	1987	1970	1987
Belgium	24.2[b]	36.4[d] (1981)	8.6[b]	12.9[d] (1981)	7.0[e]	8.0[e]
Canada	33.9[a] (1973)	42.9[d] (1986)	15.5[a] (1973)	34.5[d] (1986)	—	—
Denmark	33.9[a] (1965)	45.6[c] (1985)	14.3[a] (1965)	14.5[c] (1985)	8.0[e]	2.0[e]
Finland	42.1[a]	47.1[d] (1986)	(52.4)[a1]	19.8[d] (1986)	—	—
France	34.9[a] (1968)	40.3[c] (1982)	11.9[a] (1968)	9.4[c] (1982)	9.0[e]	7.0[e]
Germany (West)	35.8[b]	38.0[c] (1984)	13.5[b]	20.0[c] (1984)	8.0[e]	2.0[e]
Hong Kong	33.7[a] (1971)	37.7[d] (1986)	11.3[a] (1971)	17.0[d] (1986)	—	—
Ireland	25.9[a] (1966)	29.5[d] (1985)	5.7[a] (1966)	9.0[d] (1985)	4.0[e]	3.0[e]
Israel	31.1[a] (1972)	38.7[d] (1986)	6.6[a] (1972)	15.0[d] (1986)	—	—

Country					
Italy	27.6[a] (1965)	NA	(32.6)[a][2] (1965)	NA	8.0[e]	2.0[e]
Japan	39.0[a]	39.8[d] (1986)	4.8[a]	7.5[d] (1986)	—	—
Luxembourg	26.2[b]	33.3[c] (1981)	8.2[b]	5.5[c] (1981)	5.0[e]	4.0[e]
Netherlands	22.3[c] (1960)	34.8[c] (1985)	4.1[a] (1960)	7.2[c] (1985)	4.0[e]	2.0[e]
Norway	22.9[a] (1972)	44.5[d] (1986)	6.7[a] (1972)	20.1[d] (1986)	—	—
Sweden	35.4[a]	47.6[d] (1986)	14.9[a]	64.4[d] (1986)	—	—
United Kingdom	35.7[a] (1966)	38.8[c] (1981)	7.5[a] (1966)	22.7[c] (1981)	NA	NA
United States	37.4[a] (1972)	43.9[d] (1986)	17.7[a] (1972)	37.1[d] (1986)	—	—

SOURCE: The data on the representation of women in the economically active population and on women in administrative and managerial positions were taken from the *Yearbook of Labor Statistics* published by the International Labor Office (ILO). The year in which data were collected is added in the table where it deviates from the year indicated at the top of the column. For the sake of comparison, the data generated by EUROSTAT for the European Communities on the representation of women in middle and top management in member countries are provided in the last two columns. The data for the United Kingdom were not available.

a. ILO Yearbook of Labor Statistics (1973).
b. ILO Yearbook of Labor Statistics (1974).
c. ILO Yearbook of Labor Statistics (1986).
d. ILO Yearbook of Labor Statistics (1987).
e. EUROSTAT: "Women in Europe—Their Economic and Social Position" (European Communities, Luxembourg, 1987).
1. This number includes professional, technical, and related workers.
2. This number includes clerical and related workers.

and the challenges for the research community are examined in the concluding section.

THE NEED FOR AN
INTERNATIONAL PERSPECTIVE

Most research on women in management has come from the United States. The U.S. academic community, to date, however, has paid little attention to developments in other countries. Where such reference is made, it tends to be allocated to a separate section or chapter on "international experiences." In contrast, the European literature on the subject more often consciously integrates comparative observations with other countries with a view to countries learning from each other.

A cross-national perspective is valuable for several reasons (see Berthoin Antal, 1987). First, international comparative analysis provides social scientists with the "natural laboratory" they need to observe similar phenomena under different conditions in order to test and refine their hypotheses. This is particularly useful when, as in the case of women in management, the sample available within one country is still quite small. Second, cross-national comparisons help avoid oversimplistic explanations and ethnocentric biases. Third, management is increasingly becoming an international occupation: Companies send managers to work for them abroad, and those who stay at home often have to deal with foreign managers. Expatriate managers, those sent to represent their companies in other countries, have much to gain from familiarity with the status and situation of women managers in their host country, while stay-at-home-managers dealing with foreigners would benefit from a clearer understanding of the ways in which the latter view women managers in their own countries.

Problems of Definition and Data Collection

Scholars with experience in international research are very skeptical about the validity and reliability of cross-national data. Tables on labor market data are typically introduced with such caveats as "owing to the limited availability of even broadly-comparable data at the international level, the data in tables . . . are calculated at a very high level of aggregation. Movements over long periods are affected by changes in definitions. Both these factors reduce the usefulness of the results"

(Organization for Economic Co-Operation and Development [OECD] 1988, p. 147).

These limitations are especially true concerning the field of management, which, unlike, for example, medicine, has no internationally accepted body of requisite knowledge, paths of entry, or even job description. Who is a manager? Within most countries, let alone among them, there is no generally agreed upon definition concerning the tasks or level of responsibility at which one is deemed to be a manager. Furthermore, as Blum and Smith (1988, p. 540) point out: "Jobs labelled 'management' span a wide range of the job hierarchy within any organization." The data on management, scant to begin with, are of limited reliability, because they either are generated through broad international categories that do not account for significant national differences in the practice of power or are provided by companies and organizations in each country, with neither independent validation nor criteria for cross-national comparability. Studies from different countries rarely use comparable data, or measures and studies within the same country are almost never repeated so that changes cannot be tracked.

The data base incorporating information from the greatest number of countries is that of the International Labour Organization (ILO). It was therefore tapped for columns 1-4 in Table 3.1. The category "administrative/managerial" it uses is so inclusive, however, that it tends to significantly overstate the representation of women in managerial positions. To obtain a somewhat more precise overview, it is worth looking at the statistics generated by the European Community (EC; see columns 5 and 6) about the situation in its member countries, particularly because they attempt to differentiate between top and middle management. Looking at the developments over time, whichever data base is used, the fact remains that the representation of women in management has not kept pace with the increased labor force participation of women (see Izraeli & Adler, in press).

PREDICTORS FOR WOMEN'S PROGRESS INTO MANAGEMENT

An optimistic scenario shared primarily by men we have interviewed in different countries concerning the possibilities for women in corporate management views the paucity of women, their concentration at the bottom of the managerial hierarchy, and their absence from positions of real authority as a passing stage. It predicts that, with time, as a result of a dynamic set in motion by current trends, women will break through to the managerial ranks and close the gender gap. These trends include the increase in women's labor force participation and in their educational achievements, the opportunities presented by the development of new industries and managerial specializations as well as a predicted shortage of qualified labor. A closer examination of the situation and trends in different countries suggests, however, that women's integration into management is not "just a matter of time." (See also Blum & Smith, 1988, for a critique of optimistic scenarios, and see Northcraft & Gutek, in this volume, for a debate on women's progress.)

Labor Force Participation as a Predictor?

A common line of reasoning among managers who hold that "it's just a matter of time" is that women must first enter the labor force, accumulate experience and seniority, and then (with time) they will "automatically" move up the organizational hierarchy. While there is a significant amount of logic in this argument, it is essential to recognize the limits of such a dynamic. The big growth in women's labor force participation in most industrialized countries occurred in the decade from the late 1960s to the late 1970s. Compared with the proportion of women who have since accumulated human capital in all the countries for which we have data, however, gains in women's movement into and within management in the 1980s are modest.

As Table 3.1 so clearly illustrates, a high level of female labor force participation is no assurance of women's representation in management. While they have gotten a foot on the bottom rung of the ladder in most countries, possibly as a result of the routinization of certain managerial tasks, they remain absent from positions of authority. For example, in Denmark, where women are 47% of the salaried labor force, they are only 14% of the administrators/managers (according to the ILO) and 5% of "top management" (EC data) or 1%-2% of senior managers (according to a director at the Danish Employers' Confederation: Claus Helmann Hansen, 1987, pp. 4-5). In France, the proportions are 40% and 9% (ILO; or 7% in top management in EC data), respectively. In Israel, women constituted 40% of the labor force in 1988, 13% of the administrators and managers, 9% of senior managers in the public sector but less than 3% in the private sector. In Japan, women constituted 40% of the labor force in 1986 but only 0.3% of top management in the private sector and 0.8% in the public sector (Steinhoff & Kazuko, 1988). In Norway, women constituted 30% of the labor force in 1970, and 44.6% in 1978, but in 1983 they still held only 2.8% of the senior appointments in the private sector, compared with 2.5% in 1956 (Ellefsen, 1986). This pattern is typical for all the countries for which we could obtain information. It seems that the relationship between growth in the female labor force and women's representation among managers is mediated by other factors, some of which are discussed below.

Second, it appears that progress is not linear, and not every statistical increase marks a real breakthrough. For example, data for Great Britain indicate a drop of 3.5% in the proportion of women in senior management from 1975 to 1984, although an increase of similar proportions was registered at the middle and lower management levels (Hammond, 1986). A similar decline in the proportion of women among senior managers occurred in the United States between 1960 and 1980 when those who had probably benefited from the opportunities for women offered by the absence of men during World War II reached retirement age. For similar reasons, the Federal Republic of Germany is currently experiencing a drop in the number of women of high rank in the academic system. The essential question such observations across national borders raise is this: How can women maintain and expand the footholds gained in male-dominated domains rather than repeatedly pioneering their entrance when the labor market needs them?

Higher Education as a Predictor?

Common to all industrialized countries is the trend toward higher levels of educational achievement and usually a faster rate of growth in university students for women than for men. In some countries, including Finland and the United States, more than 50% of the university entrants are now women (OECD, 1985). In most countries, the gender gap in education is closing. While the traditionally female fields of study have become even more gender segregated in the last two decades, women have also entered some of the male specializations from which managers are recruited, such as economics and law. In some countries, women today constitute 40%-50% of the students in these fields (Roobeek, 1989). In most industrialized countries, however, women are still severely underenrolled in the natural sciences and technological departments of the universities, despite a gradual upward trend (Roobeek, 1989). In some countries, such as Britain, West Germany, and the Eastern European countries, women's entry into science and technology has been actively promoted by government agencies in response to a shortage of qualified labor. For example, training programs targeted at integrating young girls into apprenticeships for traditionally male occupations have been subsidized by the government and promoted by employers' associations in West Germany (see, for example, Kresbach-Gnath et al., 1983). The increase in women's educational achievement and their pursuit of "management-relevant" specializations, however, have not been matched by anywhere near equivalent increases in their opportunities for advancement into management.

Company Size or Economic
Structure as Predictors?

The verdict is not yet in on the "woman-friendliness" of companies according to their size. Some observers have stressed the relative openness of large organizations to women in management, as a function of clear career paths and the greater flexibility of resources available to such companies. Others emphasize the openness of small and medium-sized companies, because of their less differentiated job structures and less bureaucratic personnel procedures (Blum & Smith, 1988, p. 542) as well as their difficulty competing with the large companies for the "best men." It appears that size in itself is a weak predictor of an organization's response to women in management.

The overall structure of the economy in each country with regard to the ratio of large to small companies is another relevant factor in women's opportunities. In economies with few very large corporations and many small companies, the latter will offer more employment opportunities for women—with correspondingly short career ladders to climb. In Italy and Japan, for example, where 95% and 99.4% of all business organizations, respectively, are classified as small and medium-sized, women managers are concentrated in these businesses (Olivares, 1992). In contrast to the virtual absence of women in the large Japanese corporations, women play an active role in managing small—especially family-based—enterprises, a pattern that is typical of many other Asian countries (Steinhoff & Kazuko, 1988).

Academic research on women's organizational careers has focused on the large corporations and has paid insufficient attention to patterns of women's participation and achievement in middle-sized and smaller enterprises. It is likely that many women who are in fact managing the small firms in the Far East are not included in the official (ILO) statistics on "managers and administrators."

Do New Industries Offer More Opportunities?

Researchers in different countries have noted the tendency for new and especially fast-growing industries to provide easier access to women managers. They often include new occupations and positions that have not yet been assigned a particular sex label and where the competition for jobs is less fierce (e.g., Olivares, 1992). In Israel, for example (Izraeli, 1988), the rapid growth of the banking and insurance industries in the early 1970s as well as the expansion of certain managerial specializations such as marketing, personnel, and public relations created a demand for managers and consequently new opportunities for women. Similarly, the software computer occupations during the same period lacked a sex label and were indifferent to gender. The army, as one of the first big users of computers in Israel in the 1960s, trained women as programmers. During the 1970s and 1980s, however, as the occupation became more differentiated, women remained in the more routine lower status jobs while men came to dominate the more discretionary specializations. Unfortunately, women's representation in management in Apple Computer in the United States (33% of management and 40% of professionals, according to Meirs Osterling, 1989) is not duplicated in the growing high-tech industry anywhere else in the world. More research is required to analyze the conditions under which the growth of new industries creates opportunities for women managers and to establish whether they maintain their "advantage" over time.

The political implication of the optimistic scenario is that there is no need for specific interventions, beyond encouraging women to train in the "right" occupational skills. There is recognition, however, that the noninterventionist approach entails a change rate that is "moving about as fast as the next Ice Age is approaching," as a leading West German weekly quipped ("Bienen auf der Galeere," 1985, p. 74). This recognition of the need for political intervention was instrumental for women's heightened involvement in the political sphere.

Political Representation as a Predictor?

In all the countries we have examined, women have made greater headway in leadership positions in the political than in the economic sphere. Epstein, too, found that in most countries they have achieved a higher representation in government elites than in economic elites (Epstein, 1981). She explained this trend in terms of the opportunity created by a political ideology that legitimizes its claim to power on the basis of representativeness. Economic ideology, on the other hand, legitimizes managerial power in terms of rationality and efficiency (Kanter, 1977)—symbolically associated with masculinity (Hearn & Parkin, 1988).

Following recent elections in each country, women accounted for 38% of the members of Parliament in Sweden, 34.4% in Norway, 33.5% in Finland, 30.7% in Denmark, and 21.3% in the Netherlands (Hansard Society, 1990), but in all countries they account for only a minute percentage of the senior managers. The gap between the proportion of women elected to national parliaments and those promoted to management is less great in other countries, because women are still not being elected in great numbers: 12.9% of parliamentarians in Italy are women; in Spain and Israel, 6.6%; in Great Britain, 6.3%; and, in France, 5.8% (Hansard Society, 1990).

The European Parliament is an interesting case for exploring factors that influence women's access to power and their impact on matters of policy relating to women. Since the first direct elections in 1979, there have been proportionately more women members than in the national parliamentary bodies (17% at the international level and an average of 7.6% in the national parliaments in 1979 and 1984; Hörburger & Rath-Hörburger, 1988). It has been speculated that women have had easier access to the European Parliament because, lacking in significant power, this body was not as attractive to career-minded (male) politicians. Second, the women did not have to "unseat" men there in the same way that they have to fight male incumbents for political office within their countries. Unless positive action (e.g., quotas) is instituted, however, women may face difficulties maintaining and increasing their representation as the power and status of the European Parliament rises—parallel to developments observed in new industries in which women have not always been able to keep their initial foothold.

The case of the European Parliament, furthermore, shows that, where women in office have more than token representation, they can influence the substance of policy. The special commission on women's rights succeeded in placing many issues relating to women and work on the agenda over the years and generated solid information bases for policymaking. Although the European Parliament is not a lawmaking body, the calibre and scope of the discussions there influence the thinking of the European Commission and have an impact on the debate within the member countries.

One might hope that the visibility of women in political office could offer role models for women's leadership. The transfer of the role model from the political to the business sphere, however, does not appear to be simple. As one journalist observed: "Margaret Thatcher and Gro Harlem Brundtland [have] run countries of 57 million and 4 million people respectively. So why does the prospect of a woman at the helm of Philips, Volkswagen or ICI still seem such a long way off?" (Bebbington, 1988, p. 12).

BARRIERS TO MOBILITY AND ALTERNATIVE ROUTES FOR WOMEN IN MANAGEMENT

"Think Manager, Think Male"

Probably the single most important hurdle for women in management in all industrialized countries is the persistent stereotype that associates management with being male. Whichever characteristics are considered important for managers, they appear to be the ones generally identified more closely with men than with women (Brenner, Tomkiewicz, & Schein, 1989; Hearn & Parkin, 1988; Schein, 1973, 1975). The consistency of male dominance in management across the world is all the more remarkable when one considers that the actual features sought in a manager vary by culture. This is shown, for example, in the studies conducted by Geert Hofstede (1980) in the subsidiaries of a large multinational corporation and by André Laurent (1983) among managers (almost all men) from many countries who attended the leading international business school in France: INSEAD. Significant differences in cultural attitudes and expectations about the nature and responsibility of authority in management, the appropriate distribution of power, the role of expertise, and relevant time frames for fulfilling responsibilities help to explain misunderstandings experienced in business dealings between managers from different cultures.

While such studies are deconstructing the myth that it is desirable and possible to form or train the "universal manager," they have as yet left untouched the myth that management responsibilities are best fulfilled by men. The myth is embedded in their research approach: Laurent's samples contained almost no women; Hofstede's theoretical concepts have built-in gender stereotypes. It is therefore not surprising that he found men and women differ significantly only on the dimension he had labeled "masculinity" (assertiveness) versus "femininity" (nurturance) (Hofstede, 1989, pp. 191-194). He suggests that cultures that rate higher in "masculinity" (Japan, Austria, Venezuela, Italy, Switzerland) look less favorably on women in leadership positions.[2] Hofstede's own data show, however, that those cultures that rate highest in "femininity," such as Sweden, Norway, the Netherlands, and Denmark, are not the countries with the highest proportion of women managers. Sweden and Norway, the two most "feminine" countries, where "feminine" characteristics are more highly valued than "masculine" characteristics, even show a role reversal: In these countries, the women score more "masculine" than the men in the same occupations (Hofstede, 1989, p. 194). Such findings challenge the traditional argument that "if only women were more like men" they would make better headway in management.

"Management Is a Full-Time Job"

Traditional conceptions of management duties and loyalties, in all industrialized countries, appear to be based on total commitment measured in terms of time spent at the workplace. Management is presumed to be a full-time and continuous job that is incompatible with divided attention. This conception conflicts with women's biographies and traditional responsibilities in two ways. First, to balance their work inside and outside the home, many women have sought part-time arrangements. Second, women's biographies show interruptions for childbearing and child raising. Career breaks, it is believed, indicate lack of commitment, making reentry problematic.

A recent OECD (1985) study reported that at least 60% of part-time workers are women, rising to almost 90% in some countries. Among men, however, the majority are within the oldest and youngest age groups, whereas, among women, part-time work is most pervasive among the 20- to 35-year-olds (OECD, 1985) at the formative stage of the work career. There is a growing body of legislation in various countries designed to ensure that part-time employees receive appropriate social benefits (OECD, 1985). In Israel, for example, part-time employees receive virtually all the same fringe benefits given to full-time workers, including security of tenure.

"By far the majority of women work full-time. Only in a very few European countries does the proportion of all women employees who work part-time exceed 50 percent, and in many it is no more than 25 percent" (OECD, 1988, p. 150). The demand by women in management for more part-time opportunities is rising, however, despite the current "taboo" on part-time positions in management. This trend poses new challenges to organizations. Because part-time workers in general tend to receive fewer career development opportunities, the growing proportion of women who opt for part-time work tends to be overlooked in assignments to training and development programs (see, for example, Sandqvist, 1992; also Hohenberger, Maier, & Schlegelmilch, 1989). A recent survey conducted among members of the European Women's Management Development Network (EWMD) in West Germany ranked this issue as a top policy priority (Antal, unpublished data). A few organizations are pioneering such arrangements willingly; some are being forced to do so by the courts. In Britain, in the *Holmes v. Home Office* judgment in 1984, Ms. Holmes, an Executive Officer in the Home Office, won the right to return to work from maternity leave on a part-time basis. Such an arrangement was consequently extended to senior grades (Hansard Society, 1990). Until more experiments of this kind are conducted and made visible, however, the belief in full-time employment will remain unchallenged, and the potential pool of future managers will not include the large percentage of women who are currently working part-time or who wish to take an extended parental leave to care for children.

The requirement of continuous employment is another characteristic of the managerial career that conflicts with women's family roles in every country. Research now shows that, contrary to the stereotype, turnover rates are not significantly higher for women than for men, but women and men leave for different reasons: men to pursue career options or further training, women to care for the family.

Upon their return to the labor force, from the perspective of the same or the next employer, men's leave will have enhanced their human capital; women's leave is generally perceived to have resulted in their professional obsolescence. Organizations, furthermore, have traditionally been resistant to granting extended leaves of absence to care for small children, and women who take such leaves and are forced to leave the company and the labor force later face reentry problems. In most countries, however, women are returning to the labor market after a shorter interruption and in some countries recent data show that fewer women are interrupting their employment for child rearing—often opting for part-time arrangements or self-employment (OECD, 1988).

In a number of European countries, significant efforts are currently being made to alter traditional conceptions. The managerial skills required for running a household (e.g., budgeting, organizing, mediating, motivating) are being recognized as managerial skills. Women are being encouraged to include them in job applications, and personnel managers are learning to discuss them in job interviews with such employers as the British Civil Service. Some organizations have recognized the waste of human resources incurred by traditional attitudes toward women's absences and are therefore introducing parental leave schemes (discussed below).

Becoming Part of the Recruitment Pool

In many countries, there are structural and social obstacles to women's gaining access to the recruitment pools for managerial jobs. The following are some typical examples:

"Women do not have the right degree." While we have already noted the growing number of women selecting business- and management-relevant academic specializations, there are still relatively few in technologically related specializations (Roobeek, 1989). A trend among the new high-tech firms that does not bode well for women is the myth and mystification of technological knowledge (Roobeek, 1989). It is generally assumed that managers employed in such firms, almost regardless of their function, must have technological training, even though once in the job they may never be required to use their training. This presumption of technological competence combined with the stereotype of women's technological incompetence may keep these new firms off limits for women managers. From her study of women, management, and technology in Europe, Roobeek (1989) concluded that men with technological backgrounds are overvalued, hired, and then sent for management training to learn what women know so well—the soft values. "Often the problems are not technological but problems of values, attitudes and culture. The traditional view of technology as a male domain is used to exclude women" (Roobeek, 1989). Once women become engineers, however, they are more likely than men to reject the managerial option. They express a preference for practicing engineering rather than for managing people and papers.

"Women are not from the right school." In some countries, such as France and Japan, managers are recruited from among the graduates of a small number of elite universities, which, until recently, were male dominated. These institutions, such as the Grandes Écoles of France, functioned to filter women out of the paths to power (Serdjénian, 1988). Business schools and the MBA degree have, until very recently, played a relatively unimportant role in providing entry into management outside the United States and Canada, with the exception perhaps of Great Britain (Keller Brown, 1988). One of the reasons is that there were few business schools until just over a decade ago. These have grown, however, both in number and in importance in recent years and so has women's participation in them. In Italy, for example, the percentage of women among the graduates of management and business schools rose from 5% in 1975 to 15% in 1984 (Olivares, 1992). The leading international business school in France, INSEAD, reported that the past few classes have been averaging 12% women among new students. A major business school in Barcelona, IESE, currently counts 17% women among their MBA students, up from 5% 10 years ago (Bebbington, 1988). This is still much lower than the 25%-35% women in U.S. business schools (Bebbington, 1988).

In some countries, such as Switzerland and Israel, the army serves as a special kind of "school" and represents a major recruitment pool, especially for more senior managers. Swiss corporations, and especially banks, have a strong preference for promoting men who are army officers. Both the military training and the social networks of army officers are considered to be important assets for managers. In Israel, serving as a combat officer (a career path closed to women) is perceived to be excellent training for management responsibilities (Izraeli, in press). In addition, early forced retirement at age 40, and the operation of a politically well-connected network of retired generals, give the male officer seeking a second career a decided advantage in access to senior management positions. This is especially the case in the public and semi-public sectors, which account for more than half the Israeli economy.

Looking across national borders, women appear to fare better in countries with more flexible and multiple routes of entry (Handy, 1987). For example, in Great Britain, where companies are willing to accept nontechnical degrees, including those from the humanities, and to provide candidates with in-house management training, women have greater opportunities for entry. On the other hand, women may be at a disadvantage in systems that are characterized by unclear entry patterns, because they have a more difficult time learning the ropes and hidden routes (Hammond, 1988, p. 169).

Women face early deselection. In some countries, selection mechanisms distinguishing men from women are applied at an early stage in the career course. In Japan, for example, students are traditionally recruited immediately upon graduation. College men are recruited for managerial careers; women, for clerical jobs (Steinhoff & Kazuko, 1988). The apprenticeship system in Germany, which absorbs 60% of school graduates and represents the main bridge from school to work, has tended in practice to route young girls into nonmanagerial paths. In both cases, once deselected, it is almost impossible to rejoin the management route in later years.

Alternative Routes

In most countries, women have been generally more successful in gaining entry into management in the public than in the private sector (Australia and Japan are notable exceptions; OECD, 1985). The greater commitment to universalistic standards and the more regular and shorter working hours make the public sector more women-friendly, while higher wages in the private sector make it more attractive to equally qualified males (see Adler & Izraeli, 1988; Epstein, 1981). Within private sector corporations, women managers are more likely to be in staff and service positions, such as personnel, marketing, and public relations. Few are in general management.

A management option that appears to be attracting increasing numbers of women in industrialized countries is entrepreneurship. In Canada and Finland, for example, 30% of entrepreneurs are women (O'Connor, 1987). In the Federal Republic of Germany, a third of all new companies are being started by women (Assig, 1987, 1989), and 20% of businesses are owned by women (Bebbington, 1988).

Goffee and Scase (1985) suggest five types of women entrepreneurs, classified by life stage and motivation. Two types describe women who set up their own companies in midcareer, after accumulating experience in larger corporations. One type is responding to the "glass ceiling" that blocks their upward mobility, and the other type is motivated primarily by a desire for greater flexibility. Research in the United States, in particular, stresses the former—women turning to entrepreneurship when they find their careers blocked in large corporations (Morrison et al., 1987). This motive, however, is rarely mentioned in research on European countries, perhaps a reflection of the fact that women there have not yet climbed high enough to reach the "glass ceiling." Women in both Europe and North America pursue the entrepreneurship option to obtain greater flexibility in managing their family and employment responsibilities (Galante, 1986; Goffee & Scase, 1985).

A third category of entrepreneurs are women who establish their own—usually small—businesses at an early stage in their careers. Sweden, for example, has experienced a large increase in women entrepreneurs 25 to 44 years old (*EWMD News*, 1984). In contrast, a growing number of women in Great Britain start a business later in life, even close to retirement age (Doole, 1985). A final category of entrepreneurs are those women of any age for whom entrepreneurship is a response to the fear of unemployment. None of the available studies indicates that women use entrepreneurship as a stepping stone into or training ground for careers in the management of larger organizations; rather, it is an alternative chosen when work in a corporation is considered undesirable or unachievable.

Some governments have actively sought to stimulate entrepreneurship among women, sometimes to reduce unemployment, sometimes for other structural reasons. The Netherlands, for example, emphasizes the creation of jobs for women by providing women entrepreneurs with interest-free loans on the condition that only women are hired (*EWMD News*, 1984). Such a policy both supports women entrepreneurs and creates new jobs for women. Sweden, on the other hand, has introduced measures to encourage the creation of new businesses as a way of stabilizing the female population in the underpopulated north of the country (Business and Industry Information Group, 1983).

PROMOTING THE CAUSE OF
WOMEN IN MANAGEMENT

A number of different arguments contributed to the discourse on women in management in the 1980s[3] and provided employers with a rationale for adopting more women-friendly personnel policies. These are discussed under the competitive advantage, demographic, women's leadership, and entitlement arguments.

The competitive advantage argument. Economic and demographic arguments dominated discussion about the need for more women in management throughout the 1980s. The economic argument asserts that the underuse of women's human capital resources is a business issue and not solely a woman's issue. Better use of women affects productivity and efficiency in the workplace and makes business more competitive in the global community. In other words, the business community simply cannot afford not to tap women as a valuable resource for management. The impact of the competitive advantage argument depends on whether managers at the corporate level really believe women managers are an economic asset. It is questionable whether deep-rooted prejudices against women's leadership abilities and statistical discrimination are responsive to such rational arguments—especially when there exists a self-fulfilling prophecy that the absence of women in management signifies their lack of suitability.

The demographic argument. In countries such as the Federal Republic of Germany, Switzerland, and France, where the birthrates have been particularly low, demographic arguments are raised. Companies are advised to include women in their recruitment pools because of the anticipated shortage of highly qualified males in the 1990s that will result from the smaller cohorts of the "baby-bust" generation. Women in management we interviewed tended to find this logic attractive because it seemed so "objective" and calculable: Given the current birthrates, it would take so many years to produce more men that women believed they could establish themselves in management in the meantime. West German women who had used the demographic curve to press for more opportunities in management, however, discovered in 1989 how fragile a logic this could be. The opening of the wall between the two Germanies and of Eastern Europe as a whole has led to a great westward influx of (more or less) skilled men. Furthermore, the demographic argument is a double-edged sword. It does point to the need for women in the labor force but at the same time emphasizes, with perhaps greater urgency, women's important role in reproducing the next generation. Several countries have introduced policy measures to make childbearing a more attractive option, such as paid maternity or parental leave (see below).

The feminine leadership argument. A new theme heard recently in the discourse over women in management is the call for "feminine leadership" (Fossan, 1989; Loden, 1985). Those very female characteristics traditionally believed to disqualify women from management are currently lauded as particularly appropriate for meeting new management challenges. Academics, consultants, and managers themselves proclaim the "new qualities" needed for management today, linking them explicitly to the strengths they believe are characteristic of women: cooperativeness and the ability to integrate people, to listen to them, and to motivate them through nonmonetary incentives, to mention just a few. Although this logic is intended to be woman-friendly, it can be dangerous, because it carries the risk of a new form of stereotyping and ghettoization of women in functions deemed to be appropriate for "feminine" strengths (especially personnel and other generally relatively powerless domains). Furthermore, the effectiveness of this appeal and its impact on the willingness of companies to hire women has yet to be proven. To date, companies appear more willing to invest in training programs to help men "become more feminine" than to hire the women themselves (Berthoin Antal & Kresbach-Gnath, 1988).

The entitlement argument. A significant difference between the discourse about women in management in the United States and Canada, on the one hand, and European countries, on the other, is the role of the ethical dimension and claims to entitlement. Of the four types of reasoning outlined here, the ethical logic is the one that has been used least over the past decades in Europe, in contrast with the significant role women's claim to equal opportunity as a civil right played in launching the debate about equal opportunity legislation and programs in the United States. One reason for this difference may be that social equality as an ideology is inherent in the concept of the welfare state in Europe and Israel and in the social security and labor laws that it generated. The legacy of socialism that had a powerful influence over Europe recognized capital and human capital as of equal value in the process of production. The balance between the two forces of production was achieved through unionization and workers' participation in management. Social and protective legislation for working mothers was part of this concept of societal responsibility for the welfare of its members. The unions that were a major force for introducing welfare legislation were not, however, prime movers with regard to achieving equal opportunity for women, particularly not into positions of influence. Looking over the impact of the various forms of logic, more women in Europe are coming to recognize the difficulties involved in relying solely on the first three arguments and see the need in the 1990s to draw more on the power of the ethical dimension to underpin their claims.

The Role of Legislation and Public Policy

In most industrialized countries, policymakers have recognized that a nonintervention approach will not suffice to achieve greater equality between men and women at work. A variety of types of legislation have been introduced, and an evolution in the logic behind these policies can be observed in a majority of countries: from the traditional "equal rights" approach expressed mainly in negative terms forbidding discrimination, to "equal opportunity" aimed at establishing an equal starting position, to a third stage that takes unintentional systemic discrimination into account and is aimed at guaranteeing "equality of results." This new orientation involves more dynamic affirmative action programs aimed at modifying total employment systems (Vogel-Polsky, 1985). "The problem is no longer simply one of prohibiting discrimination; it is now considered lawful and necessary for measures to be directed 'preferentially' towards specific groups as a means of correcting any *de facto* inequalities that impair their chances of success in various fields" (Vogel-Polsky, 1989, p. 8).

Table 3.2 reviews the major legislation in different countries. It shows that by the late 1970s equal pay for equal work legislation had been enacted in virtually all European countries as well as Israel. Some, such as the United Kingdom, have introduced the concept of equal pay for work of equal value. Where equal value claims are made, the court is authorized to hire experts to conduct job analyses. It is essential to recognize, however, that the mere passing of legislation does not correct the underlying problem, and earning differentials between men and women remain significant issues in all European countries (OECD, 1988).

During the 1980s, all industrialized countries passed equal opportunity legislation, and subsequent additional provisions indicate the dynamism of the process of change currently taking place. The scope and specific provisions of affirmative action policies are rather diverse across countries. They include the passage of special equal employment legislation and the establishment of equality commissions. In some countries, the government applies pressure on firms to modify segregated employment patterns by setting and pursuing verifiable targets by job category and to reach adequate representation of women. Most countries encourage affirmative action on a purely voluntary basis using moral persuasion and in a few cases various monetary incentives. In some countries (e.g., Sweden, West Germany, and Norway), legislation provides general principles and guidelines for action. The implementation of these policies, however, is often dependent on the outcome of collective bargaining between employers and unions. Here, too, the process is voluntary. While the law recommends and encourages positive action, there is no obligation to take such action in any of the member states in the Council of Europe (Vogel-Polsky, 1989, p. 58), and the legal recourse available to women who feel they have been treated unfairly is, in practice, very limited.

A third category of legislation focuses on the sphere of reproduction, specifically on maternity leave. European countries with a strong welfare state system provide more generously in this area than systems, such as those in the United States, that distinguish more strictly between the public and the private spheres and where the state is assigned a lesser role in this sphere of social policy, leaving more responsibility to the company and the individual. The current status of such government policies is summarized in Table 3.3. Among the recent legislative revisions to expand earlier provisions are longer maternity leave, better economic coverage, and a shift from maternal to parental responsibility (see Galinski, 1989; Izraeli, 1992). The latter is in keeping with the policy of encouraging greater economic equality in the family. The outstanding example in this respect is Sweden, which specified equality in the distribution of family work as an aim of public policy and gave expression to that goal in the allocation of both work and family benefits (Sandqvist, 1992). For example, couples in which women's earnings equal those of their husbands enjoy certain tax benefits (see Lewis, Izraeli, & Hootsmans, 1992).

Corporate Programs for Women in Management

In the last decade, organizations in the private sector have undertaken a variety of equal opportunity initiatives. Motivated by an interest in making better use of women's human potential, in enhancing their public image, or in responding to external and internal pressures to do so, a growing number of companies report pioneering programs for promoting women in management. Most aim to assist women to balance the demands of home and employment; some, to enhance women's career opportunities within the organization. There is considerably more such activity in some European countries, such as the Scandinavian countries (for experiments in Sweden, see Bengtson, 1990) and

text continued on page 80

Table 3.2 Equal Pay and Equal Employment Opportunity Policy in OECD (Organization for Economic Co-Operation and Development) Member Countries

Country		Year	Title	Principal Implementing Measures / Enforcement Machinery
Australia	Equal Pay	1969, 1972	Major decisions by Conciliation and Arbitration Commission	Conciliation and Arbitration Commission
	Equal employment opportunity	1984	Sex Discrimination Act	Sex Discrimination Commissioner
		1984, 1987	Public Service Act Amendments	Public Service Commission
		1986	Affirmative Action Act	Human Rights and Equal Opportunities Commission; Affirmative Action Agency
Austria	Equal pay	1979	Law on equal treatment in employment (amended)	Equality Commission
	Equal employment opportunity	1985		Ministry of Labour
Belgium	Equal pay	1975	National Employment Council's Collective Labor Agreement No. 25 rendered mandatory by royal decree	Collective bargaining parties; Ministry of Labor
	Equal employment opportunity	1978	Title V of the Law on Economic Reorientation	Ministry of Labour; Labour Courts and Tribunals
Canada	Equal pay	1971	Equal pay provisions in Canadian Labour Code	Labour Standards Branch, Department of Labour
		1977	Canadian Human Rights Act	Canadian Human Rights Commission
	Equal employment opportunity	1977	Canadian Human Rights Act	Canadian Human Rights Commission
		1986	Employment Equity Act; Federal Contractors Act	Canadian Employment and Immigration Commission

74

Country	Type	Year	Law	Enforcement
Denmark	Equal pay	1976	Equal Pay Law No. 32	Conciliation and courts
	Equal employment opportunity	1978	Equal Treatment Act	Council of Equality; Ministry of Labour
Finland	Equal pay	1987	National equality agreements between Employers' and Trade Unions' Confederation	Collective bargaining parties
	Equal employment opportunity	1987	Act on equality between women and men	Equality Ombudsman
France	Equal pay	1972	Act No. 72-1143 on equal remuneration for men and women	Ministry of Labour; Delegation on the Status of Women
	Equal employment opportunity	1983	Act on professional equality between women and men	
Germany	Equal pay	1980	Code of Civil Procedure (§ 612)	Ministry of Labour and Social Affairs; Labour courts
	Equal employment opportunity	1949	Basic law	Ministry of Labour and Social Affairs; Labour courts
		1980	Code of Civil Procedure (§§ 61 1a, 61 1b, 2a)	Ministry of Youth, Family, Women and Health
		1986	Directive on professional promotion of women in Federal Administration	Ministry of Labour
Greece	Equal pay	1984	Law No. 1414/84 on the applications of the principle of equality between the sexes in employment	
	Equal employment opportunity			
Ireland	Equal pay	1974	Anti-discrimination (Pay) Act (amended by Employment Equality Act)	Employment Equality Agency
	Equal employment opportunity	1985	Anti-discrimination (Employment) Act	Labour courts
		1987	Employment Equality Act	
Israel[1]	Equal pay	1964, 1972	Equal pay between women and men	Labour courts
	Equal employment opportunity	1981, 1988	Equal employment opportunity	Department for Status of Women and Employment; Ministry of Work and Welfare

75

Table 3.2 Continued

Country	Year	Principal Implementing Measures Title	Enforcement Machinery
Italy			
Equal pay	1960	Equal Pay Agreement for the Industrial Sector	Collective bargaining parties
	1964	Equal pay law for the agricultural sector	Ministry of Labour
Equal employment opportunity	1977	Act on equal employment between the sexes	
	1983	Ministerial decree on the implementation of equal employment opportunity principles	Labor tribunals; Ministry of Labour
Japan			
Equal pay	1947	Labor Standards Law	Ministry of Labour
Equal employment	1986	Equal Employment Opportunity Law	Ministry of Labour
Norway			
Equal pay	1978	Act on equal status between the sexes	Equal Status Council; Equal Status Ombudsman; Equal Status Appeals Board
Equal employment opportunity	1978	Basic agreement between Employers' and Trade Unions' Confederation	Collective bargaining parties
Portugal			
Equal pay	1979	Act on equality in work and employment	Equality Commission; Labour Inspectorate
Equal employment opportunity	1979		
Spain			
Equal pay	1980	Workers' statute;	Labor tribunals;
Equal employment opportunity	1980	Basic Employment Law	Labour Inspectorate
Sweden			
Equal pay	1980	Act on equality between men and women at work	Equal Opportunity Ombudsman
Equal employment	1980	Major equal opportunity agreements	Collective bargaining parties

Country	Category	Year	Legislation	Enforcement body
	opportunity		between Employers' and Trade Unions' Confederation in Private and Public sector	
Turkey	Equal pay	1963	Law No. 1475	Labour courts
		1965	State Officials' Law	Administrative court
United Kingdom	Equal pay	1970	Equal Pay Act	Industrial tribunals
		1975	(in force)	
		1984	(amended)	
	Equal employment opportunity	1975	Sex Discrimination Act	Equal Opportunities Commission (EOC); Industrial tribunals
		1986	(amended)	
United States	Equal pay	1963	Equal Pay Act	Equal Employment Opportunity Commission (EEOC)
	Equal employment opportunity	1964	Civil Rights Act, Title VII	Equal Employment Opportunity Commission (EEOC)
		1968	Executive Order 11375	Office of Federal Contract Compliance Programs
		1972	Equal Employment Opportunities Act	
European Community	Equal pay	1957	Article 119, EEC Treaty	Commission of the European Communities
		1975	Council Directive 75/117/EEC on the approximation of the laws of the member states relating to the application of the principle of equal pay to men and women	
	Equal employment opportunity	1976	Council Directive 76/207/EEC on the implementation of the principle of equal treatment for men and women regarding access to employment, vocational training, and promotion and working conditions	Court of Justice of the European Communities; National courts, tribunals, or other competent authorities

SOURCE: Organization for Economic Co-Operation and Development (1988).
1. The data for Israel have been added by the authors.

Table 3.3 Maternity and Parental Leave (universal governmental measures)[a]

	Maternity Leave		Parental Leave	
	Maximum Duration	Replacement Rate[c] (in percentages)	Maximum Duration[b]	Replacement Rate[c]
Australia	52	—	—	—
Austria	16	100	Up to 1st birthday	Fixed allowance in some cases
Belgium	14	From 100 to 79.5[d]	[e]	Fixed allowance
Canada	17 or 18[f]	Up to 60[g]		
Denmark	28	90	10 weeks	Fixed allowance
Finland	17.5	80	28 weeks[h]	80%
France	16-28[i]	84	Up to 3rd birthday and over	Fixed allowance for 3rd child
Germany	14	100	Until 15th month[j]	Fixed allowance
Greece	14	100	Up to 30th month	Unpaid
Iceland	13	Fixed allowance		—
Ireland	14	60		—
Israel[l]	12[m]	75	Up to 1 year	Unpaid
Italy	20	80	Up to 3rd birthday	—
Japan	14	60		—
Luxembourg	16	100		—
Netherlands	16	100	[k]	—
New Zealand	14	—	Up to 1 year	—

Norway	28	100[l]	Up to 1st birthday	Paid (social security)
Portugal	13	100	Up to 3rd birthday	Fixed allowance in some cases
Spain	16	75	3 years	—
Sweden	12[m]	90	Up to 1st birthday[n]	90%, then fixed allowance[o]
United Kingdom	18[p]	9%[q]	—	—
United States[2]	[r]	—	up to 3 months[s]	Unpaid

SOURCE: Organization for Economic Co-Operation and Development (1990).

NOTE: — = none.

a. This table describes the general provisions in each country's labor legislation. Workers may have additional benefits under collective agreement provisions (longer leave, higher replacement rate). These benefits are not covered in the table.

b. When leave is expressed as a number of weeks, it is in addition to maternity leave; otherwise, it is given in terms of the child's age.

c. The figure indicates the replacement rate of the gross salary. If the maternity benefit is not subject to social security contribution or income tax, the net replacement rate may be higher. In some countries, there is a ceiling for the calculation of the benefit.

d. The rate equals 100% of mother's wage during the first month and then decreases according to a fixed level.

e. There is no parental leave as such. All workers are entitled to a "career interruption" leave, however (subject to approval by employer in the private sector—this leave is generally approved when it is a parental leave).

f. According to the province.

g. Up to 60% of a maximum determined annually and under unemployment insurance eligibility conditions (the first two weeks are unpaid).

h. Unpaid leave is also possible up to the child's third birthday.

i. According to the number of children.

j. Up to 18 months as of July 1, 1990.

k. Parents of a child under 4 years of age are entitled to work shorter hours (minimum of 20 hours per week) for a period of six months. Wages are paid for hours actually worked.

l. The replacement rate is equal to 100% if 26 weeks are taken or 80% for 35 weeks up to an annual income of NKr 200,000.

m. Obligatory leave for the mother in connection to child birth; afterward, it becomes a parental leave.

n. Up to 18 months as of 1991.

o. For the first 270 days, 90%, followed by a lower flat rate.

p. Does not apply to women with less than two years' employment by the same employer.

q. Six weeks at 90% of the woman's full wage and a fixed allowance for the remaining 12 weeks.

r. There is no provision as such at a national level. Some states, however, grant unpaid maternity leave; federal legislation prohibits employment discrimination against pregnant women or those who have just given birth.

s. This applies only to companies with 50 or more employees, federal workers including employees of Congress. Employees must be employed for at least one year and work for 25 hours minimum per week.

1. The data for Israel have been added by the authors.

2. The data for the United States for parental leave has been added by the editor.

Britain (Hansard Society, 1990), and considerably less in others, such as Spain, Portugal, and Greece. Examples of such in-house programs include training staff in equal opportunity policies, monitoring the position of women in the firm, developing women for managerial roles, and creating return-to-work schemes and schemes for occupational desegregation. The BBC, for example, runs a women-only engineering course (Hansard Society, 1990). The most innovative schemes in Britain and Sweden involve sensitizing men to the issues at stake and helping them to work more effectively with women by recognizing and appreciating differences and learning to deal with their own emotions (Poncet, 1990). Work and family initiatives include pregnancy and maternity provisions that improve women's statutory entitlements, provision for part-time work often premised on prior service, family leave to deal with domestic crises, child-care support including workplace nurseries, or, more common, child-care payments and flexible working arrangements.

One of the important types of recent corporate initiatives are career break schemes that offer periods of extended unpaid leave for the mother and, increasingly often, for the father after childbirth (over and above the legally established paid leave available in most countries), typically from two to five years, with provisions for maintaining contact between employer and employee during the break. Employees are usually required to be available for a minimum period of paid work during the break. The career break is designed in the first instance to address the problem of the woman manager on the fast track who postpones childbearing until she is established in her career. By that time, the company has often made a substantial financial investment in her training and has a vested interest in retaining her. It is hoped that, with time, experiences in retaining women through such schemes will encourage companies to be less reluctant to invest in women in general, thereby expanding the pool of female candidates for promotion. In Britain, the banking industry has taken the lead in developing career break schemes (Hansard Society, 1990). The experiences at the National Westminster Bank were passed through word of mouth in networks such as the European Women's Management Development Network (EWMD), and several major companies abroad—such as the pharmaceutical company BASF—followed suit. The most recent scheme was introduced by Daimler Benz in Germany, and its innovations included crediting the employees' pension fund with a third of their time away and extending the period to seven to ten years.

It must be pointed out, however, that the tendency to extend the length of schemes may well be counterproductive. It enables companies to avoid the issue of how to organize work in such a way as to make family responsibilities manageable. Its value for career women is doubtful because, even with skill maintenance programs, it is impossible to maintain high qualifications, social networks, as well as self-confidence, for such a long time outside of paid work. Furthermore, until significant numbers of men take advantage of these parental leave schemes to care for their children, they will not be particularly helpful for making the necessary changes in organizations that career women—and men—need to live balanced lives.

The Role of Multinational Corporations

Multinational corporations (MNC) have affected the opportunities for women in management on an international scale in several ways (Erwee, 1988; Solo, 1989). First, they appear to be making a positive contribution in recruiting women to management by introducing equal opportunity policies in their subsidiaries abroad. For example, U.S. multinationals committed to affirmative action, such as IBM, played a pioneering role in encouraging the introduction of equal opportunity policies in all branches across the world. This step raised the issue in many countries where equal opportunity had not yet been addressed locally (Berthoin Antal & Kresbach-Gnath, 1988). Second, particularly in Japan, foreign firms are reportedly more willing to "risk" taking on women managers than are local firms (Lansing & Ready, 1989). This has been in response to the difficulty foreign firms have encountered in recruiting the top male graduates who prefer working for Japanese corporations.

A third—and as yet underdeveloped—avenue by which multinational corporations can increase the opportunities for women in management is through international assignments. International management is a new frontier for women (Kirk & Maddox, 1988). The globalization of national economies is expanding the demand for managers required for international assignments. Some studies perceive such assignments to be an increasingly important step along the career route to senior management (Adler, 1984b). Others, however, claim that currently the great majority of U.S. multinationals do not consider international experience to be a criterion for promotion or recruitment (Moran, Stahl & Boyer Inc., 1988; Tung, 1988). In contrast, European, Japanese, and Australian multinationals, given their greater dependence on foreign markets for corporate revenues, generally place a heavy premium on the experience and skills acquired overseas (Tung, 1988). Despite these trends, the proportion of women expatriate managers is still very small. The next section examines why women are still cut off from an opportunity to work outside their home countries and why this may be changing.

WOMEN AS EXPATRIATE MANAGERS IN MULTINATIONAL CORPORATIONS[4]

Women constitute only a negligible portion of the expatriate managerial population. Of 412 U.S. and Canadian corporations with overseas subsidiaries surveyed in 1983 (Adler, 1984a), only 20% had sent a woman overseas in expatriate status and only 3% of the 13,388 current expatriates were women. In a 1988 survey of 70 corporations (Moran, Stahl & Boyer Inc., 1988), 64% reported having female expatriate employees. At first glance, this figure may seem higher than expected, but, upon closer examination, only 5% of the 4,774 U.S. expatriates currently assigned overseas by these firms were women. In both studies, we may assume an upward response bias in favor of those companies that had female expatriates.

There is very little empirical research to date on the subject of expatriate managers. Almost all of this research is on U.S. multinationals, so we know next to nothing about the number of women sent abroad by non-U.S. firms, about the policies of such companies, or about the experiences of these women. Most studies address the issue of why there are so few (U.S.) women expatriates. The most common explanations are discussed below.

Why So Few? Typical Reasons and Research Results

Motivation. According to this argument, women deselect themselves from serious consideration for overseas assignment either by not applying for available jobs or by turning down positions when offered. Challenging the "myth of women's lack of motivation," Adler (1984b) found that almost half of the 1,129 U.S. MBA students surveyed within six months of graduation seriously wanted an international career and that there was no gender difference in this respect. A reexamination of Adler's data suggests that what appears to be a problem of lack of motivation may in effect be a response to blocked opportunity (Kanter,

1977). In the same study, Adler found that "compared with the women, the men saw greater organizational rewards for pursuing an international career—including more recognition, more status, a higher salary, and faster career progress." Women, by contrast, perceived they had significantly less opportunity for getting an international assignment (Adler, 1984b). Almost 90% of the responding female MBAs felt that men's chances of being selected for an international assignment were better than theirs. Once women are in the corporate world, such beliefs concerning the probability of favorable outcomes are likely to discourage them from competing with men for international assignments. In such a case, women would have to want international assignments much more strongly than men to overcome the multiple dampers on their student-day motivations.

Availability. The "women are not available" argument is premised on the formal requisites for international assignment—namely, rank and specialization. Expatriates are disproportionately chosen from the ranks of middle and senior management; 70% of the female expatriates in the Moran, Stahl & Boyer Inc. (1988) survey and 95% in the Taylor, Odjagov, and Morley (1975) survey were from middle and upper management. The latter study, however, relates primarily to business travel. The pattern of sending higher-level managers will probably continue considering the pressure from foreign countries for more extensive employment of host country nationals in management, at least at lower levels (Zeira & Banai, 1985). An exception is the banking industry, which uses younger/more junior-level managers to a greater extent for international assignments, which may explain why banking has the largest number of women expatriates (Adler, 1988).

Suitability. Stereotypical thinking and the double standard are especially evident when corporations discuss women's marital status. Whether single or married, the female expatriate's family status is presumed to be problematic. Male managers tend to believe that a single woman, away from the social controls of her home turf, is more vulnerable to harassment and other dangers than a man (Izraeli, Banai, & Zeira, 1980). Corporations are apprehensive about sending married women because they presume that married women will have even greater spouse-related problems than married men.

Research indicates that spouse dissatisfaction is currently the single most important reason for failure of an overseas assignment (Tung, 1988). The problems they anticipate relate to both the employment and the family domains of both partners. For example, corporations worry that, because entry into a new job requires total involvement and longer than usual hours of work, the expatriate woman is thus likely to be even less available to her family abroad than in her domestic assignment. Furthermore, they believe that the repercussions of the spouse being unemployed are generally greater when the spouse is the husband. Visa restrictions on working permits, company nepotism rules that prohibit the employment of both husband and wife, and limited employment opportunities in the foreign country are among the barriers to finding employment for the accompanying spouse. The difficulties that husbands of expatriate women managers pose for MNCs are an additional reason for corporations to prefer promoting host country nationals to managerial positions.

Acceptability. The untested belief of policymakers in corporate headquarters that women expatriates will be hindered by cultural prejudice in the host country against women in managerial roles is a serious impediment. It may explain, in part, why a disproportionate number of women expatriates are sent to English-speaking countries (Moran Stahl & Boyer Inc., 1988), where the culture is more similar to that in the United States, although there is no empirical evidence that the success rate is greater in these countries than elsewhere.

Adler (1988) argues cogently that it is incorrect to generalize from a culture's treatment of local women to how it will treat a foreign woman. In the business setting, the expatriate female has a triple identity. She is a manager. She is also a foreigner and a woman. There are conditions when her being a woman will be less salient than her other identities. For example, her presence as manager is more likely to be overriding when she is in a senior position or perceived to be a highly qualified expert in her field. In ethnocentric cultures, she may be categorized first and foremost as a foreigner and treated accordingly. As Adler (1988, pp. 24-25) notes: "Asians see female expatriates as foreigners who happen to be women, not as women who happen to be foreigners." Consequently, even in cultures where women are not managers, being female need not be presumed to be a handicap.[5]

Discrimination. Prejudiced attitudes within the parent company block the selection of women and impede their effectiveness. Moran Stahl & Boyer Inc. (1988) report that human resource managers believed women expatriates would encounter more resistance from U.S. male counterparts and subordinates than from the foreign nationals. Adler's (1988) interviewees—52 women serving in Asia—confirmed that most of the women's problems stemmed from their relationships with peers and superiors in their own home companies, and not their relationships with Asian clients. They had difficulty convincing the company to grant the foreign assignment. Once overseas, they found that they did not always have the same leeway for action granted to their male colleagues and that the company limited their opportunities, scope of activity, or period of stay abroad.

Uncertainty as a Dilemma for Women Expatriate Managers

Corporate discrimination against women in decisions on placements abroad may in part be related to the structure of the expatriate managerial role. A characteristic feature of the managerial role in general, and of more senior management in particular, is uncertainty regarding what a manager should do, the qualifications required for getting the job done, and the outcome of decisions. The role of the expatriate involves even more uncertainties than that of the domestic manager. The list of requisite skills is longer, including a variety of cross-cultural skills as well as spouse and family qualities needed for them to adapt to a different cultural environment (Mendenhall, Dunbar, & Oddou, 1987; Zeira & Banai, 1985). Some of the skills required are highly diffuse. They include, for example, the ability to relate well to people from other cultures or "a supra-national attitude that transcends culture" (Adler, 1983).

The difficulty of predicting successful candidates is indicated in the high number of canceled overseas assignments. It has been estimated that between 20% to 50% of U.S. personnel sent abroad are called back prematurely from their overseas assignments and considered failures by headquarters (Copeland & Griggs, 1985; Mendenhall et al., 1987; Tung, 1981; Zeira & Banai, 1985). The average financial cost of a premature return to the parent company has been observed to range from $55,000 to $150,000 (see Mendenhall et al., 1987), not including unrealized business and damaged company reputation resulting from expatriate failure.

The organizational need for greater certainty has behavioral repercussions whose impact limits women's opportunities in the international arena. First, uncertainty intensifies the need for trust. This need, contends Kanter (1977; see also Lipman-Blumen, 1986), prompts managers to select others who are most similar to themselves and, consequently, presumably more likely to be trustworthy and predictable. This tendency to "homosocial reproduction" works against women, who are perceived, by male executives, to be different, unpredictable, and consequently not fully trustworthy (Kanter, 1977; Lipman-Blumen, 1986). Second, situations of uncertainty increase the likely use of stereotypes. In the absence of reliable knowledge about future performance, as occurs in situations where past experience is limited and/or contingencies are multiple, stereotypical beliefs about the characteristics and abilities of men and women are employed (Deaux & Wrightsman, 1984; Izraeli & Izraeli, 1985). Such a tendency results in women's deselection for more senior managerial positions.

Other corporate strategies, in addition to controlling geographic assignments to reduce risk under conditions of uncertainty, are to limit the woman's assignment to internal rather than to client contact assignments, to a staff rather than to a line position, and to a short-term rather than to an extended stay, or even to define her assignment as temporary. For example, Taylor et al. (1975), who interviewed 34 women expatriates, found that half reported interacting mainly with other company personnel while overseas. The same study found that almost all of the 284 women in the sample were on assignments of 30 days or less. Only eight stayed six months or more.

The uncertainty explanation of discrimination, because of its apparent benign rationality, implicitly legitimizes the very behavior it seeks to explain. What is ignored, furthermore, is that the strategies adopted as a protection against failure in the face of uncertainty may actually increase the likelihood of failure. For example, according to Adler (1988):

> Although this [defining the job as temporary] may appear to be a logically cautious strategy, in reality it tends to create an unfortunate self-fulfilling prophecy. As a number of women reported, if the company is not convinced that you will succeed . . . it will communicate its lack of confidence to foreign colleagues and clients as a lack of commitment. The foreigners will then mirror the company's behavior by also failing to take you seriously.

Despite the many reasons given by corporations for not sending women on international assignments and for expecting them to fail or be ineffective, women generally report having succeeded in their missions (Adler, 1988). Probably the best indicator of their success is that a large proportion were sent on a second mission.

A Rosier Future for Women as Expatriate Managers?

A number of recent macro-, organizational-, and micro-level developments would appear favorable for a greater women's presence in the expatriate community. We consider four of them here: shortage of qualified men for international assignments, legal and social pressures on MNCs, increasing familiarity of foreign managers with women in managerial positions, and upgrading human resource planning for international assignments.

Shortage of qualified men. Above and beyond the factors discussed at the outset of this chapter as contributing to the possible shortage of male managers for domestic assignments, there are a number of additional factors that may produce a shortage of qualified men specifically for international assignments, a factor that could force employers to look more favorably at women as candidates. At the same time as the demand for expatriate managers is rising, a growing number of potential male candidates appear to be becoming more reluctant to accept foreign assignments. One contributing factor is the rise in the proportion of dual-career couples (Sekaran, 1986). Increasing numbers of men who once could assume their wives would accompany them abroad are now restrained from accepting international assignments. Furthermore, given the relative lack of importance attributed to international assignments for career mobility, at least until recently, some career-minded executives prefer to stay close to home where they can perform in full view of top management and maneuver for promotions (Nye, 1988). Mergers and acquisitions and major staff cuts are making astute managers even more reluctant to stray far from home base. The difficulties in the repatriation process are an additional disincentive (Tung, 1988). Such factors reduce the competition for overseas assignments and should make senior managers more amenable to experimenting with women. Alternatively, however, they may deepen their use of host country (male) nationals or recruit managers from other English-speaking countries where the proportion of career women is significantly smaller.

Legal and social pressure on equal opportunity employers. This mode of action is more effective with large corporations that are more visible and vulnerable to governmental pressures and with companies that believe that assigning women abroad enhances the image of the company as a progressive and fair employer. For example, larger companies (in terms of sales, assets, income, number of employees, and subsidiaries) send more women overseas than do smaller ones (Adler, 1984a). Human resource managers believe that sending women on international assignments enhances the company's image, which in turn leads to better relations with employees and customers (Moran Stahl & Boyer Inc., 1988).

Increasing familiarity with women in managerial positions. A number of developments gaining momentum may tend to "normalize" the presence of women as managers. Among them are the increasing number of women in managerial positions in most foreign countries, the more frequent travel of foreign national managers to the United States, where they encounter women in managerial positions, and the growth in the number of two-career couples among the expatriate community from many countries. For example, the British magazine *International Management* reported that, among 565 senior executives from around the world who responded to a recent survey, 46.6% of the spouses of Americans had their own careers compared with 58.6% of the Swedish spouses, 48.6% of the spouses in Hong Kong, 53.8% of those in Singapore, and 40% of those in Brazil (see Nye, 1988).

The uncertainty discussed earlier as inherent in the role of the expatriate manager is also in part the result of unfamiliarity of top managers in corporate headquarters with the expectations of stakeholders in host countries and with other aspects of international assignments. Companies with accumulated experience in the international field are likely to perceive the expatriate role as less uncertain than the more recent entries into the arena. This should reduce resistance to sending women as expatriates on this score.

Upgrading human resource planning for international assignments. Few corporations treat a foreign assignment as involving a total family unit. The high rate of failure among international assignments and the high cost of that failure are among the incentives for headquarters to invest in improved training and preparation in this area (Ronen, 1989). More and better company training programs for international assignments can provide women with opportunities to prepare and prove themselves. For married women, a growing awareness among corporations of the need to treat every relocation as a "family affair" would produce policies more likely to enhance the organization's ability to cope with the needs of the expatriate husband as well (Mendenhall et al., 1987; Tung, 1982). The selection of women for international assignments, however, will likely continue to require the persistent pressure of individual women who either initially condition their acceptance of employment on the availability of such opportunities or are willing to "educate" their managers. The self-selection of women willing and able to go abroad and accounts of their successful performance will likely remain important ingredients for changing attitudes, while success stories of some firms provide models for other firms, at least in the same industry.

CONCLUSIONS: THE NEED FOR INTERNATIONAL EXCHANGE

The Role of International Organizations

One of the factors that has given greater visibility to the issue of women's roles in society is the attention they have received from international bodies. International organizations, such as the United Nations, European Community, Organization for Economic Cooperation and Development (OECD), and International Labor Organization (ILO), have played a significant role in putting women's issues on the public agendas of member countries, especially since the mid-1970s. These organizations collect and disseminate data, diffuse information about programs implemented in different countries and settings to promote equal opportunity for women at work, and exert pressure on member countries to adopt and implement such programs. Some of these organizations also provide a forum where women meet and develop lobbies and special interest and support groups. The women serve as important change agents in the various international and national public arenas.

The U.N. "Decade of the Woman" oriented attention and efforts to women's issues and mobilized activity directed to change. The U.N. Convention on the elimination of all forms of discrimination against women (which came into force in 1981 and was ratified by most European countries in the mid-1980s) is assessed by one scholar "to be the most significant clause in international law where positive action is concerned" (Vogel-Polsky, 1989, p. 79). It defined affirmative action as consonant with the principle of equality—provided that the measures adopted are temporary and aim to redress inequality. The European Community has been instrumental in pushing member states to introduce progressive legislation in several areas relating to women and employment. The expansion of the community from 9 to 12 member countries in the course of the 1980s, however, has made it more difficult to achieve the majority vote required to pass "directives," which are binding on member states. Furthermore, discussions and activities surrounding the establishment of the Single Market in 1992 have focused on the economic issues, leaving the social implications to simmer on the back burner. But there is increasing pressure to attend to the social aspects of integration, and women are playing a significant role in raising these issues, both in the European Parliament and in the European Commission. The European Women's Lobby created in the summer of 1990 to represent women's organizations is expected to help focus attention on women's concerns.

The Role of Women's International Networks

Women have been actively engaged in the processes of change described above, through representation in the various international organizations and national commissions dealing with gender equality as well as through professional associations and the activities of feminist groups. In the late 1970s, women managers began organizing support groups in a number of countries in Western Europe, sometimes affiliated with a management center. The first international association of women in management was founded in 1984 with the creation of the European Women's Management Development Network (EWMD). The EWMD, in turn, served as a catalyst for the establishment of networks for women in management in countries where they had not previously existed. While primarily European in orientation and membership, it maintains informal ties with leading figures in management organizations all over the world. By providing opportunities for women in management to share information, views, and experiences, the EWMD encourages experimentation with new approaches tried in other countries. It thereby helps to deconstruct myths about "impossible" ideas or "natural" ways of doing things.

International publications, such as Women of Europe, published by the Women's Information Service of the European Communities, and the EWMD News, stimulate cross-fertilization and contribute to breaking through traditional barriers facing women in management in every country.

Challenges to the Research Community

Interviews with European women reveal that they feel the information and learning flow between Europe and North America has been one-sided and that the time has come for a more balanced international exchange. The intensive reporting on women in management in the United States over the past years definitely helped women in other countries to articulate concerns; the visibility of U.S. success stories provided them with role models. On the other hand, Europeans and Israelis increasingly find that the United States lags behind other countries in matters related to social policy and women's dual roles. Furthermore, there is a strong sense in European countries that the U.S. focus on "how to achieve the same as men in a man's world" is quite limited (Fossan, 1989). In Scandinavian countries, Italy, the Federal Republic of Germany, and particularly Great Britain, the repertoire of issues is more diverse: "What kind of leaders do women seek to be?" "Of what kinds of organizations?" "At what personal price?" "How can we balance private and professional goals and responsibility?"

This chapter has suggested the usefulness and desirability of greater international exchange and cross-cultural research. A number of comparisons were made on the basis of existing research that suggest promising hypotheses concerning women's progress in management. We evaluated the dilemmas and prospects both for women managers in the industrialized countries outside of the United States and for women expatriate managers in U.S. multinational corporations. While the trends are positive, we see little cause for great optimism. At this stage, we need to generate a more systematic and comparable data base on the position of women in management in various countries. There is a particularly urgent need to obtain more information about women in business and political office in African, Latin American, Asian, and Eastern European countries, for this chapter was able to draw only on the scant data available on—primarily northern—European countries (see Adler & Izraeli, in press). We need to become more sophisticated in identifying the cultural as well as the masculine biases in our assumptions, our theories, and our methods. The international comparative perspective needs to be relocated from the periphery of research on women in management to the core. It needs to be mainstreamed and integrated into all our undertakings as "standard operating procedure" and not treated as an exotic "extra" to the program.

NOTES

1. The term *expatriate* is used loosely to refer to any manager sent by headquarters of a multinational corporation on a foreign assignment. No distinction is made between

"transferees" to whom the organization is committed to repatriate and other "assignees" to whom no such commitment is made. We are generally concerned with senior managers. It should be borne in mind that, when we speak of managers who believe or decide, the reference is almost always to male managers.

2. In addition to the fact that no studies have taken the gender factor into account in developing concepts and collecting data about different management cultures, no studies have developed reliable ways of analyzing the interaction between national culture and organizational culture. It is unclear, for example, the extent to which Hofstede's conclusions about national management cultures are influenced by the fact that the company under study was a U.S. (rather than a Swedish or German) multinational, with certain built-in American values and rules that filtered the perceptions and behavior of managers in each location.

3. The following section is based in part on a survey of experts on women in management in each of 16 countries. We received replies from 9: Canada, the Federal Republic of Germany, France, Great Britain, Israel, Italy, New Zealand, Norway, and Switzerland. We sought to learn when the issue of "women in management" had started to gain visibility in their countries, what rationale dominated public discourse about the need for increasing the number of women in management, and whether they had observed shifts over time. We also asked them what they believed to be the impact of developments in the United States on their countries, in which areas they believed they could learn from the United States, and in which areas they felt their own country had something special to offer.

4. The section on women expatriate managers draws heavily on the accumulated research by Nancy Adler and on an unpublished survey (1988) titled *Status of American Female Expatriate Employees Survey Results* (prepared by Moran Stahl & Boyer Inc., International Division, 900 28th St. Boulder, Colorado 80303). The survey respondents were human resource professionals who have responsibility for various aspects of international human resource management in their respective companies: 69% of the respondents were male and 31% female; 70 companies responded to the survey: 51 industrial, 19 service.

5. Dafna Izraeli's personal experience with the relative salience of her various identities support the argument. During the 1973 war in Israel, when official army orders were that women were not allowed into the Sinai, she was flown to the Sinai in an army plane as a "visiting professor" to lecture to the (male) soldiers. In the late 1970s, she conducted a study of Georgian (Russian) immigrants to Israel. At two Georgian weddings to which she was invited, she was seated at the men's table—the place reserved for such "important guests" as university researchers.

REFERENCES

Adler, N. J. (1983). Cross-cultural management: Issues to be faced. *International Studies of Management and Organizations, 13*(1-2), 7-45.

Adler, N. J. (1984a). Women in international management: Where are they? *California Management Review, 26*(4), 78-88.

Adler, N. J. (1984b). Women do not want international careers: And other myths about international management. *Organizational Dynamics, 13*(2), 66-79.

Adler, N. J. (1988). Pacific Basin managers: A gaijin, not a woman. In N. J. Adler & D. N. Izraeli (Eds.), *Women in management worldwide* (pp. 226-249). New York: M. E. Sharpe.

Adler, N. J., & Izraeli, D. N. (1988). Women in management worldwide. In N. J. Adler & D. N. Izraeli (Eds.), *Women in management worldwide* (pp. 3-16). New York: M. E. Sharpe.

Adler, N. J., & Izraeli, D. N. (Guest Eds.). (in press). *International studies of management and organization* (special issue: Competitive frontiers: Women managers in the triad).

Adler, N. J., & Izraeli, D. N. (Eds.). (in press). *Competitive frontiers: Women managers in the global economy.* Cambridge, MA: Basil Blackwell.

Assig, D. (1987). *Mut gehort dazu.* Reinbeck/Hamburg: Rowohlt Verlag.

Assig, D. (1989, Spring). Women entrepreneurship and a sense of adventure. *EWMD News, 19,* 4-5 (Ashridge, England).

Bebbington, C. (1988, December). Ladies don't climb ladders. *Eurobusiness, 1*(3), 12-17.

Bengtson, I. (1990). *Leading lady: On female managers in companies.* Stockholm: Swedish Employers' Confederation.

Berthoin Antal, A. (1987). Comparing notes and learning from experience. In M. Dierkes, H. N. Weiler, & A. Berthoin Antal (Eds.), *Comparative policy research: Learning from experience* (pp. 498-515). Aldershot, Germany: Gower.

Berthoin Antal, A., & Kresbach-Gnath, C. (1988). Women in management: Unused resources in the Federal Republic of Germany. In N. J. Adler & D. N. Izraeli (Eds.), *Women in management worldwide* (pp. 141-156). New York: M. E. Sharpe.

Bienen auf der Galeere. (1985, September 23). *Der Spiegel,* pp. 39, 74.

Blum, L., & Smith, V. (1988). Women's mobility in the corporation: A critique of the politics of optimism. *Signs, 13*(3), 528-545.

Brenner, O. C., Tomkiewicz, J., & Schein, V. E. (1989). The relationship between sex-role stereotypes and requisite management characteristics revisited. *Academy of Management Journal, 32,* 662-669.

Business and Industry Information Group. (1983). *Swedish women as entrepreneurs.* Stockholm: Author.

Copeland, L., & Griggs, L. (1985). *Going international.* New York: Random House.

Deaux, K., & Wrightsman, L. S. (1984). *Social psychology in the 80s* (4th ed.). Monterey, CA: Brooks/Cole.

Doole, I. (1985). Women in business: Is a different advisory approach necessary? *Equal Opportunities International, 4*(3), 34-36.

Ellefsen, S. (1986, Autumn). Women in management in private enterprises. *EWMD News, 9,* 5 (Ashridge, England).

Epstein, C. F. (1981). Women and elites: A crossnational perspective. In C. F. Epstein & R. L. Coser (Eds.), *Access to power: Cross-national studies of women and elites* (pp. 3-15). London: Allen & Unwin.

Erwee, R. (1988). South African women: Changing career patterns. In N. J. Adler & D. N. Izraeli (Eds.), *Women in management worldwide* (pp. 213-225). New York: M. E. Sharpe.

EWMD News. (1984, Winter). (Issue 2). Ashridge, England: European Women's Management Development Network.

Fossan, J. (1989, June 16). Women in organizations: *Implementing strategies and achieving change* (Seminar research report). Berlin: Aspen Institute.

Galante, S. P. (1986, March 24). Venturing out on their own. *The Wall Street Journal,* p. 4D.

Galinski, E. (1989). *The implementation of flexible time and leave policies: Observations from European employers.* Paper commissioned by the Panel on Employer Policies and Working Families, National Academy of Sciences, Washington, DC.

Goffee, R., & Scase, R. (1985). *Women in charge: The experiences of female entrepreneurs.* London: Allen & Unwin.

Hammond, V. (1986). Working women abroad: Great Britain. *Equal Opportunities International, 5*(1), 8-16.

Hammond, V. (1988). Women in management in Great Britain. In N. J. Adler & D. N. Izraeli (Eds.), *Women in management worldwide* (pp. 168-185). New York: M. E. Sharpe.

Handy, C. (1987). *The making of managers* (A report on management education, training and development in the U.S.A., West-Germany, France, Japan and the U.K.). London: Manpower Services Commission, National Economic Development Council, British Institute of Management.

Hansard Society for Parliamentary Government. (1990). *The report of the Hansard Society Commission on Women at the Top.* London: Author.

Harvey, M. G. (1985). The executive family: An overlooked variable in international assignments. *Columbia Journal of World Business, 20,* 84-92.

Hearn, J., & Parkin, W. P. (1988). Women, men, and leadership: A critical review of assumptions, practices and change in the industrialized nations. In N. J. Adler & D. N. Izraeli (Eds.), *Women in management worldwide* (pp. 17-40). New York: M. E. Sharpe.

Hellman Hansen, C. (1987, Summer). Denmark: A beautiful village in Europe. *EMWD News, 12,* 4-5 (Ashridge, England).

Ho, S. (1984). Women managers in Hong Kong: Traditional barriers and emerging trends. *Equal Opportunities International, 3*(4), 7-29.

Hofstede, G. (1980). *Culture's consequences: International differences in work-related attitudes.* London: Sage.

Hofstede, G. (1989). Women in management: A matter of culture. *The International Management Development Review, 5,* 250-254 (London: Sterling).

Hohenberger, L., Maier, F., & Schlegelmilch, C. (1989). Regelungen und Forderprogramme zur Teilzeitarbeit in den Landern Schweden, Norwegen, Grossbritannien, Frankreich, Niederlande, Belgien, und Osterreich. Bundesministerim fur Jugend, Familie, Frauen und Gesundheit. *Materialien zur Frauenpolitik.* Bundesministerium fur Jugend, Familie, Frauen und Gesundheit Nr. 3. Bonn, Germany.

Hörburger, H., & Rath-Hörburger, F. (1988). *Europa's Frauen Gleichberechtigt? Die Politik der EG-Lander, Gleichberechtigungder Frau im Arbeitsleben.* Hamburg: Verlag Otto Heinvetter.

Izraeli, D. N. (1988). Women's movement into management in Israel. In N. J. Adler & D. N. Izraeli (Eds.), *Women in management worldwide* (pp. 141-156). New York: M. E. Sharpe.

Izraeli, D. N. (1992). Culture, policy and women in dual earner families in Israel. In S. Lewis, D. N. Izraeli, & H. Hootsmans, *Dual earner families: International perspectives.* London: Sage.

Izraeli, D. N., & Adler, N. J. (in press). Competitive frontiers: Women managers in the global economy. In N. J. Adler & D. N. Izraeli (Eds.), *Competitive frontiers: Women managers in the global economy.* Cambridge, MA: Basil Blackwell.

Izraeli, D. N., & Izraeli, D. (1985). Sex effects in evaluating leaders. *Journal of Applied Psychology, 70*(1), 148-156.

Izraeli, D. N., Banai, M., & Zeira, Y. (1980). Women executives in MNC subsidiaries. *California Management Review, 23*(1), 53-63.

Kanter, R. M. (1977). *Men and women of the corporation.* New York: Basic Books.

Keller Brown, L. (1988). Female managers in the United and in Europe: Corporate boards, M.B.A. credentials, and the image/illusion of progress. In N. J. Adler & D. N. Izraeli (Eds.), *Women in management worldwide* (pp. 265-274). New York: M. E. Sharpe.

Kirk, W. Q., & Maddox, R. C. (1988, March). International management: The new frontier for women in management. *Personnel*, pp. 46-49.

Kresbach-Gnath, C., Ballerstedt, E., Frenzel, U., Bielenski, H., Büchtemann, C. F., & Bengelmann, D. (1983). *Frauenbeschaftigung und neue Technologien.* Munich: Oldenbourg Verlag.

Lansing, P., & Ready, K. (1988). Hiring women managers in Japan: An alternative for foreign employers. *California Management Review, 30*(3), 112-127.

Laurent, A. (1983). The cultural diversity of Western conceptions of management. *International Studies of management and Organization, 13*(1-2), 75-96.

Lipman-Blumen, J. (1986). Toward a homosocial theory of sex roles: An explanation of the sex segregation of social institutions. *Signs, 1*(3), 15-31.

Loden, M. (1985). *Feminine leadership or how to succeed in business without being one of the boys.* New York: Times Books.

Meirs Osterling, C. (1989, February 27). *Working women in the United States of America.* Lecture delivered to the EWMD, Berlin.

Mendenhall, M. E., Dunbar, E., & Oddou, G. R. (1987). Expatriate selection training and career-pathing: A review and critique. *Human Resource Management, 26*(3), 347-362.

Moran, Stahl & Boyer Inc. (1988). *Status of American female expatriate employees: Survey results.* Boulder, CO: Moran, Stahl & Boyer Inc., International Division.

Morrison, A., White, R. P., Van Velsor, E., & the Center for Creative Leadership. (1987). *Breaking the glass ceiling.* Reading, MA: Addison-Wesley.

Nye, D. (1988, February). The female expat's promise. *Across the Board,* pp. 38-43 (Conference Board, New York).

O'Connor, J. (1987, Winter). Women in enterprise: Setting up in business. *EWMD News, 14*, 3 (Ashridge, England).

Olivares, F. (1992). Women in management in Italy: A shifting scenario. In N. J. Adler & D. N. Izraeli (Eds.), *Women in management worldwide* (2nd ed.). New York: M. E. Sharpe.

Organization for Economic Co-Operation and Development (OECD). (1985). *The integration of women into the economy.* Paris: Author.

Organization for Economic Co-Operation and Development (OECD). (1988, September). *Employment outlook.* Paris: Author.

Organization for Economic Co-Operation and Development (OECD). (1990, September). *Employment outlook.* Paris: Author.

Poncet, J. F. (1990, Autumn). Words, actions and champions. *EWMD News,* p. 25 (Ashridge, England).

Ronen, S. (1989). Training the international assignee. In I. L. Goldstein (Ed.), *Training and career development* (pp. 417-453). San Francisco: Jossey-Bass.

Roobeek, A. J. M. (1989, October 25-27). Women, management and technology. In *Proceedings of the 5th annual conference of the European Women's Management Development Network* (pp. 12-22). Amsterdam, the Netherlands: European Women's Management Development Network.

Sandqvist, K. (1992). Sweden's gender-role scheme and commitment to gender equality. In S. Lewis, D. N. Izraeli, & H. Hootsmans (Eds.), *Dual earner families: International perspectives*. London: Sage.

Schein, V. E. (1973). The relationship between sex-role stereotypes and requisite management characteristics. *Journal of Applied Psychology, 57*, 95-100.

Schein, V. E. (1975). The relationship between sex-role stereotypes and requisite management characteristics among female managers. *Journal of Applied Psychology, 60*, 340-344.

Sekaran, U. (1986). *Dual career families*. San Francisco: Jossey-Bass.

Serdjénian, E. (1988). *L'egalite des chances ou les enjeux de la mixite*. Paris: Les Editions d'Organisations.

Solo, S. (1989, June). Japan discovers woman power. *Fortune Magazine*, pp. 964-969.

Steinhoff, P. G., & Kazuko, T. (1988). Women managers in Japan. In N. J. Adler & D. N. Izraeli (Eds.), *Women in management worldwide* (pp. 103-121). New York: M. E. Sharpe.

Sullivan, S. (1986, December, 15). Europe's baby bust. *Newsweek* (international ed.), pp. 18-23.

Taylor, M. L., Odjagov, M., & Morley, E. (1975). Experience of American professional women in overseas business assignments. *Academy of Management Proceedings*, pp. 454-456.

Tung, R. L. (1981). Selection and training of personnel for overseas assignments. *Columbia Journal of World Business, 16*(1), 68-78.

Tung, R. L. (1982). Selection and training procedures of U.S., European, and Japanese multinationals. *California Management Review, 25*(1), 57-71.

Tung, R. L. (1988). Career issues in international management. *Academy of Management Executive, 2*(3), 241-244.

Vogel-Polsky, E. (1985). *National institutional and non-institutional machinery established in the Council of Europe member states to promote equality between women and men: Comparative study*. Strasbourg, France: Council of Europe.

Vogel-Polsky, E. (1989). *Positive action and the constitutional and legislative hindrances to its implementation in the member states of the Council of Europe*. Strasbourg, France: Council of Europe, European Committee for Equality Between Men and Women.

Zeira, Y., & Banai, M. (1985). Selection of expatriate managers in MNCs: The host-environment point of view. *International Studies of Management and Organization, 15*(1), 33-51.

Commentary

JENNIE FARLEY

Women are pushing men out of management or so some seem to think. But the evidence around us suggests otherwise. If women are inching into management, they are managing small offices and businesses while men are still managing the big corporations, labor unions, Congress, and the world. Historian Alpern traces the progress women have made from colonial times to the current times in Chapter 2. She considers where women stood (by the hearth, mainly) when the colonies broke away from England and follows women into factories, offices, college classrooms, and, finally, in small numbers, into the executive suites and board rooms of corporations. This is a big order but the reader will take pleasure in the care with which she has tried to fill it. Her scholarship is inclusive: She documents what was happening to women of color and to immigrant women of all races as well as chronicling the more familiar story of what was going on with white women born here.

She tips her hat to women who defied expectations: entrepreneur Madame C. J. Walker, cosmetic executive Elizabeth Arden, activist first lady Eleanor Roosevelt, and publisher Katherine Graham, who was, when this was written, the only woman chief executive of a *Fortune* 500 company.

Any survey of highlights of women's work from colonial times through 1990 is bound to be criticized as superficial. But Alpern's review touches on many important points: the role legislation has played, first holding women back and, more recently, seeking to protect women, and, finally, seeking (and to some extent, succeeding) to protect women not from competing with men but from being discriminated against by them. She touches on how clerical work changed when women entered the occupation: It had been an avenue for upward mobility for men as apprentice managers. But, once women became secretaries in large numbers, there was little chance that they'd make it into management by that route. Businesswomen have been haunted by a bad image, she notes.

A major thread in her summary is the effect of war on women's employment opportunities. From revolutionary times, women's scope has broadened when men have gone to war. Colonial women ran their husbands' farms and businesses (and came to think of them as "ours") when the men were gone; women moved into "men's jobs," including work as managers when men went to fight in World War I and World War II. Doors were opened but were closed again when peace came. What could bring women into the management suites? Alpern lists four factors in her conclusion—the protection afforded by antibias laws, the presence of substantial numbers of women in the work force as a whole, the possibility of acceptance for a diversity of management styles, and substantial numbers of women working in peacetime—as providing hope for women as senior managers.

In Chapter 3, sociologists Berthoin Antal and Izraeli broaden the focus, arguing persuasively that research on these issues is enriched when it is multicultural for three reasons: Women managers in any one country are few; work in one country may suffer from ethnocentrism; and we all live in an increasingly multicultural world. They review the situation of women in management internationally, mainly focusing on data from Canada, the Federal Republic of Germany, France, Great Britain, Israel, Italy, New Zealand, Norway, and Switzerland. They draw on official sources for data from other countries as well, duly noting the problems of defining *manager* uniformly across cultures and of getting comparable evidence. With those caveats, they are able to come up with useful generalizations: High representation in the labor force does not guarantee high representation in management; in most countries surveyed, women do better in the public sector than in private companies and better in the polity (albeit poorly there) than in the corporate world.

Berthoin Antal and Izraeli consider factors that are thought to be linked with the movement of women into management: higher education (yes, but slowly), company size (still unclear what that relationship may be), and newness of industry (perhaps). In all countries, they say, management is seen as masculine; it is seen as requiring full-time commitment, and there are problems for women even getting into the recruitment pool, never mind being hired. In all industrialized countries now, there is lip service paid to the need for more women in high-level management because of (a) the dearth of men available and (b) the need in each country to use all talent available to be competitive internationally. Some argue that women's uniquely feminine talents are needed but these authors see dangers in this argument: "Although this logic is intended to be woman-friendly . . . it carries the risk of a new form of stereotyping" (Chapter 3). Indeed, it does.

All industrialized countries now have equal opportunity laws, these researchers show, but they caution at the same time that the presence of the legislation does not guarantee that women are welcomed into high-level management posts. Women everywhere are stalled at junior-level or mid-level management.

What is holding women back? The section on multinational corporations and the opportunities extended to women to do managerial work in countries other than their homelands is instructive. Berthoin Antal and Izraeli consider each argument against sending women managers abroad: Women don't want to go; there are not enough women at an appropriate level to send; neither single nor married women would be appropriate; and, finally, no women would be accepted. The reader will find that each of these arguments has been used to explain why women don't get ahead in management at home and will be saddened that they are being brought up once again to explain why only men are given the opportunity to serve abroad. Berthoin Antal and Izraeli counter each argument neatly.

Will the future be brighter? These three authors provide guarded responses. Alpern identified four conditions as conducive to progress in the United States; but, applying those standards to the situation of women in other industrialized countries, we see that they may be necessary but not sufficient.

I studied the question of the possibilities open to women in the United States in a different way, by using a record of leadership in a respected guide (Farley, 1985). *Who's Who in America* began publication in 1899; the editors chose 8,602 leaders to include. Since then, a new edition has appeared every two years or so. By the mid-1980s, each edition included some 75,000 leaders. But the ratio of leaders chosen for inclusion to the general population has always remained about the same—3 leaders chosen for every 10,000 in the U.S. population at the time. So it is an elite group.

When a leader included in *Who's Who* dies, the biographical sketch is taken out of the next edition and bound into a volume called *Who Was Who.* When I did this study, there were six volumes of *Who Was Who.* The editors of the guide also prepared a historical volume covering leaders from 1607 to 1899—a sort of "who would have been who if there had been such a thing as *Who's Who.*" To have a history of leadership from 1607 to the current time, I lined up the historical volume, each volume of *Who Was Who,* and four current editions. My research question was this: How many women? I went through the volumes page by page and, in the end, found that, of the deceased biographees, 5.5% were women and, of those still living, still 5.5%. Closer analysis showed that the percentage was rising, but slowly, slowly. What conditions made it possible for those few to make it (Farley, 1985)?

Like historian Alpern, I found that wars had had a significant effect on women's employment opportunities. And I found other conditions affecting individual women, of which one was wealth and another was family connections. Well into this century, only the well-to-do could afford to send a daughter to college—and precious few institutions accepted women. But the distinguished women's colleges have graduated many a woman leader who went on to earn high honors and a place in history as a volunteer community activist. Family connections have also always been useful: Women have sometimes made their way into politics by following a husband into office or a father into public life. Daughters of business executives have had opportunities they would not otherwise have had. Indeed, the sole woman chief executive officer of a *Fortune* 500 company at this writing, Katherine Graham of the *Washington Post,* had family connections. According to one analyst's estimate, no fewer than half the other CEOs of *Fortune* 500 companies are sons of CEOs.

Another condition I found was want. When women remained single or became widowed or divorced, they had to support themselves and sometimes their families. Most died—then as now—poor, but, every once in a while in U.S. history, there has been a woman who reported later that she had to drive into new territory because she had to earn money. Sarah Josepha Hale was a widow when she founded the first women's magazine in America, as was Katharine Gibbs when she fought to have women accepted as office workers and founded a school to train them. Is it possible that women will languish on the margins of business leadership unless there is a war or they are very rich or singularly determined singles? Does that mean that most U.S. women of low and middle income, married, mothers—that is, most U.S. women—are never going to be able to be contenders?

My study showed that U.S. women chosen to be leaders

had had the chance to go to college;

had been married;

had had children; and,

overall, over time, as a group, were moving out of the narrow band of "women's occupations" into a much wider range of jobs.

I choose to interpret this as progress—slow, very slow, but progress.

To be sure, there are other factors that have held women back: race, sexual orientation, class, religion, disability, status as immigrants. A sad example is African American women, often seen now as doubly protected by legislation. That protection is as it may be but the reality is that black women as a group are behind white men, black men, and white women in average salary—well behind.

Some say that women should not want to be managers because women will only end up being as corrupt as some men are, as insensitive to human needs (as to routinely expect a 70- or 80-hour work week), and as heedless of the environment and of people in poor countries as some corporate executives have proven to be. I say women should have the chance to show what women can do.

It won't be easy. Each reform that is proposed and is supposed to make it easier for women to make it in a man's business world has the potential to leave women worse off. Work at home on computers? Grand. Now some mothers can do two jobs at once at home in isolation. Job share? Terrific. Some women will have to take on three-quarter time jobs for half pay when they really wanted full-time jobs. Pregnancy leave? Maternity leaves? Quick ways to identify women who are not serious.

There must be massive change before women of all races and all conditions can have an equal shot at being one of the 3 people out of 10,000 Americans who are deemed famous enough to make it into *Who's Who in America,* that is, to make it beyond the middle ranks of management in business, in unions. One hope lies in women's organizations, both national and international, as suggested by Berthoin Antal and Izraeli, and in women's networks everywhere. They are reaching across traditional barriers to help one another. They are convinced that they

can make a contribution in peacetime as they have in times of war.
Needed are changes in laws and in the enforcement of them, changes in
education at all levels until it is really sex fair, transformations in home
lives and even in the way family is defined, and changes in the political
systems where women currently simply cannot generate the financial
resources to be elected in significant numbers. Yet, the idea that men
are leaders and women are helpers is deeply routed in American life. It
will take massive transformation to dig it out.

REFERENCE

Farley, J. (1985). Women leaders in America 1607-1982. In A. Hast & J. Farley, *American leaders past and present: The view from Who's Who in America.* Chicago: Marquis Who's Who Inc.

SECTION III

Individual and Organizational Issues

4

Women of Color in Management: Toward an Inclusive Analysis

ELLA L. BELL
TONI C. DENTON
STELLA NKOMO

Studies of women managers and the effect of gender in organizations have proliferated in recent years. Today, the body of literature referred to as "women in management" has become a well-recognized and important domain within management studies. Research on women in management grew out of a challenge to the prevailing paradigm in the study of management that might be summarized as "think manager, think male" (Nkomo, 1988). Women in management was to be a corrective scholarship, exposing gender biases in existing research and, more important, critiquing and challenging the male-dominated corporate hierarchy.

In the act of challenging and in many instances successfully altering the male-centered nature of scholarship in management research, however, women in management research often reflected and repeated the same "exclusivity error" that gave rise to its existence. A review of the existing body of knowledge on women in management might lead to the observation that much of the scholarship addresses the experience of only one

AUTHORS' NOTE: Preparation of this manuscript was supported by a grant from the Rockefeller Foundation (No. R88048). The authors would like to thank the anonymous reviewers for their helpful comments of earlier drafts of this chapter.

group of women managers. As such, we have learned little about the effects of race *and* gender on the status of women in management positions.

The existing approaches to the study of women in management do not include women of color[1] as an area of research, nor do major literature reviews include the problems and issues confronting women of color as an area of study (Dipboye, 1987; Freedman & Philips, 1988; Hennig & Jardim, 1977; Larwood & Wood, 1977; Nieva & Gutek, 1981; Powell, 1988). A notable exception to this practice is the recent review by Morrison and Von Glinow (1990). The omission of women of color is more implicit than explicit and occurs when authors of studies of essentially white women managers generalize their findings to "women." The term *woman* often means white, heterosexual, not differentially abled, and from a privileged background (Cannon, Higginbotham, & Leung, 1988).

The urgent need for a more inclusive research agenda is underscored by the recent Workforce 2000 report indicating that minority women will constitute the largest share of the increase in the nonwhite labor force between now and the year 2000 (Johnston & Packer, 1988). At the same time, one of the occupational groups expected to increase faster than average until 1995 is executives and managers. Women stand to make their greatest economic gains through successful employment in these fields. Among new graduates, women represent 31% of all MBAs and about 49% of all four-year business degrees (Ehrlich, 1989).

Obtaining accurate data on the number of women currently in management positions is difficult because of the variety of sources and the varying definitions used for the term *manager*. According to U.S. Department of Labor data, the proportion of management, executive, and administrative positions held by women has been rising consistently since 1970 and is currently at 42% (U.S. Department of Labor, 1991). The most recent data from the Equal Employment Opportunity Commission (EEOC, 1991)[2] indicate that in 1988 there were 4.1 million officials and managers employed in private sector firms that were required to file summary statistics. Black, Latina,[3] Asian American, and Native American women represented 3.8% of this total, while white women represented 24.8% (EEOC, 1991).[4] In 1978, the percentages were 1.8% and 15.2%, respectively (EEOC, 1990). The proportion of women who hold top management positions, however, continues to be quite small, less than 2% according to most surveys (Fierman, 1990; Powell, 1988). Not one black woman was among the top 25 black managers in corporate America in a survey conducted in 1988 by *Black Enterprise* (Harrison, King, & Gregg, 1988). Reports by Korn/Ferry International (reported by Jones, 1986) indicated that there were no

Asian American or Latina women in the senior ranks among the executives they surveyed. A major issue confronting women managers is how to break through the metaphorical glass ceiling that keeps them from the very top ranks (Morrison et al., 1987). The issue for women of color in management has been described as one of breaking a concrete ceiling that restricts their access to even middle management positions (Ray & Davis, 1988). Until we expand our knowledge toward fully understanding how both race and gender affect the experiences of women managers in organizations, we cannot hope to offer prescriptions for removing these ceilings and advancing their careers. Integrating women managers of all racial, ethnic, and class backgrounds into significant decision-making positions is part of the challenge as we approach the year 2000.

The major purpose of this chapter is to offer directives for charting the journey of women in management in inclusive terms. We draw heavily from other disciplines where the issues of gender *and* race have been addressed to a greater extent than in our own field (Cole, 1986; Hill-Collins, 1989; Hooks, 1984; Hull, Scott, & Smith, 1982; Rothenberg, 1988; Spelman, 1988). We present a variety of data—empirical, personal, and observational—to ask the reader to consider new ways of thinking about women in management. Our objectives are threefold: First, we intend to discuss the deficiencies in our current knowledge of women managers, especially those of Asian, African, and Latino descent. Second, we discuss and demonstrate the potential of three conceptual frameworks for broadening our approach to understanding the life experiences of women managers. Finally, we propose a multifaceted research agenda for the next decade that will provide an inclusive portrait of women managers' experiences in organizations. While the major focus of this chapter is on the effects of racial and ethnic differences, we do recognize that differences among women are far more complicated (Lugones & Spelman, 1983). Class, sexual orientation, and physical ability also affect their access to management. Space limitations preclude full treatment of these factors. Yet we do hope that the ideas discussed in this chapter will heighten awareness of the need to incorporate these issues into future research.

THE UNACKNOWLEDGED VOICES OF EXCLUDED WOMEN

A recent experience at a conference, attended by two of the authors, illustrates the very problems of exclusion and the major deficiencies in our approach to understanding the dilemmas of women in management. We attended a planning meeting to provide input for an upcoming national conference on the interface between employment and family and the related concerns of child care, parental leave, and alternate career paths, particularly for women. The meeting was primarily attended by nationally renowned researchers, practitioners, executives, and policymakers who were invited to attend because of their expertise. While the events at the conference may not be generalizable to all similar settings, they brought to the surface significant issues embedded in race, gender, and class.

During a full conference discussion, involving the entire group of participants, issues delineated by the white women, who were in the majority at the conference, consistently pointed to the dilemmas of women managers who decided to leave their companies or reduce their hours of employment to raise children. It was pointed out by a black woman in attendance that there are many women—single parents, working-class women, and women of color—for whom these alternatives are not always viable. If the single parent is a woman or a woman of color, it is likely that she is already disadvantaged in pay and promotions. Because of the relatively poor economic status of minority males compared with white males, an important factor inducing women of color into the work force is the need to shore up family resources. Research suggests that, while white women also suffer economically, their economic situation is not as dire as that of women of color (Malveaux, 1985). White women's relationship to white men (the highest earners in society) as daughters, sisters, or wives gives them an economic cushion (Palmer, 1983). Some of the white women's responses to these observations and accompanying attempts to broaden the issues were strong. One woman commented: "We can't include everyone in our initial research thrust, or we will 'dilute' our strategy." Another woman researcher added: "I think we should focus on managerial women—because they are the most visible—once we begin to make progress there, we can expand our agenda to include other groups." Throughout the remaining discussion, the efforts of the women of color and a small group of white women participants to encourage inclusive framing of the problem were met with anxiety and discomfort. One white female seemed to reflect the sentiments of the group in her statement, "If we make this too complex, we won't be able to get our arms around it."

The issues illustrated above can be understood from several different levels of analysis: individual, group, organizational, and societal. At the individual level, the dynamics of the conference led to exclusion of women of color and the ultimate invisibility of their issues. For example, women of color who wanted their perspectives addressed at the conference had to risk being ignored, perceived as distracting the group from the "real issues," or cast in the role of expert on minority experiences. They were unable to speak as "individuals." The outcome for the white women present was a feeling of being stereotyped as white people, viewed as part of the oppressor group, and associated with racist and prejudicial behaviors. None of these positions results in legitimate inclusion and influence.

Many of the conference events reflected group level dynamics. These dynamics include the relationships between women with differing racial backgrounds or dynamics among women who share a cultural identity. For example, black women who have grown up in the United States share the cultural identity of being black Americans. This is not to say that black women are a monolithic group without differences (notably class) but it refers to a common historical legacy and the likelihood that common cultural experiences have affected their lives (Hill-Collins, 1989). Similarly, although they may not be members of the same ethnic culture, white women share common experiences as white women. Both McIntosh (1988) and Frost (1987) refer to the privileges of whiteness as a common experience for white men and women. McIntosh (1988) describes how one's experience is affected by the ability to assume as normal the privileges that other groups receive only under certain conditions or not at all. Frost (1987) focuses on the ways such privileges affect white women in particular. She asserts that white women are subtly encouraged to assume a societal position beneath white men but above black men and women.

It is extremely significant that the white, privileged women present did not frame the experiences of minority women or working-class white women as part of "our issues" as women but referred to these issues as "adding 'other' groups." Thus privileged women not only defined themselves as constituting "women" but also the norm or standard. Minnich (1990) calls this the *prefix error*—that which does not carry a prefix is assumed to be universal. By not saying white women but implicitly meaning white women, other realities were relegated to subcategories. The point is that, when we do not say white woman manager but do say black or Asian American woman manager, we are reflecting and perpetuating a kind of knowledge in which experiences of white women managers are seen as the experiences of "women in management." This same error can be found in the women in management literature. Many researchers fail even to mention the racial composition of the sample or question whether their findings are universally applicable (e.g., Brenner, Tomkiewicz, & Schein, 1989; Schneer & Reitman, 1990; Terpstra & Baker, 1988).5 Even in studies where minority women are part of the sample, issues surrounding race or ethnicity are not explored (e.g., Freeman, 1990; Morrison et al., 1987).

Spelman (1988, p. 167) offers some explanation of intergroup dynamics when she writes, "To add race and class is to talk about the racial and class identity of black women, or of poor women. Talking about racism and classism thus ends up being talk about something experienced by some women rather than something perpetuated by others." White women's resistance to owning their privilege creates a barrier in their interactions with women of color. A common outcome of this barrier is that the voices of nonwhite, nonprivileged women remain unheard (Lugones & Spelman, 1983).

The outcome at the organizational level is that we are left with inadequate information about how to fully integrate women of different racial and class backgrounds into significant management positions. By resisting broader definitions of the problem, we risk developing strategies that support the mobility of one group of women at the cost of the mobility of other women. White women managers may find themselves inadvertently supporting organizational systems that have offered them some privileges at the expense of other oppressed groups.

Similarly, on the societal level, we are not dealing with the issues in their entirety. Instead of seeking knowledge about diverse groups of women, we continue to operate on the assumption that all women are the same. In reality, experiences of oppression and success differ according to the position of the group within the social system. Adrienne Rich (1979, p. 306) coined the term *white solipsism* to refer to the tendency "to think, imagine, and speak as if whiteness described the world." She adds that it is "not the consciously held belief that one race is inherently superior to all others, but a tunnel-vision which simply does not see nonwhite experience or existence as precious or significant." She further outlines the limitations of continuing to develop agendas for research, policy, and change that ignore issues of race and ethnicity, by indicating that the process of merely "adding on" minority issues will have "little or no long term, continuing momentum or political usefulness for inclusive social change" (Rich, 1979, p. 167).

RESEARCH ON WOMEN OF COLOR IN MANAGEMENT

The paucity of research on minority women managers underscores the very limited knowledge we have of their experiences in organizations. Much of the extant work has been impressionistic and nonempirical, appearing in predominantly black-oriented popular magazines (e.g., Davis, 1990; Harrison et al., 1988; King, 1988; "100 of the Best and Brightest," 1990; Ray & Davis, 1988; Weathers, 1981). In recent years, however, a small body of empirical research has emerged. Black women have been the major focus of much of this research to the exclusion of Latina, Asian American, and Native American women. A common issue in much of this work has been the nature of the effects of race *and* gender on black women in organizations. While most researchers have recognized the effects as cumulative, they differ on whether it is positive or negative. This research debate has centered on two competing hypotheses (Nkomo, 1988). The double advantage (colloquially referred to as "twofer") hypothesis holds that the sum effect of race *and* gender is positive and black women enjoy a preferred status in organizations compared with other groups including black males. As a consequence, they will advance faster and farther than other groups. One erroneous assumption of this view is that affirmative action policies are propelling black women ahead of other groups because they can be counted as a "double minority."[6] Some researchers have further suggested that there have been loopholes in racial discrimination that permitted black women to take better advantage of educational and economic opportunities than black males (Bock, 1971).

The origin of the double advantage hypothesis can be traced to the work of Epstein (1973), who studied the experience of black women in prestigious, male-dominated professions. She argued that the gender status of female and the race status of black did not result in negative consequences but formed a positive matrix for a meaningful career for the women in her study. Despite the doubt that has been cast on her findings (e.g., Fox & Hesse-Biber, 1984), the notion that black women enjoy a preferred status has been hard to dispel. Most recently, Jones (1986, p. 91), in a study of black managers in corporations, argued that, "if personal comfort levels are a main criterion for advancement, black women are less threatening and therefore more acceptable to white male executives and will advance faster and farther than black men." Adams

(1983), in a study of biracial groups, also concluded that, within a social context, black females are more readily accepted in roles of influence than black males.

In contrast, other writers and researchers have portrayed black women as victims of a "double whammy or double jeopardy" (Beale, 1970). King (1975) pointed out that, while sexism is injurious to black women, racism further intensifies the negative experience. Benjamin (1982), in a study of upwardly mobile black women, contended that, because of her race and sex, the upwardly mobile black woman occupies an acute marginal position in society, thereby increasing her chances of isolation.

Other empirical studies cast doubt on the validity of the double advantage hypothesis for black women managers. In a study of race and sex discrimination in the evaluation of job applicants, Hitt, Zikmund, and Pickens (1982) sent resumes to personnel directors of 200 corporations across the United States. Their results indicated that being a black female did not increase the number of positive responses compared with other race and sex groups. Irons and Moore (1985), in a survey of blacks in the banking industry, found that, although there was greater growth in the number of black women at the management level compared with black men, black women were concentrated in low-level operations jobs, small branch management, and staff functions and not in the more prestigious commercial lending or investment functions of banks. Fulbright (1985) studied the barriers to occupational mobility in a sample of black women managers. Using a combination of interview data and surveys, she found that black female managers lacked early exposure to a general business environment and lacked corporate sponsors, unlike their white counterparts.

More recently, Nkomo and Cox (1989) examined the validity of the double advantage hypothesis in the upward mobility of black managers. In a study of 283 black male and female managers, they found that although the women had higher job performance ratings than the males, were equally involved in their work, had experienced the same rate of promotion, and were at about the same hierarchical level, they nevertheless had received significantly less pay than their male counterparts as well as fewer opportunities and less line management experience. Though both groups had experienced similar promotion rates, black women in their study were more satisfied with their career progress than black men. Greenhaus, Parasuraman, and Wormley (1988), in a cross-race and cross-gender study of the careers of managers, found that black women managers felt less accepted by their organizations, perceived less discretion in their jobs, and were rated lower by their supervisors on their performance and promotability. They also found that black women were more likely to have reached a career plateau and to have experienced lower levels of career satisfaction when compared with white managers, both male and female.

These studies suggest that neither the "double advantage" nor the "double whammy" assumptions about the effects of race and gender are wholly accurate descriptions of the contemporary experience of black women managers. The intersection between race and gender may be far more complex, problematic, and contradictory than these oppositional hypotheses indicate. King (1988) has noted that the importance of any one factor (e.g., race) in explaining black women's experiences varies depending on the particular aspect of their lives under consideration and the reference groups with whom they are compared. In some cases, race may be the most significant predictor of black women's status; in other cases, gender or class may prevail. This suggests that on certain dimensions black women managers' experiences may more closely resemble those of black men or white women, or their experiences may be unique. Hicks (1981) has also cautioned against the tendency to theorize about the interrelations between social dynamics as "additive," "reciprocal," or "symmetrical"—for example, the tendency to view racism and sexism as parallel processes (Nkomo, 1988). Instead, she offers the thesis that the operation of multiple social categories may at best be systematically contradictory or nonsynchronous.

One of the deficiencies in the research exploring the effects of race and gender has been a tendency to focus on outcome variables (e.g., career satisfaction, number of promotions) without sufficiently explaining why experiences may differ. Many of the studies identify a lack of access to mentors, sponsorship, and significant work assignments as major barriers to minority women managers' performance, motivation, and mobility (Fulbright, 1985; Gordus & Oshiro, 1986; Ilgen & Youtz, 1986; Pettigrew & Martin, 1987). An implicit assumption underlying the lack of access to mentors is that white males engage in biased behavior and do not choose black women as protégés. In reality, this barrier may be grounded in more complex dynamics rooted in the social context of race. In a study of the development of cross-race and cross-gender mentor relationships in a corporate setting, Thomas (1989) found that black women managers were reluctant to be closely associated with white male executives because it conjured up images of black concubines who, without choice, served white masters during slavery.

Thomas (1989) also found that black managers, both male and female, when finding same-race mentors, were more likely to have mentor relationships outside their departments and organizations with persons who were not their immediate supervisors. This study is useful in pointing out the need for research that begins to explore the complexity and contradictory nature of the effects of race and gender.

Other than the comprehensive survey of 4,209 managers in one company by Fernandez (1981), there is very little research that provides information about the experiences and status of Latina, Asian American, and Native American women managers. Of interest, Fernandez (1981) reported some perplexing differences among the various racial/ethnic groups in their perceptions of their corporate experiences. In response to questions on sexism, black women were the most critical about the treatment of women managers in corporations. Latina, white, and Native American women were the next most critical after black women. Asian American women were the least critical of the treatment of women managers. While Fernandez's (1981) findings point to the importance of not treating women of color managers as a monolithic group, his reliance upon self-report data in a single firm suggests that the results need further study.

Although Fernandez could not determine the reasons for his findings with the methodology employed, he speculated that Asian American women managers have less sensitivity to sexism because of gender role socialization in their communities and the alternate forms of stereotyping of minorities in U.S. society. On the latter point, Asian Americans are often looked upon "favorably" by white society and viewed as the model minority (Osajima, 1988). Fox and Hesse-Biber (1984) attribute positive images of Asian American women to such things as the relatively high levels of educational attainment and the relative ease of absorption into the mainstream. Members of the Asian American community have argued that their image as the "model minority" is racially stereotypical and empirically inaccurate (Osajima, 1988). Woo (1985) specifically questions the notion of the advantaged status of Asian American women. In her examination of 1970 and 1980 census data, she found that, while education enhanced earnings capability, the relative gains made by Asian American women were not as great as those made by other women and were well below parity with white males. At the executive, administrative, and managerial levels, Asian American women tended to be self-employed or working as auditors and accountants. Woo (1985) also emphasized the importance of recognizing the differences in labor market experiences of different Asian American women's groups (e.g., Japanese versus Filipinas, foreign born versus U.S. born). In a survey of Asian Americans in professional and managerial jobs, Cabezas, Tam, Lowe, Wong, and Turner (1989) found that education and work experience yielded low returns on promotion and advancement when compared with white males.

Latina women suffer different types of stereotyping. Latina women are often depicted as passive and dominated by the "machismo" of their men (Horowitz, 1983). Images of Latina women either as passive, self-sacrificing mothers or as fiery, hot-blooded vixens are not uncommon (Williams, 1988). Recent work questions the validity of these stereotypes and attempts to offer a much more accurate description of the gender role identity and status of Latina women (Editorial Committee, 1986; Romero, 1986; Williams, 1988). Williams (1988) held interviews with 75 Mexican American couples in Texas to examine how married women defined their roles and conjugal relationships. Her data indicated that, contrary to previous research, married women were not passive but actually took a lead in decision making. The business/professional women in her study exhibited more diversity in role-making patterns than the working-class women. They were also more sensitive about negative stereotypes of Mexican Americans as incompetent and uninterested in education. While the business/professional women recognized that both their ethnicity and their gender prevented them from achieving certain goals at work, they often felt that they were demeaned more for their gender. Romero (1986) examined the legitimacy of the double advantage hypothesis for Latina women. Her analysis of 1975 and 1980 census data revealed that the slow pace of the movement of Chicanas into higher paying managerial and skilled positions did not support the claim of "preferential treatment." She noted that her results were particularly discouraging because they occurred during the affirmative action era and during a period of rising Chicana labor force participation and increased educational attainment.

What is clear from this literature is that race and racism are real constraints in the lives of women of color. Further, the meaning of gender and the relationships between women of color and men of color are confounded by racism. We cannot explain the experience of women managers by focusing solely on gender or race. The interaction between race and gender leads to different perceptions of the major issues confronting women in management positions and the needed responses. Women of color will rarely perceive their treatment as solely based on their sex (Editorial Committee, 1986; Hill-Collins, 1989; King, 1988; Williams, 1988). Their experiences in organizations are seen from the perspective of being a black woman or a Latina woman or an Asian woman. And, for the latter groups, perspectives may even be more finely shaped (e.g., Puerto Rican woman, Chinese American woman). For white women, it is important to understand how their racial identity and their contradictory access to the source of privilege, white men, affect their managerial experience. We need research approaches and theoretical models that fit women's own constructions of their identity and that will help us to understand the diversity of women's experiences as managers.

TOWARD A MORE INCLUSIVE ANALYSIS

It is important to investigate women managers' lives across racial and ethnic categories to understand what they have in common as well as their differences. Only then can we attempt to describe what is universal about their experiences. In this section, we discuss three theoretical frameworks to broaden our analysis of the experiences of women managers: (a) intergroup theory, (b) the bicultural model, and (c) the women's life context model. These frameworks are meant to be illustrative tools and do not necessarily represent the only frameworks available. We also present the results from two studies illustrating the kind of research produced by these frameworks.

Intergroup Theory

Intergroup theory, while not new, is a valuable paradigm for examining race and gender dynamics embedded in organizations (Alderfer 1986; Alderfer, Alderfer, Tucker, & Tucker, 1980; Alderfer & Smith 1982). The theory posits that two types of groups exist within organizations: identity groups and organization groups (Alderfer, 1986). The most commonly recognized identity groups are those based on gender, age, race, ethnicity, and family. An organization group is one in which members share approximately common organizational positions, participate in equivalent work experiences, and consequently have similar organizational views. When individuals enter organizations, they bring with them their identity groups. Membership in identity groups is not independent of membership in organizational groups. For example positions in upper management tend to be held by older white males and certain other positions tend to be predominated by women and minorities (Alderfer & Smith, 1982).

According to intergroup theory, individuals and organizations are constantly attempting to manage potential conflicts arising from the interface between identity and organization group memberships. How these tensions are managed depends on several factors, the most important of which is how the groups are embedded within the organization (Alderfer & Smith, 1982). Embeddedness is most concerned with how intergroup relations are shaped by the larger environment (Alderfer & Smith, 1982). Embeddedness can be either congruent or incongruent. Congruent embeddedness exists when power relations among groups at one level are reinforced by power relations at the suprasystem and subsystem levels (Alderfer, 1986). For example, congruent embeddedness is represented in situations in which white males dominate in high status management positions while women and minorities predominant in low power positions. This would essentially mirror the general power dynamics in the larger society/environment. Incongruent embeddedness would be represented by a situation where power relationships would not be consistent with suprasystem dynamics (e.g., an Asian American woman manager supervising a department consisting largely of white males).

Researchers can use the theory to study intergroup relations from several perspectives: (a) the effects of group membership on individuals, (b) the consequences for subgroups within groups as the groups deal with one another, (c) the outcomes for groups as a whole when they relate to significant other groups, and (d) the impact of suprasystem forces on the intergroup relationship in question. Intergroup theory provided the conceptual framework for a study of race relations among managers of a large business corporation (Alderfer et al., 1980). Alderfer and his colleagues examined general race relations, racial dynamics, and perceptions of the influence of race on hiring, advancement, firing, and job opinions. One theme cutting across the data from each level was the existence of both parallel and nonparallel perceptions between the racial groups (black and white employees). Each racial group (both males and females) reported that members of the other group socialized more with each other than with members of the other race, and each racial group tended to see this pattern as weaker in its own group than in the other group. On balance, blacks (males and females) evaluated one-to-one black-white relationships more negatively than did whites.

Intergroup theory emphasizes the importance of identity groups and embedded-intergroup relations in understanding the status and experience of women in management. Relationships of power and subordination between groups, behavioral patterns, language indicative of group memberships, processes of inclusion and exclusion, and pluralism versus assimilation can be understood using this theory (Alderfer, 1986). Intergroup theory can be used to study, for example, the relative status of black women and white women in management and the relationship of their status to white males and black males. An intergroup perspective explicitly recognizes identity group memberships and therefore that analysis should not rest solely upon understanding the behavior of individual actors. It also heightens our awareness of group differences among the women managers and that it may not be appropriate, for example, to assume that white women and black women share a common identity as "women." Nor would it be totally accurate to assume that black women and black men would share the same perceptions because they are of the same race.

The Bicultural Model

The bicultural model can be used to explain the stress one experiences from participation in both a minority group culture and a dominant group culture (Bell, 1986) and has been used by Bell (1990) to understand the lives of black professional women. *Biculturalism* is defined as socialization and participation within two cultural contexts (Valentine, 1971). Biculturalism creates an acute identity conflict for women of color because it results in emotional commitment to two distinct components of their lives. A bicultural life structure requires a woman of color manager to shape her professional world in a male-dominated white culture, while her personal world often remains embedded in her racial/ethnic community. At the workplace, she may be forced to sacrifice the racial/ethnic part of her identity in favor of what is normal in the dominant culture. The suppression of her identity can happen at the superficial level of dress, hairstyle, and language patterns and at much more substantive levels of social, personal, and political values (Bell, 1990).

Racial/ethnic minorities in general are expected by other members of their culture to retain allegiance to their own culture while "participating" in their adopted culture (Baumeister, 1986). Yet, circumstances often dictate that, for women of color to be successful managers, they must adopt a new identity and abandon commitment to their old culture. The behavior itself does not cause the crisis; rather, the tension comes from the implication of that behavior—specifically, the implication that one has to give up the betrayed component of identity. For women of color, the negative impact of racism on the general condition of their communities intensifies the obligation of uplifting and contributing to its alleviation (Gilkes, 1982). It is very difficult for women of color to betray this felt obligation.

The following quote from a Latina woman manager shared with the authors portrays her bicultural experience:

> I worked for an intelligent white man whom I respected, but he was not using me the way he could have. He made some interesting comments at different times, such as: "Being Hispanic here is not going to help you," and "You do not want to be known as the in-house Hispanic." He advised me to hide my calls from people with Hispanic surnames, and my Spanish newspaper. He gave me this advice even though I needed to read those papers in order to effectively do my job. The man thought he was giving me good advice. I don't think he ever knew how much he hurt me.

Another example is found in a Native American woman's experience. Mary is a manager within the banking industry. She has not mentioned her Native American heritage to most of the people with whom she works. Once, while working on a project in the Los Angeles office, she volunteered to pursue a deal with a Native American group in the area. At this time, she made it known to her boss that she had ties to the culture. Her boss, a white male, became very cold to her, making his distaste for Native Americans apparent.

Using the bicultural model, Bell (1990) examined the bicultural experience of 71 career-oriented black women. She was most interested in learning how they managed conflicts between the black and white cultural contexts of their lives. Bell found that biculturality required the black women in her study to create dynamic, fluid life structures to navigate between each culture. Each context had its own expectations and role demands, which often conflicted and led to bicultural stress. Isolation, feeling invisible, overcompensation, and denial of one's culture or racial identity were stressors related to the bicultural experience. Bicultural stress was also amplified by the fact that members of women's own communities perceived them as "traitors" willing to abandon their culture to be fully integrated into the dominant culture.

One example of the stress induced by these dual contexts occurs for an upper-level black female manager we interviewed. Nina is the *only* woman and the *only* black person on her work team. She described it as "hell at first; the men on my team didn't know what to say to me." Nina was aware that she faced more pressure than her teammates and she constantly had to prove herself. She said, "It's like starting all over." Nina's experiences ranged from overt incidents of racism and sexism to more subtle discrimination.

Women of color in management often must function not only in racially different contexts but also in gender-different contexts. The bicultural model also has relevance for understanding gender-different contexts. Women in predominantly male professions such as management are expected to shed their "feminine" or "womanly" characteristics to succeed. Women of color managers must learn to navigate in both a white- and a male-dominated organization culture. Exploring the biculturalism of a woman gives us the opportunity to understand the choices she makes in attempting to be psychically whole and to maintain a sense of cultural integration among the groups in which she has membership.

Woman's Life Context Model

A third proposed model is the woman's life context model (Bell 1986). Drawing from Bronfenbrenner's (1979) ecological system model of human development, Bell (1986) developed this model as a framework for understanding all levels of a woman's life. It is a woman-centered model that can be used to understand a woman manager's life at five levels personal or private, group, organizational, community, and societal. This lens for examining a woman's life does not assume that a woman manager's professional life exists apart from other life spheres. Its aim is to understand a woman manager's entire life structure and the interdependence among the different components.

In the life context model, a woman's life structure is composed of five major domains: (a) early life experiences and identity development (b) education, motivation, and aspirations; (c) early adult experiences— career choice, entry, and socialization; (d) public world—career development, goals, and professional affiliations; and (e) private world—significant relationships, family, leisure, spirituality, and sexuality. All of these life domains interact dynamically to shape a woman manager's career and life experiences. The model also stresses the importance of the context tual forces of culture, race/ethnicity, sociopolitical history, and class. These forces represent the landscape in which women develop and can best be explained as moderating variables. As such, they can influence each of the five major domains. For example, a woman's self-identity and subsequent self-esteem may be strongly influenced by her race or ethnicity. While this model has not been empirically tested, it holds promise for approaching the study of women managers in a holistic manner, recognizing the importance of multiple forces in shaping life and career experiences.

RESEARCH AGENDA FOR THE COMING DECADE

If we are to gather more inclusive knowledge about the experience of women of color in management, then our research on women in management must be expanded in five ways, as follows.

(1) A need exists for studies that examine both intraracial and interracial relationships among women managers and relationships between women of different socioeconomic status (e.g., managerial women versus nonmanagerial women). How women manage relationships across race and class will become more significant as the composition of the labor force changes over the decade. An important question is whether the cadre of women managers will simply reproduce and reinforce existing organizational cultures and policies or challenge and restructure them.

While studies consisting of samples of only one racial/ethnic group are valuable, it is also important to study the relational aspects of organizational experiences and outcomes. To better understand the status of white women or women of color in management, we must also address the ways in which organizations choose to assign limited opportunities among women and people of color. The relationships among women managers are affected in both obvious and subtle ways by how each is related to the source of privilege—white men. Hurtado (1989) argues that white women, as a group, are subordinated through seduction, while women of color, as a group, are subordinated through rejection.

The work of Larwood, Szwajkowski, and Rose (1988) is an example of needed research. Their study provided a test of the rational bias theory of managerial behavior in the prediction of sex and race discrimination.

Rational bias theory is based on the idea that a manager's decision about whether or not to discriminate will partly depend on the effect the decision may have on his or her career. Thus, with a norm favoring discrimination against women and blacks, rational bias theory predicts that decisions will favor males and whites. In the Larwood et al. study (1988), management students, acting in the role of managers, felt that a general business norm favors discrimination against both women and blacks. Specifically, they believed that biases favored males over females, whites over blacks, white women over black men, and white men over black women.

(2) We must move away from research that begins with a male-dominated concept of knowledge that views women managers as inadequate, incomplete, or deficient. We need research that does not focus on fixing the victim but instead examines the institutional dynamics, societal assumptions, and biases that keep groups oppressed. This call has also been made by others in the field (see Fagenson, 1990; Larwood et al., 1988). The exigencies of understanding the more subtle forms that racism and sexism have taken in contemporary society have never been more pronounced. One of the new cloaks of sexism in organizations, for example, is the belief that women with family responsibilities cannot make the necessary commitment to their managerial careers (Schwartz, 1989). Underlying this view is a patriarchal assumption that people at work exist apart from the other aspects of their lives. Research based on this assumption becomes mired in questions of why managerial women need a separate career track (Schwartz, 1989). Rejecting this assumption leads to very different questions. For example, what kinds of organizational environments reinforce women (and men) as whole people with employment, family, and community loyalties? And what are the spillover effects from one context to another?

If one were to review much of the literature on organizations, one would assume that racism takes place somewhere else, outside of the workplace, or, when the possibility is acknowledged at all, it is framed as an affirmative action issue (Cox & Nkomo, 1990; Nkomo, 1992). It is rarely acknowledged that race relations in society are reproduced in organizational, behavioral, and structural systems (Cox & Nkomo, 1990). Race and gender, along with class, are major bases of domination in society and directly influence the status of women in organizations. We cannot do research that decontextualizes women's experiences in organizations from the larger social context. Expanding our view leads to asking questions such as these: What is it about organizations that reproduce racist and sexist views of women and minorities? What are liberating organization structures and how can they be developed? How can management be changed to value the contribution of all employees?

(3) Research about women in management needs to draw extensively from many other disciplines and to open its theorizing to new perspectives. Calás and Smircich (1989) and Martin (in this volume), for example, have discussed the potential of feminist theory for understanding the gendered nature of organizations. They point to two strands of feminist theorizing as particularly useful for framing research on women in management. The women's voice or standpoint perspective attempts to demonstrate differences between male and female experiences and then positions "the difference" as another valid form of representing human experience (Calás & Smircich, 1989, p. 8; Gilligan, 1982; Hill-Collins, 1989; Martin, in this volume; Smircich, 1985). On the other hand, more recent feminist perspectives (i.e., postfeminism) question the very stability of such cultural categories as gender, race, and class and reject the notion of an essentially "male or female" or "black or white" reality or structure. Postfeminism points out how these oppositions are culturally defined categories derived from particular social and material relations (Calás & Smircich, 1989; Martin, in this volume). Once we begin to define race and gender as analytical categories and not as natural consequences of sex difference or race difference, we can then begin to appreciate the extent to which race and gender biases have suffused our belief systems, organizations, and other institutions (Harding, 1986). That is, the meaning of race and gender are socially constructed and largely defined by the dominant group in society.

In tandem, these feminist perspectives suggest that theories that reflect our wholeness as women are unlikely to come from a preoccupation with reacting to androcentric organization models based largely on the experience of white males. Nor is new knowledge likely to come from research that merely builds discourse around the acceptance of traditional organization theories and assumptions. Useful frameworks are much more likely to emerge from researchers allowing research participants to validate their manner of engaging the world and relying on their language, stories, myths, and modes of constructing reality.

(4) We must become more aware of our role as researchers in producing knowledge that is inclusive. The role of the researcher—who she is

and what she brings to the research process (e.g., her own group memberships, socialization, racial identity) and her ways of knowing the world—have an impact on the kind of research she does as well as what she can know from her work (Kram, 1985). Morgan (1983) refers to this process of exploring our own involvement in the research process, and subsequently our limitations, assumptions, and biases, as a "reflective conversation." This is particularly important when studying race. We must understand how our racial identity affects the design, collection, and interpretation of data. How we frame the conversation about the experiences of groups different from us is also critical. Setting the conversational tone is fraught with several dangers for the researcher. Often, the conversation is a new one within the discipline—as the study of race/ethnicity issues is in the field of management (Cox & Nkomo, 1990). Consequently, differences must be presented in a way that can be heard and understood as legitimate experiences (Cox, 1990).

(5) The proposed research approaches have implications for the methods used. In addition to the more traditional quantitative approaches to data collection, there is a need for triangulation of research methods using both qualitative and quantitative methods that allow the researcher to corroborate their findings in multiple ways (Jick, 1984; Van Maanen, 1984). The use of qualitative approaches is particularly helpful for the study of the largely uncharted journey of women of color in management. Such an approach will allow for organically developed research instruments that are based on the experiences of the groups we are studying and that take account of their history, culture, and position within the society (Alderfer & Smith, 1982). An exploration of the organizational commitment of women of color in management cannot simply be based on administering the traditional scale and drawing conclusions about the extent of that commitment. Researchers must recognize that women's perceptions may be shaped by the historical treatment of minorities in organizations. In other words, research designs must not treat race as a demographic or categorical variable; instead, they must explicitly incorporate the meaning of race into the construction of instruments.

We urge the adoption of clinical approaches that facilitate intervening in organizations by developing policies and practices to enhance organizations' ability to respond to women managers in constructive ways (Berg & Smith, 1985). Finally, methods are needed to examine changes in the environment, in organizations, and in women managers lives over time. Innovative variations of longitudinal approaches can be used to explore the interactions between history, environmental, and sociopolitical changes as they affect organizations. Methods such as the life history analysis (Freedman, Thornton, Cambrun, Alwin, & Young-DeMaco, 1988), oral history methodology (Lykes, 1983), and archival data are all useful in developing this kind of knowledge. For example, to understand the influence of ethnic identity on Asian American women managers, we need to read the histories of Asian American women in this country, written in their voices (Yung, 1986).

CONCLUSIONS

Research about women in management has generally referred to white women to the exclusion of women of color. Deficiencies exist in our current knowledge of women managers, particularly those who are women of color. Intergroup theory, the bicultural model, and the life context model are potentially useful frameworks for capturing the diversity in the experiences of women managers. The research agenda for the next decade must be expanded to rectify the exclusivity of our current knowledge. We believe that it is not simply a matter of adding information about women of color in management but one of fundamentally reconstructing what we think we know about women in management. The effects of race and gender are multifaceted, and analysis and interpretation in this area require sensitivity to theoretical and conceptual issues at the outset that will frame and inform methodological approaches. We must begin to identify the commonalities and differences in the experiences of women in dominant groups and women of color in management. Only then will we be in a position to prescribe policies and programs for the advancement of women of different racial and ethnic backgrounds.

NOTES

1. The term *women of color* (or, alternately, *racial, ethnic women*) designates groups that are simultaneously racial and ethnic minorities. It is used here to refer collectively to black, Latina, Native American, and Asian American women, groups that share a legacy of labor exploitation and special forms of oppression (Glenn, 1985, p. 105). This definition does

not negate the fact that there are qualitative differences in the experiences among the women represented in this definition.

2. In 1978, the figures were 15.2 for white women, 1.1 for black women, 0.4% for Latina women, 0.2% for Asian American women, and 0.1% for Native American Women.

3. Identifying the correct term for people of Spanish origin is quite difficult. We chose to use the term *Latina*, recognizing that there are variations in labor experiences among the groups (which include Mexican Americans or Chicanos, Cubans, Puerto Ricans, and Central and South Americans).

4. Data are taken from EEO-1 reports filed by private employers (a) with 100 or more employees *or* (b) 50 or more employees and (1) having federal contract or subcontracts worth $50,000 or more, or (2) acting as depositories of federal funds in any amount, or (3) acting as issuing and paying agents for U.S. savings bonds and notes (EEOC, 1989).

5. These studies represent three recent publications appearing in one of our leading journals (*Academy of Management Journal*).

6. This assumption has no valid basis because it is impossible to "count" women of color twice on the EEO-1 reports that must filed with the U.S. government. Its real basis rests in the fear of "reverse discrimination"—that somehow women of color would enjoy a preferred status in organizations.

REFERENCES

Adams, F. (1983). Aspects of social context as determinants of black women's resistance to challenges. *Journal of Social Issues, 39,* 69-79.

Alderfer, C. P. (1986). An intergroup perspective on group dynamics. In J. Lorsch (Ed.), *Handbook of organizational behavior* (pp. 190-222). Englewood Cliffs, NJ: Prentice-Hall.

Alderfer, C. P., Alderfer, C. J., Tucker, L., & Tucker, R. (1980). Diagnosing race relations in management. *Journal of Applied Behavioral Science, 16,* 135-166.

Alderfer, C. P., & Smith, K. K. (1982). Studying intergroup relations embedded in organizations. *Administrative Science Quarterly, 27,* 35-65.

Baumeister, R. F. (1986). *Identity: Cultural change and the struggle for self.* New York: Oxford University Press.

Beale, F. M. (1970). Double jeopardy: To be black and female. *New Generations, 5*(28), 40-42.

Bell, E. L. (1986). *The power within: Bicultural life structures and stress among black women.* Unpublished doctoral dissertation, Case Western Reserve University.

Bell, E. L. (1990). The bicultural life experience of career-oriented black women. *Journal of Organizational Behavior 11,* 459-477.

Benjamin, L. (1982). Black women achievers: An isolated elite. *Sociological Inquiry, 52,* 141-151.

Berg, D. N., & Smith, K. K. (Eds.). (1985). *Exploring clinical methods for social research.* Beverly Hills, CA: Sage.

Bock, E. E. (1971). Farmer's daughter effect: The case of the Negro female professional. In A. Theodore (Ed.), *The professional woman* (pp. 119-131). Cambridge, MA: Schenkman.

Brenner, O. C., Tomkiewicz, J., & Schein, V. E. (1989). The relationship between sex role stereotypes and requisite management characteristics revised. *Academy of Management Journal, 32,* 662-669.

Bronfenbrenner, N. (1979). *The ecology of human development.* Cambridge, MA: Harvard University Press.

Cabezas, A., Tam, T. M., Lowe, B. M., Wong, A., & Turner, K. (1989). Empirical studies of barriers to upward mobility of Asian Americans in the San Francisco Bay area. In G. Nomura, R. Endo, R. Leong, & S. Sumida (Eds.), *Frontiers of Asian-American studies.* Pullman: Washington State University Press.

Calás, M. B., & Smircich, L. (1989). Using the "F" word: Feminist theories and the social consequences of organizational research. *Academy of Management Best Paper Proceedings,* pp. 355-359.

Cannon, L. W., Higginbotham, E., & Leung, M. (1988). *Race and class bias in research on women: A methodological note* (Research paper). Memphis, TN: Memphis State University, Center for Research on Women.

Cole, J. B. (Ed.). (1986). *All American women: Lines that divide, ties that bind.* New York: Free Press.

Cox, T., Jr. (1990). Problems with organizational research on race and ethnicity issues. *Journal of Applied Behavioral Science, 26,* 5-23.

Cox, T., Jr., & Nkomo, S. M. (1990). Invisible men and women: An overview of research on minorities in organizations. *Journal of Organizational Behavior 11,* 419-431.

Davis, A. R. (1990). Power players: Ten Afro-American women in the corporate world. *Essence Magazine, 11,* 71-75.

Dipboye, R. L. (1987). Problems and progress of women in management. In K. S. Koziara, M. H. Moskow, & L. D. Tanner (Eds.), *Working women: Past, present, future* (pp. 118-153). Washington, DC: Bureau of National Affairs.

Editorial Committee, Center for American Studies. (1986). *Chicana voices: Intersections of class, race and gender.* Austin: University of Texas.

Ehrlich, E. (1989, March 20). The mommy track. *Business Week,* pp. 126-131.

Epstein, C. F. (1973). Positive effects of the multiple negative: Explaining the success of black professional women. *American Journal of Sociology, 5,* 913-935.

Equal Employment Opportunity Commission (EEOC). (1989). *Job patterns for minorities and women in private industry* (EEO-1 report). Washington, DC: Government Printing Office.

Equal Employment Opportunity Commission (EEOC, March). (1990). *Employment analysis report program.* Washington, DC: Author.

Equal Employment Opportunity Commission (EEOC). (1991). *Job patterns for minorities and women in private industry* (EEO-1 report). Washington, DC: Government Printing Office.

Fagenson, E. (1990). At the heart of women in management research: Theoretical and methodological approaches and their biases. *Journal of Business Ethics, 9,* 267-274.

Fernandez, J. (1981). *Racism and sexism in corporate life.* Lexington, MA: D. C. Heath.

Fierman, J. (1990, July 30). Why women still don't hit the top. *Fortune,* pp. 40-62.

Fox, M., & Hesse-Biber, S. (1984). *Women at work.* Palo Alto, CA: Mayfield.

Freedman, S. M., & Philips, J. S. (1988). The changing nature of research on women at work. *Journal of Management, 14,* 231-251.

Freedman, D., Thornton, A., Cambrun, D., Alwin, D., & Young-DeMaco, A. (1988). The life history calendar: A technique for collecting retrospective data. In C. C. Clogg (Ed.), *Sociological inquiry.* Washington, DC: American Sociological Society.

Freeman, S. J. (1990). *Managing lives: Corporate women and social change.* Amherst: University of Massachusetts Press.

Frost, D. D. (1987). *A special place for white women only.* Unpublished manuscript.

Fulbright, K. (1985). The myth of the double-advantage: Black female managers. *The Review of Black Political Economy, 14,* 33-45.

Gilkes, C. T. (1982). Successful rebellious professionals: The black woman's professional identity and community commitment. *Psychology of Women Quarterly, 6,* 289-311.

Gilligan, C. (1982). *In a different voice: Psychological theory and women's development.* Cambridge, MA: Harvard University Press.

Glenn, E. (1985). Racial ethnic women's labor: The intersection of race, gender and class oppression. *Review of Radical Political Economics, 17*(3), 86-108.

Gordus, J. P., & Oshiro, M. M. (1986). Ethnic-minority women in private corporations: The case of officials and managers. In W. A. Van Horne & T. V. Tonnesen (Eds.), *Ethnicity and women* (pp. 157-182). Madison: University of Wisconsin.

Greenhaus, J. H., Parasuraman, S., & Wormley, W. M. (1988, August 6-7). *Work experiences and career success of black and white managers.* Paper presented at the Careers Division preconference workshop: Cultural Diversity and Career Development: Individual, Organizational and Research Perspectives, Anaheim, CA.

Harding, S. (1986). *The science question in feminism.* Ithaca, NY: Cornell University Press.

Harrison, S., King, S., & Gregg, E. (1988). Special report: Black women in corporate America. *Black Enterprise, 9,* 45-49.

Hennig, M., & Jardim, A. (1977). *The managerial woman.* New York: Anchor/Doubleday.

Hicks, E. (1981). Cultural Marxism: Non-synchrony and feminist practice. In L. Sargeant (Ed.), *Women and revolution* (pp. 219-238). Boston: South End.

Hill-Collins, P. (1989). The social construction of black feminist thought. *Signs, 14*(4), 745-773.

Hitt, M. A., Zikmund, W., & Pickens, B. A. (1982). Discrimination in industrial employment: An investigation of race and sex bias among professionals. *Work and Occupations, 9,* 217-231.

Hooks, B. (1984). *Feminist theory: From margin to center.* Boston: South End.

Horowitz, R. (1983). *Honor and the American dream.* New Brunswick, NJ: Rutgers University Press.

Hull, G. T., Scott, P. B., & Smith, B. (Eds.). (1982). *But some of us are brave: Black women's studies.* Old Westbury, NY: Feminist Press.

Hurtado, A. (1989). Relating to privilege: Seduction and rejection in the subordination of white women and women of color. *Signs, 14,* 833-855.

Ilgen, D. R., & Youtz, M. A. (1986). Factors affecting the evaluation and development of minorities in organizations. In K. Rowland & G. Ferris (Eds.), *Research in personnel and human resource management: A research annual* (pp. 307-337). Greenwich, CT: JAI.

Irons, E. D., & Moore, G. W. (1985). *Black managers: The case of the banking industry.* New York: Praeger.

Jick, T. (1984). Mixing qualitative and quantitative methods: Triangulation in action. In J. Van Maanen (Ed.), *Qualitative methodology* (pp. 135-148). Beverly Hills, CA: Sage.

Johnston, W., & Packer, A. (1988). *Workforce 2000: Work and workers for the 21st century.* Indianapolis, IN: Hudson Institute.

Jones, E. W., Jr. (1986). Black managers: The dream deferred. *Harvard Business Review, 64,* pp. 84-93.

King, D. K. (1988). Multiple jeopardy, multiple consciousness: The context of a black feminist ideology. *Signs, 14*(1), 42-72.

King, M. C. (1975). Oppression and power: The unique status of the black woman in the American political system. *Social Science Quarterly, 56,* 121-128.

Kram, K. E. (1985). On the researcher's group memberships. In D. Berg & K. Smith (Eds.), *Exploring clinical methods for social research* (pp. 247-265). Beverly Hills, CA: Sage.

Larwood, L., Szwajkowski, E., & Rose, S. (1988). Sex and race discrimination resulting from manager-client relationships: Applying the rational bias theory of managerial discrimination. *Sex Roles, 18*(1/2), 9-27.

Larwood, L., & Wood, M. (1977). *Women in management.* Lexington, MA: D. C. Heath.

Lugones, M. C., & Spelman, E. V. (1983). Have we got a theory for you! Feminist theory, cultural imperialism and the demand for the woman's voice. *Women's Studies International Forum, 6*(6), 573-581.

Lykes, M. B. (1983). Discrimination and coping in the lives of black women: Analyses of oral history data. *Journal of Social Issues, 39,* 79-100.

Malveaux, J. (1985). The economic interests of black and white women: Are they similar? *The Review of Black Political Economy, 14,* 5-27.

McIntosh, P. (1988). *White privilege and male privilege: A personal account of coming to see correspondences through work in women's studies* (Working Paper No. 189). Wellesley, MA: Wellesley College Center for Research on Women.

Minnich, E. K. (1990). *Transforming knowledge.* Philadelphia: Temple University Press.

Morgan, G. (Ed.). (1983). *Beyond method: Strategies for social research.* Beverly Hills, CA: Sage.

Morrison, A., & Von Glinow, M. (1990). Women and minorities in management. *American Psychologist, 45,* 200-208.

Morrison, A. M., White, R. P., Van Velsor, E., & the Center for Creative Leadership. (1987). *Breaking the glass ceiling: Can women reach the top of America's largest corporations?* Reading, MA: Addison-Wesley.

Nieva, V., & Gutek, B. (1981). *Women and work: A psychological perspective.* New York: Praeger.

Nkomo, S. M. (1988). Race and sex: The forgotten case of the black female manager. In S. Rose & L. Larwood (Eds.), *Women's careers: Pathways and pitfalls.* New York: Praeger.

Nkomo, S. M. (1992). The emperor has no clothes: Revisiting "race in organizations." *Academy of Management Review, 17,* 487-513.

Nkomo, S. M., & Cox, T., Jr. (1989). Gender differences in the factors affecting the upward mobility of black managers. *Sex Roles, 21,* 825-835.

100 of the best and brightest black women in corporate America. (1990, January). *Ebony,* pp. 30-50.

Osajima, K. (1988). Asian Americans as the model minority: An analysis of the popular press image in the 1960s and 1980s. In G. Y. Okihiro, S. Hune, A. Hansen, & J. Liu (Eds.), *Reflections on shattered windows: Promises and prospects for Asian American studies.* Pullman: Washington State University Press.

Palmer, P. M. (1983). White women/black women: The dualism of female identity and experience in the United States. *Feminist Studies, 9*(1), 151-170.

Pettigrew, T., & Martin, J. (1987). Shaping the organizational context for black American inclusion. *Journal of Social Issues, 43*(1), 41-78.

Powell, G. N. (1988). *Women and men in management.* Newbury Park, CA: Sage.

Ray, E., & Davis, A. (1988). Black female executives speak out on: The concrete ceiling. *Executive Female, 6,* 34-38.

Rich, A. (1979). Disloyal to civilization: Feminism, racism, gynephobia. In *Lies, secrets, and silence.* New York: Norton.

Romero, M. (1986). Twice protected? Assessing the impact of affirmative action on Mexican-American women. In W. A. Van Horne & T. V. Tonnesen (Eds.), *Ethnicity and women* (pp. 135-156). Madison, WI: Board of Regents, University of Wisconsin System.

Rothenberg, P. S. (Ed.). (1988). *Racism and sexism.* New York: St. Martin's.

Schneer, J. A., & Reitman, F. (1990). Effects of employment gaps on the careers of MBAs. *Academy of Management Journal, 33,* 391-406.

Schwartz, F. (1989). Management women and the new facts of life. *Harvard Business Review, 67,* 65-76.

Smircich, L. (1985). *Toward a women centered organization theory.* Paper presented at the Academy of Management Meetings, San Diego, CA.

Spelman, E. V. (1988). *Inessential woman: Problems of exclusion in feminist thought.* Boston: Beacon.

Terpstra, D. E., & Baker, D. D. (1988). Outcomes of sexual harassment charges. *Academy of Management Journal, 31,* 185-194.

Thomas, D. A. (1989). Mentoring and irrationality: The role of racial taboos. *Human Resource Management, 28*(2), 279-290.

U.S. Department of Labor. (1993, January). *Employment and earnings.* Washington, DC: Government Printing Office.

Valentine, C. (1971). Deficit, difference and bicultural models of Afro-American behavior. *Harvard Educational Review, 41*(2), 173-157.

Van Maanen, J. (Ed.). (1984). *Qualitative methodology.* Beverly Hills, CA: Sage.

Weathers, D. (1981). Black executives: Winning under the double whammy. *Savvy, 2,* 34-40.

Williams, N. (1988). Role making among married Mexican American women: Issues of class and ethnicity. *Journal of Applied Behavioral Science, 24*(2), 203-217.

Woo, D. (1985). The socioeconomic status of Asian American women in the labor force: An alternative view. *Sociological Perspectives, 28*(3), 307-338.

Yung, J. (1986). *Chinese women of America: A pictorial history.* Seattle: University of Washington Press.

5

Stress and the Woman Manager: Sources, Health Outcomes, and Interventions

LYNN R. OFFERMANN
MICHELE A. ARMITAGE

With large numbers of U.S. workers reporting stress at work, and filing stress-related compensation requests in record numbers, occupational health and well-being is a topic of increasing concern to both men and women. As indicated by the second volume in the **Women and Work** series, this is also an area that has been slow to incorporate research on the specific hazards that the workplace may pose to women. In their introduction to that volume, Stromberg, Larwood, and Gutek (1987) indicate that most research on the health of women workers has focused on reproductive health and fetal safety and suggest that this important, but limited, focus may reflect a view of women that is ambivalent in terms of the appropriateness of their employment outside the home.

As more women enter careers in management, one area within the occupational health arena that merits far greater attention is stress and its resulting health outcomes in women managers. While there is no

AUTHORS' NOTE: We would like to thank Robert D. Caplan, Ellen A. Fagenson, George W. Rebok, and the chapter reviewers for their helpful comments on earlier drafts of this manuscript.

generally accepted definition of the term *stress,* we will use the term to mean "a combination of one or more of the following: an environmental stimulus . . . , an individual psychological or physical response, or the interaction between these two" (Ivancevich, Matteson, Freedman, & Phillips, 1990, p. 252).

Management is a challenging occupation for anyone, male or female, with many demands and stresses (Powell, 1988). For both men and women, job stress is considered both an independent risk factor in the development and fatality rate of coronary heart disease (CHD) and an indirect factor that may relate to CHD through increasing blood pressure, cholesterol, and smoking (LaCroix & Haynes, 1987).[1] Common stressors shared by women and men managers alike include role demands (conflict, ambiguity, and overload), work overload, interpersonal relations on the job, and extraorganizational conflicts (Nelson & Quick, 1985; Powell, 1988). For example, both women and men managers report equally high levels of work overload (Davidson & Cooper, 1986), a stressor to which managers are particularly vulnerable (Nelson & Quick, 1985).

Yet, women may experience additional on-the-job stresses unique to them and, likewise, possess different ways of interpreting and coping with both uniquely female and male-shared stresses. In this chapter, we examine the available literature in terms of three major sources of stress for women managers—from society at large, from their organizations, and from the women themselves. Our model of the impact of these domains on the stress and health of women managers as well as the specific factors within each domain that we will be considering appear in Figure 5.1. As shown in Figure 5.1, stress emanates from a combination of the three domains, with health outcomes affected by stress. We review work in each of the three domains separately, cognizant of the reciprocal influence of the three as shown by the two-way arrows. For example, while individuals and organizations mirror the social system of which they are a part, as people and organizations change, underlying societal assumptions and values may change as well (albeit slowly). Likewise, the behavior of individual women managers may change organizational assumptions and behavior toward women, just as organizational policies and practices may affect the behavioral reactions of women managers. Any complete understanding of the effects of stress on women managers needs to examine stressors from each of these domains as well as consider their combined potential. Furthermore, individual differences may also moderate the amount of stress experienced from these combined sources through individual appraisal of events and coping mechanisms as well as by directly moderating the health outcomes experienced under stress.

Within each domain, we highlight a number of critical stressors for women managers. These particular stressors should not be taken as an exhaustive listing; they do, however, reflect those treated at least to some degree in the research literature and about which conclusions can be drawn. Unfortunately, the literature on the effects of stress on the health of women managers is not yet well developed, with much speculation and little conclusion. We present what is known to date as well as areas in need of greater attention. Although we have labeled some of the specific stressors "shared" to indicate that they are relevant to the stress responses and outcomes of both men and women, all shared stressors discussed here may operate differently for men and women. For example, while balancing career and family demands can be a source of stress for both women and men managers (hence "shared"), we will present data indicating that women are differentially affected.

Stressors faced equally by all managers or all workers are not presented here. Our goal is to examine factors involved in stress production and health outcomes that are either unique to women managers or that appear to express themselves differently for women and men managers. The effects of some of these factors may also differ by a manager's race. Our focus is on factors relevant to women managers of all races; specific racial issues are dealt with in greater detail in Bell, Denton, and Nkomo's chapter in this book. Following a consideration of stress factors, we present intervention options designed to reduce stress where possible and alleviate the negative health impacts of those that remain. We conclude by raising important issues for future research and application.

SOURCES AND OUTCOMES OF STRESS

Social Systemic Sources

Both persons and employing organizations exist within a larger sociocultural system of values, practices, expectations, and stereotypes defining appropriate roles for men and women. This system of extraorganizational processes influences intraorganizational structures as well as individual behavior in organizations. These forces, which are firmly grounded and highly resistant to change, include the career-family interface, off-the-job support, and attitudes toward women in management that engender discrimination.

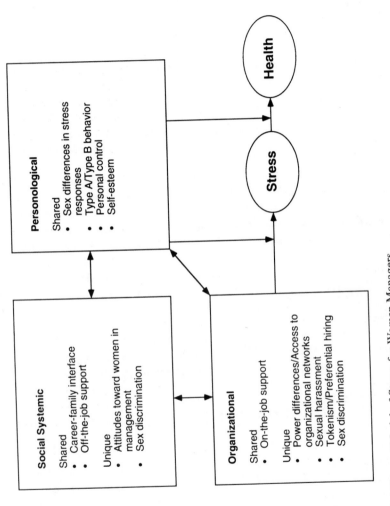

Figure 5.1. A Multifaceted Model of Stress for Women Managers

Personological

Shared
- Sex differences in stress responses
- Type A/Type B behavior
- Personal control
- Self-esteem

Social Systemic

Shared
- Career-family interface
- Off-the-job support

Unique
- Attitudes toward women in management
- Sex discrimination

Organizational

Shared
- On-the-job support

Unique
- Power differences/Access to organizational networks
- Sexual harassment
- Tokenism/Preferential hiring
- Sex discrimination

Health

Stress

134

Career-family interface. Although a potential source of stress for both women and men managers, conflict between career and family roles can be particularly high for women managers. Summarizing five studies comparing women and men holding MBA degrees, Olson and Frieze (1987) showed that, although women MBAs were less likely than men to be married and have children, 56% to 65% of the women were married and 35% to 78% had children. Thus most of these women faced both job and family responsibilities. Women managers consistently report significantly higher job/family role strain accompanied by higher mental and physiological outcomes than men managers. The more job-family conflicts women managers report, the greater their irritation, anxiety, and depression (Greenglass, 1987). Findings that women managers report greater stress than men managers due to conflicts with their partners, childbearing, and other home conflicts suggest that, although career demands may be equal for both partners, married women managers still do not receive the support they need (Davidson & Cooper, 1986).

Data show that women professionals still assume primary responsibility for home and child-care activities (Googins & Burden, 1987; Jick & Mitz, 1985; Zappert & Weinstein, 1985). Among married couples, fathers reported spending 10-15 hours less each week on home and child-care tasks than full-time employed mothers, giving fathers a combined weekly job-home load of 68.92 hours while mothers reported 83.91 hours (Googins & Burden, 1987). For single parents, most of whom are women, the burden is likely to be far greater as they struggle to cover all functions themselves without a partner to free them for required business travel, conventions, or other after-hours professional obligations.

The extra burdens of managing career and family that women face may result in negative mental and physiological health outcomes. Employed women (white-collar professionals, clerical, and blue collar) with three or more children are at higher risk for developing coronary heart disease (CHD) than those without children and housewives with three or more children (Haynes & Feinleib, 1980). These effects were most pronounced among clerical workers, however. Findings from a study of Swedish managers and clerical workers showed that physiological indicators of stress including heart rate and excretions of the stress hormone epinephrine were high on the job for both men and women managers at levels above their clerical counterparts. However, while physiological reactions of men managers suggested a rapid unwinding after work (at home), women managers' blood pressure remained high and their levels of the stress hormone norepinephrine actually increased (Frankenhaeuser et al., 1989). These findings are consistent with reports from women managers that they are unable to relax due to their chronically heavy work load both on and off their jobs (Davidson & Cooper, 1986). Thus the balance of paid work and family is more likely to generate negative outcomes for women managers than men (see Parasuraman & Greenhaus, this volume, and Lewis and Cooper, 1988, for a more in-depth examination of job-family issues).

Off-the-job support. The support off the job may be provided by family, friends, neighbors, and community. Support from family and friends has been positively associated with psychological well-being and negatively associated with stress for women workers (Pugliesi, 1988). A great deal of research documents that those with social support show better psychological adjustment to stressful events, have reduced risks of mortality from certain diseases, and show faster recovery from diagnosed illnesses (House, Landis, & Umberson, 1988). In fact, women from a mixed-occupational sample reported that off-the-job support was the most effective moderator of life and job stress (Etzion, 1984).

Studies of sex differences in the total amount of off-the-job support received have produced inconsistent results, with one study of managers showing women reporting lower levels than their male counterparts (Davidson & Cooper, 1986), while other studies with mixed-occupational samples have found women reporting either no differences (Fusilier, Ganster, & Mayes, 1986) or more off-the-job support than men (Etzion, 1984). Differences such as these are not surprising given a literature that uses myriad (often unique) measures of support and that often fails to consider the diversity encompassed by a term like social support. Not only can support come from different sources (such as friends or family) but supportive behaviors may include providing emotional support, such as sympathy or advice, and/or direct assistance such as financial aid and help with chores and child care. A more differentiated view of social support is now emerging, with the realization that there are different kinds of social support, that some people may make better use of the supportive resources available to them, and that some efforts by well-meaning others to be supportive may actually aggravate existing stress (Taylor, 1990). These differentiations are critical to understanding the impact of support on health for both women and men.

Attitudes toward women in management and sex discrimination. Sex typing of social roles and the resulting normative expectations appear to have great influence on women's advancement in male-dominated professions (Nelson & Quick, 1985). Gender stereotypes have typically defined the characteristics associated with "successful managers," with women normally perceived as not fitting these criteria. Results from Schein's well-known 1973 and 1975 studies showed that male and female managers rated successful managers as similar to men in general but not women in general and that women were not believed to possess the essential attributes (e.g., leadership, self-confidence, objectivity, forceful-ness, ambition) to be successful managers. Recent findings indicate that, although women managers no longer show this differential rating pattern (Brenner, Tomkiewicz, & Schein, 1989), men managers today are still far less likely to associate characteristics of successful managers with charac-teristics of women in general than they are with men in general (Brenner et al., 1989; Heilman, Block, Martell, & Simon, 1989). Furthermore, Heilman et al. (1989) found that characteristics that distinguished women from men and successful managers were negative in connotation, such as bitter, selfish, quarrelsome, and power hungry.

Such evidence that men managers still define the "successful man-ager" by stereotypical masculine characteristics suggests that women managers who do not exhibit these masculine attributes may experience stress-inducing roadblocks along their career paths. Women who pos-sess other, more feminine, attributes that make them good managers may be excluded from the opportunities granted to men. This may harm the organization as well as the individual, in that it has been suggested that women may possess some unique characteristics that are leadership assets (Lipman-Blumen, 1988). Organizations need to focus more on the outcomes of behavior, that is, effective task performance, rather than the stylistic means of accomplishment to achieve both the success-ful integration of women managers and successful organizational per-formance (Thomas, 1989).

The belief that women are less suited for management than men engenders discrimination, which is a great barrier to women's mobility and a significant source of stress for them (Nelson & Quick, 1985). Although legislation has reduced the degree of overt discrimination, a subtle yet debilitating form still exists informally in many organizations as organizations struggle to mesh law with traditional attitudes. Northcraft and Gutek, as well as Lee, discuss this issue in greater detail later in this book.

Organizational Sources

By its very nature, management is a diverse occupation. Two managers with the same title in the same organization may do very different work under very different circumstances. Stress in women managers may well relate not only to societal pressures and personal characteristics brought by the manager to the job but also to the nature of the tasks involved and the circumstances under which these tasks are performed. These organizational variables include formal and informal policies and practices as well as the amount of support and resources provided by the organization. Organizational factors particularly implicated in stress responses for women managers include on-the-job support, sex differences in access to power and opportunity networks, sexual harassment, tokenism and preferential hiring, and sex discrimination. Although our focus is on the concerns of women managers, it should be noted that some of these factors may also be experienced by minority men managers.

On-the-job support. Support may be provided within an organization by supervisors or coworkers as well as externally from family and friends. Davidson and Cooper (1986) found that women managers reported less on-the-job support than men managers. More than half of these women occupied lower management positions, compared with less to 27% of the men. Another study using an equal-proportioned sample where 50% of both men and women occupied middle management positions similarly reported significantly less supervisor support among women managers than men (Greenglass, 1988). Ohlott, Ruderman, and McCauley (1990) similarly found women managers reporting both less supervisor support and a lack of support from top management.

On-the-job support has been negatively associated with psychological, physiological, and behavioral problems. Women managers with low perceived supervisor support have reported high job anxiety, depression, psychosomatic symptoms, irritation, anger, drug use, and intent to turnover (Greenglass, 1985, 1987). Women first-line supervisors also reported high job anxiety as well as low job satisfaction when they perceived low supervisor and coworker support (Greenglass, 1988). High coworker support significantly predicted low job stress and low psychological distress for a sample of Hispanic managerial and professional women (Amaro, Russo, & Johnson, 1987). Although long-term associations with physical disease for women managers are unknown, a study with clerical workers found that those who developed CHD were more likely to report nonsupport from their supervisors than those who did not develop CHD (Haynes & Feinleib, 1980). These results are consistent with the common conclusion in the social support literature that social support is associated with better health (e.g., Cohen & Wills, 1985).

Power differences/access to organizational networks. Increases in the number of women in management do not necessarily mean equal jobs at equal pay. Most of today's managerial women are in lower-level positions with less authority and less pay (Morrison & Von Glinow, 1990). In keeping with traditional stereotypes of women as supportive, many women managers have been relegated primarily to staff roles in organizations, away from the high visibility line roles with direct responsibility for profit and loss. Some have termed the segregation of women into staff positions as the creation of a "velvet ghetto," a comfortable place with few opportunities for escape to higher organizational levels with greater power (e.g., Morrison et al., 1987). These limitations may have implications for stress production. Women managers who perceive that their skills are underused are more likely to report anxiety, depression, and psychosomatic symptoms (Greenglass, 1985).

Women often occupy less central positions in organizational networks, giving them less access to the main power holders in the organization (Brass, 1985). As a result, they typically have been shown to have less upward influence than men (Brass, 1985; Trempe, Rigny, & Haccoun, 1985). For women managers, this can be a double negative, because less upward influence often reflects itself in less downward influence as well. Managers who have better relationships with their immediate superior tend to have greater access to resources and support from above through upward influence. These same managers then have resources to give to subordinates in the form of rewards, information, or privileges, which earns them status with their own subordinates (Graen, Cashman, Ginsburgh, & Schiemann, 1977). Having responsibilities without the power or resources to adequately perform them has been suggested to be a risk factor in the development of psychological strain and disease (e.g., Karasek, 1979).

Sexual harassment. One by-product of unequal power between women and men is sexual harassment, which both expresses male power and keeps women in subordinate positions (Hemming, 1985). Tangri, Burt, and Johnson (1982) found that 42% of women and 15% of men reported being sexually harassed at work during the prior two years. Other surveys have produced prevalence rates for women of more than 90% (Faley, 1982). Further, the number of sexual harassment complaints rose from 4,272 in 1981 to 7,273 in 1985 (Terpstra & Baker, 1988). Sexual harassment is not limited to women in low-level positions. A study by Terpstra and Baker (1988) of charges filed in Illinois showed that 11% of complaints were from administrative and managerial personnel. Other studies have shown that women in male-dominated occupations are more likely to suffer harassment than women in mixed or traditionally female jobs (Gutek & Morasch, 1982; Lafontaine & Tredeau, 1986) and are more likely to report negative outcomes resulting from harassment such as quitting or being fired (Gutek & Morasch, 1982).

Sexual harassment has been clearly linked to reported stress. Crull and Cohen (1984) found that 99.5% of women harassed by a superior and 88.2% of women harassed by a nonsuperior experienced symptoms of psychological stress such as nervousness or depression. About a third of these harassed women experienced physical stress symptoms such as headaches, stomachaches, or changes in weight or blood pressure. Problems were severe enough for about a third of women harassed by superiors and about a fifth of women harassed by nonsuperiors to have sought some form of help (medical, psychological, worker compensation) in relieving stress.

On the positive side, organizations rated by women as pursuing equal employment opportunities have been shown to have significantly fewer reports of harassment than low opportunity companies (Lafontaine & Tredeau, 1986). This is a clear indication that organizations can have an impact on the likelihood of stress being experienced by women managers from harassment as well as limit their own corporate liability. Given that men tend to label fewer behaviors as sexual harassment than women (Konrad & Gutek, 1986), interventions may begin by simply developing an awareness of how particular behaviors are perceived by others as well as by emphasizing the organization's commitment to a harassment-free workplace.

Tokenism/preferential hiring. Although legislation has forced organizations to more actively recruit and promote women into management positions, benefits to women may be mixed unless care is taken in implementation. Women managers may be cast in the position of *tokens* individuals who numerically compose less than 15% of the entire group, who are often hired as a result of external pressure, and who are less than fully accepted by their peers (Kanter, 1977). Their small numbers make them more visible by contrast and often cast upon them extra burdens such as representing their category (women) as well as themselves, not making the dominant members (men) look bad or engendering their resentment, being socially isolated and kept outside the informal network of the organization, and being cast in stereotypical roles (Kanter, 1990). These extra performance pressures no doubt engender additional stress for women managers above and beyond traditional managerial demands. Although women in the field of management are beyond numerical tokenism, now constituting more than a third of all managers (Powell, 1993), women are still scarce in some firms and at top corporate levels throughout the country and therefore are likely to suffer from these additional pressures.

Women who perceive that their selection reflects the organization's need for a woman in the position rather than their own competence and fit for the job have been shown to have lower satisfaction with work, supervision, and coworkers, lower organizational commitment, and more stress in the form of role conflict and ambiguity than women who do not see sex as relevant to their selection (Chacko, 1982). Women perceiving sex-based preferential selection have been shown to take less credit for successful outcomes, to devalue their leadership performance and skills, and to view themselves as more deficient compared with those in a system of merit-based selection (Heilman, Simon, & Repper, 1987). Men receiving such sex-based preferential selection show no such self-devaluation. Both men and women, however, have reported greater stress under preferential selection compared with merit-based selection (Heilman, Lucas, & Kaplow, 1990). These data highlight the importance of ensuring that affirmative action policies are not free of merit criteria and that the importance of merit and prior task competence in selection are emphasized both to those chosen and to others already in the organization.

Sex discrimination. Once hired, women managers are more likely to experience sex discrimination and pay inequity than men managers (Greenglass, 1987). Such women are more likely to report greater mental and physical stress as a consequence (Davidson & Cooper, 1986; Nelson & Quick, 1985). Women middle and senior managers with high perceived sex discrimination have reported high anxiety, depression, intent to turnover, and low job satisfaction (Greenglass, 1987).

Discrimination may cause women to perceive that stress is beyond a woman manager's control. Davidson and Cooper (1986) found that women managers associated their stress with external discrimination-based pressures such as prejudice, sex discrimination, and being a minority in a male-dominated profession. Men managers, on the other hand, attributed pressure to intrinsic job factors such as leadership aspects and pay rate. As a result of discrimination, women's access to informal organizational networks that provide direction and support to men managers may be obstructed (Nelson & Quick, 1985). Some women managers may respond by lowering their expectations of career success in their organizations to reduce the difference between their aspirations and perceived opportunity. Others remain in junior and middle management positions, experiencing frustration from a "glass ceiling"—an impenetrable boundary where they can see, but not reach, the top of the corporation (Morrison et al., 1987).

Personological Sources

The literature examining sex-linked individual difference variables in stress and stress responses is large and conflicting. Researchers disagree as to whether employed women experience greater stress than employed men or nonemployed women (Nelson & Quick, 1985) or whether there are no sex differences in degree of job stress (Martocchio & O'Leary, 1989). Others believe that employed women, particularly women in high status occupations, enjoy mental and physical health advantages over nonemployed women (Baruch, Beiner, & Barnett, 1987).

The explanation for these disparate views may lie in the different methodologies and samples used by each study. Unfortunately, most studies of women and job stress fail or are unable to differentiate key potential moderators from the social systemic and organizational domains such as the nature of the job, occupational status or level, additional family responsibilities, levels of organizational and personal support, and equal employment opportunity practices. The largest number of studies compare employed and nonemployed women; others combine managers with other professionals and compare them with clerical staff or nonemployed women. We will discuss commonly found sex differences in stress with a focus on the much smaller number of studies using samples of women managers. These sex differences include physiological and psychological responses to stress, Type A behavior patterns, personal control, and self-esteem.

Sex differences in stress responses. Men often have been found to show greater physiological reactions to stress on some measures, with consistent evidence that male excretions of the stress hormone epinephrine rise more during exposure to achievement tasks or stressors than do female excretions (Polefrone & Manuck, 1987). There is also evidence, however, that undergraduate women aspiring to traditionally masculine fields more closely resembled men in the degree of epinephrine excretion in an achievement-oriented task (Collins & Frankenhaeuser, 1978). Managerial women have also been found to have serum cholesterol levels equal to the high level exhibited by men and higher than that of women in the general population (Frankenhaeuser et al., 1989).

A major issue that needs to be addressed is whether such physiological similarity in responses between men and those women seeking traditionally male careers portends an equal gender similarity in mortality rates from stress-related diseases. In comparison with other groups of women, a study of female mortality in Wisconsin found that, while death rates of employed women as a group were typically lower than the rates for housewives, for the 60- to 64-year-old group, white-collar workers experienced significantly higher death rates than housewives, with saleswomen, professional women, and women managers showing the highest death rates (Passanante & Nathanson, 1985). Other research with women and men managers and graduate students found that the link between stress and illness was stronger for women than for men (Matheny & Cupp, 1983). Will women pursuing traditionally male occupations such as management lose their traditional mortality advantage relative to men? Although mortality rates continue to improve for both men and women, sex differences in mortality rates have been narrowing in recent years. Increasing work force participation by women has been cited as one possible explanation (Rodin & Ickovics, 1990). A study by Detre, Feinleib, Matthews, and Kerr (1987) of senior-level government employees, however, suggests that the traditional mortality advantage of women appears reduced in these demanding jobs (most of which included supervisory functions). Currently, however, there are insufficient data to draw conclusions on this important question.

One of the most commonly found sex differences related to stress and health has been that women report higher levels of psychological distress while men are more prone to physical illness (see Jick & Mitz's,

1985, review). This finding seems to generalize across job type and country, with similar conclusions reported from studies with managers and MBA students in the United States (Matheny & Cupp, 1983; Zappert & Weinstein, 1985) and Great Britain (Cooper & Davidson, 1982) as well as other employed adults in the United States and abroad. Reasons suggested for these differences range from genetics to differences in work situations (even among individuals occupying jobs with similar titles/responsibilities) to social psychological explanations based on differential appraisals of situations and their meaning. Although there is evidence that women business school graduates were four times more likely to report seeing a mental health professional in the last three years than their male classmates (Zappert & Weinstein, 1985), other work shows that men are less likely to associate a low sense of well-being and depressive symptoms as signs of emotional problems (Kessler, Brown, & Broman, 1981). Men may therefore be less likely to report psychological distress and to seek treatment for emotional problems than women despite identical symptoms. In this respect, traditional sex-role stereotypes may make it easier for women to acknowledge problems and get assistance, deterring later problems. Men managers have been shown to be more likely than women to turn to alcohol for relief (e.g., Davidson & Cooper, 1986), a "solution" that may bring on its own long-term physical problems. Another possibility is that women are more vulnerable to poor mental health due to their typically greater involvement in providing support for others (Belle, 1982) and their greater exposure to negative events in their social networks that affect them emotionally and that may elicit requests from others for support (Kessler, 1985). In any case, separating actual symptoms (physical or psychological) from reported ones is a challenge researchers must face squarely before sex differences in stress responses will be fully understood.

Type A behavior. Extensive work has been done characterizing people with the Type A behavior pattern as prone to stress and likely to suffer physical health consequences such as an increased risk of CHD (e.g., Booth-Hewley & Friedman, 1987). Type A behavior is typified by chronic feelings of time pressure or urgency, a competitive achievement orientation, and increased hostility and aggression (Glass, 1977). In contrast, Type B behaviors are less harried and angry. Women managers and professionals have been found to score high on Type A behaviors, with 90% scoring at or above the 65th percentile (Lawler, Rixse, & Allen, 1983). A recent study with both male and female first-line supervisors found that female Type A scores were significantly higher than male scores (60th percentile versus 50th percentile; Greenglass, 1988). These findings are disturbing given data from the well-known Framingham study showing that employed women who score high on tests for Type A behavior are twice as likely to develop CHD as their male Type A counterparts (Davidson & Cooper, 1986). Moreover, Type A women have been found to occupy higher occupational levels, have more demanding jobs, report more stress in their jobs, and, for those also married, report poorer physical health than Type B women (Kelly & Houston, 1985). Although Type A behavior has been associated with stress and poor health for both women and men executives, it has been shown to be even more predictive for women executives (Cooper & Melhuish, 1984).

Attention needs to be given to women managers as well as men in attempts to modify Type A behaviors on the job, particularly focusing on the hostility component that many researchers now view as most predictive of CHD (Taylor, 1990). Traditional assumptions about women as being more immune to CHD problems than men could have life-threatening implications, particularly for Type A women managers, if equal need for treatment modifying coronary-prone behaviors is not recognized. Fortunately, research suggests that Type A behavior can be successfully reduced through behavior counseling, thereby lowering rates of subsequent cardiac morbidity and mortality (Friedman et al., 1986).

Although the link between Type A behaviors and CHD has been among the most widely studied associations between personality and disease, the utility of the Type A concept has been questioned. New reports that higher levels of anxiety, depression, and extraversion show similar associations with higher disease risk (particularly CHD) as the Type A characteristics of anger, hostility, and aggression have led some to call for the broader study of a "disease-prone personality" (Friedman & Booth-Hewley, 1987). As yet, however, such study has not advanced enough to consider sex differences in susceptibility among managers.

Personal control. Of all the factors considered in relation to stress responses, perceived control over one's environment has been suggested to be particularly important (Taylor, 1990). Differences in coping strategies employed by men and women, and among women in general, may lead to different interpretations of stress and its consequences (e.g., Matheny & Cupp, 1983). The ability to deal with stress effectively depends upon one's perceptions of personal control and individual resources, which in turn are affected by individual self-efficacy, hardiness, locus of control, and self-confidence (Kobasa, 1987; Matheny & Cupp, 1983; Nelson & Quick, 1985). Frankenhaeuser (1977) argued that increased personal control may reduce physiological stress reactions. When life events are perceived to be beyond one's control, the relationship between stress and illness is significantly stronger than when they are perceived to be within one's control. This finding has been shown to be stronger for a mixed sample of women managers and graduate students than for their male counterparts (Matheny & Cupp, 1983).

Women managers who possess a high internal locus of control believe that they control their own outcomes and may create beneficial consequences from stress. A high internal locus of control permits managers to act upon stressful situations to achieve better outcomes whereas managers with an external locus of control may more readily resign themselves to negative outcomes (Nelson & Quick, 1985). Work by Robinson and Skarie (1986) indicates that women professionals with a high internal locus of control report lower sex-role traditionality, less fear of success, and less job role stress (i.e., role overload and ambiguity, nonparticipation) than those with low internal control. The authors suggest that interventions designed to increase perceptions of control may help women managers reduce job stress.

Personal control also figures in Kobasa's (1979) concept of individual "hardiness," defined as a personality variable reflecting a deep commitment and involvement in one's activities, perceived control over one's life, and acceptance of changes as challenges. She found that executives (primarily male) who reported high stress and low illness scored higher on hardiness than those who reported high stress and high illness. She suggests that using internal resources to adopt more active coping styles may reduce dysfunctional outcomes under chronic stress, at least for individuals like executives whose jobs allow for commitment, control, and challenge. A more recent view suggests that hardiness may be an effective coping skill that can be developed through intervention programs (Ivancevich et al., 1990).

Self-esteem. Men and women who are high in self-esteem and low in self-denigration are less likely to show negative effects under stress than those low in self-esteem and high in self-denigration, and women as a group score lower on self-esteem and higher on self-denigration than men (Kobasa, 1987). Women with these characteristics may therefore have an increased vulnerability to stress. Employed women, however, have reported higher self-satisfaction than those not employed (Meddin, 1986), and self-esteem has been positively associated with psychological well-being for employed women (Pugliesi, 1988). In addition, one study has shown that women employed in professional positions were similar to men professionals in their self-esteem (Sekaran, 1986).

Women managers who have high self-esteem and self-confidence, particularly those with a high internal locus of control, perceive themselves as capable of making their own opportunities and dealing with challenges as well as with the stresses that both may cause (Nelson & Quick, 1985). Women managers' ability to perform well may also be affected by self-esteem. For example, Davidson and Cooper (1986) found that women managers who lacked assertiveness and confidence scored poorly on work performance factors and high on occupational stress. Therefore, while women managers may or may not show lower self-esteem than their male counterparts, due to its potential stress-related effects, self-esteem should be considered in examining their individual responses to stress.

Summary

We have shown that each of these three domains—social systemic, organizational, and personological—can create undesirable levels of stress for women managers. Together, they interact in complex ways that may affect the nature and level of the stress produced. For example, it has been shown that availability of and responses to supervisor support (an organizational variable) may differ for Type A or Type B women (a person variable), with Type A women supervisors reporting significantly less support from their supervisors than Type Bs (Greenglass, 1988). Type B women reported that supervisor support was more important than support from coworkers, family, and friends for ameliorating job stress. Type A women were more likely to refuse support, like their Type A men counterparts. Previous work by the same researcher (Greenglass, 1987), however, indicated that, although there was a positive relationship between on-the-job anger and sex discrimination for Type A managerial women but not Type B women, this anger was reduced as supervisor support increased. This suggests that having a supportive supervisor may moderate angry responses to sex discrimination in Type A women managers. Given the relationship between anger in Type As and CHD, such moderation may be associated with better health, particularly if anger is replaced by problem-focused approaches for reducing discrimination. Thus responses to work support appear to reflect an interaction between person and organization-level variables.

Responses to sex-based preferential selection similarly appear to reflect a person-organization interaction, with recent work indicating that initial self-confidence in leadership affects responses. Persons initially confident of their task-relevant abilities on a leadership task (men as well as the women who received pretask positive feedback) did not show negative effects of preferential selection; those initially less self-confident women (without positive or with negative pretask feedback) and men (with negative pretask feedback) suffered greater self-devaluation (Heilman et al., 1990). While not all women are less confident of their leadership abilities than men, the societal expectations presented earlier make sex differences in leadership self-confidence more likely. Other interactions may involve person and systemic variables such as individual differences in sensitivity to sex-stereotypic expectations (perhaps through self-esteem or locus of control) or systemic-organizational interactions involving the effects of legal requirements on organizational practices or policies.

It is clear that women managers are exposed to numerous stressors, singly and in combination, and that their health may be jeopardized as a result. Actions taken by organizations now to prevent and control stress responses in women managers may reduce the loss of valuable management talent. While stress management programs need to deal with all the stressors shared by women and men managers, the unique stressors faced by women and their different responses to shared ones merit separate consideration.

INTERVENTION OPTIONS

Stress costs U.S. businesses an estimated $75-$150 billion a year (Fielding, 1986), a figure predicted to grow as health costs and employment increase. As a result, organizations have taken a serious interest in stress management interventions (SMIs) both to reduce costs and as an investment in valued human resources. Programs can focus on reducing existing stress and/or on choosing healthier long-term behaviors, such as smoking cessation, exercising, and eating properly. The majority of SMIs reported in the literature are designed for both women and men employees (Ivancevich et al., 1990), and rigorous evaluations of program effectiveness are lacking, with only 21% of SMIs formally evaluated (Fielding, 1986). A thorough review of SMIs and their effectiveness is beyond the scope of this chapter (see Ivancevich et al., 1990). Rather, we highlight intervention issues and options that have been suggested, and, more rarely, put in place, that deal with stress for women managers. These options can be considered to be systemic-, organization-, or person-oriented, depending on the primary change target of the intervention (see Figure 5.2).

Systemically-Oriented Interventions

The pervasive social forces discussed earlier can have potent health effects that are too immediate and significant to wait for long-term sociocultural change. Interventions designed to mitigate the effects of known systemic forces can be implemented now along with others focusing on the individual and organization. Legislative changes mandating minimum amounts of leave time for family reasons will clearly help alleviate stress. Until recently, the United States lagged behind most industrialized nations in failing to provide any form of guaranteed parental leave to employees. Today, while paid leave is offered by more than 100 countries, the United States is not among this group (see the chapter by Antal & Izraeli in this volume; Offermann & Gowing, 1990). Clear national commitment to equal employment opportunity would likewise relieve stress. Increased national awareness of women and health issues is critical, and additional government funding of research on occupational health for women is needed.

In addition to national governmental intervention, local communities could be more involved in providing support for employed parents in the form of supporting day-care facilities and providing information clearinghouses on available resources, extended school day options, and job sharing banks. In many communities, women themselves have spearheaded efforts to demand these supports. For women managers, professional associations should also provide avenues for lobbying for changes aimed at making women's needs salient. Efforts on the wider systemic front will assure women that their needs are valid and important and that women are entitled to action.

Organization-Oriented Interventions

Organization-oriented SMIs employ environmental strategies to increase employee control and support and decrease conflicts and demands.

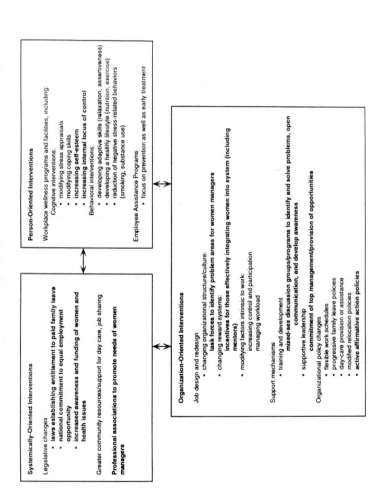

Figure 5.2. Intervention Options for Stress Management in Women Managers

NOTE: Boldface indicates options likely to hold particular relevance for women.

They fall into three categories: job design and redesign, support mechanisms, and organizational policy changes. Job design and redesign techniques may involve changing organizational structure and culture, reward systems, training and development opportunities, and leadership relationships as well as intrinsic job factors such as control and work load (Ivancevich & Matteson, 1986). Task forces have also been established to identify issues particularly likely to affect women, such as harassment and job-family conflicts, and to act as change agents (Morrison & Von Glinow, 1990). Reward systems can incorporate incentives that award bonuses to managers who become mentors or effectively integrate women managers into the system (Morrison & Von Glinow, 1990; Nelson & Quick, 1985). There is evidence that improving job design by increasing control and support and decreasing demands can improve psychological and physiological health and be cost effective (House & Cottington, 1986; Ilgen, 1990).

Support mechanisms may include mixed-sex coalitions to reduce power imbalances among managers by empowering the weaker and enhancing their perceptions of control (Ruben, 1986). In most cases, this will mean the empowerment of women managers. Workplace social support networks can also be established for men and women managers, which include single-sex and mixed-sex discussion groups (Naffziger, 1986). Senior managers can also show support by exhibiting commitment and providing opportunities for women managers (Morrison & Von Glinow, 1990).

As the number of employees with both career and home responsibilities increases, so does the recognition that organizational assistance is necessary to facilitate employee health and maintain organizational attractiveness (Googins & Burden, 1987). The feminization of the managerial profession is pressing organizations to develop corporate policies that minimize stressors. Support benefit packages can be developed from any combination of the following policies: (a) flexible work schedules (e.g., flextime, part time, job sharing, 4/40 workweek, work at home); (b) family (maternity/paternity) leave; (c) adequate day care; (d) modified relocation policies; and (e) vigorous affirmative action policies (e.g., career management, organizational support; Davidson & Cooper, 1986; Freedman & Phillips, 1988; Googins & Burden, 1987).

Person-Oriented Interventions

Theoretically, stress management interventions should be developed to prevent or reduce the effects of stress by attempting to change individual factors, organizational factors, their interaction, or interactions with broader systemic factors. In practice, however, organizations overwhelmingly prefer to consider stress an individual problem and therefore support person-oriented interventions that focus on individual behaviors, appraisals, and coping skills (House & Cottington, 1986; Ivancevich et al., 1990; Singer, Neale, Schwartz, & Schwartz, 1986). Cognitive interventions help managers modify stress appraisals, self-perceptions, and coping skills. They include encouraging participants to think differently (i.e., cognitive restructuring) through the use of rational emotive therapy techniques and positive self-talk. Behavioral interventions are designed to help the individual gain physiological and mental control over stress responses as well as to change maladaptive behaviors. They include biofeedback, relaxation training, developing new adaptive skills such as in assertiveness and time management, and life-style change programs emphasizing exercise, diet, and smoking cessation. Job training, education, and retraining programs, as well as expanded employee assistance programs that incorporate prevention and treatment, may also provide help to the individual.

Person-oriented interventions attempt to create a person-environment fit by altering the person rather than the environment. By focusing entirely on the individual, however, organizational and systemic influences that interact with individual factors are excluded, and only symptoms are treated. Failing to change environmental causes perpetuates resulting stress responses and prevents their dissolution. Both researchers and labor unions have argued that person-oriented interventions "inoculate" employees but do not remove objective stressors from the organizational environment, which requires changes in organizational policies and practices (Ganster, Mayes, Sime, & Tharp, 1982; House & Cottington, 1986). Therefore the organizational sources of stress for women managers discussed earlier may not be addressed. Organization-level interventions are needed to assess the manner in which both the organizational and the extraorganizational systems affect harassment, tokenism, discrimination, power and opportunity imbalances, and job-family conflicts that clearly can cause stress for women managers. Likewise, systemic factors implicated in stress for women managers also are largely ignored. For example, person-based interventions may be perceived as placing responsibility for stress on the individual (male or female). Thus, if women are stereotypically perceived as having specific traits and behaviors that make them deficient as managers (Heilman et al., 1989; Schein, 1973), a strict personological perspective on stress may have even greater impact on them, signaling that they in particular are inadequate. This in turn can create a vicious cycle by undermining self-confidence and increasing stress.

SMI Development

Consistent with our model, researchers have argued for a multidimensional approach to SMI development that incorporates biological, psychological, and environmental perspectives (Singer et al., 1986). Evidence that personality traits and job characteristics jointly affect employed women's job stress supports the need for a combination of person-oriented and organization-oriented interventions (Abush & Burkhead, 1984). Systemically-oriented programs would provide additional assistance. Therefore adopting comprehensive SMIs is suggested to be most effective in managing stress for all paid workers (Singer et al., 1986) and may be particularly suited to addressing the unique combination of stressors typical of women managers.

Organizations should begin SMI development by identifying stressors through a comprehensive needs analysis assessing individual and organizational needs, levels of control, support, and conflict, extraorganizational demands, cultural and sex-role orientations, and individual differences (Ilgen, 1990; Ivancevich & Matteson, 1986). A needs analysis can suggest appropriate formats for training, participation, duration, costs, and evaluation (Naffziger, 1986). Information can be collected from both men and women by using interviews, questionnaires, objective ratings, informal discussions, and focus groups. Conducting both single-sex and mixed-sex discussion groups will provide an understanding of both gender perspectives. It is also important to examine current organizational practices, such as selection, placement, and performance appraisal systems, and to determine their consequences for women managers to end sex-typed biases (Freedman & Phillips, 1988; Morrison & Von Glinow, 1990).

Decisions must be made regarding whether participation will be voluntary and will include both sexes. Researchers recommend that both sexes participate to avoid singling women out and to provide an opportunity for men and women to collaboratively change maladaptive interactions, facilitate communication, and ameliorate conflict through enhanced awareness and mutual problem solving (Naffziger, 1986). Single-sex programs may have the unintended effect of conveying expectations of sex-linked deficiency that undermine the confidence of women managers and reinforce traditional sex-typed attitudes about them both to others and to themselves. The belief in the value of full, mixed-sex participation is reflected in a current trend toward developing SMIs that help managers work together to manage diversity and reduce discrimination by flexible use of single- and mixed-sex discussion groups (Morrison & Von Glinow, 1990). Despite these trends and recommendations, however, "women-only" programs are still widely implemented (Morrison & Von Glinow, 1990).

Transferring information learned in training back to the job environment is essential to preventing a relapse into old behaviors and attitudes. SMIs rarely incorporate relapse prevention, however (Ivancevich et al., 1990). Using adult learning theory principles and encouraging both men and women to participate in the program design and reinforcement process will facilitate transfer as well as provide supports and checks on the job (Naffziger, 1986). Measurements collected at pretraining and posttraining intervals for both women and men can assess the degree of change and determine intervention effectiveness (Ivancevich & Matteson, 1986; Naffziger, 1986).

ISSUES FOR RESEARCH AND APPLICATION

The study of stress and health in women managers is just beginning. While the most critical need is for future research to break down research findings by both sex and occupation, additional concerns are discussed below.

Methodological Issues

The quality of the data being generated in the literature varies widely. It is important for future research to be conducted in a manner that allows building a cumulative knowledge base for comparisons and analyses. The recent meta-analysis conducted by Martocchio and O'Leary (1989) was only able to use 15 of 65 identified stress studies in the literature due to lack of quantitative information, inadequate information on effect size, exclusion of either men or women from the sample, or failure to compare male and female stress levels. Of the 15 used, 5 failed to report occupational group, again limiting comparisons and conclusions about to what group(s) a particular set of findings might be relevant. Pertinent information on potential moderators such as sex, race, occupation, and marital and family status must be routinely collected and reported.

The measures used present additional concerns. Most psychological measures of stress are based on self-reports, the accuracy of which may be questioned. The ability to separate physical symptoms from reported feelings is a key to understanding sex differences in mental health. Physiological measures of stress should not be unequivocally accepted as valid either, because such reactions may be influenced by many factors other than stress or be produced by stressors outside of the job environment. One suggestion for improvement is the use of multiple measures (Martocchio & O'Leary, 1989), which may include combinations of both self-report and physiological assessments. Whatever measures are used, evidence of reliability and validity should be presented—a basic tenet of good research that is widely violated in this area.

Conceptual Issues

In addition to moving away from solely self-report data, it is important to embark on longer-term studies of occupational stress (Haw, 1982). Organizations are not static entities, and the working environment for many women managers has, is, and will continue to change. As societal changes force organizational changes, and more women enter into and progress in management positions, their reactions and responses may be altered along with their environment. Longitudinal research is critically important in examining effects of both age cohort and time on stress responses. Such longer-term research may also help disentangle the interactive effects of the three domains outlined here as relevant to the stress and health of women managers.

More research is needed on the antecedents of success for women managers as well as on the behaviors of women who become successful (Freedman & Phillips, 1988). Often, there is the implication that women should be more like men to succeed. This implication can produce stress for the women involved, and acting on it may prove unsuccessful as well. For example, work with women executives by Morrison et al. (1987) suggests that trying to be "one of the boys," adopting male behaviors wholesale, are characteristics of women managers who failed to reach the level of success expected of them.

The model presented in this chapter can help guide future research by providing a coherent theoretical framework. Organizational factors that activate or deactivate systemically derived stereotypical information processing need to be examined (Freedman & Phillips, 1988). The impact of affirmative action policies and other organizational practices on the stress levels of women managers also warrants further exploration. To date, a limited range of person variables have been studied. Other personal factors that may help ameliorate stress effects include self-efficacy (Bandura, 1986), self-awareness, and private self-consciousness (Nelson & Quick, 1985). Possibilities for interactions between domains call for a close examination of these components as a totality, for that is the way they will be experienced by the women exposed to them.

Application Issues

Although research on SMIs has improved significantly in the last decade, many limitations still exist. Sex differences in the impact of interventions need to be explored, and the specific needs of women managers need to be addressed. The ability to effectively evaluate programs has been limited by inexplicit program goals, lack of objective measures of stress, exclusion of important interacting organizational and situational factors, and inadequate methodologies and designs characterized by nonrepresentative samples and a lack of matched control subjects (Fielding, 1986; Ivancevich et al., 1990). Ongoing baseline and follow-up measures of a broad range of criteria would provide much needed information to program developers (House & Cottington, 1986). In addition, cooperative research across organizations would provide a larger pool of data from which organizations could select those interventions most likely to be effective for their particular needs (Morrison & Von Glinow, 1990). Alternative techniques need to be compared (Ivancevich & Matteson, 1986), and factors predicting and increasing participation in stress programs need to be examined (Ilgen, 1990).

In addition, work on the methodological and conceptual issues described above would inevitably help application. Full understanding of the stressor-stress-outcome *process* is critical in scientifically driving the design and implementation of intervention programs (Nelson & Quick, 1985). The link between specific strategies and theoretical constructs is poorly understood and sorely needs elaboration (Morrison & Von Glinow, 1990).

CONCLUSION

The number of women in management is growing steadily. White males no longer constitute the majority of the work force (Johnston &

Packer, 1987), and future productivity may well depend on an organization's ability to integrate women and minorities into the mainstream of organizational life (Offermann & Gowing, 1990). Opening the doors of management to women will not be enough to enhance organizational effectiveness; the companies that succeed will be those that find ways to allow the women selected to thrive and prosper as well as their male counterparts.

Today's managerial women are the vanguard of a far larger group of future women managers, and as such we do not yet know enough about the long-term health effects that they will face as they age. Although we can assess current stress levels, the health outcomes, particularly in terms of diseases such as CHD, do not follow immediately on current stress and await much later evaluation. Yet the study of today's managerial women can tell much about the possible health outcomes of the women who follow them as well as how those outcomes can be improved. Getting women into positions of management to the detriment of their health would be a Pyrrhic victory; yet, using health concerns as a camouflage for societal ambivalence about women in managerial positions is equally damning. Organizations *can* be more responsive to the needs of women managers for true equal opportunity in an equal environment, including a concern about their health and well-being as well as that of their male peers. Demographic patterns and the demands of the managerial work force suggest that such responsiveness may be the most productive, as well as the most humane, solution.

NOTE

1. Note that, while stress has been implicated in the development or exacerbation of many physical ailments and diseases, CHD is by far the most widely studied.

REFERENCES

Abush, R., & Burkhead, E. J. (1984). Job stress in midlife working women: Relationships among personality type, job characteristics, and job tension. *Journal of Counseling Psychology, 31,* 34-44.

Amaro, H., Russo, N. F., & Johnson, J. (1987). Family and work predictors of psychological well-being among Hispanic women professionals. *Psychology of Women Quarterly, 11,* 505-521.

Bandura, A. (1986). *Social foundations of thought and action.* Englewood Cliffs, NJ: Prentice-Hall.

Baruch, G. K., Beiner, L., & Barnett, R. C. (1987). Women and gender in research on work and family stress. *American Psychologist, 42,* 130-136.

Belle, D. (1982). The stress of caring: Women as providers of social support. In L. Goldberger & S. Breznitz (Eds.), *Handbook of stress* (pp. 496-505). New York: Free Press.

Booth-Hewley, S., & Friedman, H. S. (1987). Psychological predictors of heart disease: A quantitative review. *Psychological Bulletin, 101,* 343-362.

Brass, D. J. (1985). Men's and women's networks: A study of interaction patterns and influence in an organization. *Academy of Management Journal, 28,* 327-343.

Brenner, O. C., Tomkiewicz, J., & Schein, V. E. (1989). The relationship between sex role stereotypes and requisite management characteristics revisited. *Academy of Management Journal, 32,* 662-669.

Chacko, T. I. (1982). Women and equal opportunity: Some unintended effects. *Journal of Applied Psychology, 67,* 119-123.

Cohen, S., & Wills, T. A. (1985). Stress, social support, and the buffering hypothesis. *Psychological Bulletin, 98,* 310-357.

Collins, A., & Frankenhaeuser, M. (1978). Stress responses in male and female engineering students. *Journal of Human Stress, 4,* 43-48.

Cooper, C. L., & Davidson, M. J. (1982). The high cost of stress on women managers. *Organizational Dynamics, 10,* 44-53.

Cooper, C. L., & Melhuish, A. (1984). Executive stress and health: Differences between men and women. *Journal of Occupational Medicine, 26,* 99-104.

Crull, P., & Cohen, M. (1984, March). Expanding the definition of sexual harassment. *Occupational Health Nursing,* pp. 141-145.

Davidson, M. J., & Cooper, C. L. (1986). Executive women under pressure. *International Review of Applied Psychology, 35,* 301-326.

Detre, K. M., Feinleib, M., Matthews, K. A., & Kerr, B. W. (1987). The federal women's study. In E. Eaker, B. Packard, N. Wenger et al. (Eds.), *Coronary heart disease in women* (pp. 78-82). New York: Haymarket Doyma.

Etzion, D. (1984). Moderating effect of social support on the stress-burnout relationship. *Journal of Applied Psychology, 69,* 615-622.

Faley, R. H. (1982). Sexual harassment: Critical review of legal cases with general principles and preventive measures. *Personnel Psychology, 35,* 583-600.

Fielding, J. E. (1986). Worksite health promotion and stress management. *Advances, 6,* 36-40.

Frankenhaeuser, M. (1977). Job demands, health, and well-being. *Journal of Psychosomatic Research, 21,* 313-321.

Frankenhaeuser, M., Lundberg, U., Fredrikson, M., Melin, B., Tuomisto, M., & Myrsten, A. (1989). Stress on and off the job related to sex and occupational status in white-collar workers. *Journal of Organizational Behavior, 10,* 321-346.

Freedman, S. M., & Phillips, J. S. (1988). The changing nature of research on women at work. *Journal of Management, 14,* 231-251.

Friedman, H. S., & Booth-Hewley, S. (1987). The "disease-prone" personality: A meta-analytic view of the construct. *American Psychologist, 42,* 539-555.

Friedman, M., Thoresen, C. E., Gill, J. J., Ulmer, D., Powell, L. H., Price, V. A., Brown, B., Thompson, L., Rabin, D. D., Breall, W. S., Bourg, E., Levy, R., & Dixon, T. (1986). Alteration of Type A behavior and its effects on cardiac occurrences in post myocardial infarction patients: Summary results of the recurrent coronary prevention project. *American Heart Journal, 112,* 653-665.

Fusilier, M. R., Ganster, D. C., & Mayes, B. (1986). The social support and health relationship: Is there a gender difference? *Journal of Occupational Psychology, 59,* 145-153.

Ganster, D. C., Mayes, B. T., Sime, W. E., & Tharp, G. D. (1982). Managing organizational stress: A field experiment. *Journal of Applied Psychology, 67,* 533-542.

Glass, D. C. (1977). *Behavior patterns, stress, and coronary disease.* Hillsdale, NJ: Lawrence Erlbaum.

Googins, B., & Burden, D. (1987). Vulnerability of working parents: Balancing work and home roles. *Social Work, 32,* 295-300.

Graen, G., Cashman, J., Ginsburgh, S., & Schiemann, W. (1977). Effects of linking pin quality on the quality of working life of lower participants. *Administrative Science Quarterly, 22,* 491-504.

Greenglass, E. R. (1985). Psychological implications of sex bias in the workplace. *Academic Psychology Bulletin, 7,* 227-240.

Greenglass, E. R. (1987). Anger in Type A women: Implications for coronary heart disease. *Personality Individual Differences, 8,* 639-650.

Greenglass, E. R. (1988). Type A behavior and coping strategies in female and male supervisors. *Applied Psychology: An International Review, 37,* 271-288.

Gutek, B. A., & Morasch, B. (1982). Sex-ratios, sex-role spillover, and sexual harassment of women at work. *Journal of Social Issues, 38,* 55-74.

Haw, M. A. (1982). Women, work, and stress: A review and agenda for the future. *Journal of Health and Social Behavior, 23,* 132-144.

Haynes, S. G., & Feinleib, M. (1980). Women, work, and coronary heart disease: Prospective findings from the Framingham Heart Study. *American Journal of Public Health, 70, 133-141.*

Heilman, M. E., Block, C. J., Martell, R. F., & Simon, M. C. (1989). Has anything changed? Current characterizations of men, women, and managers. *Journal of Applied Psychology, 74,* 935-942.

Heilman, M. E., Lucas, J. A., & Kaplow, S. R. (1990). Self-derogating consequences of sex-based preferential selection: The moderating role of initial self-confidence. *Organizational Behavior and Human Decision Processes, 46,* 202-216.

Heilman, M. E., Simon, M. C., & Repper, D. P. (1987). Intentionally favored, unintentionally harmed? Impact of sex-based preferential selection on self-perceptions and self-evaluations. *Journal of Applied Psychology, 72,* 62-68.

Hemming, H. (1985). Women in a man's world: Sexual harassment. *Human Relations, 38,* 67-79.

House, J. S., & Cottington, E. M. (1986). Health and the workplace. In L. H. Aiken & D. Mechanic (Eds.), *Applications of social science to clinical medicine and health policy* (pp. 392-416). New Brunswick, NJ: Rutgers University Press.

House, J. S., Landis, K. R., & Umberson, D. (1988). Social relationships and health. *Science, 241,* 540-545.

Ilgen, D. (1990). Health issues at work: Industrial-organizational psychology opportunities. *American Psychologist, 45,* 273-283.

Ivancevich, J. M., & Matteson, M. T. (1986). Organizational level stress management interventions: A review and recommendations. *Journal of Organizational Behavior Management, 8,* 229-248.

Ivancevich, J. M., Matteson, M. T., Freedman, S. M., & Phillips, J. S. (1990). Worksite stress management interventions. *American Psychologist, 45,* 252-261.

Jick, T. D., & Mitz, L. F. (1985). Sex differences in work stress. *Academy of Management Review, 10,* 408-420.

Johnston, W. B., & Packer, A. H. (1987). *Workforce 2000: Work and workers for the twenty-first century.* Indianapolis, IN: Hudson Institute.

Kanter, R. M. (1977). *Men and women of the corporation.* New York: Basic Books.

Kanter, R. M. (1990). Token women in the corporation. In J. Heeren & M. Mason (Eds.), *Sociology: Windows on society.* Los Angeles: Roxbury.

Karasek, R. A. (1979). Job demands, job decision latitude, and mental strain: Implications for job redesign. *Administrative Science Quarterly, 24,* 285-308.

Kelly, K. E., & Houston, B. K. (1985). Type A behavior in employed women: Relation to work, marital, and leisure variables, social support, stress, tension, and health. *Journal of Personality and Social Psychology, 48,* 1067-1079.

Kessler, R. C. (1985). Sex differences in vulnerability to undesirable life events. *American Sociological Review, 79,* 620-631.

Kessler, R. C., Brown, R. L., & Broman, C. L. (1981). Sex differences in psychiatric help-seeking: Evidence from four large-scale surveys. *Journal of Health and Social Behavior, 22,* 49-64.

Kobasa, S. C. (1979). Stressful life events, personality, and health: An inquiry into hardiness. *Journal of Personality and Social Psychology, 37,* 1-11.

Kobasa, S. C. (1987). Stress responses and personality. In R. C. Barnett, L. Beiner, & G. Baruch (Eds.), *Gender and stress* (pp. 308-329). New York: Free Press.

Konrad, A. M., & Gutek, B. A. (1986). Impact of work experiences on attitudes toward sexual harassment. *Administrative Science Quarterly, 31,* 422-438.

LaCroix, A. Z., & Haynes, S. G. (1987). Gender differences in the health effects of workplace roles. In R. C. Barnett, L. Beiner, & G. K. Baruch (Eds.), *Gender and stress* (pp. 96-121). New York: Free Press.

Lafontaine, E., & Tredeau, L. (1986). The frequencies, sources, and correlates of sexual harassment among women in traditional male occupations. *Sex Roles, 15,* 433-442.

Lawler, K. A., Rixse, A., & Allen, M. T. (1983). Type A behavior and psychophysiological responses in adult women. *Psychophysiology, 20,* 343-350.

Lewis, S. N. C., & Cooper, C. L. (1988). Stress and dual-earner families. In B. A. Gutek, A. H. Stromberg, & L. Larwood (Eds.), *Women and work* (Vol. 3, pp. 139-168). Newbury Park, CA: Sage.

Lipman-Blumen, J. (1988, August). *Connective leadership: A female perspective for an interdependent world.* Invited address, American Psychological Association, Atlanta.

Martocchio, J. J., & O'Leary, A. M. (1989). Sex differences in occupational stress: A meta-analytic review. *Journal of Applied Psychology, 74,* 495-501.

Matheny, K. B., & Cupp, P. (1983). Control, desirability, and anticipation as moderating variables between life change and illness. *Journal of Human Stress, 9,* 14-23.

Meddin, J. R. (1986). Sex differences in depression and satisfaction with self: Findings from a United States national survey. *Social Science Medicine, 22,* 807-812.

Morrison, A. M., & Von Glinow, M. A. (1990). Women and minorities in management. *American Psychologist, 45,* 200-208.

Morrison, A. M., White, R. P., Van Velsor, E., & the Center for Creative Leadership. (1987). *Breaking the glass ceiling: Can women reach the top of America's largest corporations?* Reading, MA: Addison-Wesley.

Naffziger, D. W. (1986). The smooth transition. *Training and Development Journal, 40*(4), 63-65.

Nelson, D. L., & Quick, J. C. (1985). Professional women: Are distress and disease inevitable? *Academy of Management Review, 10,* 206-218.

Offermann, L. R., & Gowing, M. (1990). Organizations of the future: Changes and challenges. *American Psychologist, 45,* 95-108.

Ohlott, P. J., Ruderman, M. N., & McCauley, C. D. (1990, August). *Women and men: Equal Opportunity for development?* Paper presented at the meeting of the Academy of Management, San Francisco.

Olson, J. E., & Frieze, I. H. (1987). Income determinants for women in business. In A. H. Stromberg, L. Larwood, & B. A. Gutek (Eds.), *Women and work* (Vol. 2, pp. 173-206). Newbury Park, CA: Sage.

Passanante, M. R., & Nathanson, C. A. (1985). Female labor force participation and female mortality in Wisconsin 1974-1978. *Social Science Medicine, 21,* 655-665.

Polefrone, J. M., & Manuck, S. B. (1987). Gender differences in cardiovascular and neuroendocrine response to stressors. In R. C., Barnett, L. Beiner, & G. K. Baruch (Eds.), *Gender and stress* (pp. 13-38). New York: Free Press.

Powell, G. N. (1993). *Women and men in management.* (2nd ed.). Newbury Park, CA: Sage.

Pugliesi, K. (1988). Employment characteristics, social support, and the well-being of women. *Women and Health, 14,* 35-58.

Robinson, S. E., & Skarie, E. K. (1986). Professional women: Job role stresses and psychosocial variables. *American Mental Health Counselors Association Journal, 8,* 157-165.

Rodin, J., & Ickovics, J. (1990). Women's health: Review and research agenda as we approach the 21st century. *American Psychologist, 45,* 1018-1034.

Ruben, D. H. (1986). The management of role ambiguity in organizations. *Journal of Employment Counseling, 23,* 120-130.

Schein, V. E. (1973). The relationship between sex-role stereotypes and requisite management characteristics. *Journal of Applied Psychology, 57,* 95-100.

Schein, V. E. (1975). Relationships between sex role stereotypes and requisite management characteristics among female managers. *Journal of Applied Psychology, 60,* 340-344.

Sekaran, U. (1986). Significant differences in quality-of-life factors and their correlates: A function of differences in career orientations or gender? *Sex Roles, 14,* 261-279.

Singer, J. A., Neale, M. S., Schwartz, G. E., & Schwartz, J. (1986). Conflicting perspectives on stress reduction in occupational settings: A systems approach to their resolution. In M. F. Cataldo & P. J. Coates (Eds.), *Health and industry: A behavioral medicine perspective* (pp. 162-192). New York: John Wiley.

Stromberg, A. H., Larwood, L., & Gutek, B. A. (1987). Series editors' introduction. In A. H. Stromberg, L. Larwood, & B. A. Gutek (Eds.), *Women and work* (Vol. 2, pp. 9-19). Newbury Park, CA: Sage.

Tangri, S. S., Burt, M. R., & Johnson, L. B. (1982). Sexual harassment at work: Three explanatory models. *Journal of Social Issues, 38,* 33-54.

Taylor, S. E. (1990). Health psychology: The science and the field. *American Psychologist, 45,* 40-50.

Terpstra, D. E., & Baker, D. D. (1988). Outcomes of sexual harassment charges. *Academy of Management Journal, 31,* 185-194.

Thomas, R., Jr. (1989, August). [Invited presentation]. C. Dexter (Chair), Managing Diversity in the Workplace symposium conducted at the meeting of the Academy of Management, Washington, DC.

Trempe J., Rigny, A., & Haccoun, R. (1985). Subordinate satisfaction with male and female managers: Role of perceived supervisory influence. *Journal of Applied Psychology, 70,* 44-47.

Zappert, L. T., & Weinstein, H. M. (1985). Sex differences in the impact of work on physical and psychological health. *American Journal of Psychiatry, 142,* 1174-1178.

6

Dangerous Liaisons? A Review of Current Issues Concerning Male and Female Romantic Relationships in the Workplace

LISA A. MAINIERO

More so than ever before, women and men are meeting, dating, and marrying spouses whom they met in their workplaces. Current incidence rates for office romances at work are reported to be surprisingly high. In a 1988 *Newsweek* poll, 78% of respondents reported they knew or worked with employees who were involved in an intimate relationship with another coworker in their firm ("Love in the Office," 1988). Of the 175 respondents surveyed by Anderson and Hunsaker (1985), 85% reported that they were aware of one or more office romances in their firm.

But *should* women and men engage in romantic involvements at work? Do women enhance or harm their professional credibility as a result of such "dangerous liaisons"? Or have workplace norms about gender and sexuality changed to the point where women can participate in such relationships without fear of career reprisals?

AUTHOR'S NOTE: The author wishes to thank the anonymous reviewers who contributed helpful suggestions and comments for this chapter and, especially, editor Ellen Fagenson for her support and comments.

These are the questions that concern corporate women who are considering a romantic relationship at work. Although there are many different types of relationships in which women and men can be involved at work—that is, friendships, competitive coworker relationships, and the like—this chapter will focus on the complexities that concern romantic relationships between male and female managers.[1]

Three areas will provide a framework for the issues detailed in this chapter. First, the literature on office romance will be reviewed to determine common issues and concerns. Second, a model of the power dynamics for couples who become involved in such relationships will be advanced. Third, the implications of these relationships for management practice, and for women, will close the chapter.

This review will cover office romances, that is, relationships that occur between single male and female employees that are (a) characterized by mutual sexual attraction and (b) made known to others through the participants' actions. It is important to underline the mutuality of involvement in this definition, as this is what distinguishes office romances from unwanted sexual advances. Sexual harassment occurs when mutuality of interest does not exist, and discussion of this topic is beyond the scope of this review (see Gutek, 1985, for an excellent treatment of this subject). Office romance, on the other hand, takes place between willing parties who consciously make the decision to act upon their attraction out of their own free choice.

Couples who make a public declaration of their romance to coworkers as well as couples who are suspected by coworkers of a romance are included in this definition. This is because suspected romances affect coworker reactions as much as do openly disclosed romantic relationships in the office. The study of office romance is unique in this respect because it is important that researchers note the effects the romance may have on observers as well as participants. In nonoffice romances, the perspective of observers is rarely considered because the focus is on participant experiences only.

The literature on office romance comprises four areas: (a) survey studies designed to present an overview of the issues concerning romantic relationships at work (e.g., Anderson & Hunsaker, 1985; Ford & McLaughlin, 1987; Mainiero, 1989; Powell, 1986; Quinn, 1977; Warfield, 1987), (b) qualitative case studies detailing the dynamics of office romances (e.g., Clawson & Kram, 1984; Collins, 1983; Crary, 1987; Mainiero, 1989), (c) position papers that outline management strategies and the concerns for women (e.g., Goodman, 1983; Mead, 1978), and

(d) popular magazine reports (e.g., "Love in the Office," 1988; "Men at Work," 1989; "Romance in the Workplace," 1984) and newspaper articles that disclose reader surveys or anecdotal case information.

The survey data that have been collected on this subject (Anderson & Hunsaker, 1985; Ford & McLaughlin, 1987; Mainiero, 1989; Powell 1986; Warfield, 1987) generally are based on convenience samples that range from 50 to more than 200 respondents. Questions are posed to respondents concerning their observations of office romances in their firms. For example, Quinn (1977) surveyed 211 participants in an airport setting to identify the factors influencing the formation, evolution, and organizational impact of romantic relationships at work Anderson and Hunsaker (1985) and Powell (1986) surveyed more than 200 part-time MBA students. Ford and McLaughlin (1987) mailed questionnaires to more than 100 personnel administrators; Mainiero (1989) surveyed 100 corporate women in wide-ranging occupations Warfield (1987) gathered data on fewer than 50 employed women. Case studies also are based on convenience samples and range from 4 couples studied (e.g., Collins, 1983) to more than 50 couples (Mainiero, 1989) Crary (1987), Jamison (1983), Spruell (1985), and Schultz (1980), however, based their case findings on limited observations and anecdotal data.

This literature is diverse, varied, and mixed. Information about the experiences of couples who participate in office romances, as well as coworker reactions to romantic involvements at work, often are combined in the same study. In this chapter, participant and observer reactions will be distinguished from one another to discuss the complexities of the personal relationship and the effect the romance has on coworkers.

PARTICIPANT DYNAMICS IN ROMANTIC RELATIONSHIPS AT WORK

Participant dynamics, defined as the factors that affect the quality of the experience of romantically involved couples, can be categorized into five major areas: (a) social and organizational trends, (b) participant motives, (c) issues of risk and disclosure, (d) role conflict, and (e) the effects on the couple's work motivation.

Social and Organizational Trends

A number of reasons have been advanced to explain the occurrence of office romances. The majority of these reasons parallel the literature in social psychology that indicates that proximity, intensity of tasks, and similarity of interests are primary factors in the development of attraction (Berscheid & Walster, 1969). According to Quinn's (1977) survey of 211 respondents, ongoing geographic proximity was a factor in 63% of the romances reported by observers. Clawson and Kram (1984) suggested that the intensity of the work relationship contributes to sexual attraction among the mentor-protégé cases they studied. In addition, many newspaper reports and magazine articles have suggested anecdotally that employees are turning to the workplace rather than social activities outside of work to socialize with workers with whom they already are well acquainted (see "Love in the Office," 1988, for a more complete description of current trends).

The sex composition of the workplace also may be a factor. In a study by Haavio-Mannila, Kauppien-Toropainen, and Kandolin (1988), in which they interviewed more than 200 men and women in Helsinki, token men and women reported more workplace romances than those in sex-segregated workplaces. The availability of women in a male workplace precipitated sexual attraction for the men; for women, it was apparently necessary to share the same task to become emotionally involved with a man at work. For both men and women, about one half of the workplace romances resulted in sexual relationships.

Participant Motives

What motivates employees to become romantically involved with one another in a work setting? Four motives were attributed by observers in the Quinn (1977) and Anderson and Hunsaker (1985) surveys: (a) love motives, applying to those involvements characterized by a strong sense of commitment that might lead to a permanent relationship; (b) ego motives, defining romances in which one participant seeks personal rewards such as excitement, adventure, and sexual experiences from the other; (c) job motives, characterizing relationships in which one party pursues job-related benefits such as job security or financial rewards through participation in the relationship; and (d) power motives, defining involvements in which one participant enters into the relationship to gain deflected or assumed power, influence, recognition, or visibility. In the Anderson and Hunsaker (1985) survey, 30% of the men and 38% of the women were thought to be in love by the participant who described such relationships; 37% of the women and 40% of the men were judged as ego motivated; and power motives were attributed to

16% of the women and 12% of the men studied. Less than 18% of the men and 9% of the women were viewed as job motivated.

A reading of some of the case and anecdotal literature suggests that misaligned motives may explain some of the reasons some office romances go sour. For example, if one participant began an office romance on the basis of love, and the other party entered into the liaison to achieve deflected power, the misaligned motives of each party eventually may lead to the relationship's dissolution (Collins, 1983; Spruell, 1985). A recent survey reported in the popular press ("Men at Work," 1989) of more than 100 men reported that 46% of respondents who had participated in an office romance indicated that the primary reason for the breakup of the romance was that they were not suited to the women whom they had been dating. Only 14% indicated that the strain of maintaining the work relationship concurrently with the personal relationship was a contributing factor. This suggests that more office romances end as a result of personal, rather than professional, reasons, as do romantic relationships in general.

Issues of Risk and Disclosure

Fears about a public breakup often cause romancers in the office to keep their involvement a secret. According to Anderson and Hunsaker (1985), approximately 70% of the cases studied reported that couples tried to keep their relationships a secret. Collins (1983), Spruell (1985), and Jamison (1983) each identified concerns about the dissolution of the relationship to be one of the reasons couples were reluctant to go public about their romances. Mainiero (1989) found that 65% of the 100 women managers surveyed believed that romantic involvements could ruin professional relationships in the office should the couple dissolve their union.

Many managers, especially women, fear potentially adverse effects on their careers that may result from an office involvement (Anderson & Hunsaker, 1985; Clawson & Kram, 1984; Collins, 1983; Quinn, 1977) and, as such, attempt to keep romantic liaisons a secret. There is good reason for such fears on the part of women. According to an American Association for Personnel Administrators' survey conducted by Ford and McLaughlin (1987), more than 42% of 245 personnel administrators agreed with the statement, "A known office romance has a strong and negative influence on the careers of those involved." A study conducted by Powell (1986) of more than 300 MBA students showed their discomfort with sexual intimacy and work: Female respondents surveyed saw less positive value in sexual intimacy in the workplace, believed that an employee's personal life is not the business of management, desired more managerial action to discourage sexual intimacy, regarded sexually oriented behavior by others as less acceptable, and were less inclined than were men respondents to engage in sexually oriented behavior themselves.

Among the 100 executive women surveyed by Mainiero (1989), 65% believed "professional relationships could be ruined" and 63% felt "careers could be threatened" as a result of a romantic office involvement. Yet, when these same participants were asked to rate the outcomes associated with actual romances they had observed in their offices, less than 40% indicated that romancers had been adversely affected. This may suggest that perceptions concerning the risks associated with office romances remain strong, but in actuality such negative outcomes may be exaggerated.

Because perceptions about adverse outcomes remain strong, many couples hope their office romance will not be discovered. This decision to retain privacy may depend largely on office norms and corporate cultures. Quinn (1977) found that work group process characteristics, such as work group rules, supervisory style, coworker group norms, and other factors, may affect the decision to take the risk of making a romance public. Mainiero (1989) reported that more than half the managers in firms described by respondents as "conservative, traditional, and reactive" felt compelled to keep their romances a secret for as long as possible. Of those surveyed from such firms, 68% believed the risks outweighed the benefits, especially for women. But only 28% of those who worked for firms they characterized as "creative, innovative, and liberal" work environments felt compelled to hide their romantic liaisons. In addition, more than 48% of respondents who indicated they worked for such firms felt the risks and the benefits applied equally to men and women managers.

Experiencing Role Conflicts

Couples who pursue romantic relationships at work successfully learn quickly that balancing personal and professional roles in the office can be quite stressful. Much of the case research and anecdotal literature describes role conflict as a potential problem for those involved in office romances (Clawson & Kram, 1984; Collins, 1983). Two types of role conflicts are cited throughout the case literature: (a) those that stem from personal role demands that interfere with the role expectations of the work situation and (b) those that are generated by work demands that encroach upon personal time. Collins's (1983) case study of four romantically involved executive couples shows vividly how conflicts between personal and professional roles complicate the lives of romantically involved couples at work. For example, in one case, the lovers attended a presentation ceremony dinner along with the company's top people. During dinner, someone at the table suggested to the male executive that it was inappropriate to bring his lover along as her corporate status was not the same as the other executive guests. In another case noted by Collins (1983), a female coworker met regularly with a group of employees to air complaints about their boss. Once it became known that this coworker was dating the boss, the informal communication among group members ended.

Crary (1987) studied the experiences of couples who become involved in intimate relationships at work. At issue for many couples was how to manage a balance between personal intimacy and professional distance. One male interviewee discussed a romantic relationship he developed with one of his female coworkers. He found it difficult to spend time with his lover in the office and, when she visited him in his department, he became "short" with her and became irritable with others with whom he worked. Coping with the stresses and strains of competing demands of intimacy and distance interfered with his work performance, so he broke off the relationship.

On the other hand, there are times when the blend of personal and professional roles benefits the couple. Mainiero (1989) identified several cases in which couples reported their personal and professional relationships were enhanced by an office romantic involvement. One couple described a situation in which a work deadline had to be made, and the couple worked together at home to meet the deadline. In another case, a couple reported that they benefited from each other's critical comments regarding management style and work behaviors.

No firm conclusions can be drawn concerning how couples should cope with role conflicts or manage the tension between personal intimacy and professional distance. In general, it appears that each member of the couple must learn to strike a balance with the other in a way that does not sacrifice the rewards of the personal relationship by single-mindedly pursuing work outcomes and vice versa.

Effects on the Couple's Work Motivation

Questions about the extent to which the romancers' work motivation may actually be affected by an office romance have not been fully answered in the literature to date; results are mixed across studies on this subject. For example, the Quinn (1977) survey found only 14% of the men and 17% of the women were observed as performing lower quality work by participants who reported on their romances. In the Anderson and Hunsaker (1985) survey, 20% of the women and 16% of the men also were observed as performing lower quality work. The results from both these reports, however, also indicated positive outcomes on work motivation as well. For example, respondents in the Anderson and Hunsaker (1985) survey observed that 29% of the women who were involved in office romances became more productive when they were involved in a relationship where the male was in a superior position; 21% of the women and 9% of the men romantically involved at work were seen by observers as more productive.

The case and anecdotal literature offers similar mixed results: Collins (1983), Spruell (1985), Jamison (1983), and Schultz (1980) offer both positive and negative examples of how couples' productivity was affected by their participation in an office romance. It is difficult, therefore, to develop any firm conclusions concerning the effects of romantic relationships on the productivity of romancers in the office. Mainiero (1989) suggested that the work motivation of couples may ebb and flow based on the stage of the personal relationship. The productivity of each couple may also vary depending on the work tasks and job demands placed on each member as much as on the needs of the personal relationship. Future research may answer these questions.

OBSERVER DYNAMICS REGARDING ROMANTIC RELATIONSHIPS AT WORK

One of the most important questions about office romance is the impact on coworkers in the work group. *Observer* dynamics, defined as how work group members react to couples involved in office romances, have been studied in two ways: (a) coworker suspicions and fears concerning the romance and (b) negative and positive coworker reactions.

Coworker Suspicions and Fears

Although many couples prefer to keep their romances a secret, maintaining the privacy of an office affair is a difficult task. Coworkers are particularly sensitive to minor changes in behavior and typically become aware of romances in their workplaces well before they are made public. Quinn (1977) identified several "behavioral tip-offs" that alerted coworkers to the possibility of a suspected office romance. For example, 78% of the couples were seen away from work together; 47% took long lunches; 42% had intense discussions behind closed doors; and 58% spent an unusual amount of time chatting.

Sometimes, however, unfair attributions are made by coworkers who assume that two employees are involved romantically when in reality this is not the case. According to Mary Cunningham in her (1984) book, *Powerplay: What Really Happened at Bendix,* such suspicions concerning her alleged romantic relationship with William Agee were unfounded yet subsequently destroyed her career at Bendix. The suspicions of coworkers can wreak untold damage, and even simple friendships in some cases may become truly "dangerous." As Clawson and Kram (1984) note, there are some workplace relationships, such as cross-gender mentoring relationships, that run the risk of arousing the suspicions of coworkers that a more intimate relationship has formed even if it has not. According to these authors, it is possible that men who fear such accusations may be reluctant to mentor women, and this may impede women's developmental progress unless concerns about distance and personal intimacy are well managed.

The gossip coworkers generate about suspected office romances in their midst also can be disruptive. Collins (1983) argues that coworkers fear "pillow talk": the sharing of private information that may disrupt informal communication channels. According to a survey by Powell (1986), coworkers also fear that romances, especially those between a superior and a subordinate, will turn into sexual harassment. Ford and McLaughlin (1987) found in their survey that personnel managers strongly believed an office romance has a negative effect on work productivity. And Quinn (1977) documented a number of fears concerning deflected power or status associated with office romances that occur between upper- and lower-level personnel.

Positive and Negative Coworker Reactions

A number of negative effects on work group members have been documented (Anderson & Hunsaker, 1985; Collins, 1983; Driscoll & Bova, 1980; Horn & Horn, 1982; Quinn, 1977). For example, respondents in the Quinn (1977) and Anderson and Hunsaker (1985) studies reported a number of negative behavior changes, such as increased hostility in the work group, distorted communications, lowered output and productivity, slower decision making, threatened image or reputation of the unit, redistributed work, lowered morale, gossip, and acts of sabotage directed at couples who acted in an unprofessional manner. In one case reported in Quinn and Lees (1984), the president of a large corporation delegated an increasing number of tasks to his secretary with whom he was having an affair. Over time, coworkers became upset about the president's lack of availability. Messages to him became delayed, and the distorted information flow caused communication problems that led to lowered morale and productivity among those who reported to him directly.

The literature in this area is rather mixed, however, as positive effects of office romances on work group morale also have been reported. Positive effects include improved communication, morale, and productivity; improved coworker relationships; increased teamwork and cooperation between departments; and a sense of "love in the air" that energizes overall departmental productivity (Anderson & Hunsaker, 1985; Jamison, 1983; Quinn, 1977; Schultz, 1980; Spruell, 1985). In one case reported by Anderson and Hunsaker (1985), a woman manager dating another employee was able to personally coach her lover on his style as a manager in a way that improved work group morale. In another case reported by Westoff (1985), a couple dating across departments were able to resolve a work conflict that was impeding the progress of both departments on their personal time.

Ironically, most managers have concluded that the negative effects outweigh the positive benefits in most office romances (see Anderson & Hunsaker, 1985; Quinn, 1977). Yet, case analyses suggest that such strong negative responses may not be entirely justified. There may be a continuing discrepancy between global attitudes on this subject and assessments of individual cases, a discrepancy that parallels some of the literature on prejudice. Among the 100 executive women surveyed by Mainiero (1989), 53% of the women reported they "did not believe there were any benefits" to office romances. Yet, when these same women were asked to rate actual romances they had observed, more than 40% reported romancers were "easier to get along with" and cited a number of positive outcomes, such as improved productivity, morale, and teamwork as a consequence of the romance.

It is important to note, however, that observers' attributions concerning the positive and negative consequences of office romances may be suspect due to personal biases—positive and negative—of the observers themselves. Second, it is possible that romances may share both positive and negative consequences; for example, at the beginning of a romance, the relationship may improve motivation and morale but, as the relationship falls apart, negative outcomes such as conflict and emotionalism may cancel out earlier positive effects. The literature remains mixed in this area; no firm conclusions can be developed at this stage.

Regardless of the diverse findings on the positive and negative outcomes associated with office romances, it appears that about half of the working population are generally tolerant of romantic liaisons among couples in their workplaces, as long as the couples are not otherwise married. According to Quinn (1977), 56% of the men and 63% of the women were willing to tolerate romantic relationships among single coworkers. The Bureau of National Affairs (1988) report stated that coworkers are tolerant of office liaisons as long as the couple acts in a professional manner. Powell (1986) found widespread agreement with the statement: "It is all right for someone to look for a marriage partner at work." Of the 756 adults surveyed through a *Newsweek* Gallup Poll ("Love in the Office," 1988), 47% indicated they approved of unmarried coworkers having an intimate relationship at work, and 52% staunchly defended the rights of couples who marry to remain at work once married.

PSYCHOLOGICAL, SOCIAL, AND SOCIOLOGICAL INTERPRETATIONS

This review of the literature on office romances suggests that the research in this area is quite diverse and requires a unifying perspective. A model that discusses psychological, social, and sociological interpretations of the phenomenon may help to make sense of some of thi diversity. In this section, a model of the power dynamics of office romances will be discussed to unify portions of this diverse research.

A Model of Power Dynamics in Office Romances

Mainiero (1986) presented a model of power dynamics in office romances (see Figure 6.1) based on social exchange theory, which suggested two central propositions:

1. Balanced power relationships (such as peer relationships) may lead to a synergistic office romance with positive outcomes for the involved members. Imbalanced power relationships (such as relationships across hierarchial levels) may lead to the exploitation of one partner with negative repercussions for both the involved couple and the work group.

2. The greater the evidence that one of the parties is exploiting the relationship for personal gain (such as unfair promotions, raises, task reallocations, or other actions perceived to be inappropriate by coworkers), the stronger the attempts of work group members to break down the coalition.

A Psychological Interpretation of Internal/External Dynamics

Proposition 1 offers, in essence, a psychological interpretation of the internal dynamics of the relationship for the couple by borrowing from the literature on power dynamics of dating relationships. This literature (Blood & Wolfe, 1960; McDonald, 1980; Safilos-Rothschild, 1977; Sprecher, 1985) presents a social exchange perspective of power in dating relationships that is a function of the relative dependency of each partner on the other for resources being exchanged in the relationship.

To apply this model to office romances, Mainiero (1986) theorized that two domains of resources, task and career dependencies, are exchanged in most organizational relationships. For example, an employee who values career advancement may work hard to impress his or her boss to gain the support necessary for a future promotion. In this case, working hard (task domain) is exchanged for organizational rewards (career domain). But, when an office romance evolves, a sexual domain of exchange is added. Resources such as affection, sex, and companionship commonly exchanged in dating relationships may threaten to upset the normal balance of task and career domains.

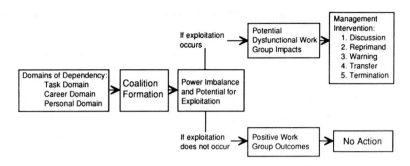

Figure 6.1. A Model of Power Dynamics in Organizational Romances
SOURCE: Reprinted from Mainiero (1986); used by permission.

According to Emerson (1962), dependency and power are inversely related in personal relationships such that, the more dependent one party is on another, the less power he or she will hold in that particular social relation. If one party is more dependent on the other for the resources exchanged, then an imbalance of power occurs in the social relation. Balanced relationships are at least temporarily stable; imbalanced relationships suggest the potential for exploitation of the more dependent (least powerful) member.

In hierarchical office romances—that is, romances that cross the lines of authority in an organization—there is potential for exploitation of the relationship as it may become unbalanced once the sexual dimension is added. In other words, a subordinate could exploit the relationship by providing sexual favors to the boss in return for a promotion. Or, conversely, a boss may manipulate a subordinate by threatening to withdraw from the relationship unless certain work deadlines are accomplished. This is why office romances become "dangerous liaisons." Coworkers fear that *sex can be traded for power in an office setting* across hierarchical levels.

There is substantial evidence in the literature that suggests that the majority of negative effects occur in hierarchical liaisons where the potential for the misuse of sexual favors is greatest. The majority of negative perceptions in the Powell (1986) study, in Collins's (1983) case analyses, and in the Bureau of National Affairs (1988) report occurred in relationships that crossed hierarchical levels, such as direct reporting boss-subordinate pairs, rather than those involving lateral or peer relationships. Similar results were reported in the Anderson and Hunsaker (1985) and Quinn (1977) studies as well.

This may be because office lovers at the same lateral level in the organization do not have the authority to promote one another, nor can they provide any form of organizational rewards other than that which is legitimately theirs commensurate with their position. Hierarchical romances, however, offer the potential that coveted organizational rewards (such as raises, promotions, favorable task assignments, autonomy in work hours) may be unfairly exchanged for personal gain because the relative power of the participants remains unequal.

In the case analyses reported by Mainiero (1989), hierarchical romances were evaluated by coworkers far more negatively than peer romances; 79% of romantic boss-subordinate relationships were rated as "more difficult" and "unproductive" by observers; more than 60% of the observers indicated that they "resented the relationship" because the involved couple "showed favoritism" toward one another as a result of the romance. Yet, only 21% of peer relationships were similarly negatively evaluated. As an example, one woman manager wrote in a comment:

> In my office, a woman was hired into the company while dating our boss. Management was aware of the romance before the woman was hired, [but] I feel it was an extremely out-of-line decision and makes working with this woman awkward for other employees. The woman has preferred treatment as to time off and salary arrangements. I totally disapprove and management has hit the bottom of my respect scale.

The Bureau of National Affairs (1988, p. 37) similarly concluded:

> The type of romance considered to be most disruptive of office routine and most negative in its consequences is an affair between a supervisor and a subordinate. . . . These romances cause jealousy and suspicion among coworkers and can result in lowered productivity. Such involvements can lead to charges of favoritism when the two parties to the romance are not of equal rank. Coworkers of the romantically linked pair can have feelings of jealousy, anger, and abandonment.

Because what work group members fear most is the *potential* for exploitation and manipulation in the relationship (Anderson & Hunsaker, 1985; Collins, 1983; Jamison, 1983; Quinn, 1977), the mere potential for unfair exchange may be sufficient to raise the wrath of coworkers. In one case reported in Mainiero (1989), a woman reported that her fiance, who was also her boss, was "stricter with me than with other employees because he wants to be sure no one thinks he's playing favorites—hence he's unfair to me. . . [But] coworkers still refuse to [believe] we're on the level."

The potential for sexual manipulation is a particular fear of men more than women. According to Gutek (1985), men believe that women's sexuality offers women an unfair advantage in a workplace environment where more men than women serve in management positions. To the extent that people use sexuality at work, women are the ones most expected to do so. This stereotype probably emerged because men assume women to be the "carriers" of sexuality, because, to men, sexuality is viewed as a resource to be used. In her study on sexual harassment, Gutek (1985) reported that women also indicated that their male supervisors offered them the opportunity to use sexuality in exchange for organizational rewards, such as promotions. Such offers would not ordinarily be made between heterosexual men reporting to one another in a manager-subordinate relationship.

In addition to hierarchical relationships, there are other types of workplace relationships that also may present the potential for dangerous exploitation. For example, cross-departmental relationships where inappropriate information exchange could occur, service provider/professional-client relationships, and vendor-competitor relationships may also create professional conflicts of interest. The landmark legal case of *Gina Rulon-Miller v. IBM* (1984) illustrates such a conflict when Rulon-Miller was fired for dating the employee of a competitor. The court ruled against IBM, and Rulon-Miller was reinstated. (For further discussion of the legal implications of office romances, see the chapter by Lee in this book.)

A Social Interpretation of Work Group Reactions

The second proposition offers a social interpretation of work group reactions toward office romances based on the literature on power and coalition formation. Power analyses of coalition formation suggest that, when a coalition forms that has different goals than those of the other group members, attempts to break down the coalition occur (Coser, 1973; Pfeffer, 1981). Blau (1964) further suggests that the power differences may provoke a range of reactions on the part of group members, including social disapproval, outright hostility, and/or a desire for group members to retaliate against the coalition. This would suggest that, when exploitation—real or imagined—is attributed to the couple, coworkers would take action to break down the coalition. In other words, when organizational rewards are perceived by coworkers as being traded for personal gain, such as when one member is promoted unfairly, receives an unwarranted raise, or is allowed to arrive late or leave earlier than other workers, such actions are likely to create resentment on the part of coworkers, which may, in turn, provoke negative reactions.

There is growing evidence in the literature to support this second proposition. Quinn (1977) noted that, as power behavior changes in relationships became more pronounced, coworkers are more willing to take action against the couple. Comparative case analysis reported in Mainiero (1989) of hierarchical romances in which one of the romancers used the relationship for personal gain showed that other coworkers used a variety of tactics to disrupt the relationship or retaliate against the couple. For example, in several cases, anonymous notes were sent to the personnel office complaining about an affair. Other strategies included extraloud lunchroom conversations within earshot of higher-ups to discuss an unfair raise or convention travel, notes sent to the offending couple, and, in one case, graffiti in the men's room depicting a man who was willing to misuse his power in exchange for sexual favors. Anderson and Hunsaker (1985) also found that retaliation tactics included complaints about the relationship, blackmail, ostracism, and acts of sabotage.

This analysis would therefore suggest that employees who misuse sex in exchange for a promotion would incur the wrath of coworkers. In one case studied by Mainiero (1989), a lower-level woman manipulated her boss with sexual favors in exchange for a highly visible task force assignment. He became very dependent on her and was ready to leave his family for her. She was less committed to him, and, once she was promoted, she broke off the relationship. Coworkers were resentful of the woman's blatant manipulations. In the words of one observer,

> When she was appointed to the task force, it was a fatal mistake. It's one thing to have an affair. It's another to let yourself be used as a pawn in someone else's schemes. . . . We were all seething [with the news]. I mean, I didn't care about the task force myself, but there was this other guy who was really good, interested, and deserved the appointment. We were [justifiably] upset.

Coworkers found ways to retaliate against the couple. As reported by one observer of this incident:

> We joked about them—and found ways to insult them at first. [Then] the joking and insults grew into concerted action. Some people actually dropped hints about the affair when they could be overheard by a division vice president. Others made the woman look bad—I remember there was this report that the woman had due that suddenly was misplaced. . . . Eventually we made life so miserable [for the couple] that they were both asked to leave.

Reports of women (and men) advancing their careers as a result of romantic relationships at work (or "sleeping their way to the top") are less prevalent than the public might imagine. In Warfield's (1987) survey of female managers, less than one third of the respondents noted a case in their firm in which a woman successfully advanced her career through sexual encounters with higher-ups. Respondents in the Warfield (1987) study described a number of negative effects, such as coworker resentment, ruined credibility, and limited likelihood of future advancement.

Gutek (1985) also found relatively little evidence that women routinely or even occasionally use their sexuality to gain organizational goals. Only 1 woman out of 800 in her sample said she used sex to achieve her current position; many more women reported that they were fired or quit after becoming involved with a man at work. Despite common gender-stereotypical perceptions that women can and will use their sexuality to get ahead at work, the Gutek (1985) study concluded that there is virtually no evidence that women have succeeded or advanced at work by using their sexuality.

For those who attempt to do so, more often than not the career advancement prospects of both members of the couple are arrested once the judgment of the higher-level member of the couple is questioned by upper management. As one example, Mainiero (1989) reported a case in which a male division manager was plateaued as a consequence of his romantic liaison with a female subordinate. Coworkers caused an uproar when the division manager promoted his lover for the second time in the same year. Once news of the romantic relationship reached the upper ranks, the division manager was sidelined. The female subordinate's department was reorganized so that she managed only one third as much staff as before.

Such outcomes occurred under conditions where coworkers felt that the relationship had adversely affected workplace equity. For romantic relationships among peers, retaliation was unnecessary because manipulation of organizational rewards for personal gain rarely, if ever, occurred.

A New Proposition Based on a Sociological Interpretation

Sociological interpretations suggest that the power ascribed to individual employees based on their status or level of authority in the organization influences workplace dynamics (Kanter, 1977; Pfeffer, 1981). One possible explanation of why women as a group believe they have more at risk by pursuing an office romance may be because women attribute to their gender a greater risk of negative career consequences. It is possible, however, that such risks may be more attributable to women's limited power as a group in organizations than to their gender. Unger (1986) and Kanter (1977) have suggested that gender serves as a carrier variable for status in organizational settings. Recent demographic data suggest that approximately 5% of the nation's top executive positions are held by women (U.S. Department of Labor, 1991). Once more women are promoted to positions of power, attributions of risk may equalize between men and women.

Stereotypes about who has more to lose—the woman or the man—by participating in an office romance may already be changing as demographic patterns begin to shift. A survey in *Glamour* magazine ("Men at Work," 1989) of more than 100 men reported that more than 40% of the men surveyed believed it was now possible for a man to sleep his way to the top of the corporation. More than 50% of the men surveyed said they would be willing to date their female superiors. Only 6% of respondents, however, actually had become romantically involved with their female bosses.

Those men who do may be subject to the same negative repercussions that have traditionally affected women. According to Mainiero (1989), lower-level men who are romantically linked to upper-level women are evaluated by coworkers in a similar negative fashion as are women if the personal relationship is exploited to gain organizational rewards. In one case, for example, coworkers were resentful of a man dating his (female) boss, whom he then dumped once he was promoted and transferred to a larger division. In another case, a lower-level man was transferred because he was perceived as less valuable by management as a consequence of his dalliance with a high potential female boss. Very few cases (n = 9) of reverse-stereotypical romances were present due to the convenience nature of the sample; however, among those cases noted, lower-level men who misused a dating relationship with a female boss generated negative reactions among coworkers similar to those generated by women.

A new proposition based on this sociological interpretation may therefore be advanced for future research and study:

3. As the ratio of men to women equalizes across organizational levels, others' perceptions about the risks associated with office romances should be attributed less to gender and more to participants' relative power in the organization.

Future research in organizations that are female dominant (e.g., where women hold proportionally more powerful positions, such as in nursing, publishing, or the cosmetics industries) may provide support for this hypothesis. Further research is necessary to determine whether this hypothesis can be supported.

IMPLICATIONS FOR RESEARCH, MANAGEMENT PRACTICE, AND CORPORATE POLICY

The literature on office romances is quite diverse and allows for many possible avenues for future research. One area that would benefit from additional exploration is the effect of corporate norms on the incidence rates of office romances in different firms. Only limited research has taken place that addresses this issue; future research might specify further how differences in corporate cultures affect couples' assessments of risk. Do businesses that actively support women react more positively to workplace liaisons? Are more negative effects attributed to women than men in conservative cultures? Research in this area is strongly encouraged as corporate culture may be a primary factor that explains differences in attitudes and reactions.

A second area worthy of investigation concerns what factors other than hierarchical level may provoke negative reactions on the part of coworkers. Romantically involved parties in competing departments, for example, may create a conflict of interest situation that may upset coworkers. The work flow between the two competing departments could become distorted should the couple share or withhold confidential departmental information. New research on the conditions that provoke negative reactions will explain more clearly the complicated and sometimes mixed reactions to this phenomenon.

Third, it is important to determine the specific effects a romance may have on the couple. More research on the role conflicts couples experience, and how they handle them, is sorely needed to help couples cope with their dual roles and the stress associated with such complications. Ways in which couples may more productively handle the emotional detachment of an office breakup also may be needed as the incidence of office romance rises.

Fourth, the impact of office romance on productivity concerning the couple and the work group requires further exploration. The literature in this area is mixed. Future research is needed to specify the conditions that may cause productivity to increase or decrease. Variables such as whether a hierarchical romance is involved, whether the couple works for the same department, and the stage of the romance (dating/married) may each have an impact on couples' productivity and, consequently, on coworker reactions.

Fifth, only limited research has taken place that addresses the issues for gay and lesbian couples who find romance in the workplace. Equally little attention has been paid to the experiences of minority and interracial couples who work together. In addition, as yet, no qualitative assessments have been made concerning the impact of extramarital affairs on coworkers. Coworker reactions to office romances may vary depending upon whether both members of the couple are single, otherwise married, or divorced. Each of these areas may provide fruitful issues for future research.

Given the complexities of behaviors, attitudes, perceptions, and outcomes associated with office romances, one might conclude that engaging in such relationships is indeed "dangerous" and should be avoided at all costs. When Cupid's arrow strikes, however, no one can predict where it may land. Managers are as likely to fall in love with one another at work as in other social circumstances. As a consequence, many authors have suggested the need for organizational policies concerning office romances (Collins, 1983; Jamison, 1983; Mead, 1978; Powell, 1986; Spruell, 1985). Much controversy, however, has been generated about such policies regarding workplace romances because managers fear legal accusations of intruding on employee privacy if they interfere. As noted by Lee elsewhere in this book, managers will be held responsible for enforcing the policies they adopt.

It may be largely for this reason that policies concerning office romance remain relatively rare. A 1985 *Fortune* magazine survey sent to human resource managers at 220 *Fortune* 500 companies showed that 94% said they had not developed formal policies regarding personal/romantic relationships. More than one third said their companies tried to overlook such relationships, and a fifth said they felt such problems would resolve themselves.

Legal precedents concerning office romances also are unclear. The interpretation of the legalities of job terminations varies from state to state, but most corporations are protected by the employment-at-will statue, which states that terminations may be made for good reason or no reason but not for illegitimate reasons (see *Crozier v. UPS,* 1983, or *Rodgers v. IBM*, 1980, for discussions on this matter). Legally, in most states, corporations can enforce policies concerning dating relationships at work. But the majority of corporations have not yet developed policies concerning office romance as distinct from policies concerning sexual harassment or nepotism (see the survey in "Love in the Office," 1988, or the report in "Romance in the Workplace," 1984).

Collins (1983) suggested that policies concerning office romance should require one member of the couple to leave the firm. She suggests that the lower-level member of the couple should be the one asked to leave, as she considers this employee less valuable to the organization as a whole. Policy statements such as this one, however, are untenable for a variety of reasons: (a) The lower-level member of the couple may not always be less valuable, (b) the lower-level member of the couple is more likely to be female than male and such a practice would be discriminatory against women, and (c) the romance may have no deleterious effects on the work group to support cause for dismissal.

Powell and Mainiero (1990) suggest an alternative approach based on work performance rather than personal reasons. To fire employees simply because they have become romantically involved and there is potential for damage neglects the fact that many romances have beneficial effects on worker productivity, office morale, and motivation. To require that one member of the couple leave the firm because the couple is romantically involved or has married seems inappropriate. But, if work performance is adversely affected by an office romance, then management has a legitimate reason to take action to improve the situation. If the romance has not caused any adverse effects, no action should be necessary.

CONCLUSION

Do office romances represent "dangerous liaisons" for women managers in the modern-day corporation? Certainly, there always is an element of danger in the sense that it may be difficult to detach emotionally from a coworker or supervisor who had once been a lover should the relationship dissolve. But this element of risk is present in any personal relationship.

The danger, it appears, from an office romance results more from the career consequences that romancers may experience than adverse personal outcomes. This review suggests that hierarchical romances that exploit the power of one party over the other indeed may be dangerous simply because such relationships provoke strong negative reactions from coworkers. Such negative reactions may tarnish one's credibility in a corporation to the point where career advancement is threatened. Lateral romantic relationships between peers may be less "dangerous," however, as coworkers are more willing to tolerate peer liaisons because power is unlikely to be exploited when the couple is of equal standing.

The issues for women managers on this area remain complex and confounded. As the representation of men and women managers becomes more equivalent throughout the 1990s, the issues may become less gender focused and more a function of the underlying systemic issues, such as power, level, or status. It is a testament to how much women as a group have achieved that the office is now a viable place to meet a future spouse *and* pursue a career. Once women are able to pursue personal relationships without risk to their professional goals, we will know that parity with men truly has been achieved.

NOTE

1. The focus of this chapter is on heterosexual romantic relationships in the workplace. For readers interested in the dynamics of homosexual relationships, see Beth Schneider's chapter, "Invisible and Independent: Lesbian's Experiences in the Workplace" in Stromberg and Harkess (1988).

REFERENCES

Anderson, C., & Hunsaker, P. (1985). Why there's romancing at the office and why it's everyone's problem. *Personnel, 62,* 57-63.

Berscheid, E., & Walster, E. (1969). *Interpersonal attraction.* Reading, MA: Addison-Wesley.

Blau, P. (1964). *Exchange and power in social life.* London: John Wiley.

Blood, R., & Wolfe, D. (1960). *Husbands and wives.* New York: Free Press.

Bureau of National Affairs. (1988). *Corporate affairs: Nepotism, office romance, and sexual harassment.* Washington, DC: Author.

Clawson, J., & Kram, K. (1984, May-June). Managing cross-gender mentoring. *Business Horizons,* pp. 22-32.

Collins, E. (1983). Managers and lovers. *Harvard Business Review, 61,* 142-153.

Coser, W. (1973). *The functions of social conflict.* New York: Plenum.

Crary, M. (1987, Spring). Managing attraction and intimacy at work. *Organizational Dynamics,* pp. 26-41.

Crozier v. UPS (Calif Ct App, 1983, 115 LRRM 3535).

Cunningham, M. (with Brewer, F.). (1984). *Powerplay: What really happened at Bendix.* New York: Simon & Schuster.

Driscoll, J., & Bova, R. (1980). The sexual side of enterprise. *Management Review, 69*(7), 51-62.

Emerson, R. (1962). Power-dependence relations. *American Sociological Review, 27,* 33-41.

Ford, R. C., & McLaughlin, F. S. (1987). Should Cupid come to the workplace? An ASPA survey. *Personnel Administrator, 32*(10), 100-110.

Goodman, E. (1983, September 27). When love enters the executive suite. *Boston Globe,* Sec. D.

Gutek, B. (1985). *Sex in the workplace.* San Francisco: Jossey-Bass.

Haavio-Mannila, E., Kauppien-Toropainen, K., & Kandolin, I. (1988). The effect of sex composition in the workplace on friendship, romance, and sex at work. In B. Gutek, A. Stromberg, & L. Larwood (Eds.), *Women and work* (Vol. 3). Newbury Park, CA: Sage.

Horn, P., & Horn, J. (1982). *Sex in the office: Power and passion in the workplace.* Reading, MA: Addison-Wesley.

Jamison, K. (1983). Managing sexual attraction in the office. *Personnel Administrator, 28*(8), 45-50.

Kanter, R. M. (1977). *Men and women of the corporation.* New York: Basic Books.

Love in the office. (1988, February 15). *Newsweek,* pp. 48-52.

Mainiero, L. (1986). The power dynamics of organizational romances. *Academy of Management Review, 11*(4), 750-762.

Mainiero, L. (1989). *Office romance: Love, power and sex in the workplace.* New York: Rawson Associates/Macmillan.

McDonald, G. (1980). Family power: The assessment of a decade of theory and research 1970-79. *Journal of Marriage and the Family, 42,* 841-854.

Mead, M. (1978, April). A proposal: We need taboos on sex at work. *Redbook,* pp. 31-38.

Men at work: Is sex on their minds. (1989, January). *Glamour,* pp. 124-129.

Pfeffer, J. (1981). *Power in organizations.* Marshfield, MA: Pitman.

Powell, G. (1986). What do tomorrow's managers think about sexual intimacy in the workplace? *Business Horizons, 29*(4), 32-33.

Powell, G., & Mainiero, L. (1990). What human resource managers need to know about office romances. *Leadership and Organization Development Journal, 11*(1), 18.

Quinn, R. (1977). Coping with Cupid: An analysis of the dynamics in organizational romances. *Administrative Science Quarterly, 22,* 30-45.

Quinn, R., & Lees, P. (1984). Attraction and harassment: Dynamics of sexual politics in the workplace. *Organizational Dynamics, 13*(2), 35-46.

Rodgers v. IBM (DC W Pa, 1980, 115 LRRM 4608).

Romance in the workplace: Corporate rules for the game of love. (1984, June 18). *Business Week,* pp. 70-72.

Gina Rulon-Miller v. IBM (Calif CT Appls, 1984, 117 LRRM 3309).

Safilos-Rothschild, C. (1977). *Love and sex roles.* Englewood Cliffs, NJ: Prentice-Hall.

Schneider, B. (1988). Invisible and independent: Lesbian's experiences in the workplace. In A. Stromberg & S. Harkess (Eds.), *Women working.* Mountain View, CA: Mayfield.

Schultz, T. (1980, May). In defense of the office romance. *Savvy,* pp. 54-64.

Sprecher, S. (1985). Sex differences in bases of power in dating relationships. *Sex Roles, 12*(4), 449-461.

Spruell, G. (1985). Daytime dramas: Love in the office. *Training and Development Journal, 39*(2), 20-33.

Unger, R. K. (1986). *Sex, gender, and social change.* New York: Plenum.

U.S. Department of Labor (1991). *A report on the glass ceiling initiative.* Washington, DC: Government Printing Office.

Warfield, A. (1987). Coworker romances: Impact on the work group and on career-oriented women. *Personnel, 64*(5), 22-35.

Westoff, L. (1985). *Corporate romance.* New York: Times Books.

7

Personal Portrait: The Life-Style of the Woman Manager

SAROJ PARASURAMAN
JEFFREY H. GREENHAUS

The literature on women in management has focused extensively on women's access to and advancement in managerial positions (see Dipboye, 1987, and Morrison & Von Glinow, 1990, for reviews). Far less attention has been devoted to issues related to the life-style of the woman manager. What are the implications of a managerial career for the personal lives of women managers? Do characteristics of their personal lives affect the career success and advancement of women managers? Conversely, do characteristics of women's careers and career outcomes affect the nature and quality of their personal lives?

Answers to these questions should be of interest to women planning to enter or already in managerial careers, the spouses and families of women managers, and human resource professionals. Systematic examination of these and related issues would (a) enable women to gain an

AUTHORS' NOTE: The authors thank Edwin L. Makamson, doctoral student in management at Drexel University, for his valuable assistance in locating references and for his helpful comments on earlier drafts of this chapter. The constructive comments and suggestions of Stewart D. Friedman, the reviewers, the series editor, and the editor of this volume are also acknowledged with thanks.

expanded understanding of the factors that impinge on career success and personal well-being, and thereby the determination of effective strategies for career management and life-style balance; (b) inform organizational career development programs responsive to the career experiences and needs of women managers; and (c) stimulate careers researchers to modify and expand current theories of career development to incorporate the unique factors that affect women's careers.

A *New York Times* poll indicates that 4%-8% of women and 33% of men think that women have "given up too much" for the gains achieved in the workplace ("Women's Gains on the Job," 1989). Although 70% of women with full-time jobs reported that women had equal or better than equal chances of promotion where they worked, most feel that progress has been achieved at the expense of time with their children and the quality of their family lives. A similar view was expressed by Stanford University economist Victor R. Fuchs, who commented that women's progress in the labor market has been offset by the loss of leisure time and the decline of marriage, with employed women more likely to divorce than nonemployed women ("Women's Gains on the Job," 1989). Moreover, it has been suggested that the primary responsibility for housework and child care shouldered by the majority of employed women entails their working a "second shift" (Hochschild, 1989) and that the problems of balancing the demands of a career and family life inhibit the realization of the career potential of women managers.

The perspectives noted above indicate that the employment and personal spheres of women managers' lives are inextricably linked, and a deeper understanding of the life-style of the woman manager necessitates an examination of the relationships between her career and family life experiences. Thus the purpose of this chapter is to examine different facets of the career and personal life experiences of women managers, the interdependencies among them, which collectively shape their life styles, and affect their outcomes and well-being in both domains. In examining these issues, we draw on the literature on women managers whenever available, supplemented by the research on women professionals and on employed women in general. The chapter is organized into the following sections: (a) life-style choices, (b) career experiences of the woman manager, (c) family life experiences of the woman manager, (d) linkages between career and family life domains, (e) theoretical perspectives on life-style choices, and (f) conclusions.

LIFE-STYLE CHOICES

The literature on women managers indicates little evidence of women making conscious decisions about what life-style to adopt. It appears that, in the initial stages of their entry into managerial roles, the heightened expectations of women were accompanied by inadequate attention to the ramifications of a highly involved career, or of the possibility of conflict between career and other life roles, as well as by unfounded optimism concerning women's ability to "have it all"— that is, a successful managerial career, a fulfilling marriage, and children (Hardesty & Jacobs, 1986). Underlying this optimism was a lack of recognition of the reality that "careers were originally designed to suit traditional men whose wives raised their children" (Hochschild, 1989, preface). According to Blair Sheppard, director of the Human Resource Management Center at Duke University, "The whole career ladder in the U.S. is predicated on the life cycle of a man" (Fierman, 1990, p. 58). Reports of women leaving the corporate world for self-employment and/or motherhood and time with their children (Basler, 1986; Taylor, 1986) may indicate some disenchantment with a vision of life that includes family, career, and happiness (Fierman, 1990). It has been suggested that "the 1980's effectively destroyed the notion that they [women] could have it all" (Fierman, 1990, p. 40). Thus women (and perhaps men) are becoming aware of the need to make choices to achieve a well-rounded life (Hardesty & Jacobs, 1986).

The need for women to choose among different life-style options has only recently been articulated by women in management researchers (Marshall, 1984; Morrison, White, & Van Velsor, 1987). Such life-style choices include decisions about the importance of a career relative to other areas of life; whether and when to marry; whether and when to have children; arrangements for managing housework and child care; managing relationships with spouses, relatives, and friends; and managing competing demands from various life roles (Marshall, 1984). In the two sections that follow, we provide an overview of key elements in the career and family life experiences of women managers as a backdrop for the analysis of the factors affecting women's life-style choices.

CAREER EXPERIENCES OF
THE WOMAN MANAGER

This section on career experiences of the woman manager provides the context in which the interdependencies between women managers' careers and family lives are analyzed. The research findings indicate that two salient categories of career experiences are likely to be related to the family experiences of women managers. The first category encompasses four aspects of career commitment, that is, career aspirations, job involvement, career interruptions, and multiple domain involvement. The second category of career experiences focuses on career success in terms of job performance, career advancement, salary, and job attitudes. The research results summarized in Table 7.1 indicate that, despite equivalent or higher job involvement than men, women managers aspire to positions lower in the managerial hierarchy than men, are more likely to experience career interruptions than men, and tend to place somewhat higher priority on family life relative to careers than men. While their job performance is equal to or greater than that of men, their salaries are, however, lower, with the salary differential increasing over time. Notwithstanding this, it is surprising that women managers report high levels of job and career satisfaction.

FAMILY EXPERIENCES OF
THE WOMAN MANAGER

The family life experiences of women managers relevant to understanding their life-styles include marital status, spouse characteristics, structure of marital relationships, parenthood, division of housework and child care, and leisure. The profile that emerges from the findings summarized in Table 7.2 is that a majority of women managers are not married (they are single, divorced, or widowed) or, if married, have no children. Their career priority is lower than that of their husbands; they spend more time on housework and child care than their spouses; and they have little leisure time or time for themselves.

It should be noted that the gender differences reported in the studies cited in Tables 7.1 and 7.2 may be influenced by individual, organizational, and/or societal factors (Fagenson, 1990), although the investigators may

text continued on page 194

Table 7.1 Summary of Research Findings on Career Experiences of Women Managers (Part 1)

Experiences	Findings	Illustrative Sources
Career Commitment:		
Career aspirations	Women managers aspire to lower managerial positions.	Harlan & Weiss, 1982 Hennig & Jardim, 1977
Job involvement	Job involvement of women managers is equal to or higher than that of men.	Lorence, 1987 Marshall, 1984 Moen & Smith, 1986
Career interruptions	Women managers are more likely to interrupt their careers than men.	U.S. Bureau of the Census, 1984 Davidson & Cooper, 1987 Strober, 1982
	Women MBAs are more likely to experience employment gaps than men with MBAs, but the impact of an employment gap on income is greater for men than for women.	Schneer & Reitman, 1990
Multiple domain involvement	Women managers are ambivalent about their involvement in a career, due to the competition for their time and attention from other life roles.	Howard & Bray, 1988
	Women executives, administrators, faculty, and professionals are more likely to be family accommodated (family first in priority, career second) than men.	Taylor & Spencer, 1988

190

Career Success:

Job performance	The job performance of women managers is equal to or higher than that of men.	Fernandez, 1981 Greenhaus, Parasuraman, & Wormley, 1990 Moses & Boehm, 1975 Tsui & Gutek, 1984
Career advancement	Women progress more slowly up the managerial hierarchy than men.	Dipboye, 1987 Morrison, White, & Van Velsor, 1987
Salary	Women managers earn lower salaries than men.	U.S. Bureau of the Census, 1987a Dipboye, 1987
	Despite similar starting salaries, over time, women MBAs' salaries average about 80% of those of men with MBAs.	Devanna, 1987 Strober, 1982
Job attitudes	Women managers report similar levels of job satisfaction as men managers.	Howard & Bray, 1988 Strober, 1982
	Women managers report higher career satisfaction than men managers.	Greenhaus et al., 1990

Table 7.2 Summary of Research Findings on Career Experiences of Women Managers (Part 2)

Experiences	Findings	Illustrative Sources
Marital status	Women managers are less likely to be married than men managers.	Davidson & Cooper, 1984 Harlan & Weiss, 1982 Howard & Bray, 1988 Valdez & Gutek, 1987
	A larger proportion of executive women (52%) than executive men (4%) are single, divorced, separated, or widowed.	Hellwig, 1985 Powell, 1988 U.S. Bureau of the Census, 1987b
Spouse characteristics	Professional and managerial women tend to marry men with equal or higher educational and occupational achievement; men tend to marry women with lower academic and occupational achievements, who are likely to be nonemployed or employed in less demanding jobs.	Howard & Bray, 1988 Kanter, 1977
Structure of Marital Relationships:		
Income	The majority of employed women earn substantially less than their husbands.	Bianchi, 1984 U.S. Bureau of Labor Statistics, 1989
	Only 15% of women in two-career relationships earn more than their husbands.	U.S. Bureau of the Census, 1984
	Of women MBAs, 50% earned incomes that were 15% lower than that of their husbands.	Strober, 1982
Career priority	Women managers and professionals in two-career relationships place lower priority on their own careers compared with their husbands.	Greenhaus, Parasuraman, Granrose, Rabinowitz, & Beutell, 1989

Gender role ideology	Gender role ideology helps to determine the priority women accord to a career versus home.	Hochschild, 1989
	Gender role ideology and expectations influence the reactions of spouses to women managers' occupational attainments.	Bailyn, 1970 Beutell & Greenhaus, 1982 Hiller & Philliber, 1982 Ross, Mirowsky, & Huber, 1983
Commuter marriages	A growing number of employed women are involved in commuter marriages (estimated to number 700,000 couples in 1982).	Gerstel & Gross, 1984 Leo, 1982 Macklin, 1987
Parenthood	Nearly 57% of women managers in the 25-34 age group and 25% of women in the 35-44 age group are childless.	U.S. Bureau of the Census, 1987b
	Executive women are significantly more likely to be childless (61%) than executive men (3%).	Powell, 1988
	Employed women in general, and women managers and professionals in particular, tend to be late first-time parents.	Bloom, 1984 Langer, 1985 Marshall, 1984
Housework and child care	Employed women, including women managers, work significantly longer hours each week on housework and child care than employed men.	Bernardo, Shehan, & Leslie, 1987 Hochschild, 1989 Piotrkowski & Repetti, 1984 Robinson, 1988 Strober, 1982
	Despite more hours spent on housework than men, a majority of employed women report that their husbands do their fair share around the house.	"Women's Gains on the Job," 1989 Yogev, 1981
Leisure	Employed women have significantly less leisure time per week than employed men.	Firestone & Shelton, 1988 Shaw, 1985
	A majority of married employed women with and without children report that they lack enough time for themselves.	Hochschild, 1989 "Women's Gains on the Job," 1989

not have explicitly examined these factors or controlled for them. The role of organizational and sociocultural factors in explaining the differential career and family experiences of women is illustrated in the following section on linkages between the career and family domains.

LINKAGES BETWEEN CAREER AND FAMILY DOMAINS

An appreciation of the life-style issues faced by women managers requires an understanding of the mutual interdependencies between their careers and other life pursuits. In this section, we examine women managers' involvement in their career and family domains, and the critical linkages between them that shape their life styles. As Figure 7.1 indicates, we propose that women managers' family experiences have direct and indirect effects on their career outcomes. Moreover, the literature also indicates that career experiences have direct and indirect effects on women's family outcomes. In other words, women managers' involvements, demands, and accomplishments in the employment and family domains are mutually interdependent (Gutek, Repetti, & Silver, 1988).

We first discuss how family experiences affect the career experiences and outcomes of women managers and then examine the impact of career experiences on family experiences and outcomes. Although the cross-sectional nature of most of the research precludes inferences regarding causality (Gutek et al., 1988), we use the literature to establish the presence of relationships among variables and to examine the conceptual basis for inferring reciprocal causal relationships.

The Impact of Family Experiences on the Career Domain

It has been frequently observed that extensive family responsibilities, especially those involving marriage, child care, and household activities, can impede women managers' career achievements (Gutek et al., 1988; Olson & Frieze, 1987). Involvements in the family domain produce extensive work-family conflicts to which women respond by reducing their employment involvement, which, in turn, restricts career opportunities and advancement. The literature provides support for the existence of these linkages (Bourne & Wikler, 1982; Olson & Frieze, 1987; Strober, 1982).

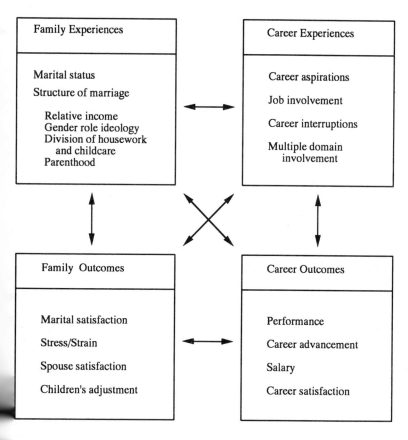

Figure 7.1. Linkages Between Career and Family Domains of Women Managers

Employed women who are married and/or those who have children tend to experience high levels of career-family conflict because of the conflicting pressures arising from these two domains (Greenhaus & Beutell, 1985; Holahan & Gilbert, 1979; Pleck, Staines, & Lang, 1980; Sekaran, 1986). Moreover, women who experience extensive role conflict and time pressures from their career and family roles may reduce their level of career involvement (Bourne & Wikler, 1982) or curtail their time commitment to their jobs (Kingston & Nock, 1985; Pittman & Orthner, 1988) in an effort to alleviate the conflict.

The extent to which women subordinate their career aspirations to meet their family's needs depends upon women's own value systems and priorities (Powell, Pozner, & Schmidt, 1984; Taylor & Spencer, 1988), the degree of support provided by their husbands (Houseknecht & Macke, 1981), the age-based needs of their children (Brett & Yogev, 1988) as well as the availability of organizational support in the form of flexible work schedules and facilities or assistance for child care. Reduced career involvement may take the form of restricted time devoted to the job, seeking a less demanding job and/or refusing a promotion, less psychological investment in a career, cutting back on job-related travel, or unwillingness to relocate (Chapman, 1987; Dipboye, 1987; Hochschild, 1989; Markham, 1987). Such strategies for managing career-family conflicts, however, can impede women managers' career advancement (Markham, 1987; Olson & Frieze, 1987; Strober, 1982). To quote *Business Week* ("Companies Start to Meet," 1983, p. 191), "Careers almost inevitably suffer when [women] curtail work schedules." According to economist Sylvia Ann Hewlett, the impact of taking time off to have a child and spending time with the child through preschool is a reduction in future earnings of 13%-19% for the rest of the woman's career (Basler, 1986).

Family role involvements can have a negative impact on career achievements even when the women themselves may not choose to reduce their career involvement. Based on long-held stereotypes, organizations often assume that married women (especially those with children) will and should play a primary caretaker role within their families (Rosen & Jerdee, 1973; Schwartz, 1989). Given the assumption that these women will subordinate their careers to their family responsibilities, such organizations are unlikely to invest in the development of their women managers in the form of training, sponsorship, and assignment to jobs that provide power and opportunity (Devanna, 1987; Lewis & Cooper, 1988).

In an attempt to prevent such adverse effects on their career advancement, and to dispel the stereotype that women with children are not serious about their careers, some women adopt a "superwoman" or "supermom" strategy, combining extensive career involvement with a frenzy of activity at home, including extraordinary efforts to spend more time with children. According to Hochschild (1989), supermoms develop a conception of themselves as being "on-the-go, organized, competent," and perceive themselves as women without need for rest or time for themselves (p. 195). Over time, however, this strategy may be seen as ineffective by the women themselves (Beutell & Greenhaus, 1982), and may ultimately detract from successful careers and satisfying marriages.

Family experiences can also influence career outcomes through their effects on family outcomes. Symptoms such as irritability, anxiety, depression, and fatigue that are produced by family role overload (Pearlin, 1975) may intrude into the job domain (Greenhaus & Parasuraman, 1986), and inhibit a woman manager's involvement, performance, or success (Holmstrom, 1972; Hunt & Hunt, 1982; for a more detailed discussion of stress experienced by managerial women, see Chapter 5 in this volume by Offermann & Armitage).

Husbands' attitudes and behavior can have substantial effects—positive and negative—on the ways in which their wives balance career and family activities. Not only may women seek their husbands' approval in selecting managerial positions (Taylor & Spencer, 1988), but their career involvement can be reduced in response to their husbands' career needs (Brett & Yogev, 1988) and husbands' perception of their wives' failure to fulfill the maternal role (Chassin, Zeiss, Cooper, & Reaven, 1985). Moreover, ambivalent or hostile feelings on the part of the husband (Campbell, 1986) can affect a woman's job involvement and career success. For example, there is evidence that some women avoid family tension and competitive feelings in their husbands by moving to lower-status jobs (Hiller & Philliber, 1982) or by making compromises that limit their career success (Campbell, 1986; Gutek et al., 1988; Hochschild, 1989; Sekaran, 1986).

On the other hand, husbands may be supportive in a number of respects. They can restructure their own jobs to participate more extensively in family activities, thereby reducing their expectations regarding their wives' family involvement. Although this form of support is not unheard of, Brett and Yogev (1988) found that men were less likely to restructure their jobs than women, and that husbands of managers and professionals were particularly unlikely to restructure their jobs. Second, husbands can provide other forms of instrumental support (Vanfossen, 1981), such as sharing the work load at home (Baron, 1987; Hochschild, 1989), hiring outside services, and participating in a commuter marriage (Douvan & Pleck, 1978). Third, husbands can be supportive by encouraging their wives to pursue their career needs and by embracing the success that their wives achieve. Despite initial acceptance of the notion of an egalitarian marriage, however, some couples find it difficult to sustain such a relationship (Campbell, 1986). The erosion of egalitarian ideals over time arises from husbands' resentment of their wives career commitment and success, which threatens their happiness by taking their wives' attention away from them. The maintenance of egalitarian relationships is also jeopardized by husbands' regression to unconsciously held traditional expectations and the lack of peer and societal support for men who are involved with their wives and children (Campbell, 1986; Wilk, 1986).

In summary, extensive involvements in family activities can have a debilitating effect on women managers' career achievements. A woman's family situation can (a) produce career-family time conflicts that are resolved through a reduced level of career involvement, (b) produce symptoms of strain that intrude into the job domain, (c) reinforce organizational stereotypes that limit women's opportunities for development and advancement, and (d) provoke husbands' feelings of competition or jealousy to which women may respond by curtailing their career involvement and success.

The Impact of Career
Experiences on the Family Domain

Just as family experiences can influence the course of a woman manager's career, so can her career experiences affect the nature of her family and personal life. As noted earlier in this chapter, women managers are less likely to be married and are more likely to be childless than their male counterparts. These findings suggest that women who are strongly committed to their managerial careers have chosen not to marry or, in the event of marriage, not to have children.

Another significant factor related to the lower marriage rates found among managerial women is the propensity of professional and managerial women to marry men with equal or higher educational and occupational achievements (Howard & Bray, 1988), a group that is in short supply. The tendency of high status women to marry later or not at all also has been ascribed to their own preference for avoiding traditional dependent relationships (Howard & Bray, 1988), the preference of potential husbands for nonthreatening wives (Mueller & Campbell, 1977; Preston & Richards, 1975), and the sheer difficulty of establishing intimate relationships while pursuing a time-consuming and exhausting career (Morrison et al., 1987).

In some cases, career-oriented women anticipate the time conflicts that they would experience between their career roles and their spouse or parent roles and choose to avoid such conflicts by minimizing their family involvements (Marshall, 1984). This is particularly true of older women managers, who tend to view marriage and employment as mutually exclusive. Devanna (1987) reported that 63% of a sample of women executives said that they gave up their marriages, family plans, and social relationships to be successful. Such sacrifices, though voluntarily made, may nevertheless be deeply painful. To quote a senior woman executive on the personal price she had paid for success, "I would never want my mother to know how much it hurts me to be childless" (cited in Fierman, 1990).

Not all women managers choose to eschew marriage and family life. The arrival of children, however, compounds the problems of career-family conflicts. Given their desire to spend some time with their children during infancy, the typically short maternity leaves and the limited availability of flexible work schedules sometimes act as a catalyst for women extending their temporary leaves permanently (Hardesty & Jacobs, 1986). There is also evidence that some women who are frustrated or stalled in their careers display an interest in having children (Gerson, 1986; Hardesty & Jacobs, 1986; Morrison et al., 1987). These findings imply that children are thought to be an interference when the woman is actively pursuing career advancement and that women, like men (Bray, Campbell, & Grant, 1974), may turn more toward their families when their careers no longer provide substantial opportunities for satisfaction or success. Having children also becomes a socially acceptable and possibly face-saving way for some women to deal with hitting the limits of opportunity within the corporate setting and/or the limited satisfactions derived from corporate life (Hardesty & Jacobs, 1986).

It seems that women managers' career experiences are more likely to strain their marriages when they pose a threat to their husbands. For example, wives who are employed in nontraditional jobs, or who achieve higher occupational status and higher or equivalent salaries than their husbands, tend to experience increased marital instability and divorce (Fendrich, 1984; Hiller & Philliber, 1982; Philliber & Hiller, 1983). This finding is consistent with the negative relationship observed between wives' income and husbands' marital satisfaction (Simpson & England, 1981). Other research, however, suggests that it is the hours worked by the woman, not her earnings, that have a greater impact on marital dissolution, especially in middle-class families where the husband disapproves of his wife's employment (Spitze & Smith, 1985). In a similar vein, Garland (1972) reported that wives' occupational status did not threaten their husbands as long as the wives accorded priority to family over career and did not earn more than their husbands. Wilk (1986) notes that it is not the professional status or income per se of the woman manager that seems to be the critical factor but the underlying meaning and value attributed by both partners to her career. Thus the research seems to suggest that the marital stability and happiness of women managers are strongly affected by husbands' reactions to their wives' employment, status, success, and earnings.

In addition to their effects on marital relationships, women managers' career experiences can influence other facets of their personal lives. Because of role overload, women managers have been found to have difficulties "unwinding" after leaving their place of employment (Frankenhaeuser et al., 1989; Marshall, 1984) and can experience extensive stress and conflict (Davidson & Cooper, 1987), especially if they hold jobs that are highly complex and demanding (Greenhaus et al., 1989; see also Chapter 5 in this volume by Offermann & Armitage).

In short, many women in managerial roles may pay an emotional price for success. Boardman, Harrington, and Horowitz (1989) found that 80% of the successful professional middle-aged women they studied incurred significant costs in terms of family and intimate relationships, leisure time, and health. The most frequently mentioned personal sacrifices by the women executives interviewed by Morrison et al. (1987) were personal free time and time with friends as well as nurturing friendships. A majority of the women managers and professionals in Hochschild's (1989) study reported that they cut back on their personal needs and gave up such activities as reading, watching television, exercise, visits with friends, and time alone. Apparently, giving up personal leisure time is pervasive among employed women, especially those with children (Hochschild, 1989; "Women's Gains on the Job," 1989).

Despite the potential for impairment in marital and social relationships, women managers' career experiences also can have a positive effect on their family and personal lives. Women's employment can enhance their self-esteem and emotional well-being (Barnett & Baruch, 1985; Baruch & Barnett, 1986), especially if they are employed out of choice (Ross et al., 1983) and hold jobs that are sufficiently challenging and interesting (Valdez & Gutek, 1987). Moreover, women who hold managerial jobs not only contribute to the financial well-being of the family but also have more power and influence within the family (Bahr,

1974; Sekaran, 1986) and can be more interesting and compatible spouses (Marshall, 1984). Certainly, many husbands provide enthusiastic support to their wives and lead enriched lives in the process (Baron, 1987; Hochschild, 1989; Houseknecht & Macke, 1981; Marshall, 1984).

Finally, women's employment can have beneficial effects on their children's development. Although nearly a third of the women and men employed full time who participated in the *New York Times* poll think that children suffer the most when a woman tries to combine a career with marriage and children ("Women's Gains on the Job," 1989), an earlier *Fortune* study of employed mothers and fathers (Chapman, 1987) indicated that 86% of the women and 78% of the men thought that the children of employed parents benefit from having parents who can serve as interesting role models. Moreover, boys and girls reared in two-career families tend to hold egalitarian sex-role attitudes (Stephan & Corder, 1985) and are likely to be independent (Knaub, 1986; Symons, 1984). Although children of employed mothers may receive somewhat less time or attention on occasion (Chapman, 1987; Knaub, 1986), the quality of parent-child relations depends more on employed mothers' role satisfaction and job-related attitudes than on the time spent with children (Piotrkowski & Katz, 1983).

In summary, women managers' involvement in the career domain can substantially affect their family experiences and outcomes. Women's level of involvement in their careers can affect their personal well-being, can influence their decisions regarding marriage and parenthood, and can affect the quality of their family relationships.

THEORETICAL PERSPECTIVES ON LIFE-STYLE CHOICES

The findings reviewed in the previous section indicate that the life-styles of women managers are shaped by a complex set of factors and suggest a number of theoretical perspectives that can explain the selection and consequences of alternative life-styles. Based on role theory (Goode, 1960), much of the research in this area implicitly or explicitly takes a role conflict and/or role overload perspective. This perspective is based on the premise that individuals have limited resources in terms of time and physical, mental, and emotional energy (Marks, 1977) and that the demands and competing requirements of multiple roles (e.g., career and family) create interrole conflict and role overload and attendant role strain on individuals. An alternative perspective to the scarcity notion is energy expansion (Marks, 1977) that accompanies role accumulation (Sieber, 1974). According to Sieber (1974) and Marks (1977), multiple roles can be energizing and can result in positive outcomes for individuals through role privileges, resources for status enhancement and role performance, personal enrichment, and buffers against failure in any one role. In other words, multiple involvements can provide a variety of sources of stimulation, gratification, and social validation.

Although the decision of women managers to remain single supports a role conflict perspective, and the decision of married women managers to have children supports a role accumulation perspective (Valdez & Gutek, 1987), a third relevant perspective is based on the proposition that well-being is more a function of role quality than the number of roles occupied (Baruch & Barnett, 1987). According to this view, the quality of women's experiences as paid workers, wives, and mothers is a better predictor of self-esteem and emotional well-being than role occupancy per se (Baruch & Barnett, 1987).

Two additional concepts relevant to explaining alternative life-styles are role salience and gender role ideology. According to Greenhaus and Beutell (1985), career-family conflict is more likely to occur when both career and family have high salience for the individual. Thus women who place substantially greater emphasis on their career relative to family (or vice versa) may avoid extensive career-family conflict because there are not equally strong role pressures arising from the career and family domains. In addition, women's gender role ideology can influence their self-role expectations (traditionally oriented women may hold high expectations for themselves as wives and mothers) and the salience of different life roles (traditionally oriented women may place substantially greater emphasis on family over career). Because of its effects on self-role expectations and role salience, a woman's gender role ideology can also influence her reactions and adjustments to the role expectations of key members of her role set, especially her spouse (Hochschild, 1989).

The perspectives described above are evident in varying degrees in the life-style choices and subsequent modifications made to them by women managers. Based on the empirical findings reviewed in the previous sections and the qualitative data provided in some studies, it appears that women managers may be grouped into three life-style orientations.

The career-primary orientation (Schwartz, 1989) includes women who are strongly career committed, have accorded top priority to achieving success in their careers (Marshall, 1984; Morrison et al.,

1987), and have chosen to subordinate their personal and social lives (Devanna, 1987). Illustrative of the latter is a comment by a woman executive interviewed by Marshall (1984, p. 179): "If you want to succeed you have to be prepared to sacrifice quite a few of the normal things, but then all life is trade-offs isn't it?" The career-primary life orientation is analogous to Taylor and Spencer's (1988) career-accommodated life orientation in which career comes first and family comes second. While single, divorced, and married but child-free women are prominently represented in this group (Devanna, 1987; Marshall, 1984; Strober, 1982), it also includes women who are married and have children (Morrison et al., 1987), most of whom have maintained career continuity with only minimal interruptions for childbirth (Hellwig, 1985). In fact, the career success of these women has been attributed to the decision to "put their career first, and squeeze in whatever else in life they can around it" (Morrison et al., 1987, p. 114). It is important to note that, in the case of married career-primary women, their husbands' attitudes toward their careers and the support provided by them is an important enabling factor in their success (Marshall, 1984). Notwithstanding this success, however, Morrison et al. (1987) predict that a majority of these women executives will opt out and seek alternative life-styles.

The second life-style orientation is the family-primary orientation, which includes women who are career involved but place primary emphasis on family and pursue their careers within the constraints of family demands and obligations (Marshall, 1984). This group exemplifies Taylor and Spencer's (1988) family-accommodated life orientation (family first, career second). This configuration of priorities may reflect a woman's own values and interests and is reflected in the statement: "I don't want to be a person who does nothing but work. I've got too many interests, obligations and satisfactions outside" (Marshall, 1984, p. 180). It may also reflect a woman's accommodation to her husband's preferences and needs, however (Brett & Yogev, 1988; Chassin et al., 1985). This group perhaps represents the majority of married women in two-career relationships, whose career involvement is bounded by the need not to inconvenience the family (Hunt & Hunt, 1982).

The third life-style orientation, described as career *and* family, includes women who place equal emphasis on career and family and expect to successfully combine a rapidly advancing career with extensive involvement in marriage and parenthood. This type of life-style is likely to produce extensive role conflict and stress. There is some evidence that the quality of their careers and personal life experiences have prompted some women with this life-style orientation to reassess their values and priorities (Gallese, 1985). In some cases, the reassessment has been motivated by the impediments to upward mobility encountered by them; in others, reassessment resulted from the sheer difficulty of juggling the demands of both career and family (Hardesty & Jacobs, 1986; Morrison et al., 1987). The high standards of performance they set for themselves in their major life roles further exacerbate the conflicts experienced (Marshall, 1984). Recognition of the personal costs incurred (Morrison et al., 1987), and concerns about having children and maintaining their identity as women (Marshall, 1984) also played a role for them in reconsidering their options.

The above categorization of women's life-style orientations as career primary, family primary, and career and family does not imply that women's life orientations remain unchanged over time. It appears reasonable to expect that movement among the three life-style orientations occurs over the course of women's careers and life stages. For example, a woman who starts out with a career-primary orientation in her early career or when she is single may shift to a career and family orientation following marriage or parenthood. Alternatively, a woman who initially places equal emphasis on career and family may adopt a family-primary orientation following parenthood and early childhood years but move back to career and family orientation when the children are older. It is also possible that a woman with a career and family orientation may move toward a career-primary orientation following divorce or death of a spouse.

Because there have been few longitudinal studies of women's careers, empirical evidence concerning changes in women's life-style orientations is sparse. There are some reports that suggest that the dilemmas and ambivalence felt by women with a career and family orientation have been resolved in diverse ways. Some have scaled down their career commitment and made career shifts or interruptions to accommodate the family (Basler, 1986; Morrison et al., 1987). Others have quit or plan to leave the corporate world, choosing self-employment as a career option that allows greater autonomy, flexibility, and self-expression (Chapman, 1987; Gallese, 1985; Morrison et al., 1987). It is possible that a small number of women have reacted to the conflict by reducing their family involvements through divorce, extensive use of paid child care and home care help, or through psychological withdrawal from the family unit.

A woman manager's life-style orientation is not only subject to change over time, but it may also be influenced by her cultural and ethnic background. Research suggests that race and gender interact to influence career experiences (Thomas & Alderfer, 1989). Bell's (1986) bicultural perspective illustrates the stress experienced by minority women who function in two worlds: the majority-dominated employment culture and the minority-dominated community culture. Because women of color may be subject to different experiences than white women in their careers (Fernandez, 1981) and in their family lives (Clay, 1975; Norton & Glick, 1976), it is possible that the interdependencies between career and family domains are shaped by the combination of women's ethnicity and societal attitudes. (The impact of ethnicity on women managers' careers and life experiences is discussed further in the chapter by Bell, Denton, and Nkomo in this book.)

CONCLUSIONS

To sum up, women managers do not represent a homogeneous group in terms of their life-styles. In choosing an acceptable life-style, women face a number of dilemmas, and their choices are governed significantly by the complex linkages that exist between their career and family roles. These linkages both affect and are affected by women's (and men's) gender role ideology, the salience of career and family roles, the quality of experiences within these roles, the responsiveness of organizations to the family needs of women (and men), and the broader sociocultural milieu.

This review has deliberately emphasized descriptive rather than prescriptive analyses. Our goal was to understand women managers' life-style choices and dilemmas through an examination of the interdependence of their career and family involvements. One can view this interdependence in two ways. On the one hand, it places burdens on women by forcing them to make difficult, often irreversible choices and by limiting their career (or family) accomplishments and satisfactions. On the other hand, the interdependence of career and family can be viewed as a natural reflection of the human dilemma of seeking meaning and balance in life. It is evident, however, that neither the career systems of organizations nor career theories have fully recognized the extensiveness of these interdependencies in the case of women or their implications for the pattern, continuity, and progress of women's careers.

What is unfortunate is not that women's career and family involvements are interdependent and sometimes limiting. Rather, it is the gender asymmetries (Crosby, 1987) in the interdependence that are both troublesome and inequitable. Women have had to base their life-style decisions on factors that men have generally not had to consider, and consequently their career accomplishments have been limited by factors that have not impeded men's accomplishments. Although the recommendations for innovative changes in corporate policies (Galinsky, 1985) to accommodate the family roles of employees are appropriate, and partially address the problems encountered by women in combining a career and a family life, they appear to implicitly sanction the gender inequalities in family relationships described in the previous section. Concomitant changes are needed in the structure of marital relationships if women are to participate as truly equal partners in pursuing enriched lives in both the career and the family domains. Such changes would recognize and support the need for balance in the lives of both men and women.

The life-style choices and dilemmas reported in this chapter do not inherently belong to women, although they have fallen unfairly on their shoulders. It is hoped that these interdependencies will be shared by future generations of women and men managers whose career and life-style decisions will be based on personal and family preferences rather than on gender-based stereotypes. It is also hoped that the ideas expressed in this chapter will stimulate empirical research that sheds additional light on the complex and dynamic factors that influence the life-styles of women managers and lead to the reformulation of career models and theories that acknowledge and incorporate variables that uniquely shape the career experiences of women.

REFERENCES

Bahr, S. J. (1974). Effects on power and division of labor in the family. In L. W. Hoffman & F. I. Nye (Eds.), *Working mothers.* San Francisco: Jossey-Bass.

Bailyn, L. (1970). Career and family orientations of husbands and wives in relation to marital happiness. *Human Relations, 23,* 97-113.

Barnett, R. C., & Baruch, G. K. (1985). Women's involvement in multiple roles and psychological distress. *Journal of Personality and Social Psychology, 49,* 135-145.

Baron, A. S. (1987). Working partners: Career-committed mothers and their husbands. *Business Horizons, 30*(5), 45-50.

Baruch, G. K., & Barnett, R. C. (1986). Role quality, multiple role involvement, and psychological well-being in midlife women. *Journal of Personality and Social Psychology, 51,* 578-585.

Baruch, G. K., & Barnett, R. C. (1987). Role quality and psychological well-being. In F. J. Crosby (Ed.), *Spouse, parent, worker: On gender and multiple roles* (pp. 63-73). New Haven, CT: Yale University Press.

Basler, B. (1986, December 7). Putting a career on hold. *The New York Times*, pp. 152-153, 158.

Bell, E. L. (1986). *The power within: Bicultural life structures and stress among black women.* Unpublished doctoral dissertation, Case Western Reserve University, Cleveland, OH.

Bernardo, D. H., Shehan, C. L., & Leslie, G. R. (1987). A residue of tradition: Jobs, careers, and spouses' time in housework. *Journal of Marriage and the Family, 49,* 381-390.

Beutell, N. J., & Greenhaus, J. H. (1982). Interrole conflict among married women: The influences of husband and wife characteristics on conflict and coping behavior. *Journal of Vocational Behavior, 21,* 99-110.

Bianchi, S. A. (1984). Putting off children. *American Demographics, 6*(9), 30-33, 45.

Boardman, S. K., Harrington, C. C., & Horowitz, S. V. (1989). Successful women: A psychological investigation of family class and educational origins. In B. A. Gutek & L. Larwood (Eds.), *Women's career development* (pp. 66-85). Newbury Park, CA: Sage.

Bourne, P. G., & Wikler, N. J. (1982). Commitment and cultural mandate: Women in medicine. In R. Kahn-Hunt, A. K. Daniels, & R. Colvard (Eds.), *Women in work* (pp. 111-122). New York: Oxford University Press.

Bray, D. W., Campbell, R. J., & Grant, D. L. (1974). *Formative years in business.* New York: John Wiley.

Brett, J., & Yogev, S. (1988). Restructuring work for family: How dual-earner couples with children manage. *Journal of Social Behavior and Personality, 3*(4), 159-174.

Campbell, B. M. (1986). *Successful women, angry men.* New York: Random House.

Chapman, F. S. (1987, February 16). Executive guilt: Who's taking care of the children? *Fortune,* pp. 30-37.

Chassin, L., Zeiss, A., Cooper, K., & Reaven, J. (1985). Role perceptions, self-role congruence and marital satisfaction in dual worker couples with pre-school children. *Social Psychology Quarterly, 48*(4), 301-311.

Clay, W. L. (1975). The socioeconomic status of blacks. *Ebony, 29,* 40-44.

Companies start to meet executive women halfway. (1983, October 17). *Business Week,* pp. 191-195.

Crosby, F. J. (1987). Preface. In F. J. Crosby (Ed.), *Spouse, parent, worker: Gender and multiple roles* (pp. ix-xiv). New Haven, CT: Yale University Press.

Davidson, M. J., & Cooper, C. L. (1984). Occupational stress in female managers: A comparative study. *Journal of Management Studies, 21*(2), 185-205.

Davidson, M. J., & Cooper, C. L. (1987). Female managers in Britain: A comparative perspective. *Human Resource Management, 26,* 217-242.

Devanna, M. A. (1987). Women in management: Progress and promise. *Human Resource Management, 26,* 469-481.

Dipboye, R. L. (1987). Problems and progress of women in management. In K. S. Koziara, M. S. Moskow, & L. D. Tanner (Eds.), *Working women: Past, present, and future* (pp. 118-153). Washington, DC: BNA Books.

Douvan, E., & Pleck, J. (1978). Separation and support. In R. Rapoport & R. N. Rapoport (Eds.), *Working couples.* London: Routledge & Kegan Paul.

Fagenson, E. A. (1990). At the heart of women in management research: Theoretical and methodological approaches and their biases. *Journal of Business Ethics, 9,* 267-274.

Fendrich, M. (1984). Wives' employment and husbands' distress: A meta-analysis and a replication. *Journal of Marriage and the Family, 45,* 871-879.

Fernandez, J. P. (1981). *Racism and sexism in corporate life: Changing values in American business.* Lexington, MA: Lexington.

Fierman, J. (1990, July 30). Why women still don't hit the top. *Fortune,* pp. 40-42, 46, 50, 54, 58, 62.

Firestone, J., & Shelton, B. A. (1988). An estimation of the effects of women's work on available leisure time. *Journal of Family Issues, 9*(4), 478-495.

Frankenhaeuser, M., Lundberg, U., Frederikson, M., Melin, B., Malawian, M., Myrsten, A. L., Hedman, M., Bergman-Losman, B., & Wallin, L. (1989). Stress on and off the job as related to sex and occupational status in white collar workers. *Journal of Organizational Behavior, 10,* 321-346.

Galinsky, E. (1985). Family life and corporate policies. In T. B. Brazelton & M. Yogman (Eds.), *In support of families.* Boston: Harvard University Press.

Gallese, L. R. (1985). *Women like us: What is happening to the women of the Harvard Business School, class of 75—The women who had the first chance to make it to the top?* New York: William Morrow.

Garland, T. N. (1972). The better half? The male in the dual profession family. In C. Safilios-Rothchild (Ed.), *Toward a sociology of women.* Lexington, MA: Xerox.

Gerson, K. (1986). Briefcase, baby or both? *Psychology Today, 20*(11), 30-36.

Gerstel, N., & Gross, H. (1984). *Commuter marriage: A study of work and family.* New York: Guilford.

Goode, W. J. (1960). A theory of role strain. *American Sociological Review, 25,* 483-496.

Greenhaus, J. H., & Beutell, N. J. (1985). Sources of conflict between work and family roles. *Academy of Management Review, 10,* 76-88.

Greenhaus, J. H., & Parasuraman, S. (1986). A work-nonwork interactive perspective of stress and its consequences. *Journal of Organizational Behavior Management, 8*(2), 37-60.

Greenhaus, J. H., Parasuraman, S., Granrose, C. S., Rabinowitz, S., & Beutell, N. J. (1989). Sources of work-family conflict among two-career couples. *Journal of Vocational Behavior, 34,* 133-153.

Greenhaus, J. H., Parasuraman, S., & Wormley, W. M. (1990). Effects of race on organizational experiences, job performance evaluations, and career outcomes. *Academy of Management Journal, 33,* 64-86.

Gutek, B. A., Repetti, R. L., & Silver, D. L. (1988). Nonwork roles and stress at work. In C. L. Cooper & R. Payne (Eds.), *Causes, coping, and consequences of stress at work* (pp. 141-174). New York: John Wiley.

Hardesty, S., & Jacobs, N. (1986). *Success and betrayal.* New York: Franklin Watts.

Harlan, A., & Weiss, C. A. (1982). Sex differences in factors affecting managerial career advancement. In P. A. Wallace (Ed.), *Women in the workplace* (pp. 59-100). Boston: Auburn House.

Hellwig, B. (1985, April). The breakthrough generation: 73 women ready to run corporate America. *Working Women,* pp. 98-101, 146-148, 150.

Hennig, M., & Jardim, A. (1977). *The managerial woman.* New York: Anchor/Doubleday.

Hiller, D. V., & Philliber, W. W. (1982). Predicting marital and career success among dual worker couples. *Journal of Marriage and the Family, 44,* 53-62.

Hochschild, A. (1989). *The second shift.* New York: Viking.

Holahan, C. K., & Gilbert, L. A. (1979). Conflict between major life roles: Women and men in dual career couples. *Human Relations, 32,* 451-467.

Holmstrom, L. (1972). *The two-career family.* Cambridge, MA: Schenkman.

Houseknecht, S. K., & Macke, A. S. (1981). Combining marriage and career: The marital adjustment of professional women. *Journal of Marriage and the Family, 45*, 877-884.

Howard, A., & Bray, D. W. (1988). *Managerial lives in transition.* New York: Guilford.

Hunt, J. G., & Hunt, L. L. (1982). Dual-career families: Vanguard of the future or residue of the past. In J. Aldous (Ed.), *Two paychecks: Life in dual-earner families* (pp. 41-59). Beverly Hills, CA: Sage.

Kanter, R. M. (1977). *Men and women of the corporation.* New York: Basic Books.

Kingston, P. W., & Nock, S. L. (1985). Consequences of the family work day. *Journal of Marriage and the Family, 47*, 619-630.

Knaub, P. K. (1986). Growing up in a dual career family: The children's perceptions. *Human Relations, 35*, 431-437.

Langer, J. (1985). The new mature mothers. *American Demographics, 7*(7), 29-31, 50.

Leo, J. (1982, January 25). Marital tales of two cities. *Time*, pp. 83-84.

Lewis, S. N. C., & Cooper, C. L. (1988). Stress in dual-career families. In B. A. Gutek, A. H. Stromberg, & L. Larwood (Eds.), *Women and work: An annual review* (pp. 139-168). Newbury Park, CA: Sage.

Lorence, J. (1987). A test of "gender" and "job" models of sex differences in job involvement. *Social Forces, 66*, 121-143.

Macklin, E. D. (1987). Nontraditional family forms. In M. B. Sussman & S. K. Steinmetz (Eds.), *Handbook of marriage and the family* (pp. 317-353). New York: Plenum.

Markham, W. T. (1987). Sex, relocation, and occupational advancement. In A. H. Stromberg, L. Larwood, & B. A. Gutek (Eds.), *Women and work: An annual review* (Vol. 2, pp. 207-231). Newbury Park, CA: Sage.

Marks, S. R. (1977). Multiple roles and role strain: Some notes on human energy, time and commitment. *American Sociological Review, 42*, 921-936.

Marshall, J. (1984). *Women managers: Travellers in a male world.* Chichester, U.K.: John Wiley.

Moen, P., & Smith, K. R. (1986). Women at work: Commitment and behavior over the life course. *Sociological Forum, 1*, 450-475.

Morrison, A. M., & Von Glinow, M. A. (1990). Women and minorities in management. *American Psychologist, 45*, 200-222.

Morrison, A. M., White, R. P., Van Velsor, E. & the Center for Creative Leadership (1987). *Breaking the glass ceiling: Can women reach the top of America's largest corporations?* Reading, MA: Addison-Wesley.

Moses, J. L., & Boehm, V. R. (1975). Relationship of assessment center performance to management progress of women. *Journal of Applied Psychology, 60*, 527-529.

Mueller, C. W., & Campbell, B. G. (1977). Female occupational achievement and marital status: A research note. *Journal of Marriage and the Family, 39*, 587-593.

Norton, A. J., & Glick, P. C. (1976). Marital instability: Past, present, and future. *Journal of Social Issues, 32*, 5-19.

Olson, J. E., & Frieze, I. H. (1987). Income determinants for women in business. In A. H. Stromberg, L. Larwood, & B. A. Gutek (Eds.), *Women and work: An annual review* (Vol. 2, pp. 173-206). Newbury Park, CA: Sage.

Pearlin, L. I. (1975). Sex roles and depression. In N. Dalen & H. Ginsberg (Eds.), *Life span developmental psychology.* New York: Academic Press.

Philliber, W. W., & Hiller, D. V. (1983). Relative occupational attainment of spouses and later changes in marriage and wife's work experience. *Journal of Marriage and the Family, 45*, 161-170.

Piotrkowski, C. S., & Katz, M. H. (1983). Work experience and family relations among working class and lower middle-class families. In H. Z. Lopata & J. H. Pleck (Eds.), *Research in the interweave of social roles: Vol. 3. Families and jobs.* Greenwich, CT: JAI.

Piotrkowski, C. S., & Repetti, R. L. (1984). Dual-earner families. *Marriage and Family Review, 7*(3/4), 99-124.

Pittman, J. F., & Orthner, D. K. (1988). Gender differences in the prediction of job commitment. *Journal of Social Behavior and Personality, 2,* 227-228.

Pleck, J. H., Staines, G. L., & Lang, L. L. (1980). Conflicts between work and family life. *Monthly Labor Review, 103*(3), 29-32.

Powell, G. N. (1988). *Women and men in management.* Newbury Park, CA: Sage.

Powell, G. N., Pozner, B. Z., & Schmidt, W. H. (1984). Sex effects on managerial value systems. *Human Relations, 37,* 909-921.

Preston, S. H., & Richards, A. T. (1975). The influence of women's work opportunities on marriage rates. *Demography, 12,* 209-222.

Robinson, J. P. (1988). Who's doing the housework? *American Demographics, 10*(12), 24-28, 63.

Rosen, B., & Jerdee, T. (1973). Sex stereotyping in the executive suite. *Harvard Business Review, 52*(2), 55-58.

Ross, C. E., Mirowsky, J., & Huber, J. (1983). Dividing work, sharing work, and in-between: Marriage patterns and depression. *American Sociological Review, 48,* 809-823.

Schneer, J. A., & Reitman, F. (1990). Effects of employment gaps on the careers of M.B.A.'s: More damaging for men than for women? *Academy of Management Journal, 33,* 391-406.

Schwartz, F. N. (1989). Management women and the facts of life. *Harvard Business Review, 67*(1), 65-76.

Sekaran, U. (1986). *Dual-career families: Contemporary organizational and counseling issues.* San Francisco: Jossey-Bass.

Shaw, S. (1985). Gender and leisure: Inequality in the distribution of leisure time. *Journal of Leisure Research, 17*(4), 266-282.

Sieber, S. D. (1974). Toward a theory of role accumulation. *American Sociological Review, 39,* 567-578.

Simpson, I. H., & England, P. (1981). Conjugal work roles and marital solidarity. *Journal of Family Issues, 2* 180-204.

Spitze, G., & Smith, S. J. (1985). Women's employment, time expenditure, and divorce. *Journal of Family Issues, 6*(3), 307-329.

Stephan, C. W., & Corder, J. (1985). The effects of dual-career families on adolescents' sex-role attitudes, work and family plans, and choices of important others. *Journal of Marriage and the Family, 47,* 921-929.

Strober, M. H. (1982). The MBA: Same passport to success for women and men? In P. A. Wallace (Ed.), *Women in the workplace* (pp. 25-44). Boston: Auburn House.

Symons, G. L. (1984). Career lives of women in France and Canada: The case of managerial women. *Work and Occupations, 11,* 331-352.

Taylor, A., III. (1986). Why women managers are bailing out. *Fortune, 114*(6), 16-23.

Taylor, J. C., & Spencer, B. A. (1988). Lifestyle patterns of university women: Implications for family/career decision modeling. *Journal of Social Behavior and Personality, 3*(4), 265-276.

Thomas, D. A., & Alderfer, C. P. (1989). The influence of race on career dynamics: Theory and research on minority career experiences. In M. B. Arthur, D. T. Hall, & B. S. Lawrence (Eds.), *Handbook of career theory* (pp. 133-158). New York: Cambridge University Press.

Tsui, A. S., & Gutek, B. A. (1984). A role set analysis of gender differences in performance, affective relationships, and career success of industrial middle managers. *Academy of Management Journal, 27,* 619-635.

U.S. Bureau of the Census. (1984). Male-female differences in work experiences, occupation and earnings: 1984. In *Current population reports* (Household Economic Studies, Series P-70, No. 10). Washington, DC: Government Printing Office.

U.S. Bureau of the Census. (1987a). *Money income of households, families and persons in the United States: 1987* (Series P-60, No. 162). Washington, DC: Government Printing Office.

U.S. Bureau of the Census. (1987b). Household and family characteristics: March 1987. In *Current population reports* (Population Characteristics, Series P-20, No. 424). Washington, DC: Government Printing Office.

U.S. Bureau of Labor Statistics. (1989). *Labor force statistics derived from the current population survey.* Washington, DC: Government Printing Office.

Valdez, R. L., & Gutek, B. A. (1987). Family roles: A help or a hindrance for working women? In B. A. Gutek & L. Larwood (Eds.), *Women's career development* (pp. 157-169). Newbury Park, CA: Sage.

Vanfossen, B. E. (1981). Sex differences in the mental health effects of spouse support and equity. *Journal of Health and Social Behavior, 22,* 130-143.

Wilk, C. A. (1986). *Career women and childbearing.* New York: Van Nostrand Reinhold.

Women's gains on the job: Not without a heavy toll. (1989, August 21). *The New York Times,* pp. A13-A14 ff.

Yogev, S. (1981). Do professional women have egalitarian marital relationships? *Journal of Marriage and the Family, 43,* 865-871.

Commentary

MARY ANNE DEVANNA

The previous four chapters provided an interesting perspective on the evolution of the literature focused on the concerns of women in management. In the 1960s and 1970s, the central issue of concern in the managerial workplace was that of equity—an attempt to explain women's ability to gain access to and to succeed in male-dominated professions. In the 1980s, we have seen a substantial shift to the problems women face as they try to balance their personal and professional lives.

In the area of discrimination, the popular press pushes the notion that one of the few male preserves left is the executive suite, which is separated by the proverbial "glass ceiling" from an organization that otherwise could be classified as a meritocracy. In "Women of Color in Management: Toward an Inclusive Analysis," Bell, Denton, and Nkomo reminded us of how far we still have to go to ensure equal treatment at all levels of the organization for those who are different than the majority.

The authors suggested that the racist and sexist views of society at large are replicated in organizations and produce the differential treatment accorded women and members of minority groups. They suggested different ways to enrich our understanding of the issues facing not just the majority women, who happen to be white, but also the issues that confront women of color. The contribution is important. We must understand the phenomenon if we are to deal with it.

The emphasis on differences instead of similarities, however, contains its own set of issues. It raises the specter that we will increase our

212

understanding of why groups have problems succeeding in organizations but it will also provide a rationale that justifies their slow progress. It is useful to remember that there are usually greater differences within groups than there are between groups and that research studies that include men in their samples and that compare the relative progress of individuals whose preparation and performance are the same, but who can be differentiated by gender, race, or ethnicity from the dominant group, go beyond description to provide a basis for action. This happens because such studies focus attention on the shortcomings of organizations and not on groups of individuals trying to succeed in organizations.

In "Personal Portrait: The Life-Style of the Woman Manager," Parasuraman and Greenhaus talked about the trade-offs women make to achieve managerial success. Here we have an acknowledgment that differences within the group are significant. What is useful to bear in mind is that men also are involved in trade-offs and that career-primary men frequently pay a price in terms of their relationships both with their wives and with their children. Indeed, in a *Fortune* article that focused on both men and women, more men than women reported that they had turned down a job and/or refused a geographic move because it was not in the best interests of their family.

The fact that society is more willing to accept the idea of a wife at home caring for house and family than it is to accept a husband in the same role results in more career-primary men who report being married with children than we find among career-primary women.

Thus society's values are played out in the organization. But we should not confuse the sacrifices demanded by organizations of those who aspire to reach the top with gender discrimination. The price being extracted in today's environment is significant for both men and women. Trade-offs happen because there are only 24 hours in a day. Workweeks that exceed 60 hours a week and that demand extensive travel make it very difficult to balance work and family life.

If we were not moved by the Parasuraman and Greenhaus chapter to look at the trade-offs that both organizations and their employees are being forced to make, we should have been moved from our inertia by reading "Stress and the Woman Manager: Sources, Health Outcomes, and Interventions" by Offermann and Armitage. The failure of the health community to recognize the changing demographic factors for those subjected to workplace stress puts a generation of women at risk. This area provides a fertile field for longitudinal, cross-cultural, crossgender study. We know that poor nations pay a price in terms of health and mortality rates for their children and their adults. We would benefit from knowing what price is being paid by different groups whose work fuels the corporate engine in successful, highly industrialized European countries and Japan as well as other countries. It may help us to make better judgments about the trade-offs between standard of living and quality of life.

In the chapter "Dangerous Liaisons? A Review of Current Issues Concerning Male and Female Romantic Relationships in the Workplace" by Mainiero, we considered a renewed interest in the thorny problem of romance in the office. Clearly, romance in the workplace is not a new issue. Our current preoccupation with the subject focuses on the increased probability that the liaison will involve two highly visible middle- to senior-level executives.

Mainiero focused on both the participant dynamics of those involved in the relationship and the reactions of coworkers to the romance. As might be expected, some of the personal outcomes are positive and some dysfunctional, and some organizational outcomes are neutral or positive while others have deleterious outcomes.

Clearly, large organizations that have the ability to use the talent of managers in relatively independent areas through internal movement have an advantage over those that can only use the talents of the couple in the same area. The greatest danger that emerges from the perspective of the organization is the perception of unfairness on the part of other employees. It is not only in hierarchical relationships that the possibility of favoritism arises. It also comes into play in internal customer-supplier relationships when one party has the ability to provide resources (information, material, or access to decision makers) to the other in a way that provides them with a competitive advantage over others or that violates the best interests of the company in terms of the way resources should be allocated. The fundamental issue is that we are not meant to be totally objective about those we love—we are supposed to support them.

These chapters taken together are reminders of how far we have come and how far we still have to go to create an organizational reality that is both fair and humane. Just as women in general have provided a litmus test to show just how good an organization is at promoting people based on their abilities and not their gender, women of color can help us to understand that the battle below the glass ceiling is far from over. In addition, they help us to gain a perspective that is not confounded by conflicts between career and family, with respect to the barriers that

ᴧose who are "different" than those in power still face. A society's
ᴩrogress ultimately depends on the ability of its organizations to use the
ᴨlents of all of its members. To the extent that they can only use those
f a dominant group, whether white men or Japanese men, their growth
ᴙill ultimately be constrained by their inability to manage diversity.
'he best of the nondominant group will flock to those organizations that
ᴨovide them the opportunity to excel, not merely to survive.

The chapters focusing on trade-offs forced us to look again at the way
ᴨ which organizations, and the social system in which they are embed-
ᴇd, are structured. Can we find a way to increase organizational
ffectiveness in a way that enhances the quality of our lives and not
ᴨerely our standard of living?

It is sometimes useful to remind ourselves of how far we have come
ᴐ that we may have the strength to continue the struggle. Women have
ᴦgnificantly changed their status and options in the United States. To
ᴨderstand just how much progress they have made, one need only
ᴨavel abroad and see the constraints facing women in many other parts
f the world. Future progress will be affected by our ability to formulate
ᴨew paradigm in organizations that redefines success from upward
ᴨobility to a competence-based sense of contribution. Organizations
ᴇed such a paradigm shift to gain the involvement of the many rather
ᴨan the few and thus to enhance their global competitive position. It is
ᴨce to know that the paradigm shift will also enhance the opportunities
f the many no longer at the expense of the few.

SECTION IV

Future Directions and Systemic Issues

8

Point-Counterpoint: Discrimination Against Women in Management— Going, Going, Gone or Going But Never Gone?

GREGORY B. NORTHCRAFT
BARBARA A. GUTEK

This chapter is unusual in that it uses a debate format. The two authors each take a side and make a case for that point of view, citing and reviewing literature supportive of that view. In this chapter, discrimination against women is defined as overt or covert differential treatment based on gender. In the first part of the chapter, Gregory Northcraft argues that discrimination will disappear. Then Barbara Gutek argues that discrimination is here to stay.

POINT: DISCRIMINATION AGAINST
WOMEN IN MANAGEMENT—GOING, GOING, GONE?

The 1980s were a time of unprecedented advances for women. Women were awarded Rhodes scholarships, long a fortress of all-male traditionalism. In another traditionally all-male bastion, girls were provided the opportunity to play Little League baseball side by side with their male counterparts. In

1984, Geraldine Ferraro became the first woman to be nominated to the most prestigious management team in the United States, and by 1989 women in 16 states were running for governor (Behrens, 1990).

In 1964, Title VII of the Civil Rights Act legally guaranteed women freedom from employment discrimination. Now, more than 25 years later, it is time to ask whether the intent of that legislation has been fulfilled for women in management. Statistically, of course, gender parity among the ranks of the corporate elite remains a long way off. In 1972, women accounted for 39% of the total work force in the United States and held only 20% of managerial jobs; by 1987, those figures had risen to 45% of the total work force and 38% of administrative and managerial jobs (Williams, 1988). Even now, however, women account for less than 2% of top executive positions (Williams, 1988)—perhaps as little as 0.5% (Fierman, 1990)—yet account for 42% of managers (U.S. Department of Labor, 1993).

There is an important time lag at work in these statistics. Even as women make progress in management, their lack of seniority will keep them from "catching up" in the corner offices and executive suites for some years to come. The average age of a *Fortune* 1,000 CEO is around 58 (Horton, 1987); even if absolute equity had been attained in the hiring of women in the 1970s, it would still be years from now before that equality would "trickle up" to the executive suites. The real question is this: Are the barriers that traditionally have barred women's progress in management disappearing? Two of these barriers will be discussed: perceptions of women as managers and evolving practices in the U.S. work force.

Stereotypes and Women in Management

The stereotype that men and women have different managerial styles and that the managerial style of males is better suited to the pursuit of corporate excellence, has been a troubling barrier to the advancement of women in management. Naturally, this stereotype need not be based in truth for it to be a barrier for women. If the people who do the hiring (whether men *or women*) have this view in their minds, it will (perhaps subconsciously) influence their evaluations of applicants' potential.

Are women stereotyped as inferior managers? It would seem so. A variety of research in the 1970s (e.g., Massengill & DiMarco, 1979; Powell & Butterfield, 1979; Schein, 1973, 1975) found that both men and women perceived successful managers to possess more character istics typically associated with males than characteristics typically associated with females. These results were still holding up well in the late 1980s: Women managers are perceived as less aggressive and independent than their male counterparts, though typically possessing better interpersonal skills (e.g., Brenner, Tomkiewicz, & Schein, 1989; Frank, 1988; Heilman, Block, Martell, & Simon, 1989). One version of this stereotype lays blame for these differences at the feet of childhood experiences and our culture's socialization processes. Women play cooperative games as children, while men learn to compete (Bardwick & Douvan, 1971). Consequently, women are seen to focus on collaboration and group goal attainment at the expense of personal achievement—an emphasis on vicarious achievement perfectly in keeping with the maternal child-rearing role (Schwartz, 1989).

In fact, researchers have found little to differentiate between the managerial or leadership styles of men and women (e.g., Donnell & Hall, 1980; Goktepe & Schneier, 1988). The larger issue, however, is the importance of perceived differences between male and female managerial style (whether real or imagined) to corporate placement decisions. Contingency theories of management (e.g., Fiedler, 1964) downplay the existence of a single effective management style and instead emphasize the importance of matching managerial competencies and situational demands. In the eyes of contingency theory, different is just different and not necessarily better. Even if female and male managers are perceived to have unique competencies, then some situations should favor each managerial style.

Furthermore, Williams (1988) notes that U.S. corporations in the 1980s were undergoing something of a "Darwinian struggle" to become more globally competitive. One facet of this struggle has been increasing acceptance of the human resources approach to management. The human resources approach emphasizes interpersonal communication, collaboration, and the development of subordinate potential (Miles, 1965) to fully realize a work force's potential. This suggests that those unique competencies available in the female managerial stereotype may fit the current needs of U.S. corporations at least as well as or better than those available in the male managerial stereotype.

Whether U.S. corporations look far enough into the female managerial stereotype—or, better still, into the actual capabilities of women—to discover the "fit" of women as managers is another matter, however. If they do, the prognosis for women in management looks particularly good. Assume that women can handle managerial work, whether because stereotypical differences between male and female managers do not exist or because these differences favor women as managers in some circumstances. Eventually, one would expect the weight of the evidence—positive experiences of corporations with women as managers—

to dissolve stereotypes against women as managers. This is the basis of the "contact hypothesis"—that contact with members of a negatively stereotyped group will dispel unreasonably negative stereotypes (Amir, 1969; Gutek & Konrad, 1990). This assumes that contact is at worst neutral with respect to the negative stereotypes. Unfavorable contact may simply reinforce negative stereotypes (Webster, 1961). Research on women managers has demonstrated the hypothesized salutary effects of contact on negative stereotypes. Men and women managers supervised by women have been found to have more positive opinions toward women as managers (Ezell, Odewahn, & Sherman, 1981).

One problem with contact as a remedy to inappropriate negative stereotypes about women as managers has been the relative paucity of contact exemplars (i.e., women managers and executives) in the U.S. work force. That is changing, however. Only 2% of MBA graduates in the 1950s—the cohort that we would expect to see taking over executive suites today—were women; in contrast, 1989 found women representing 37% of the graduating classes of MBAs in the United States (Fierman, 1990). These numbers become even more striking when the absolute increase in the number of MBA graduates (an increase from 5,000 in 1960 to 70,000 in 1984) is taken into account (Snook, 1987). Overall, this means 250 times as many managerially trained women entering the U.S. work force today compared with 1960, and that's a lot more contact. The critical point is that all this female managerial expertise is more than just an index of progress on the problem—it is also part of the solution. Increases in the proportion of female managers and executives should similarly increase the power and prestige of women and the perceived value of their work contributions (Schneer, 1985).

Evolving Practices in the U.S. Work Force

Even as increasing contact of U.S. workers with competent women managers should alleviate prejudice and discrimination against women in management, evolving business practices may also favor the rise of women in management.

In response to pieces in business publications about the "mommy track"—companies that favor career-primary women while discriminating against women who are equally interested in home lives and careers (Ehrlich, 1989)—"daddy track" articles have recently begun to appear, which chronicle the experiences of male executives who have throttled back their careers to devote greater attention to family lives (Ball, 1989; Machan, 1990; O'Connell, 1990). The message of these articles is a simple one: While only women have babies, some men are as committed to being daddies as some women are committed to being mommies. Apparently, some men want to give up single-minded pursuit of their careers for parental pursuits. In turn, the wives of these men could have opportunities to have families *and* be single-minded about *their* careers, much as traditional men have always done.

While this arrangement seems uncharacteristic of or unacceptable to the macho, primary-earner male mentality, other changes in business practices in the United States are conspiring to make it more palatable. One such development is the increasing acceptance by U.S. corporations of flextime scheduling. The latitude allowed flextime workers in deciding what hours to work means that employees can fit working hours around their other obligations like child care. In the 1980s, the number of companies in the United States using some form of flextime work scheduling doubled; about 1.5% more companies adopt flextime work scheduling every year (Thomas, 1987).

The position of women in management also may be helped by the increasing use of "telecommuting" in the U.S. work force. Between 1982 and 1987, the number of corporate employees working at home and dialing into the office tripled from 20,000 to 60,000; in the 1990s, the number of professionals working at home is expected to reach 13 million—more than 11% of the U.S. work force (Castro, 1987). Annual projections see the telecommuting work force growing at least 7% to 9% per year during the early 1990s (Bacon, 1989).

In the face of the "daddy track," increased acceptance of flextime work scheduling and telecommuting could mean that some women may not have to juggle their career and home life obligations—their husbands may be willing to do it instead. Flextime scheduling and telecommuting provide ways for men to retain career involvement while becoming primary caregivers for their children at home. Men may not be ready to give up their work lives completely. The structures and practices, however, are in place for them to allow their wives *primary* attention to a career, with a family life to boot—an arrangement men have enjoyed for centuries. Further, as changes in U.S. business practices make it easier for men to shoulder a larger share of parental burdens, these changes in norms should also help corporations *forget* parenting obligations as a consideration in the career advancement of women (much as currently they are probably forgotten for men).

Of course, the idea that a spouse could free up more work time for a parent-manager isn't too helpful when there is no spouse, and this too is a particularly female problem. Three times as many women as men between the ages of 25 and 64—prime time for managers and would-be executives—head up single-parent families (Exter, 1990). Here again, changing business practices may be bringing some welcome relief and support. Large corporations such as Johnson & Johnson and Campbell Soup Company have begun to open their checkbooks to fund services (like on-site day-care centers) designed to keep working mothers at work. Some smaller companies that sense the importance of the issue but can't afford the price of day-care centers instead have substituted assistance in the form of day-care referral services and "summer camps" (Machan, 1990).

If You Can't Join 'Em, Beat 'Em

Some of the most important changes in U.S. business that favor the rise of women in management come from women helping themselves in two important ways: female "networking" and entrepreneurship.

In a 1987 survey of women by Advance Research Management Consultants, "old boy networks"—power cliques of male executives at the top of organizations—were one of the three most cited forms of professional discrimination against executive women. One female corporate VP noted: "It's tough. The ways I am excluded are very subtle . . . before meetings or during the break, I am often left by myself while the men chat with each other" (Watts, 1989a, p. 32). Being "left out" at this level can prove critical. Preliminary deals may be struck during informal social gatherings (such as golf games), and social functions that exclude women also exclude them from important opportunities to cultivate professional connections.

Traditionally, women have not been able to help themselves much in this area. The small number of women executives—as noted earlier, less than 2% of all executives (Williams, 1988)—has made it difficult for women to form viable networks just among themselves. This picture appears to be changing, however. Women's business networks are on the increase. In New York City, for example, the number of formal professional and management women support organizations grew by 25% in just two years (1987 to 1989). High powered executive women's groups have been springing up around the country, such as the Executive Women's Council of Greater Baltimore and Houston's River Oaks Business Women's Exchange Club (Smith, 1986). In one survey by Korn/Ferry, 78% of senior female executive respondents reported that they were "actively grooming" women below them for top management positions; only 14% reported that they had been mentored by women (Watts, 1989b). In 1988, the Clairol Mentor Program for women was inaugurated; leading women executives from 11 different industries are asked to mentor an aspiring woman in their field. In 1988, the Small Business Administration (SBA) also established a mentoring program—the Women's Network for Entrepreneurial Training. In the SBA's program, successful women business owners are paired up with women who are just getting businesses off the ground. The SBA's program has proven so successful that many of the mentors have requested additional opportunities to sponsor female entrepreneurial aspirants (Watts, 1989b). Further, as the number of women in management continues to grow, the problem of management women not having other women with whom to network should decrease. In fact, as women become more plentiful in top management, men soon will not be able to afford to exclude knowledgeable and insightful women from their informal executive inner circles.

The success of the SBA's mentoring program also points out another avenue by which women are finding their way to the top in organizations—namely, by starting or owning those organizations. No doubt, employees are unlikely to discriminate against women when women own the company or occupy critical decision-making positions (Larwood, Szwajkowski, & Rose, 1988). In this arena, the amount of change in the 1980s has been astonishing. In the 10 years between 1974 and 1984, *three times* as many women as men took over or started up businesses on their own; during the same 10 years, the number of self-employed women increased 75%—twice the rate at which women were entering the U.S. work force (Horton, 1987). By 1989, nearly one third of all small businesses in the United States were owned by women, compared with *less than 5%* in 1972. A congressional report has gone on record with the estimate that by the year 2000 as many as 50% of small businesses in the United States will be owned by women (Nelton, 1989). Between 1980 and 1986, sole proprietorships owned by women increased by 62.5% (2.5 million to 4.1 million); those owned by men increased by only 33.4% during the same period (Nelton, 1989).

These women's new ventures are not just cottage industries, either. During the 1980s, *Savvy Woman* magazine began publishing an annual list of America's top women business owners. In 1984, the cutoff point for companies to make the list was $5 million in annual sales. By 1988, the cutoff had risen to $24 million in annual sales, and 21 companies on the 1988 list had revenues of more than $100 million; 3 companies on the list had revenues exceeding $1 billion (Nelton, 1989).

As women have gained footholds in management during the 1980s across a wide variety of industries, their gains in experience have come to be reflected in the *types* of businesses that women start up or own. Even today, about 80% of women-owned businesses are concentrated in services or retailing (Nelton, 1989). Between 1980 and 1985, however, the number of women-owned sole proprietorships in transportation (a traditional male stronghold) increased 124%, compared with only a 35% increase across the industry as a whole (Nelton, 1989).

According to the SBA, the world of high finance (investment banking in particular) remains a last bastion of all-male top management (Nelton, 1989). But even that is changing. Between 1986 and 1989, companies owned and run by women and minorities increased their share of municipal bond underwriting from $700 million to $11.2 billion—from 0.4% of the total pie to more than 11% (Nathans, 1990).

The "Bottom Line"

In the final analysis, the strongest argument for the disappearance of barriers against women in management is bound to be economic. Economics has been volunteered as one argument to explain why men traditionally have kept women out of management—namely, that it is in the economic interests of men to have women subjugated and relegated to the role of staying at home as an inexpensive source of child care and domestic labor (Gornick & Moran, 1971). But economics is a sword that cuts both ways.

According to *Workforce 2000*, a 1987 report on prospective work demographic patterns in the 1990s, women will provide 55% of the net increase in the U.S. work force. In contrast, white males—top management's traditional source of talent—will provide only 15% of the increase (Williams, 1988). As noted by Felice Schwartz, president of a firm that advises organizations on women in management, the handwriting on this wall is clear: "Companies will either have to dip deeper into the pool of less-qualified white males for future managers, or attract, retain, and promote top women and minorities" (Williams, 1988, p. 129). In short, soon clubby male "old boy" networks will have to open their doors to women and minorities or risk the loss of their competitive edge.

The latest movement in management and hiring circles toward valuing diversity in a work force (e.g., Mandell & Kohler-Gray, 1990) can only increase this pressure. Major U.S. corporations like Corning and Honeywell have begun to understand that, in hiring management talent, different really can be better (Solomon, 1990). First, a company that values diversity in its work force and hires or promotes more minorities or women into management circles is expanding the diversity of its idea base. More perspectives, more opinions, and more values—if managed well—should mean greater creativity and greater adaptability for an organization. Second, organizations that value diversity are going to be those more willing to reject traditional managerial stereotypes and hire the most qualified person for the job—whether that person is male or female. That translates into *not* having to dip deeper into the pool of less qualified males.

To be sure, some firms already have learned these lessons. Avon's CEO H. B. Waldron (a man, no less!) believes that managing diversity in their work force will directly affect Avon's success and profitability in the 1990s: "The companies providing a receptive and supportive environment for women and minorities will be the companies that can hire the cream of the crop" ("In Diversity," 1987, p. 7). With this goal in mind, Avon's top management team has established a support network to monitor issues and concerns related to work force diversity. Members of the network bring their concerns—including career-related issues for minorities and women—to a "multicultural committee." This committee in turn meets monthly to monitor the company's progress toward its work force diversity goals. Avon's efforts in promoting work force diversity earned it one of Catalyst's 1988 Annual Corporate Leadership Awards. That this type of program should be deserving of an award confirms the visibility and importance in corporate circles currently attached to the work force diversity issue. And Avon finds good company— including such firms as W. L. Gore and Campbell Soup—in its belief that the pursuit of excellence must fly in the face of traditional gender or racial managerial stereotypes (Peters & Austin, 1984).

The EEOC's Uniform Guidelines on Employee Selection of 1978 certainly encourage this position. The Uniform Guidelines do not require employers to select managers only on the basis of merit—that is, suitability for the job, independent of race or gender. The Uniform Guidelines do, however, codify the view that, to comply with Title VII of the Civil Rights Act of 1964, personnel actions (in particular, hiring and promotion decisions) should be based on statistically validated job-related considerations (Gatewood & Feild, 1990).

In the end, of course, changes in the ways businesses do business in the United States (such as the growing acceptance of flextime scheduling or the valuing of work force diversity) can only open doors for women. Eventually, women managers will stand on their own merits. For most women, that is probably all they ever wanted; the progress of women in management in the 1980s (e.g., Baum, 1987) suggests that it's all they'll ever need.

COUNTERPOINT: DISCRIMINATION— GOING BUT NEVER GONE?

There is no denying that progress has been made. The mere fact that a whole book is devoted to women in management is an indication of that progress. Other indications of progress for women in management are evident in both sections of this chapter. It does not necessarily follow, however, that, because there is progress, discrimination eventually will completely disappear. The counterpoint argument is based on the belief that there are and probably always will be overt and subtle discrimination against women, including expectations and role responsibilities that differ from those of men. The conclusion that discrimination against women managers never will completely disappear is based on four arguments and bodies of evidence: (a) the salience of gender, (b) role responsibilities outside the workplace, (c) existing workplace factors, and (d) the limitations of legislation.

Salience of Gender

Gender, along with race, is one of the most salient human characteristics (Bem, 1981; Laws, 1979); therefore people will always notice whether an individual is male or female. The saliency of gender has at least two implications for women managers. First, because gender is so salient, people attribute their own and others' behavior to their genders. When someone sees a woman behave in a manner consistent with a female stereotype, it is quite understandable that her behavior should be attributed to her gender—even though it might actually be caused by some organizational or systemic factor or even some other genetic factor (Fagenson, 1990b). People may especially notice the instances in which a woman behaves differently than one of her male colleagues even though most of her behavior may be quite similar to her male colleagues.

Second, the salience of gender means that there are two categories of managers, male managers and female managers, who are viewed as different than each other. In theory, two different categories can be equally valued, but, in practice, as the Supreme Court contended in its 1954 ruling on segregated schools, there is no such thing as separate but equal. If men and women managers are viewed as different, they are likely to be viewed as unequal on many dimensions. But, might one ask, does the fact that women and men are not equal on many dimensions mean that women managers will be valued less than men? If women managers are considered deficient relative to men in some areas, will not men managers be considered deficient to women managers in other areas?

According to some scholars (e.g., Broverman, Broverman, Clarkson, Rosenkrantz, & Vogel, 1970; Lipman-Blumen, 1984), the mere fact that men and women are viewed as different and unequal on many dimensions puts women at a distinct disadvantage because men have more power, and therefore characteristics associated with men will be valued more than the characteristics associated with women. Lipman-Blumen (1984) argued that men control social institutions and they structure them to their advantage. Women, the less powerful group, must constantly negotiate or manipulate the situation because they do not create the rules, regulations, and norms of society. In short, they are always second best.

While a trait associated with women, like nurturance, is valued in managers, it is less valued than traits associated with men, like toughness, rationality, and leadership. Indeed, Schein's (1973, 1975) widely cited research showing that people believe that women lack the requisite management characteristics has recently been replicated (Brenner et al., 1989).

Why should women be viewed as lacking requisite management characteristics when the research findings in general suggest that men and women in management are and/or behave quite similarly (see, for example, Donnell & Hall, 1980; Fagenson, 1990a)? The fact that men control most organizations and that gender is the most salient social characteristic means that men will be able to appropriate the most desirable traits for themselves and/or give value to the traits they possess. To achieve a workplace devoid of discrimination, gender would need to lose some of its salience so that women would be evaluated as individuals and not associated with stereotypes about women.[1]

Family Role Responsibilities

Family role responsibilities of men and women form another set of factors that subtly discriminate against women managers. In fact, they may well be the single biggest impediment to attainment of a discrimination-free environment for women managers as well as other working women. It has frequently been argued and documented (e.g., Hochschild & Machung, 1989; Lapidus, 1988; Lewis & Cooper, 1988; Nieva, 1985; Roby & Uttal, 1988) that women's family responsibilities are greater and take more time than men's family responsibilities. This is true of responsibilities of family of procreation as well as family of origin. Women's roles as mother and wife in the family of procreation and daughter in the family of origin require more time and energy than the comparable male roles. Even though women managers have resources not available to other employed women, they spend more time on family activities than male managers.

Role responsibilities in family of procreation. The two major roles in family of procreation are spouse and parent. The relationship of these two roles to the work role has been studied extensively by researchers under the rubric of work-family conflict or interrole conflict (e.g., Beutell & Greenhaus, 1982, 1983; Cooke & Rousseau, 1984; Gutek, Nakamura, & Nieva, 1981; Herman & Gyllstrom, 1977; Lewis & Cooper, 1988; Pleck, 1985; Repetti, 1987). In this case, the responsibilities of the two family roles are often considered together because it may be difficult to disentangle time spent in one versus the other.

Women, managers included, spend significantly more time than men in family tasks. For example, in their examination of husbands' and wives' detailed time diaries, Berk and Berk (1979) found that, although the husbands of employed wives assumed some of the burden of child care and household work, they did not match their wives in total hours spent in these two domains. In fact, these authors concluded—10 years before Hochschild and Machung's more influential *Second Shift* (1989)—that employed wives essentially hold down two full-time jobs: one in the labor force and one in the home.

After an extensive literature review and secondary analysis of two national data sets that include detailed information on work and family time, Pleck (1985) concluded that husbands of employed wives did not spend more time in family work than husbands of housewives. This is true whether time is measured in absolute number of hours or in percentage of total time spent, although these two methods of collecting time information yielded somewhat different results. Early studies (e.g., Blood & Wolfe, 1960) suggested that, as women became more involved in the labor force, men would become more involved with family work—but this result seems to be an artifact of measurement. Blood and Wolfe (1960), for example, asked respondents for proportional amounts of work performed by a respondent and his or her spouse. As Pleck (1985) noted, such questions are easy for respondents to answer but they do not provide information about how much work each spouse performs individually. When amount of time spent by each spouse individually is used, women clearly spend more time in family work than men (Berk & Berk, 1979; Hoffman, 1977; Robinson, 1977). The finding that men may spend proportionally more time in family work when a wife is employed comes from the fact that women who are employed spend less time in family work than women who are housewives. Men's time in family work is relatively constant whether or not the wife is in the paid labor force. Thus the available data through the 1970s suggest that women have reduced their own time spent on family tasks to compensate for their greater involvement in the paid labor force, but, so far, men appear to have made minimal adjustment to their wives' time spent in paid work. The situation could well change, of course. But, so far, although one may hear many individual stories of househusbands and fathers who take on primary child-care duties, these cases appear to be rare enough so as not to have affected the overall relationship between wife's labor force involvement and husband's time in family work.

The above analysis is complicated by at least one factor not yet considered: the differential definition of roles. This is associated with what Pleck (1977) called the *differential permeability of roles*, by which he meant the extent to which work roles are "allowed" to spill over to family roles and vice versa. Pleck contended that, for men, work is allowed to interfere or spill over to family, while, for women, sex-role expectations (if not employers and colleagues) allow family responsibilities to spill over to work. We would like to make a somewhat different distinction between women's and men's family roles, namely, the extent to which performing in one role fulfills the expectations associated with the other role.

In the case of men, fulfilling one's work role traditionally was tantamount to fulfilling one's family role as a "good provider" (Bernard, 1981). In short, working many hours and advancing within the corporation to provide a stable income for the family is part of the good provider role that men and women see as a major contribution of men to their families despite the fact that their paid work represents time away from their families. Thus moving up the ranks of management, which provides well for the family, is viewed as part of the roles of husband and father. Women, on the other hand, are not seen as fulfilling or contributing to either the wife or the mother role when they advance in management in order to provide an adequate income for their families. Instead, women are more often expected to provide a stable home situation than they are financial security. Women managers are sometimes viewed as "selfish" or self-centered for "wanting to have it all." They may be viewed as neglecting their families because they are employed in professionally demanding jobs.

In short, the way work and family roles are defined for men and women differs in the direction of encouraging women to spend more time than men in family tasks. Male managers may feel that they are more than fulfilling their family roles by virtue of the fact that they are doing a good job in their work role. Female managers may feel reluctant to ask their husbands to do half of the family work. Both may prefer instead to hire outside household help—usually supervised by the wife rather than by the husband. For women, on the other hand, performance as a manager has little to do with how she is evaluated—by others or herself—in her family role. In fact, if there is any relationship, it is likely to be slightly negative, that is, the more a woman is succeeding in management, the more she may be viewed as neglecting or even failing in her family obligations.

Family of origin. Although there is little research available on family responsibilities in families of origin, traditionally, women in their general role as caregivers have had responsibility for maintaining ties with the family of origin and physically caring for aging parents. In traditional families, women have also had responsibility for maintaining ties with their husband's family of origin through phone calls, handling family occasions like birthdays and anniversaries, and helping his parents when assistance is needed. These responsibilities take much less time than the responsibilities of the family of origin and may be inconsequential during the time when one's children are small and require the most work. As people live longer and their lives may be prolonged even more through extensive medical intervention, the specter of seeing one's parents through a protracted illness or years of life in which they are not able to care for themselves looms large. Daughters may be expected to provide more nurturance and care for their parents than sons.

Changing family role responsibilities. These role responsibilities may be more difficult to change than factors in the workplace for two reasons. First, they require men as well as women to change their behavior and, second, women seem to accept or perhaps welcome a certain level of unequalness in family responsibilities.

Legislation since the 1960s has focused on increasing access for women (and minorities) to male-dominated occupations, including access to the educational programs that prepare people for many of those jobs (Jacobs, 1985). In the first women's movement in the 1800s, the suffragettes focused on opportunities for political equality; in the second women's movement in the 1960s and 1970s, feminists focused on jobs as a route to equality with men. Men were asked to do very little directly except to keep from preventing equal opportunity for women. Women would make the changes by taking math and science in high school and college, entering male-dominated jobs, and learning to be assertive and to dress for success. The assumption seemed to be that, if women were given an opportunity to have access to all jobs, equality eventually would follow.

In the case of family role responsibilities, however, equality will only come about if *someone other than women* take on a greater share of these role responsibilities. Men as a group, the government, or employers, or all of the above will have to take on a greater share of the chores and responsibilities currently assumed by mothers, wives, and daughters of aging parents if women are to have equal opportunity outside the workplace. Without equal opportunity outside the workplace, there can be no real equality inside the workplace. As Hochschild and Machung (1989) have graphically depicted, women today work a second shift. While particularly dedicated women—the superwomen—may be able to hold second jobs and still compete with men on their first job, most women cannot. Some other women may work two shifts for a while but, not surprising, may burn out after 5, 10, or 15 years and opt for some alternative.

A second reason it may be more difficult to change family role responsibilities than workplace factors is that women seem to accept some amount of unequalness in family responsibilities. While the data suggest that many women would like their husbands to contribute more in the way of housework and child care (Burley, 1989; Pleck, 1985; Repetti, 1987), it is not clear that women expect their husbands to perform half of such chores. Women do not necessarily report more career-family conflict than men even when they spend more time in the two domains than men. In several studies, women reported no more career-family conflict than men (e.g., Greenhaus, Bedian, & Mossholder, 1987; Herman & Gyllstrom, 1977; Holahan & Gilbert, 1979a). Gutek, Searle, and Klepa (1991) examined the way hours spent in a domain (paid-work domain versus family domain) translate into perceived conflict between employment and family. They found that women managers who, on average, spent significantly more time on housework and child care than male managers did not report more family interference with their paid work (i.e., family-to-paid-work conflict). On the other hand, women reported significantly more interference from paid work with family (i.e., career-to-family conflict) than men when the amount of time on the job was equivalent.

These apparently differential expectations in how the sexes should divide family responsibilities—that is, the actual involvement in career and family—may be changing or may change in the future. Because many women would like their husbands to spend more time in family work, their expectations in this area may escalate when or if men in general do contribute more to family tasks and responsibilities. Women's apparent acceptance of a disproportionate share of family responsibilities may wane if men show evidence of being willing to take on 50% of family responsibilities.

Avoiding family responsibilities. Finally, it should be noted that, perhaps because family responsibilities weigh so heavily on women, many women managers, like women in other professions, do not take on family roles. Women managers are much less likely than men to be married, and, if they are, they tend to have few if any children (Gutek, Searle, & Klepa, 1991; Herman & Gyllstrom, 1977; Powell, 1988). Paradoxically, as families of procreation get smaller, the tasks associated with the family of origin may increase. An only child or only daughter will probably have more responsibilities for aging parents than those who can share those responsibilities with many siblings.

While deciding that they cannot "have it all" may well be a solution for some women, many others are unwilling to forgo marriage and motherhood for a career in management. Furthermore, the specter of management ranks composed of married men with children and unmarried women hardly smacks of equality. The impediments to equal treatment posed by women's family responsibilities represent a difficult dilemma.

Workplace Factors

A number of workplace factors work against women managers achieving parity with men. Many of these (such as lack of role models) are widely discussed elsewhere and will not be reviewed here. Four factors, either not widely discussed with respect to women managers, or not widely discussed at all, will be briefly reviewed here: (a) sex segregation of work and the entrenched position of men in power positions in the workplace, (b) the requirement of relocating for many professional and managerial jobs, (c) women's (realistic?) expectations for relatively low wages and advancement, and (d) differential pay of men and women managers. The last point is widely discussed, but here the emphasis is not on the findings but on the method by which the topic is studied.

Sex segregation of work. The sex segregation of work is exceptionally well documented (e.g., Beller, 1984; Blau & Ferber, 1985). Under affirmative action plans, women have begun moving into male-dominated jobs, and labor statistics reflect the growing number of women in male-dominated jobs such as management (Beller, 1984), but the number of men moving into traditional women's jobs is miniscule. Thus traditional women's jobs, both clerical and professional, are just as sex segregated as ever (Steinberg & Cook, 1988). Thus the labor force as a whole is barely less sex segregated than it was in the past. Strober (1984) argued that jobs are sex segregated precisely because men in general are able to select the most desirable jobs for themselves and likewise avoid the less desirable jobs. Although women have been allowed to enter management, most women are still entering the labor force in traditionally female jobs that men avoid and that are unlikely to lead to managerial positions (see Rosenbaum, 1985). And, if most women are continuing to enter positions that have little opportunity for advancement into management, will discrimination ever completely disappear?

Relocation as job requirement. Markham (1987) labeled relocation as "the great cruncher" because it appears to be an important component of advancement in professional and managerial jobs and there are clear sex differences. Women are less likely than men to relocate so as to advance in a career (Markham, 1987) and are much more likely than men to move to help a spouse or significant other advance in a career (Gutek & Burley, 1988). One of the many possible reasons women are not as mobile as men is that women's spouse/significant others are less likely to willingly follow than the average man's spouse or significant other (Gutek & Burley, 1988).

Women's (realistic?) expectations. Several studies show that women tend to have lower expectations in the workplace than men. Beginning with O'Leary's (1974) pioneering review, several research studies have shown that women expect less than men in the way of rewards and promotion opportunities. These lower expectations are no doubt realistic because they reflect women managers' status in the work force; that is, women do earn less money; they achieve a lower dollar return for every year of education relative to men; they are less frequently promoted; and they do not rise as far in general as men (e.g., Konrad & Langton, 1989; Konrad & Pfeffer, 1990; Olson & Frieze, 1987). Although the expectations may be realistic, research by Martin, Price, Bies, and Powers (1987) suggests that in some cases women who believe they have a chance for advancement shy away from it. In any event, whatever the origin of low expectations, they also are likely to affect women's progress—or lack thereof—toward equality with men in the workplace.

Pay differentials. Pay differentials between the sexes have been widely documented and researched and show no sign of dropping (Konrad & Langton, 1989; Olson & Frieze, 1987; Spitze, 1988; Stevenson, 1988). Many people believe that women in general are subject to sex discrimination at work (Crosby, 1982; Schneer & Reitman, 1990), and some are inclined to think that their own organizations favor men over women (Gutek, 1988). Relatively few women report that they themselves are victims of sex discrimination (Crosby, 1984), although women managers may be an exception; Schneer and Reitman (1990) found that almost half of a group of women managers had experienced some sex discrimination. Nevertheless, the proportion is much smaller than one might expect given the figures on salary differences between men and women in management, for example.

The research on pay differences tends to use the following paradigm: Researchers attempt to explain sex differences in pay with other differences between men and women such as number of years of experience, level of education, tenure in an organization, specialization, and the like (e.g., Olson & Frieze, 1987). These studies exhibit some consistency in findings. First, they are usually able to account for some of the difference between men's and women's salaries in general or in particular fields like management by taking into account factors such as years of experience or education. Second, none of the studies are able to account for all of the difference. (See a discussion of this issue in Konrad & Langton, 1989; Madden, 1985; O'Neill, 1985.) Researchers seem to differ in their interpretation of the studies. Some people contend that other differences not yet measured will account for all of the difference whereas others contend that the difference will not be eliminated no matter how many or which legitimate factors are considered. (Compare, for example, O'Neill, 1985, with Madden, 1985.) In short, they contend that the unexplained variance in men's and women's pay is due to sex discrimination.

Limitations of Legislation

Why should we not use legislation to change some of the inequalities between men and women today? As a society, we can choose to provide free child care for all parents, free extended care for the aged, and the like. Legislation has played an important role in the changes that have occurred to date in providing women with greater access to education and jobs. While important laws have been passed in that area, only recently has there been legislation passed relevant to family roles and responsibilities. (See the chapter by Lee in this volume for a more in-depth discussion of this issue.) The United States is one of the only industrialized countries that has restrictive legislation in this area. (For more discussion of this issue, see Berthoin Antal & Izraeli in this volume.) The cost, time, and energy of having and raising children are directly on the shoulders of the family. It is for individual couples to negotiate with each other how they will divide the responsibilities of maintaining their relationship as well as having and raising children. While legislation can no doubt be used to provide relief for families, there are two reasons legislation cannot be viewed as a fail-safe court of last resort: the cost of social programs and the fragility of laws relative to social roles and practices.

The first argument, the cost of social programs, is somewhat analogous to the above argument about the need for men to change. Someone other than women themselves has to do something. It may have been easier to legislate equal opportunity in the workplace than relief for families because the former is much less expensive than the latter. Equal opportunity legislation entails certain costs of implementing and enforcing the legislation, but those costs pale in comparison with the cost of government—or corporations—assuming responsibility for the care of the country's children or dependent elderly. Although, in the long run, child care and elderly care may save companies money via reduced turnover and absenteeism of employees, these are long-term benefits that may be neglected when short-term interests (cost of day care) prevail. Walsh and Kelleher (1987, p. 132) noted: "In the past, industry's interest in child care has been ephemeral, reflecting shortages in the labor pool or changes in prevailing social norms." The only time in U.S. history when government and businesses have expended effort to assist families with child care was during World War II. Deaux and Ullman (1983) note that, of the 3,000 day-care centers operating during the war, 2,800 were closed after the war.

The second argument is about the fragility of legislation relative to the other factors we have considered in this chapter. Legislation is not immutable; it can be challenged relatively easily as advocates of freedom of choice have discovered. While it is not easy to overturn legislation, it does happen with much greater frequency of occurrence than changes in some of the forces working against equality between the sexes. Legislation can be changed much more easily than the saliency of gender or sex roles.

As important as new legislation and overturning previous laws is the simple failure to enforce existing laws. Neglecting to enforce existing laws, often on grounds of cutting expenses, is a fairly common practice, especially for laws that do not have the full support of the citizenry (Walsh & Kelleher, 1987; see also Lee in this volume). The extent to which current legislation protects equal opportunity in the workplace and in education, as well as the extent to which any future legislation about family policy is enforced, depend a great deal on the existing political climate and the current set of officeholders and judiciary.[2]

A Final Caveat

> At this very moment, business is the wide-open field for female self-expression. . . . Women are revolutionizing business offices. They are, in fact, the unheeded revolution itself—a wave of the great ocean of the industrial revolution that has been sweeping through the world. (Buchanan, 1942, p. ix)

This statement was not written in the past 10 years but almost 50 years ago. The revolution predicted by Buchanan (1942) did not happen in the 1950s, 1960s, or 1970s. The optimistic ring of Buchanan's (1942) book is an example of all too many accounts written over the past half century. Buchanan is not the only one who has contended that the country was on the verge of true equality between the sexes. The optimistic accounts turned out to be overstatements. Why should the current situation be any different?

POINT AND COUNTERPOINT:
SOME COMMON GROUND?

The preceding pages have argued both sides of the issue of the fate of women in management. First, the case was presented that the winds are changing, that the future for women in management looks good, and that discrimination against women in the workplace should be "going, going, gone." Next, we have heard that women have no chance: Equality in the workplace—let alone equality in the executive suite—is flat-out "an unobtainable goal." Can both of these positions be correct?

The fact is that both of these positions *are* true—all the pieces *are* in place for very favorable change, and the current situation *is* dismal. This picture becomes a bit clearer when viewed through the GOS (gender-organization-system) perspective (e.g., Fagenson, 1990b). The GOS perspective highlights the importance of different levels of analysis— individual (e.g., gender), organizational, and systemic—in understanding perceptions of the suitability of women as managers. Both the point and the counterpoint address issues at all three levels.

Both arguments acknowledge the importance of *individual*-level variables (specifically, gender) in understanding how women will be received as managers. Strong stereotypes are in place that prevent women from moving up, and the salience of gender ensures that those stereotypes will be elicited. But the salience of gender also can be women's salvation. As women succeed and the numbers of women in management increase, the salience of gender may work to dissolve the stereotypes that hold women back, especially if women are able to obtain more powerful top management positions.

Of course, the success of women as managers (and thereby the increase of their numbers in the management ranks) is dependent upon the *organizational*-level variables that free or oppress women. More flexible work scheduling and increased availability of work-provided child care provide women better opportunities to succeed. But these provisions do not erase the harsh realities (like differential training and sex segregation of work) that will hold women back if these practices are allowed to continue. Short of tearing down these barriers, even favorable changes in work force practices may not substantially enhance women's progress. Worse yet, as long as these organizational barriers remain in place, favorable changes like work-scheduling flexibility and the possibility of telecommuting may be used to perpetuate the subjugation of women in inferior organizational roles or isolate them at home where they cannot accomplish as much while combining work with child care. The increasing entrepreneurship of women might then come to represent an exodus of female talent from U.S. corporations and the gender segregation of business in the United States rather than the success of women in business.

Whether these organizational barriers against women in management disappear may well depend upon the fate of *system*-level variables—variables that reflect the larger social system in which organizations function. The point and counterpoint arguments address three system-level variables: family, economics, and legislation. As noted in the counterpoint, family role responsibilities remain predominantly the province of women. Today, the "daddy track" remains something of an urban myth, perhaps quite limited in its scope. Herein lies a critical distinction for women in management: Although daddy-trackers certainly exist, they are at best an emerging trend and not sufficiently normative to be of immediate help.

Someday, economic pressures may help tradition-minded husbands see the light—that often what works best is having the *best* wage earner be the *primary* wage earner, whether the wife or husband (or that there is positive value to having an egalitarian marriage). For this to happen, more companies have to recognize the economic importance of hiring and paying the best, whether male or female. Again, some companies like "women-friendly" Pitney-Bowes (Konrad, 1990) are already there and have a firm commitment to women and diversity because it makes good economic sense. But this is no norm either and may never become one unless staunch traditionalists are somehow forced to abandon their prejudicial personnel practices and find out who can and can't do the work. Perhaps the changing demographic patterns of the U.S. work force soon will leave them no alternative.

Legislation concerning women in management—a key to forcing traditionalists to change—probably best exemplifies the tension of this point-counterpoint. The point argument notes the intent of the Uniform Guidelines in underscoring the appropriateness of *merit* as the basis for personnel decisions. Yet the counterpoint argument stresses that legislation really has not served its purpose in remedying discrimination against women. In fact, this ambivalence was played out in arguments for and against the Civil Rights Bill of 1990 (e.g., Biskukpic, 1990). As initially proposed and passed by Congress (and vetoed by then President Bush), the bill called for a return to the merit standards of the Uniform Guidelines—merit standards that had eroded through the 1980s by court opinions—and additionally offered the possibility of punitive damages for discriminators. On the other hand, after much argument about the 1991 reincarnation of the bill, it finally did pass and became law although the compromise that was struck to assure its passage reduced its effectiveness for women. Thus the fate of the systems-level variables remained in doubt and, with them, the future of women in management. The potential for favorable change exists, but, until that potential is realized, it is only the opportunities for women in management that will be going, going, gone.

NOTES

1. An extension to the notion of salience of gender is the gendered nature of organizations. Gender is such a salient characteristic that jobs and indeed whole organizations take on male or female characteristics. Hearn and his colleagues (e.g., Hearn & Parkin, 1987; Hearn, Sheppard, Tancred-Sherriff, & Burrell, 1989) go one step further to describe the sexuality of organizations. They argue that the processes of organizations reflect and maintain dominant forms of sexuality in the culture; that is, organizations are male dominated and heterosexual.

2. If organizations believe that affirmative action laws and values will not be policed, they may allow their own affirmative action efforts to lapse, especially if they view affirmative action programs, and the collecting and reporting of affirmative action data, as a burden.

REFERENCES

Amir, Y. (1969). Contact hypothesis in ethnic relations. *Psychological Bulletin, 71*, 319-342.

Bacon, D. C. (1989, October). Look who's working at home. *Nation's Business*, pp. 20-31.

Ball, A. L. (1989, October 23). The daddy track. *New York Magazine*, pp. 52-60.

Bardwick, J. J., & Douvan, E. (1971). Ambivalence: The socialization of women. In V. Gornick & B. Moran (Eds.), *Women in sexist society* (pp. 225-241). New York: Mentor.

Baum, L. (1987, June 22). Corporate women: They're about to break through. *Business Week*, pp. 72-78.

Behrens, L. (1990, February 18). The options will blossom in the '90s and beyond. *Chicago Tribune*, pp. 6-6.

Beller, A. (1984). Trends in occupational segregation by sex and race, 1960-1961. In B. Reskin (Ed.), *Sex segregation in the workplace: Trends, explanations, remedies*. Washington, DC: National Academy Press.

Bem, S. (1981). Gender schema theory: A cognitive account of sex-typing. *Psychological Review, 88*, 354-364.

Berk, R. A., & Berk, S. F. (1979). *Labor and leisure at home: Content and organization of the household day*. Beverly Hills, CA: Sage.

Bernard, J. (1981). The good-provider role: Its rise and fall. *American Psychologist, 36*, 1-12.

Beutell, N. J., & Greenhaus, J. H. (1982). Interrole conflict among married women: The influence of husband and wife characteristics on conflict and coping behavior. *Journal of Vocational Behavior, 21*, 99-110.

Beutell, N. J., & Greenhaus, J. H. (1983). Integration of home and nonhome roles: Women's conflict and coping behavior. *Journal of Applied Psychology, 68*, 43-48.

Biskukpic, J. (1990, February 10). A bipartisan Hill coalition unveils rights measure. *CQ*, p. 392.

Blau, F., & Ferber, M. (1985). Women in the labor market: The last twenty years. In S. Stromberg, L. Larwood, & B. Gutek (Eds.), *Women and work: An annual review* (pp. 19-50). Newbury Park, CA: Sage.

Blood, R., & Wolfe, D. (1960). *Husbands and wives: The dynamics of married living.* New York: Free Press.

Brenner, O. C., Tomkiewicz, J., & Schein, V. E. (1989). The relationship between gender role stereotypes and requisite management characteristics revisited. *Academy of Management Journal, 2*, 662-669.

Broverman, I. K., Broverman, D. M., Clarkson, F. E., Rosenkrantz, P. S., & Vogel, S. R. (1970). Sex-role stereotypes and clinical judgments of mental health. *Journal of Counseling and Clinical Psychology, 28*, 59-78.

Buchanan, A. (1942). *The lady means business.* New York: Simon & Schuster.

Burley, K. (1989). *Work-family conflict and marital adjustment in dual career couples: A comparison of three time models.* Unpublished doctoral dissertation, Claremont Graduate School, Claremont, CA.

Castro, J. (1987, October 26). Staying home is paying off. *Time*, pp. 112-113.

Cooke, R. A., & Rousseau, D. M. (1984). Stress and strain from family roles and work role expectations. *Journal of Applied Psychology, 69*, 252-260.

Crosby, F. (1982). *Relative deprivation and working women.* New York: Oxford University Press.

Crosby, F. (1984). The denial of personal discrimination. *American Behavioral Scientist, 27*, 371-386.

Deaux, K., & Ullman, J. (1983). *Women of steel.* New York: Praeger.

Donnell, S. M., & Hall, J. (1980, Spring). Men and woman as managers: A significant case of no significant differences. *Organizational Dynamics*, pp. 60-77.

Ehrlich, E. (1989, March 20). The mommy track: Juggling kids and careers in corporate America takes a controversial turn. *Business Week*, pp. 126-131.

Exter, T. (1990). Look ma, no spouse. *American Demographics, 12*(3), 63.

Ezell, H., Odewahn, C. A., & Sherman, J. D. (1981). The effects of having been supervised by a woman on perceptions of female managerial competence. *Personnel Psychology, 34*, 291-299.

Fagenson, E. A. (1990a). Perceived masculine and feminine attributes examined as a function of individual's sex and level in the organizational power hierarchy: A test of four theoretical perspectives. *Journal of Applied Psychology, 75*, 204-211.

Fagenson, E. A. (1990b). At the heart of women in management research: Methodological approaches and their bases. *Journal of Business Ethics, 9*, 267-274.

Fiedler, F. E. (1964). A contingency model of leadership effectiveness. In L. Berkowitz (Ed.), *Advances in Experimental Social Psychology, 1*, 149-190.

Fierman, J. (1990, July 30). Why women still don't hit the top. *Fortune*, pp. 40-62.

Frank, E. J. (1988). Business students' perceptions of women in management. *Sex Roles, 19*, 107-118.

Gatewood, R. D., & Feild, H. S. (1990). *Human resource selection.* Hinsdale, IL: Dryden.

Goktepe, J. R., & Schneier, C. R. (1988). Sex and gender effects in evaluating emergent leaders in small groups. *Sex Roles, 19,* 29-35.

Gornick, V., & Moran, B. K. (1971). *Woman in a sexist society.* New York: Mentor.

Greenhaus, J. H., Bedian, A. G., & Mossholder, K. W. (1987). Work experiences, job performance, and feelings of personal and family well being. *Journal of Vocational Behavior, 31,* 200-215.

Gutek, B. A. (1988). Women in clerical work. In A. Stromberg & S. Harkess (Eds.), *Women working* (2nd ed., pp. 42-60). Mountain View, CA: Mayfield.

Gutek, B. A., & Burley, K. (1988, August 12-16). *Relocation, family, and the bottom line: Results from the Division 35 Survey.* Paper presented at the APA Annual Convention, Atlanta.

Gutek, B. A., & Konrad, A. M. (1990). *A theory of contact in organizations* (Working paper). Tucson: University of Arizona.

Gutek, B. A., Nakamura, C., & Nieva, V. (1981). The interdependence of work and family roles. *Journal of Occupational Behavior, 2,* 1-16.

Gutek, B., Searle, S., & Klepa, L. (1991). Rational versus gender role explanations for work-family conflict. *Journal of Applied Psychology, 76* (4) 560—568.

Hearn, J., & Parkin, W. (1987). *"Sex" at "work": The power and paradox of organizational sexuality.* New York: St. Martin's.

Hearn, J., Sheppard, D. L., Tancred-Sheriff, P., & Burrell, G. (1989). *The sexuality of organization.* Newbury Park, CA: Sage.

Heilman, M. E., Block, C. J., Martell, R. F., & Simon, M. C. (1989). Has anything changed? Current characterizations of men, women, and managers. *Journal of Applied Psychology, 74,* 935-942.

Herman, J. B., & Gyllstrom, K. K. (1977). Working men and women: Inter- and intra-role conflict. *Psychology of Women Quarterly, 1,* 319-333.

Hochschild, A., & Machung, A. (1989). *Second shift: Inside the two-job marriage.* New York: Penguin.

Hoffman, L. W. (1977). Maternal employment: 1979. *American Psychologist, 34,* 859-865.

Holahan, C. K., & Gilbert, L. A. (1979a). Conflict between major life roles: Women and men in dual career couples. *Human Relations, 32,* 451-467.

Holahan, C. K., & Gilbert, L. A. (1979b). Inter-role conflict for working women: Career versus job. *Journal of Applied Psychology, 64,* 86-90.

Horton, N. R. (1987, December). More challenges for the managerial woman. *Management Review,* pp. 5-6.

In diversity there is strength. (1987, June). *Management Review,* p. 7.

Jacobs, J. (1985). Sex-segregation in American higher education. In L. Larwood, A. H. Stromberg, & B. A. Gutek (Eds.), *Women and work: An annual review* (Vol. 1, pp. 191-214). Newbury Park, CA: Sage.

Konrad, A. M., & Langton, N. (1989). *Labor market effects on male-female earnings inequality.* Paper presented at the annual meetings of the Academy of Management, Washington, DC.

Konrad, A. M., & Pfeffer, J. (1990). Do you get what you deserve? Factors affecting the relationship between productivity and pay. *Administrative Sciences Quarterly, 35,* 560-577.

Konrad, W. (1990, August 6). Welcome to the woman-friendly company where talent is valued and rewarded. *Business Week,* pp. 48-55.

Lapidus, G. (1988). The interaction of women's work and family roles in the U.S.S.R. *Women and work: An annual review* (Vol. 3). Newbury Park, CA: Sage.

Larwood, L., Szwajkowski, E., & Rose, S. (1988). Sex and race discrimination resulting from manager-client relationships: Applying the rational bias theory of managerial discrimination. *Sex Roles, 18*, 9-29.

Laws, J. L. (1979). *The second X: Sex role and social role.* New York: Elsevier.

Lewis, S., & Cooper, C. (1988). Stress in dual-earner families. *Women and work: An annual review* (Vol. 3). Newbury Park, CA: Sage.

Lipman-Blumen, J. (1984). *Gender roles and power.* Englewood Cliffs, NJ: Prentice-Hall.

Machan, D. (1990, April 16). The mommy and daddy track. *Forbes*, pp. 162-164.

Madden, J. F. (1985). The persistence of pay differentials: The economics of sex discrimination. In L. Larwood, A. Stromberg, & B. Gutek (Eds.), *Women and work: An annual review* (Vol. 1, pp. 76-114). Newbury Park, CA: Sage.

Mandell, B., & Kohler-Gray, S. (1990, March). Management development that values diversity. *Personnel*, pp. 41-46.

Markham, W. T. (1987). Sex, relocation, and occupational advancement: The "real cruncher" for women. In A. H. Stromberg, L. Larwood, & B. A. Gutek (Eds.), *Women and work: An annual review* (Vol. 2, pp. 207-232). Newbury Park, CA: Sage.

Martin, J., Price, R. L., Bies, R. J., & Powers, M. (1987). Now that I can have it, I'm not so sure I want it: The effects of opportunity on aspirations and discontent. In B. Gutek & L. Larwood (Eds.), *Women's career development* (pp. 42-65). Newbury Park, CA: Sage.

Massengill, D., & DiMarco, N. (1979). Sex-role stereotypes and requisite management characteristics: A current replication. *Sex Roles, 5*, 561-570.

Miles, R. E. (1965, July/August). Human relations or human resources? *Harvard Business Review*, pp. 148-163.

Nathans, L. J. (1990, February 12). What do women want? A piece of the muni business. *Business Week*, p. 66.

Nelton, S. (1989, May). The age of the *woman* entrepreneur. *Nation's Business*, pp. 22-26.

Nieva, V. (1985). Work and family linkages. In L. Larwood, A. Stromberg, & B. Gutek (Eds.), *Women and work: An annual review* (Vol. 1). Beverly Hills, CA: Sage.

O'Connell, L. (1990, June 20). More men moving onto the nurturing "daddy track." *Arizona Daily Star*, p. 1C.

O'Leary, V. (1974). Some attitudinal barriers to occupational aspirations in women. *Psychological Bulletin, 81*, 809-826.

Olson, J. E., & Frieze, I. (1987). Income determinants for women in business. In A. Stromberg, L. Larwood, & B. Gutek (Eds.), *Women and work: An annual review* (Vol. 2, pp. 173-206). Newbury Park, CA: Sage.

O'Neill, J. (1985). Role differentiation and the gender gap in wages. In L. Larwood, A. Stromberg, & B. Gutek (Eds.), *Women and work: An annual review* (Vol. 1, pp. 50-75). Newbury Park, CA: Sage.

Peters, T. J., & Austin, N. K. (1984, June). Diamonds in the rough. *Savvy*, pp. 38-46.

Pleck, J. (1977). The work-family role system. *Social Problems, 4*, 417-427.

Pleck, J. (1985). *Working wives/working husbands.* Newbury Park, CA: Sage.

Powell, G. (1988). *Women and men in management.* Newbury Park, CA: Sage.

Powell, G. N., & Butterfield, D. A. (1979). The "good manager": Masculine or androgynous? *Academy of Management Journal, 22*, 395-403.

Repetti, R. L. (1987). Linkages between work and family roles. In S. Oskamp (Ed.), *Applied social psychology annual: Family process and problems* (Vol. 7, pp. 98-127). Newbury Park, CA: Sage.

Robinson, J. P. (1977). *How Americans use time: A social-psychological analysis of everyday behavior.* New York: Praeger.

Roby, P., & Uttal, L. (1988). Trade union stewards: Handling union, family, and employment responsibilities. *Women and work: An annual review* (Vol. 3). Newbury Park, CA: Sage.

Rosenbaum, J. E. (1985). Persistence and change in pay inequalities: Implications for job evaluation and comparable work. In *Women and work: An annual review* (pp. 115-140). Newbury Park, CA: Sage.

Schein, V. E. (1973). The relationship between sex role stereotypes and requisite management characteristics. *Journal of Applied Psychology, 57*, 95-100.

Schein, V. E. (1975). The relationship between sex role stereotypes and requisite management characteristics among female managers. *Journal of Applied Psychology, 60*, 340-344.

Schneer, J. (1985). *Gender context: An alternative perspective on sex differences in organizations.* Paper presented at the annual meetings of the Academy of Management, San Diego, CA.

Schneer, J. A., & Reitman, F. (1990). Effects of employment gaps on the careers of MBA's: More damaging for men than women? *Academy of Management Journal, 22*, 391-406.

Schwartz, F. (1989, January/February). Management women and the new facts of life. *Harvard Business Review*, pp. 65-76.

Smith, L. (1986, November/December). NAFE turns networking upside down. *The Executive Female*, pp. 22-26.

Snook, J. L. (1987). *The history of GMAC.* Los Angeles: Graduate Management Admissions Council.

Solomon, C. M. (1990, April). Careers under glass. *Personnel Journal*, pp. 96-105.

Spitze, G. (1988). The data on women's labor force participation. In A. Stromberg & S. Harkess (Eds.), *Women working* (2nd ed., pp. 42-60). Mountain View, CA: Mayfield.

Steinberg, R. J., & Cook, A. (1988). Policies affecting women's employment in industrial countries. In A. Stromberg & S. Harkess (Eds.), *Women working* (2nd ed., pp. 307-328). Mountain View, CA: Mayfield.

Stevenson, M. H. (1988). Some economic approaches to the persistence of wage differences between men and women. In A. Stromberg & S. Harkess (Eds.), *Women working* (2nd ed., pp. 97-100). Mountain View, CA: Mayfield.

Strober, M. (1984). Toward a general theory of occupational sex segregation: The case of public school teaching. In B. Reskin (Ed.), *Sex segregation in the work place: Trends, explanations, remedies.* Washington, DC: National Academy Press.

Thomas, E. G. (1987, Spring). Workers who set own time clocks. *Business and Society Review*, pp. 49-51.

U.S. Department of Labor, Bureau of Labor Statistics (1993). *Employment and earnings,* vol. 40. Washington, DC: Government Printing Office.

Walsh, D. C., & Kelleher, S. E. (1987). The "corporate perspective" on the health of women at work. In A. H. Stromberg, L. Larwood, & B. Gutek (Eds.), *Women and work: An annual review* (Vol. 2, pp. 117-142). Newbury Park, CA: Sage.

Watts, P. (1989a, November/December). Breaking into the old-boy network. *The Executive Female*, pp. 32-72.

Watts, P. (1989b, July/August). Lending a helping hand. *The Executive Female*, pp. 38-40 ff.

Webster, S. W. (1961). The influence of interracial contact on social acceptance in a newly integrated school. *Journal of Educational Psychology, 52*, 292-296.

Williams, M. J. (1988, September 12). Women beat the corporate game. *Fortune*, pp. 128-138.

9

The Legal and Political Realities for Women Managers: The Barriers, the Opportunities, and the Horizon Ahead

BARBARA A. LEE

The low proportion of women in management is well documented (Hymowitz & Schellhardt, 1986) and some of the reasons for their underrepresentation have been discussed in earlier chapters. Unfavorable treatment of women is not confined to the corporate sector; women are also underrepresented in public sector management and in "management" ranks in the military. (In fact, women are excluded from combat positions, which effectively precludes them from attaining most top military ranks and jobs.) Exclusion of women from combat has been sanctioned by the U.S. Supreme Court (*Rostker v. Goldberg,* 1981) on national security grounds.

Although sex discrimination in employment has been illegal since 1964 under federal law, and for even longer under some state civil rights laws, it persists in many employment settings. Furthermore, systemic discrimination against women, such as occupational segregation and depressed wages for employees in female-dominated occupations, remains a serious social problem that is seemingly impervious to legislative or judicial solutions. Despite some gains by women (e.g., the application of the civil rights laws to formerly all-male social and service clubs; *Bohemian Club v. FEHC,* 1987; *Roberts v. U.S. Jaycees,*

246

1984), discrimination against women in hiring, promotion, and job assignments; sexual harassment; discrimination based on reproductive ability; and stereotyping persist.

When women managers consider their options in combating sexism and discrimination, they may find that, although such conduct is barred by law, it can be difficult to obtain redress. The mere fact of belonging to, or aspiring to belong to, the management team complicates the decision to litigate. Filing a claim of gender discrimination can result in discharge, a stalled career, or, at best, strained relationships between the woman manager and her colleagues (Bumiller, 1988).

In addition, if a woman manager does decide to pursue a discrimination claim with a civil rights agency or in court, success is not assured. Even "winning" a lawsuit may not result in a workplace free of gender discrimination. Nor can a lawsuit necessarily change fundamental problems such as the failure of most U.S. businesses to accommodate women's roles as mothers, daughters, wives, and employees.

This chapter examines a few areas of concern to female (and often to male) managers and describes how the courts and legislatures have responded. The first section gives a brief overview of the antidiscrimination laws used most frequently to redress sex discrimination. It also reviews evidence that most plaintiffs in sex discrimination cases in general, and plaintiffs in managerial positions in particular, have usually been unable to prove their claims in court and suggests some reasons for this low success rate. This is followed by a brief analysis of the Civil Rights Act of 1991, which reversed several decisions of the U.S. Supreme Court that were widely viewed as hostile to the ability of women and minorities to prevail in employment discrimination lawsuits.

The chapter then examines a series of gender-related problems that women managers may face and assesses how the courts and enforcement agencies have dealt with these problems. Fetal vulnerability policies, an issue that may exclude women from managerial positions in corporations with manufacturing operations, involve a clash between equal employment opportunity and the health of unborn children. Following that, the much criticized "mommy track" and its legal and practical implications for managers of both sexes are examined. Next, the interplay between sexual harassment, sex discrimination, and romantic relationships at work is discussed in the context of the disinclination of many women managers to report incidents of harassment.

The chapter concludes with some comments on recent and pending legislation and suggests areas where either legislation or changes in corporate practice could reduce the difficulties faced by women managers. It also questions the ability of judges and legislators to address some of these intractable issues.

NONDISCRIMINATION LAWS AND HOW THEY WORK

Sex discrimination in employment is prohibited by several federal laws as well as by the laws of most states. The primary source of federal protection for employed women is Title VII of the Civil Rights Act of 1964. That law covers all employment-related decisions, such as hiring, job assignment, transfer, promotion, discharge, and so on (42 U.S.C. sec. 2000e et seq.). Women of color can attack race discrimination under a second law, Section 1981 of the Civil Rights Act of 1870 (42 U.S.C. sec. 1981), which protects the right of all persons to "make and enforce contracts" regardless of color or citizenship status. A third, less comprehensive federal law, the Equal Pay Act, requires employers to pay women who do "equal work" the same wage that male workers receive (29 U.S.C. sec. 206[d]).

Executive Order 11246 (amended by Executive Orders 11375 and 12086) prohibits sex discrimination by recipients of federal contracts exceeding $10,000. The Executive Orders also require federal contractors to develop affirmative action plans and to practice affirmative action. Neither Title VII, Section 1981, nor the Equal Pay Act requires affirmative action (although Title VII has been interpreted to permit affirmative action under certain circumstances).

Although Title VII's prohibitions on sex discrimination are very clear, proving sex discrimination in hiring, promotion, discharge, or other employment decisions is quite difficult for most plaintiffs. Unless there is a "smoking gun" or some other obvious evidence that discrimination has occurred, the employer may defend against a Title VII charge by saying that the woman's performance was inadequate, her absences excessive, her attitude poor, or the like. When an employer asserts this type of a defense and there is no direct evidence of discrimination, the plaintiff must then prove that this defense is a pretext—that it is, in fact, a lie—and that the only plausible reason for the negative decision she is challenging is sex discrimination. Most plaintiffs have great difficulty proving pretext unless either they can show written evidence that their gender was the primary reason for the negative employment decision or some management witness admits that discrimination occurred.

Women in or seeking managerial positions have even more difficulty than most plaintiffs in establishing sex discrimination under Title VII because judges tend to defer to the company's judgment vis-à-vis both the criteria used to evaluate these types of employees and the actual judgments made. Even though using subjective criteria (such as "leadership" and/or "aggressiveness") to evaluate candidates for promotion often allows gender bias to infect the evaluation (*Price Waterhouse v. Hopkins,* 1989), legal scholars have documented the tendency for judges to rule against women who claim that promotion or evaluation systems at upper management levels are discriminatory, especially when subjective criteria are used to make employment decisions (Bartholet, 1982; Ginesky & Rogoff, 1976; Waintroob, 1979-1980).

Although women challenging sex discrimination in pay have fared reasonably well when they are comparing their pay with that received by men performing identical jobs, women working in female-dominated occupations, such as nursing, teaching, and service industries (i.e., insurance), have had difficulty obtaining compensation equivalent to that paid to individuals in male-dominated occupations (engineering, skilled crafts; *Lemons v. City and County of Denver,* 1980). Proponents of the comparable worth doctrine have argued that employers should pay individuals based upon what the job they do is worth to the employer, not based upon the market value of their services (Treiman & Hartmann, 1981). Women attempting to challenge the practice of paying lower salaries to workers in female-dominated occupations have had virtually no success in the courts (*AFSCME v. Washington,* 1985), although some states, such as Minnesota and Iowa, have passed laws requiring comparable worth in the public sector (Evans & Nelson, 1989). Thus women in female-dominated occupations face a double burden: barriers to advancement into management careers and wage discrimination across the occupation (Sorensen, 1989).

THE OUTCOME OF DISCRIMINATION CLAIMS

As noted above, it is very difficult for women claiming discrimination to prove their case in court. In a study of sex discrimination cases in which rulings on the merits (as opposed to rulings on technical legal procedure) were issued by federal courts between 1971 and 1980 (Maschke,

1989), women won only 34% of the time. This study did not, however, distinguish between women managers and lower-level employees. Similarly, a study of all discrimination cases litigated under Title VII by college faculty between 1972 and 1984 revealed that only one fifth of the plaintiffs whose cases were tried on the merits were successful, although women faculty filing class action lawsuits and white women suing predominantly black colleges were more successful (5 of 12, or 42%, and 4 of 4, or 100%, respectively; LaNoue & Lee, 1987, pp. 31-32).

An analysis of the success rates of women managers challenging alleged sex discrimination in significant employment decisions, such as hiring or promotion, was performed for this chapter. Federal court decisions issued between 1983 and 1989 where women managers challenged negative hiring or discharge decisions were reviewed. In these cases, women managers (or prospective managers) prevailed only 29% of the time in hiring denials and in 37% of the discharges.[1] Given the difficult burden of proof that plaintiffs face, as well as judicial deference to the employer's evaluation of the plaintiff, this outcome is not surprising, but it is discouraging for women contemplating filing sex discrimination charges.

This analysis also indicates that far fewer women managers pursue a sex discrimination claim to its conclusion than women seeking entry to (or promotion to) blue-collar, skilled trades, or other nonmanagerial jobs. (Data on the number of discrimination cases actually filed, but either withdrawn or settled, are not available.) In the cases decided between 1983 and 1989, a comparison of women managers with women in blue-collar, skilled trades, or other nonmanagerial jobs revealed that only 9% of the sex discrimination claims challenging negative hiring decisions had been brought by women who were managers, and only 13% of the discharge claims involved women managers. This low litigation rate by women managers not only reflects the career-related disincentives to litigation mentioned earlier but also reflects the pre-1992 limits on damages, for, under the prior version of Title VII, plaintiffs were limited to two years of back pay and were denied punitive damages, often making the cost of litigation higher than the financial gains. The low reinstatement rates also suggest that many women managers may decide that litigation is not worth the cost (Posner, 1989).

Added to the dismal record in court is the personal toll that discrimination litigation takes on plaintiffs. These cases may take five to ten years to resolve once they are filed. Plaintiffs have reported broken marriages, cleavages in families, and ruined careers, whether or not they actually won their lawsuits (LaNoue & Lee, 1987). Challenging a negative employment decision while still working for the defendant employer is an especially unpleasant experience, for colleagues and friends often feel torn between loyalty to a friend and concern about their own careers (Theodore, 1986). Plaintiffs who win their cases and are either reinstated in their old jobs or win while they are incumbents often perceive negative effects on their careers. Some perceive either overt retaliation by the employer or covert actions such as isolation or shunning (LaNoue & Lee, 1987; Theodore, 1986).

Most women who successfully challenge employment discrimination are employed elsewhere long before the verdict is reached (Posner, 1989). This is necessary because of the requirement that plaintiffs mitigate the extent of back pay liability by accepting a similar position with another employer during the pendency of the lawsuit. Given the poor probability of success and the severe emotional toll that litigation exacts, this approach is clearly the recommended one. But this practical strategy—giving up on the former position or career—means that even the infrequent victories for women plaintiffs are incomplete. The civil rights laws require that plaintiffs who win be "made whole" (42 U.S.C. sec. 2000e et seq.) by reinstatement and the recovery of monetary losses. The experience of plaintiffs demonstrates that this requirement may be an illusion for many plaintiffs and that even victorious plaintiffs can never be made completely whole when discrimination occurs.

RECENT CHANGES IN CIVIL RIGHTS DOCTRINE

The early 1990s witnessed a vigorous debate about the civil rights laws and pitted the U.S. Supreme Court and the president against much of Congress. Although the debate is too lengthy to describe in this chapter, it involved opinions issued by the U.S. Supreme Court in several cases in 1989 that sharply limited the ability of plaintiffs to prevail in lawsuits under Title VII of the Civil Rights Act of 1964 and Section 1981 of the Civil Rights Act of 1870. As a result, after more than two years of debate, Congress passed and President Bush signed the Civil Rights Act of 1991.

The overall impact of the new law should make it somewhat easier for plaintiffs to prevail in discrimination lawsuits, and it also increases the amount of money that plaintiffs can be awarded if their lawsuits are successful. This latter change is particularly important, because the very low ceiling on damages under the previous version of Title VII often made it difficult for potential plaintiffs to find a lawyer willing to take the case, as legal fees often exceeded the amount of damages plaintiffs could be awarded in these cases.

Another change that the new law brings is to permit the plaintiff to request a jury trial. Before Congress passed the new law, all Title VII cases were tried before a judge; juries were not permitted. Because a plaintiff's chances of winning a lawsuit increase substantially when a jury is making the decision, this change in the law is an important victory for plaintiffs.

Other changes are more technical but important both to litigation strategy and to the plaintiff's ability to prevail. This section of the chapter will briefly describe the change, the Supreme Court case that stimulated the change, and the implications for plaintiffs.

Plaintiffs' burdens in disparate impact cases. Prior to spring 1989, if plaintiffs in "disparate impact"[2] discrimination cases could show that women were substantially underrepresented in certain job categories, the employer was then required to prove the "business necessity" of the policies or practices alleged to be excluding women from these jobs. For example, certain physical tests required for entrance to police and fire fighting jobs have been found to exclude women disproportionately and have been challenged successfully on that basis.

The U.S. Supreme Court, in *Wards Cove Packing Co. v. Atonio* (1989), made it much more difficult for plaintiffs to shift this burden of proof to the employer. The Court said that gross statistical disparities are not enough; the women must show a direct cause-and-effect relationship between each challenged practice or policy and the underrepresentation of women. Furthermore, the court appeared to lighten the employer's burden, should the plaintiffs successfully show this relationship, by permitting the employer to provide evidence that the challenged policy had a "legitimate employment goal" rather than "business necessity"— a substantial diminution of the employer's defense burden (Lee, 1989-1990). This case sharply limited the ability of groups of women to challenge employer practices that, although appearing to be neutral, in fact work to the disadvantage of women; unfortunately, it has taken such class action litigation to convince some employers to eliminate such practices (*EEOC v. AT&T*, 1978; *Kyriazi v. Western Electric Co.*, 1979).

Most of the controversy over the Civil Rights Act of 1991 was over language to reverse *Wards Cove*. The bill's sponsors wished to restore the "business necessity" requirement for employers. Despite the fact that courts had been applying the "business necessity" test for nearly 20 years without encouraging employers to adopt quotas, employer organizations (and the White House) asserted that the bill's language would require employers to use hiring and promotion quotas to avoid being sued over imbalances in the work force.

The new law codifies the "business necessity" requirement, stating that the employer must demonstrate that "the challenged practice is job related for the position in question and consistent with business necessity" (sec. 105[a]) and also permits a plaintiff, or group of plaintiffs, to challenge the combined effect of an employer's practices if their individual effects cannot be separated. These provisions of the bill are, to many civil rights advocates, the centerpiece of the new law.

When does the harm occur? Another case decided by the Supreme Court in 1989 was particularly devastating for women working in nontraditional jobs, because their recent arrival often results in very low seniority compared with that of most of their male colleagues. The case was especially troubling because it had the practical effect of precluding women from challenging the application of a discriminatory seniority system if the harm to them occurred more than six months after the seniority system was adopted. Under Title VII, a woman has only six months after the discrimination occurs to file a complaint. (Although extending the time limits was proposed in an earlier version of the new law, the final version leaves the six-month time limit unchanged.)

In *Lorance v. AT&T Technologies, Inc.,* a seniority system that disadvantaged workers in one particular job category was adopted in 1979. Three years later, several women were laid off in accordance with that new seniority system. When they filed Title VII claims, they were told that the discrimination occurred when the seniority system was adopted, not when the layoffs occurred, even though at the time the system was adopted no layoffs were contemplated.

The Supreme Court agreed with this interpretation of Title VII, even though it would have required women to challenge a policy that had not yet been applied to them and perhaps never would be. The case cut off legitimate discrimination claims as untimely and encouraged speculative claims before discrimination actually occurred.

The Civil Rights Act of 1991 overruled *Lorance*. The new law permits individuals to challenge a seniority system that they believe is discriminatory "when the seniority system is adopted, when an individual becomes subject to the seniority system, or when a person aggrieved is injured by the application of the seniority system" (sec. 112). This benefits all workers and removes the pressure to challenge a seniority system that has not yet disadvantaged, but has the potential to disadvantage, women. The new law speaks only to seniority systems, however; lower courts may continue to follow *Lorance* if other kinds of employer policies (leave of absence policies, for example) are challenged.

A victory for women of color. A post-Civil War law forbidding race (but not sex) discrimination in the "making of contracts" (42 U.S.C. sec. 1981) has been used for decades by women of color to challenge race discrimination in employment. Women of color have used this law frequently because Section 1981's two-year filing period gives them more time to file a discrimination charge than the six-month filing limit of Title VII, thus permitting claims to be brought under Section 1981 that could not be litigated under Title VII. Section 1981 also permits punitive damages to be awarded (until late 1991, Title VII did not). Also, there is no requirement in Section 1981 that a woman first file a discrimination charge with the Equal Employment Opportunity Commission (as Title VII requires); she can hire a lawyer and sue in court immediately, as long as the suit is initiated within two years of the alleged discrimination.

The law had been used for decades to challenge many forms of employment discrimination (discharge, failure to promote), but racial harassment charges had not been brought under Section 1981 until recently. When a black woman attempted to challenge racial harassment under this law, the Supreme Court said that the law could only be used to challenge hiring decisions or other situations where the "making of a contract" is involved. This opinion, *Patterson v. McLean Credit Union* (1989), sharply limited the ability of women of color to challenge racial harassment or other forms of employment discrimination and to obtain appropriate remedies. Because women of color often face double discrimination (Scarborough, 1989), this outcome was a setback for their efforts to redress illegal employer conduct under the law.

The Civil Rights Act of 1991 overturned *Patterson* by defining the right to make and enforce contracts to include "the making, performance, modification and termination of contracts, and the enjoyment

of all benefits, privileges, terms and conditions of the contractual
relationship" (sec. 101). It permits women of color to challenge harassment, discharge, failure to promote, or other negative employment actions
under this law, as long as they are alleging race, not sex, discrimination.
Sex discrimination must still be challenged under Title VII.

The new law creates an anomaly for women, in that damages are
capped for women suing under Title VII, but no such cap exists in
Section 1981. Thus white women challenging sex discrimination or
sexual harassment are limited to $300,000 in compensatory and puni-
tive damages (plus back pay) if they work for large companies and lower
amounts (the minimum cap is $50,000) if the employer has 100 or fewer
employees (sec. 102), while minority women (and minority men) who
can challenge race discrimination under Section 1981 may obtain un-
limited compensatory and punitive damages. If minority women wish
to challenge sex discrimination or sexual harassment, they too will face
the damage limits of Title VII.

Gender stereotyping. The Supreme Court in 1989 reached one conclusion favorable to women plaintiffs, although it is unlikely that this
case, or the language in the new law that codifies its result, will greatly
improve the unfavorable odds that women plaintiffs face. In *Price
Waterhouse v. Hopkins* (1989), the plaintiff demonstrated successfully
that the men evaluating her for partnership used unfavorable gender
stereotypes to decide against her. In this case, the plaintiff was able to
obtain the kind of evidence that many plaintiffs in discrimination
lawsuits cannot: She provided testimony that she had been told to walk
and talk more femininely, to wear makeup, and to have her hair styled
if she wanted to be named a partner in the firm (1989). The Court
returned the case to the trial court, which ruled in Spring 1990 that Price
Waterhouse must give Hopkins a partnership (Lewin, 1990).

The Court ruled that, if a plaintiff demonstrates that the decision was
infected with gender stereotyping, then the burden shifts to the employer to prove that the same decision would have been reached absent
the illegal stereotyping. Given the propensity of the courts to defer to
employers' judgments of employees, this case may mean only that the
employer is still victorious but has a slightly heavier evidentiary burden. For those plaintiffs who are so clearly superior that there is no
credible reason, absent stereotyping, that a negative decision would
have been made, this case may make discrimination cases somewhat

easier to win. But few plaintiffs are able to present the strong evidence of gender stereotyping that infected Ann Hopkins's partnership decision; stereotyping is often subtle, unspoken, and, sometimes, even unconscious.

Language in the Civil Rights Act of 1991 goes beyond *Price Water house* to provide that, if gender is "a motivating factor" in an employment decision (but not the sole motivating factor), a legal violation may be established (sec. 107). If a plaintiff can establish that gender was a motivating factor, the employer will then be required to prove that it would have "taken the same action in the absence of the impermissible" stereotyping (sec. 107) rather than the normal requirement in claims of intentional discrimination that the employer present a "legitimate nondiscriminatory reason" for the negative decision. This provision may improve plaintiffs' chances of prevailing in these "mixed motive" cases.

Protections for consent decrees. The 1991 law contains other provisions that may aid plaintiffs in their quest for fair treatment. Section 108 of the law protects employment decisions taken under the aegis of a consent decree[3] from later attack by an individual or group not protected by the consent decree. For example, if a group of women challenged an employer's practices that had the effect of limiting the number of women who received promotions, and the court issued a consent decree requiring the employer to promote certain numbers or percentages of women to reverse prior discriminatory treatment, males could not attack subsequent promotion decisions made under the authority of that consent decree. This provision of the law overturns *Martin v. Wilks* (1989), which permitted challenges to consent decrees even a decade or more after they were ordered by a court. This change in the law removes the "double bind" that *Martin* created for employers in that decisions made under consent decrees could be challenged, and decisions that violated consent decrees could also be challenged.

The 1991 law contains various other provisions that will aid women plaintiffs—for example, extending the protections of Title VII to U.S. citizens working abroad for U.S. firms or their subsidiaries, as long as compliance with Title VII does not violate the law of the host country. (The law does not apply to foreign corporations or their employees or to non-U.S. citizens working for U.S. companies.) The law also outlaws race or gender norming on standardized tests and creates a "Glass Ceiling Commission" to conduct a study and develop recommendations concerning the elimination of barriers to the advancement of women and minorities in the workplace.

The overall effect of the Civil Rights Act of 1991 will be to improve the chances of prevailing for plaintiffs in discrimination lawsuits, although it does not remove many of the disincentives to litigation (career concerns, possible employer retaliation, and the financial and emotional burden of a lawsuit). The opportunity to present one's case to a jury, the heavier burden on employers who introduce gender stereotypes into employment decisions, and expanded compensatory and punitive damages (although capped), however, help to equalize the balance of power that heretofore has generally favored employers in these cases.

THE CURRENT STATUS OF
AFFIRMATIVE ACTION

Although the new civil rights law reverses many Supreme Court decisions hostile to the interests of potential plaintiffs, it did not address that Court's decisions regarding affirmative action. Given congressional silence on this matter and recent changes in the composition of the Supreme Court, it is possible that the current protections afforded women and minorities under affirmative action doctrine may be weakened or even eliminated.

More than a decade ago, the U.S. Supreme Court declared in *United Steelworkers of America v. Weber* (1979) that Title VII permitted private companies to implement voluntary affirmative plans. That ruling has been the foundation for all subsequent affirmative action litigation. These rulings generally have permitted, in situations where women or minorities are underrepresented in certain job categories or overall in an organization, that gender or race be viewed as a "plus" factor in hiring and promotion decisions (*Firefighters v. Cleveland,* 1986; *Johnson v. Transportation Agency of Santa Clara County,* 1987). Conversely, however, race or gender may not be used to make layoff decisions (*Firefighters v. Stotts,* 1984; *Wygant v. Jackson Board of Education,* 1986).

Women were handed an important affirmative action victory by the Supreme Court in *Johnson v. Transportation Agency of Santa Clara County* (1987). In that case, the Court ruled that a state agency could rely on an affirmative action plan (that had targeted several job categories where women were either unrepresented or underrepresented) to select a woman for a position despite her slightly lower overall rating. *Johnson* is the first (and, to date, the only) time the Supreme Court has addressed gender-based affirmative action, and it remains a significant precedent.

The precedent is not immune to reversal, however. Only five justices joined the majority in *Johnson,* and three of these have since retired, to be replaced with conservative justices. What these events portend for affirmative action is unclear, but two 1989 Supreme Court decisions involving affirmative action may foreshadow a weakening of the heretofore favorable treatment of affirmative action.

In early 1989, the Supreme Court's new conservative majority struck down a set-aside plan used by the city of Richmond, Virginia (*City of Richmond v. J. A. Croson,* 1989). Although the case involved the awarding of construction contracts rather than employment, the Court's analysis could be easily translated to employment. In a second case, the Court ruled that white males could challenge promotions made under the guidance of an affirmative action plan at any time, even if the employer had acted under the dictates of a consent decree (*Martin v. Wilks,* 1989). *Martin* has since been nullified by the Civil Rights Act of 1991.

While neither *Croson* nor *Martin* specifically overturns *Johnson,* they suggest a hostility to affirmative action that may eventually lead to strict limitations on its use or, in fact, its abolition, as Justices Scalia, Rehnquist, and White's dissents in *Johnson* state that they believe that Title VII does not permit any gender-conscious employment decisions, even if their purpose is to remedy past discrimination. Given the fact that the new civil rights law does not address affirmative action, the conservative Court could outlaw affirmative action by interpreting Title VII's language forbidding the use of gender in making employment decisions as prohibiting *any* consideration of gender (or race) in making employment decisions. More challenges to affirmative action are on the Court docket; we can expect more limitations to, or perhaps even the abolition of, this doctrine in the coming decade.

EQUAL OPPORTUNITY CONFRONTS BIOLOGY

One reality of gender differences that the civil rights laws have not been able to diminish is the biological differences between the sexes, particularly in their reproductive capacity. The fact that women are the childbearers has posed difficulties in the workplace.

In recent years, medical evidence that certain chemicals and other substances found in some workplaces (especially production facilities) may harm unborn babies has stimulated some employers to exclude all women of childbearing age from certain jobs. This has been done despite the evidence that many of these substances also affect male workers' reproductive organs, which, in turn, may cause birth defects (Hatch, 1984; Randall, 1985).

This issue poses legal, financial, and public relations problems for employers. If gender is used to exclude workers from jobs, that is clearly sex discrimination. If a worker bears a baby with birth defects and sues the employer for subjecting the mother to dangerous substances, that poses both a financial and a public relations problem for the company. Even if the mother signs a statement waiving her rights to sue should her baby have physical or medical abnormalities, the baby has an independent right to take legal action against the employer—a right that the mother cannot waive.

On the other hand, many women believe that the decision to expose themselves (and their actual or potential fetuses) to dangerous substances is a personal decision. Furthermore, employer policies that prohibit "fertile" women (defined as women of childbearing age who cannot prove that they are sterile) from performing certain jobs also exclude women who have completed their families, women who plan not to bear children, women in homosexual relationships, and women who are celibate. These women argue that the employer has no right blindly to exclude women on the basis of their age and gender and that such policies unfairly exclude many women who will never be harmed from the high-paying jobs that only men are permitted to fill.

This issue is important for women aspiring to management careers in production industries because such careers usually require experience as a plant-level supervisor. If women cannot work in certain jobs, or, in some cases, in any job on the factory floor, this may effectively preclude them from management positions in these industries.

The courts have struggled with the biology-equal opportunity conundrum in good faith, but have not been able to develop an approach that protects the interests of both women and fetuses equally. In the few cases that have been litigated, the lower courts have generally ruled that the employer may bar "fertile" women from certain jobs if there is proof of potential harm to a fetus, whether or not the woman is or will ever be pregnant, as long as the reproductive risk to males is shown to be lower. In a recent decision, however, the U.S. Supreme Court ruled that such policies violate Title VII and are impermissible.

The lower courts gave great deference to the employers' assertions that concern for the safety of a potential fetus outweighed women's interest in freedom from discrimination. In *Wright v. Olin* (1984), a federal court ruled that Olin's policy of excluding all women under age 63 from certain "restricted" jobs, unless they could prove they were physically incapable of bearing children, did not violate the civil rights laws. Olin had presented extensive scientific evidence that benzene, used in its manufacturing processes, was clearly harmful to a fetus, even at levels that would not affect the mother's health. Olin also showed that males were not similarly affected and that the company had made reasonable efforts to reduce the levels of benzene but could not achieve a level of exposure that was safe for a fetus. The court ruled that this approach was appropriate, given the medical evidence and the company's efforts to accommodate women to the degree that safety permitted.

More recently, the U.S. Court of Appeals for the Seventh Circuit ruled that Johnson Controls, which manufactures automobile batteries, could bar all "fertile" women from jobs in which they are exposed to lead (*UAW v. Johnson Controls,* 1991). The plaintiffs who sued were middle-aged women who asserted that they had been passed over for promotion to supervisory jobs or were displaced from higher paying, but hazardous, jobs by younger men. Only if the women could prove to the satisfaction of the company doctor that they were unable to bear children could they be exempted from the policy. The judges, in ruling for the company, cited medical evidence that exposure to lead can cause learning problems or other mental harm to a fetus. A dissenting judge objected, stating that endorsing such an exclusionary policy would deny 15 to 20 million women access to jobs that involve possible exposure to toxic chemicals.

Shortly after Johnson Controls's victory in the Seventh Circuit, a California appellate court ruled that the same policy *did* violate California's state nondiscrimination law (*Johnson Controls v. California FEHC,* 1990). This contrary result was possible, in part, because the California court was interpreting state law, while the Seventh Circuit was interpreting Title VII, a federal law. In March 1991, the U.S. Supreme Court reversed the ruling of the Seventh Circuit, unanimously finding a clear violation of Title VII.

The Court ruled that Johnson Controls's policy classified women on the basis of gender and childbearing capacity, rather than fertility, and was not applied to men despite evidence that they too were at risk. The Court stated that the company could only assert a "safety defense" if "sex or pregnancy actually interferes with the employee's ability to perform the job" (1991) and that no such showing had been made. Furthermore, the Court rejected the company's claim that such a ruling would expose it to liability for potential birth defects of employees children, noting the potential financial burden of a nondiscriminatory employment policy was never an appropriate defense to a discrimination claim. Potential liability for claims by the employee-parents of a baby with birth defects was "remote," according to the Court, as long as the company informed its employees of the potential risk to their unborn children posed by the lead to which they were exposed.

The *Johnson Controls* case does not address the question of whether an employer may exclude women from certain jobs if there is no evidence that exposure can harm a male's reproductive ability (as was the case in *Olin*). While such exclusionary policies are understandable from a risk-avoidance perspective, they place an unfair burden on women working in manufacturing industries. If work in the industry involves exposure to teratogens (substances that harm a fetus even if they do not harm the mother), the woman may have to choose between bearing children and attaining a management position in the organization. Although many women have deferred motherhood to pursue a career, their choice has not been this draconian.

These policies and other attempts to account for the biological differences between the genders, such as laws granting preferential treatment to women on the basis of pregnancy, are criticized by proponents of individual liberty and freedom of choice (Kirp, Yudof, & Franks, 1986). Such policies hark back to the "protective" labor legislation of the early part of this century that excluded women from working at night, or from working in certain jobs (for example, bartending), or that restricted women to a shorter workweek than men, all of which also reduced their earning potential. On the other hand, despite the Court's words in *Johnson Controls,* it is likely that employers still will face substantial potential legal liability if an employee becomes pregnant, bears a baby with medical or physical problems, and sues the company. Until companies are able or willing to reduce the exposure levels of harmful substances effectively, or until employers' liability for birth defects in such a situation is reduced or eliminated, there is still little incentive for employers to grant women unfettered access to jobs involving teratogens.

THE "MOMMY TRACK": IS IT LEGAL?

Another issue related to the biological differences between the sexes is the propensity for women to interrupt their careers for childbearing and, for some women, for child rearing as well (Posner, 1989). Despite the fact that more than half the employed women bearing children in 1987 returned to work within 12 months of giving birth (U.S. Bureau of the Census, 1989), leaving a job temporarily to give birth to a child or to care for a newly adopted child may be viewed as causing delays or disruptions in a woman manager's career.

Some states, such as California, have attempted to "equalize" the biological inequality by requiring (a) that employers give women at least a minimal maternity and parental leave and (b) that the employer hold the woman's job (or an equal position) for her until she returns. The law applies only to disabilities based on pregnancy. But feminists disagree about whether pregnant women and recent mothers should receive more favorable treatment than other individuals with non-pregnancy-related disabilities (a form of "benign" discrimination). Some argue that pregnancy should be treated like any another disability and not receive additional protection (Williams, 1984-1985) so as to reduce potential discrimination against women by employers who are unwilling to bear what they view as the additional costs of hiring women.

A dramatic example of this debate is the furor over the purported "mommy track," originating in law firms that permit women attorneys to work part time and that either take them off the partnership track or give them additional years before the partnership decision is made (Graham, 1986). Creating a separate career path for working women who are mothers has, to the dismay of many, been advocated by Felice Schwartz as the solution to the problem of the allegedly lower productivity and high turnover of women managers who are also mothers (1989).[4] Schwartz has proposed that corporations identify "career-primary" women—those who decide to devote their energies to their jobs and who either forgo children or who are "satisfied to have others raise" them (1989, p. 69). These women, Schwartz proposes, should be treated just like "fast-track" men. Corporations should "recognize them early, accept them, and clear artificial barriers from their path to the top" (p. 69).

But the majority of employed women, Schwartz states, are "career-and-family women" who want both to have a career and to play an active role in the rearing of their children. For these women, the corporation should provide flexibility and support services and may in turn place them in positions of less responsibility in recognition of their limited commitment to their careers.

For many, the dichotomy that Schwartz sets up is a false one. All employed mothers, including "career-primary" women, would benefit from the assistance Schwartz suggests should be given to women on this "mommy track" (as, of course, would employed fathers), and corporations should "clear artificial barriers" from the paths of all employed persons who seek career advancement. Two legal issues are involved: (a) Does the "mommy track" give more (or less) favorable treatment to women than to men during the time that the woman's children are young? (b) Does this track discriminate against women at a later stage in their careers when they may wish to return to the "fast track"?

Legislation and judicial precedent shed little light on the legality of providing preferences for women on the basis of pregnancy or childbirth, although treating women *less* favorably on the basis of pregnancy or childbirth is illegal. Title VII of the Civil Rights Act of 1964 forbids discrimination on the basis of pregnancy but is silent on whether women may be given more favorable treatment because of pregnancy. As a result, Title VII has been interpreted to allow a California law to treat pregnant workers more favorably than employees with other disabilities, but Title VII has also been used to uphold a Missouri law that some would argue penalizes women for childbearing.

A challenge to a California law that required employers to reinstate women returning from childbirth to the same or a similar job, but made no such provision for workers returning from other kinds of disability leaves, was upheld by the U.S. Supreme Court in *California Federal Savings and Loan v. Guerra* (1987). In the same year, however, the Supreme Court rejected the argument that Missouri's unemployment compensation law, which states that resignation because of pregnancy or childbirth is voluntary quitting and thus excludes the worker from coverage, was unlawful sex discrimination because men do not bear this burden (*Wimberly v. Labor & Industry Commission of Missouri,* 1987). An early Supreme Court case, *Phillips v. Martin Marietta* (1971), held that employers cannot assume, without evidence, that female employees have greater child-care responsibilities than males, but the case would probably permit "parent track" policies if they were applied equally to male and female employees.

To the degree that corporations offered the options suggested by Schwartz to new (or prospective) mothers and not to new fathers, one might argue that the policies were applied in a discriminatory fashion. On the other hand, corporations that have offered paid parental leave or part-time work options to men have reported that men very seldom, if ever, take advantage of them (Alexander, 1990b, p. B-1; Hall, 1989, p. 4). To the degree that the "career-and-family" track is offered only to women, it not only discriminates against men but it perpetuates the stereotype that child rearing is the woman's responsibility.

The second question poses the more serious legal and policy issue for corporations: Will the approach that Schwartz is advocating work to exclude women from upper management cadres because male executives will assume that women who have or plan to bear children are "career-and-family" women rather than "career-primary" women? Furthermore, does this approach relegate a woman once and forever to one particular category, when an individual's career aspirations, personal goals, and priorities may change several times over the course of a lifetime? Can a career-and-family tracker ever move into the career-primary track? Is it sex discrimination if she is not permitted to?

One of the serious problems with Schwartz's dichotomy is that it perpetuates stereotypes of women that have been an important cause of sex discrimination in employment. Making employment decisions based on sex stereotypes violates Title VII, which says that women must be treated as individuals, not as members of a group to whom a stereotype may be applied, even if that stereotype is often accurate (Taub, 1980). Thus one could argue that placing a woman on a "mommy track," with little hope of movement to the "fast track," is per se sex discrimination because it presumes that the employed mother will always place a lower priority on her job. Not making the "career-and-family" track available to men also unfairly stereotypes them as uninvolved in child-rearing responsibilities. Corporations considering the use of a two-track system should use care to make sure that such practices are completely voluntary, that both sexes have an equal opportunity to take advantage of them, and that individuals who do reduce their working hours or take advantage of parental leave policies are regularly given the opportunity to move back to the "fast track" or its equivalent.

SEXUAL HARASSMENT, DISCRIMINATION, AND OFFICE ROMANCE

A form of sex discrimination that has stubbornly refused to disappear from the workplace is sexual harassment.[5] Although the popular notion of harassment involves male boss to female secretary, women at all levels, including women managers, are victims, and some men are as well. In fact, women managers may endure harassment from both subordinates and superiors as well as from peers (Clarke, 1986).

It is difficult to ascertain the extent of sexual harassment in the workplace because many, if not most, cases of harassment go unreported (Gutek, 1985, p. 71). There are strong disincentives, especially for women in management, to report harassment, particularly if the harasser happens to be the woman's boss. Yet, women challenging sexual harassment in the workplace have generally received a positive reaction from the courts (Maschke, 1989; York, 1989), although the outcomes of charges filed with at least one state civil rights agency have not tended to favor women (Terpstra & Baker, 1988).[6]

Although lower federal courts first ruled favorably on women's sexual harassment claims in 1976 (*Williams v. Saxbe,* 1976), it was not until a decade later that the U.S. Supreme Court dealt with this issue in *Meritor Savings Bank v. Vinson* (1986). *Meritor* is a significant case because it permits a woman who can prove that she was harassed by a supervisor to sue the company successfully, even if she did not report the harassment.[7]

Meritor is also important because it discusses the ways in which an employer can reduce its liability in the event of coworker harassment (called "hostile or offensive environment" harassment). The Court criticized the employer in *Meritor,* a bank, which had no policy specifically prohibiting sexual harassment, required the victim to report the harassment to her supervisor (the harasser), and had not established explicit penalties for sexual harassment. In this situation, the Court commented, one could hardly expect a victim to report harassment, and the mere fact of not reporting the harassment should not preclude a finding of liability against the bank.

Conversely, the Court suggested, and the EEOC has confirmed in guidelines to its investigative staff, if an employer develops an explicit sexual harassment policy, adopts a reporting system that permits a victim to make the report to a neutral party, and establishes specific penalties for sexual harassment, a victim's failure to report hostile or offensive environment harassment may result in a finding of no liability on the part of the employer (EEOC, 1990, p. 405:6697).

Although women managers certainly have been subject to harassment by supervisors (Clarke, 1986), it is more likely that they will be exposed to the "hostile or offensive environment" harassment that is inflicted upon them by coworkers, clients, or subordinates. Women managers are more likely than nonmanagerial women to take business trips, to be required to entertain business clients, or to attend social functions sponsored by the business. Harassment is more likely to occur in these settings. Furthermore, women managers are more likely to come ir contact with male employees (or customers or clients) than are non managers, and increased contact with men increases the potential for and frequency of harassment (Gutek, 1985).

For women encountering the hostile environment form of sexua harassment, the legal remedies are not so easily obtained. There are strong disincentives for women managers to report harassment: the possibility that they will not be believed, the potential for being labeled a "troublemaker" (Bumiller, 1988), or a belief that they "deserved" the harassing treatment (Gutek, 1985). These, and other difficulties, faced Anita Hill when she alleged that now confirmed Supreme Court Justice Clarence Thomas engaged in sexual harassment. Although women have obtained relief for hostile environment harassment (for example, *Broderic v. Ruder*, 1988), they have usually done so only when they could show tha the workplace was pervaded by sexual activity and after showing that they were exposed to this environment over a long period of time.

And what if the harassment is the result of a formerly consensual love affair with a coworker or superior? Although the EEOC Guidelines state that unwanted behavior of a sexual nature is illegal harassment (EEOC Guidelines, 1980), the woman may not receive a sympathetic ear, either from the employer or from a judge, if she admits that the sexual conduc began voluntarily and became unwelcome at some later point.

Office romance. A romantic relationship between coworkers, or be tween supervisor and subordinate, can present a host of problems, onl some of which have legal implications. The relationship may caus morale problems for other employees, may cast doubt upon the objec tivity of one or both of the lovers, and may stall or destroy the career c one or both participants (see the chapter by Mainiero in this book for more in-depth discussion of these matters).

Although most corporations do not have nepotism policies or policie forbidding coworkers to date (Bureau of National Affairs [BNA], 1988a those businesses that enforce such policies have occasionally encountere legal problems. For example, in *Rulon-Miller v. IBM* (1984), a femal manager fired for dating a former coworker employed by a competitc was awarded damages for wrongful discharge and emotional distres: It is likely that Rulon-Miller won because IBM had a written polic against interfering in its employees' private lives unless a negativ effect on the business had been demonstrated; no such effect had bee

hown. If, however, a business can present evidence that the romance
as creating a morale problem, performance problems for one or both
f the pair, or other negative impacts on the business, rules against
ating coworkers have been upheld in court (*Crozier v. United Parcel
ervice,* 1983; *Ward v. Frito-Lay, Inc.,* 1980).

And what if an employee is promoted or receives favored treatment
om a lover who is a supervisor? Do other employees, perhaps better
ualified, have a legal claim? Some courts have answered these "par-
mour claims" in the affirmative. In *King v. Palmer* (1985), a nurse who
as passed over for promotion in favor of a less-well-qualified woman
ho was having an affair with the supervisor sued the employer,
lleging sex discrimination. (It was not sexual harassment because
xual favors had not been demanded from the plaintiff; nor did the
laintiff allege a hostile environment.) The court agreed that it was sex
iscrimination against the plaintiff because the promotion decision had
een influenced by the sexual relationship.

King has not been followed in subsequent cases, however. For exam-
le, courts have ruled that, if both males and females are passed over
r promotion in favor of a participant in a sexual relationship, no Title
II violation has been found (*DeCintio v. Westchester County Medical
enter,* 1987; *Polk v. Pollard,* 1989). New policy guidelines issued by
e EEOC say that "Title VII does not prohibit isolated instances of
referential treatment based on consensual romantic relationships," but
ey add that, if there is "widespread favoritism" based on the granting
f sexual favors, a hostile environment may be found, because a mes-
ge is conveyed that "managers view women as sexual playthings"
EOC, 1990). Although this legal doctrine is still developing, it seems
ear that, if the plaintiff can allege that preferential treatment of a
oworker because of a sexual relationship created a hostile environment
he argument used in *Broderick*), the court will entertain the claim as
xual harassment (Shearer, 1989).

WHAT IS ON THE LEGAL AND
POLITICAL HORIZON?

This chapter has explored several persistently troublesome legal and
ractical issues for women managers. Some of the problems are not
sily amenable to legal solutions, such as the debate between the

protection of fetuses (or potential fetuses) and equal employment op
portunity. Other problems are more effectively addressed by changes
corporate practices, such as more flexible work structures for emplo
ees with young children.

The recently enacted Family and Medical Leave Act, which entitle
certain employees to unpaid leave to care for newborn or adopte
children or family members who are ill, is a small step on the pa
toward more flexible work structures. However, because women a
more likely to use family leave than are men, some experts worry th
the law could actually result in employer reluctance to hire or promo
women. And for women who are single parents, the economic cons
quences of using unpaid family leave may be prohibitive.

Despite this long awaited law, the United States is well behind oth
industrialized nations in its attention to work and family issues (see t
Berthoin Antal & Izraeli chapter for more discussion of this issue). F
example, workers in Sweden are entitled by law to 12 months leave
90% of their salary when a child is born or adopted, and their job mu
be held for them. They are also given, by law, 60 days of leave ea
year, with pay, to care for sick children (Edlund & Nystrom, 1988). T
government provides funding for day care, primarily at the municip
level. Not surprisingly, participation by women in the work force
Sweden is 80% (Flanagan, 1987), while the participation rate for wom
in the United States in 1987 was 56% (U.S. Bureau of the Census, 198

The changing demographic patterns of America's work force[8] m
pressure employers to provide the family-oriented employment be
efits that some, but by no means all, employers have begun to gi
their workers. Sporadic articles in *The Wall Street Journal* chronic
the attempts of employers to help workers, both men and women,
have rewarding careers and attend to the needs of their famili
(Trost & Hymowitz, 1990, p. B-1). These articles also report surve
of both male and female employees that show a developing disinc
nation to put career ahead of family (Trost & Hymowitz, 1990,
B-1). The fact that such employer policies are newsworthy sugges
their novelty.

Given the current political climate, it is unlikely that family-orient
laws, such as Sweden's, will be in place anytime soon. It appears th
thus far at least, only when a company believes such policies to be

its best economic interest, to keep valued female (and male) managers, will it adapt to meet their needs (Hymowitz, 1990, p. B-1).

But enlightened corporate policies related to combining career and family will not be sufficient to keep top women managers, according to another survey. Even if a company has a full array of family-oriented policies, women managers who want greater responsibility, more attention to their professional development, or more recognition will leave anyway and are leaving at rates higher then similarly dissatisfied men (Deutsch, 1990, p. F-27). Continuing problems with discrimination, inability to break the "glass ceiling" into upper management, and dissatisfaction with their work assignments were cited by both white and minority women managers far more than family issues as reasons for leaving a job (Alexander, 1990a, p. B-1; Trost, 1990, p. B-1). A top (male) manager at a large insurance company believes that "a complex web of reasons, including stereotyping by male managers who are more comfortable working with other men, and a lack of assertiveness by women on 'managing the political process of their career development' " is responsible for the barriers to the advancement of women into top leadership roles (Trost, 1990, p. B-4).

The findings of these surveys suggest that the legal system, and perhaps the political system as well, are still not well positioned to address many of the problems faced by women managers. Given the low success rate of litigation and the disinclination of women managers to use the courts in the first place, the civil rights laws may not present much of a disincentive to companies that continue to discriminate against women. Although legislators are more responsive to the views of constituents than are judges, the business lobby is powerful and can kill or delay legislation, as was the case under the Bush adminstration for the Family and Medical Leave Act. President Clinton seems committed to political and social change and has made women's issues a high priority, but societal and attitudinal changes may be slow to arrive. At least until the political and social climate clearly establishes itself as being favorable to the concerns of women managers over the long run, they must look beyond the legal system for solutions and, as some women managers have already done, either persuade their employers to meet their needs or, perhaps, vote with their feet.

NOTES

1. For this analysis, the index to decisions published in the BNA (1988b) Fair Employment Practice Cases from 1983 through 1989 was consulted. Every published decision in federal trial or appellate courts relating to sex discrimination against women in hiring, promotion, and discharge was reviewed (sex discrimination cases against men were not included). Outcomes of all such cases where a decision was rendered on the merits were categorized by manager and nonmanager and by win or loss.

2. A claim of "disparate impact" involves the charge by one or a group of individuals that an employer's practice, although facially neutral, disproportionately excludes certain classes of people from hiring, promotion, and so forth and is thus discriminatory. Disparate impact cases are usually, but not always, class action cases.

3. A consent decree is a voluntary settlement between parties to a lawsuit that, upon acceptance by the court, becomes the judgment of the court and is legally binding on the parties.

4. Although Posner (1989) also states that data demonstrate that women are less "productive" than men because of the time they spend out of the labor market and because of their higher representation among part-time workers, Donohue (1989) suggests that this viewpoint is shortsighted. He argues that such a definition of productivity is inappropriate, saying that the greater propensity of men to be alcoholics, for example, is a more telling example of productivity differences between the sexes than work force participation rates.

5. The EEOC (1980) defines sexual harassment as "unwelcome sexual advances, requests for sexual favors, and other verbal or physical conduct of a sexual nature . . . when (1) submission to such conduct is made either explicitly or implicitly a term or condition of an individual's employment, (2) submission to or rejection of such conduct by an individual is used as the basis for employment decisions affecting such individual, or (3) such conduct has the purpose or effect of unreasonably interfering with an individual's work performance or creating an intimidating, hostile, or offensive working environment" (29 C.F.R. 1604.11).

6. Although these studies may seem contradictory, one plausible explanation lies in the cost differences between state agency proceedings and a trial. Filing a charge with a state civil rights agency does not require the assistance of an attorney, so there is little incentive for women with weak or marginal cases to refrain from filing charges. The cost of litigation is substantial, not only because an attorney is involved but because other necessities, such as the copying of documents, deposition costs, and expert witness fees, must be paid.

7. This form of harassment is called "quid pro quo" and involves harassment by an individual who has the power to affect or alter a woman's employment status (such as the power to hire, promote, fire, or give her a raise). The other form of sexual harassment, "hostile or offensive environment" harassment, may be engaged in by supervisors, coworkers, clients, customers, or any other person with whom the employee comes in contact because of a business relationship (for example, a machine repairperson).

8. The "baby-boom" generation is reaching middle age; in 15 years or less, there will be fewer people, both men and women, to move into middle management positions. This situation should pressure employers to give greater attention to preserving a precious resource—their potential managers—by providing more flexible employment policies.

REFERENCES

AFSCME v. Washington, 770 F.2d 1401 (9th Cir. 1985).

Alexander, K. (1990a, July 25). Minority women feel racism, sexism are blocking the path to management. *The Wall Street Journal,* p. B-1.

Alexander, S. (1990b, August 24). Fears for careers curb paternity leaves. *The Wall Street Journal,* p. B-1.

Bartholet, E. (1982). Application of Title VI to jobs in high places. *Harvard Law Review, 95,* 945-1027.

Bohemian Club v. Fair Employment and Housing Commission, 187 Cal. App. 3d 1 (1986), *appeal dismissed,* 52 Fair Employ. Prac. Cases 848 (U.S., 1987).

Broderick v. Ruder, 685 F. Supp. 1269 (D.D.C. 1988).

Bumiller, K. (1988). *The civil rights society: The social construction of victims.* Baltimore: Johns Hopkins Press.

Bureau of National Affairs (BNA). (1988a). *Corporate affairs.* Washington, DC: Author.

Bureau of National Affairs (BNA). (1988b, October). State law chart. *Fair Employment Practice Manual, 451,* 102-104.

California Federal Savings and Loan Association v. Guerra, 107 S.Ct. 683 (1987).

City of Richmond v. J. A. Croson Co., 109 S.Ct. 706 (1989).

Clarke, L. W. (1986). Women supervisors experience sexual harassment too. *Supervisory Management, 31*(4), 35-36.

Crozier v. UPS, 150 Cal. App. 3d 1132 (1983).

DeCintio v. Westchester County Medical Center, 807 F.2d 304 (2d Cir. 1986), *cert. denied,* 108 S.Ct. 89 (1987).

Deutsch, C. H. (1990, April 29). Why women walk out on jobs. *The New York Times,* p. F-27.

Donohue, J. J., III. (1989). Prohibiting sex discrimination in the workplace: An economic perspective. *University of Chicago Law Review, 56*(4), 1337-1368.

Edlund, S., & Nystrom, B. (1988). *Development in Swedish labor law.* Stockholm: Swedish Institute.

EEOC Guidelines, 29 C.F.R. Sec. 1604.11(a), et seq. (1980).

EEOC. (1990, January 12). *Policy statement* (No. 915.048). Washington, DC: Author.

EEOC v. American Tel. & Tel., 556 F.2d 167 (3d Cir. 1977), *cert. denied,* 438 U.S. 915 (1978).

Evans, S. M., & Nelson, B. J. (1989). *Wage justice: Comparable worth and the paradox of technocratic reform.* Chicago: University of Chicago Press.

Firefighters v. Cleveland, 478 U.S. 501 (1986).

Firefighters v. Stotts, 467 U.S. 561 (1984).

Flanagan, R. J. (1987). Efficiency and equity in Swedish labor markets. In B. Bosworth & A. M. Rivlin (Eds.), *The Swedish economy* (pp. 125-184). Washington, DC: Brookings Institution.

Ginesky, A. B., & Rogoff, A. R. (1976). Subjective employment criteria and the future of Title VII in professional jobs. *Journal of Urban Law, 54,* 165-236.

Graham, D. (1986, December). It's getting better, slowly. *ABA Journal,* pp. 54-58.

Gutek, B. A. (1985). *Sex and the workplace.* San Francisco: Jossey-Bass.

Hall, D. T. (1989). Moving beyond the "mommy track": An organization change approach. *Personnel, 66*(12), 23-29.

Hatch, M. (1984). Mother, father, worker: Men and women and the reproductive risks of work. In W. Chavkin (Ed.), *Double exposure: Women's health hazards on the job and at home* (pp. 161-179). New York: Monthly Review Press.

Hymowitz, C. (1990, June 18). As Aetna adds flextime, bosses learn to cope. *The Wall Street Journal*, pp. B-1, B-4.

Hymowitz, C., & Schellhardt, T. D. (1986, March 24). The glass ceiling. *The Wall Street Journal*, pp. D-1, D-4 to D-5.

Johnson v. Transportation Agency of Santa Clara County, 107 S.Ct. 1442 (1987).

Johnson Controls v. California FEHC, 267 Cal. Rptr. 158 (Cal. App. 4 Dist., 1990).

King v. Palmer, 598 F. Supp. 65 (D.D.C. 1984), *rev'd*, 778 F.2d 878 (D.C. Cir. 1985).

Kirp, D. L., Yudof, M. G., & Franks, M. S. (1986). *Gender justice*. Chicago: University of Chicago Press.

Kyriazi v. Western Electric Co., 476 F. Supp. 335 (D.N.J. 1979).

LaNoue, G. R., & Lee, B. A. (1987). *Academics in court: The consequences of faculty discrimination litigation*. Ann Arbor: University of Michigan Press.

Lee, B. A. (1989-1990). Subjective employment practices and disparate impact: Unresolved issues. *Employee Relations Law Journal, 15,* 403-417.

Lemons v. City and County of Denver, 620 F.2d 228 (10th Cir. 1989).

Lewin, T. (1990, May 19). Winner of sex bias suit set to enter next arena. *The New York Times*, p. L-7.

Lorance v. AT&T Technologies, Inc., 109 S.Ct. 2261 (1989).

Martin v. Wilks, 109 S.Ct. 2180 (1989).

Maschke, K. J. (1989). *Litigation, courts and women workers*. New York: Praeger.

Meritor Savings Bank v. Vinson, 106 S.Ct. 2399 (1986).

Patterson v. McLean Credit Union, 109 S.Ct. 2363 (1989).

Phillips v. Martin Marietta Corp., 411 F.2d 1, *vacated and remanded*, 400 U.S. 542 (1971).

Polk v. Pollard, 52 Fair Empl. Prac. Cases 538 (La. App. 1989).

Posner, R. A. (1989). An economic analysis of sex discrimination laws. *University of Chicago Law Review, 56*(4), 1311-1335.

Price Waterhouse v. Hopkins, 109 S.Ct. 1775 (1989).

Randall, D. (1985). Women in toxic work environments: A case study and examination of policy impact. In L. Larwood, A. H. Stromberg, & B. A. Gutek, *Women and work* (Vol. 1). Beverly Hills, CA: Sage.

Roberts v. U.S. Jaycees, 468 U.S. 609 (1984).

Rostker v. Goldberg, 453 U.S. 57 (1981).

Rulon-Miller v. IBM, 162 Cal. App. 3d 241 (1984).

Scarborough, C. (1989). Conceptualizing black women's employment experiences. *Yale Law Journal, 98,* 1435-1478.

Schwartz, F. N. (1989, January-February). Management women and the new facts of life. *Harvard Business Review*, pp. 65-76.

Shearer, R. A. (1989). Paramour claims under Title VII: Liability for co-worker/employer sexual relationships. *Employee Relations Law Journal, 15,* 57-66.

Sorensen, E. (1989). The wage effects of occupational sex composition: A review and new findings. In M. A. Hill & M. R. Killingsworth (Eds.), *Comparable worth: Analyses and evidence*. Ithaca, NY: Cornell University Press.

Taub, N. (1980). Keeping women in their place: Stereotyping per se as a form of employment discrimination. *Boston College Law Review, 21,* 345-418.

Terpstra, D. E., & Baker, D. D. (1988). Outcomes of sexual harassment charges. *Academy of Management Journal, 31*, 185-194.

Theodore, A. (1986). *The campus troublemakers: Academic women in protest.* Houston: Cap and Gown.

Treiman, D. J., & Hartmann, H. I. (Eds.). (1981). *Women, work and wages: Equal pay for jobs of equal value.* Washington, DC: National Academy Press.

Trost, C. (1990, May 2). Women managers quit not for family but to advance their corporate climb. *The Wall Street Journal,* pp. B-1, B-4.

Trost, C., & Hymowitz, C. (1990, June 18). Careers start giving in to family needs. *The Wall Street Journal,* pp. B-1, B-4.

United Auto Workers v. Johnson Controls, 50 Fair Empl. Prac. Cases 1627 (7th Cir. 1989), *rev'd,* 111 S.Ct. 1196 (1991).

U.S. Bureau of the Census. (1989). Labor force participation, 1987. In *Statistical abstract of the United States.* Washington, DC: Government Printing Office.

United Steelworkers of America v. Weber, 443 U.S. 193 (1979).

Waintroob, A. R. (1979-1980). The developing law of equal employment opportunity at the white collar and professional level. *William and Mary Law Review, 21*, 45-119.

Ward v. Frito-Lay, Inc., 95 Wis. 2d 372 (Wis. App. 1980).

Wards Cove Packing Co. v. Atonio, 109 S.Ct. 2115 (1989).

Williams, W. W. (1984-1985). Equality's riddle: Pregnancy and the equal treatment/special treatment debate. *New York University Review of Law and Social Change, 13*, 325-380.

Williams v. Saxbe, 12 Fair Empl. Prac. Cases 1093 (D.D.C. 1976).

Wimberly v. Labor & Industrial Commission of Missouri, 107 S.Ct. 821 (1987).

Wright v. Olin, 34 Fair Empl. Prac. Cases 1226 (W.D.N.C. 1984).

Wygant v. Jackson Board of Education, 476 U.S. 267 (1986).

York, K. M. (1989). Defining sexual harassment in workplaces: A policy capturing approach. *Academy of Management Journal, 32*, 830-850.

10

Feminist Practice in Organizations: Implications for Management

PATRICIA YANCEY MARTIN

[Jones] is at the top of his special breed in American business. His skills encompass every conceivable attribute of the compleat [*sic*] corporate executive, save those in the subjective area of sentimentality, the appearance of kindness, or an inherent willingness to give a man in error a second chance. It is not that he couldn't, if he cared, acquire the polish of gentleness, but rather that he regards it as a superfluous characteristic. . . . [Jones's] favorite phrase is, "I'll cut his balls off." (William Rodgers, 1969, pp. 249-250, about an IBM executive in the 1960s)

The women structured their days to include as much sharing as possible; it was a deliberate process, a major goal of every day. . . . Sharing was facilitated by their view of themselves as being in the center of things rather

AUTHOR'S NOTE: An earlier draft of the chapter was presented in the session on Democratic Practice in Feminist Organizations at the Annual Meeting of the Eastern Sociological Society, Boston (March 1990). I am indebted to Joan Acker, Rebecca Bordt, Celia Davies, Robin Leidner, Irene Padavic, Barbara Reskin, Ruth Wallace, and Carmen Siriani for their suggestions for revision. I thank Robin Leidner and Carmen Siriani for initially encouraging me to write the chapter. The suggestions of Ellen Fagenson and of several anonymous referees were especially helpful to me in shaping the final draft.

than at the top; it's more natural to reach out than to reach down. . . . Implicit in such structurings is the notion of group affiliation rather than individual achievement as having the highest value. (Sally Helgesen, 1990, pp. 27, 49, about four U.S. women executives)

As feminists articulate their methods, they can become more aware of what they do, and thus do it better. Thinking about method is empowering. When I require myself to explain what I do, I am likely to discover how to improve what I earlier may have taken for granted. In the process, I am likely to become more committed to what it is that I have improved. (Bartlett, 1990, p. 831, making a case for feminist legal methods in the practice of law)

Many managers and scholars (Collinson, Knights, & Collinson, 1990; Hardesty & Jacobs, 1986; Helgesen, 1990; Watson, 1990) want to transform the corporation from a context that favors men and male-associated norms and practices—such as those described in *THINK* (the first quote)—to one that (also) values women and woman-associated norms and practices—like those described by Helgesen (in the second quote). Some scholars claim that corporations cannot be transformed—but must be dismantled and replaced—because reforms will be undermined by hierarchy, bureaucracy, patriarchy, or the participation of men (Blum & Smith, 1988; Ferguson, 1984). Others, including the writer, are somewhat more sanguine (see Bergmann, 1986; Morrison & Von Glinow, 1990; O'Farrell & Harlan, 1984).

The opening quotes from Rodgers and Helgesen are highly gender typed. Rodgers's is a stereotypically *masculine* conception of management. Writing in the late 1960s, he praises Jones's macho toughness, enjoyment of power over others, and eschewal of the softer emotions, such as kindness or forgiveness. Helgesen, 20 years later, idealizes her subjects' *feminine* management style, which values relationships, coordination, and the well-being of the collective. Although both depictions are stereotypical, each has considerable popular appeal.

Helgesen's quote reflects a recent theme in the literature, which claims that women's ways of managing are more effective and humane than men's ways are (e.g., Gilson & Kane, 1987; Hardesty & Jacobs, 1986; Lenz & Myerhoff, 1985; Loden, 1985; Maccoby, 1988; Naisbitt & Aburdene, 1985, 1990). The claim is that women and girls are more relationship centered, nurturing, and sensitive than men and boys are, due to different socialization experiences, and thus women make superior managers. While this literature emphasizes the virtues of *feminine* values and practices, it rarely mentions *feminist* values and practices. Although reasons for this are unknown, I suspect that many managers view feminism and feminists with distaste. Corporate managers probably are wary of feminists, believing—correctly—that feminists' visions of the workplace and its obligations to women and, indeed, all employees are different than prevailing conceptions and practices. In support of this view, Martin, Seymour, Godbey, Courage, and Tate (1988) found that corporate managers—women and men—were less favorable than feminists were toward policies and benefits to help employees fulfill their family obligations.

The third quote, from legal scholar Katharine Bartlett (1990), challenges feminist lawyers to clarify the nature and form of feminist legal methods for use in the practice of law. *Feminist legal methods* are strategies for practicing law that are calculated to enhance the status of women (and other excluded groups) and to produce feminist outcomes. (See Martin, 1990a, for a discussion of feminist outcomes relative to individual and collective transformation.) Bartlett specifies three methods for use by feminists to improve the treatment of women in the legal system and urges men as well as women to employ them. Like this chapter, Bartlett defines feminism as political orientation and practice aimed at improving the status of women. Although most women experience the disadvantages of gender inequality and discrimination, *not all* women are feminists, and, although most men benefit from sexist arrangements and practices, some men *are* feminists. As political orientation and practice, feminism is neither determined by nor synonymous with gender. In this view, men as well as women can practice feminist management.

This chapter invites managers to join the author in an exercise parallel to Bartlett's by considering the implications of feminism for management. Women's experiences in corporations are different than those of men. The corporation's ways of doing business produce privilege for many majority men and exclusion and exploitation for many women and minority men (Boyd, Mulvihill, & Myles, 1990; Morrison & Von Glinow, 1990; Reskin & Ross, 1990). Compared with (majority) men, women suffer disadvantages of authority, compensation, promotion, better jobs, and control over monetary and human resources. If feminism can challenge prevailing conceptions of corporate purpose, improve the way management is practiced, and enhance women's status in and treatment by the corporation, the exercise will have been worthwhile.

BACKGROUND

Women's representation in corporations has increased dramatically since World War II (Morrison & Von Glinow, 1990) and women's representation in managerial, executive, and administrative positions has doubled in only 20 years. In 1970, 18.5% of all managers, executives, and administrators in the United States were women but, by 1980, women were more than 30% and, by 1992, approximately 42% of this group (Reskin & Ross, 1990; U.S. Department of Labor, 1993).

Despite their increased numbers, women continue to be disadvantaged in corporations. For example, they are segregated into a limited number of jobs (e.g., secretary, receptionist, or other nonexempt positions; Kanter, 1977; Reskin & Hartmann, 1986), are often targets of sexual harassment (Gutek, 1985, 1989), and are excluded from job ladders that lead to senior management posts (Baron, Davis-Blake, & Bielby, 1986). Women managers are crowded into lower and middle hierarchical levels (Reskin & Ross, 1990) and have minimal jurisdiction or authority over others, especially over men (Bergmann, 1986; Boyd et al., 1990). Nearly all senior management posts are occupied by men, with women holding only 5% of these positions (U.S. Department of Labor, 1991).

Women's increased presence in management is, according to some scholars, due to the increase in women employees generally and to occupational and market shifts toward a white-collar, information-based, service economy (Boyd et al., 1990; Lorence, 1989). The apparent *gender desegregation* of management must be assessed in light of the *gender resegregation* within management that has also occurred (Reskin & Ross, 1990). According to Boyd, Mulvihill, and Myles (1990), women managers have been recruited and hired primarily to manage other women and, like the women they manage, they are crowded into lower and middle hierarchical levels. Women rarely manage men. In general, women have few subordinates, make few final decisions, have little control over financial resources, have few to no male subordinates, and are overrepresented in smaller enterprises (Boyd et al., 1990; Brown, 1988; Reskin & Ross, 1990).

Women's increased representation in management is thus a mixed benefit. Now prevalent in middle management, women are rare in senior management posts. This is due, I suggest, to the *normative masculinity* of management. Despite women's influx, managerial work remains *normatively* the job of married (white) men who can—and do—devote full time to the job and who can rely on their wives to take care of children, marriage, and home (Acker, 1990; Cockburn, 1988; Hearn, Sheppard, Tancred-Sheriff, & Burrell, 1989). Because of this, women have less legitimacy as managers, especially when the position brings authority over men, substantial resources, and major decisions (Boyd et al., 1990; Brenner, Tomkiewicz, & Schein, 1989; Chase & Bell, 1990).

Men's numerical predominance in the highest paid, most coveted, and most powerful positions also hurts women. As Reskin (1988) notes, those who control powerful positions in hierarchies are able to protect themselves by enforcing succession rules that secure their privileged status. Men control the powerful positions in practically all corporate hierarchies. Thus men make the rules that select, and reward, their successors—persons like themselves who, they presume, share their circumstances, interests, and goals—that is, other (majority) men (Kanter, 1977). For these and related reasons, Connell (1987) depicts the work organization as hegemonically (predominately) masculine. Male-associated norms, in combination with the dominance of male persons, give masculinity and men high status and influence.

Women managers who are mothers and wives must discharge home and family obligations while trying to fulfill the expectations associated with their male-normative management jobs (Hardesty & Jacobs, 1986). That this is burdensome for them may be nominally acknowledged but expectations and practices that reward managers for giving their all to the job continue to hold sway (see, for example, Jackall, 1988). Men are typically freer than women are to devote *most* of their time and energy to a management job.

Corporations will have to change so as to treat women commensurately with men. But can—and will—they change? How might change be accomplished? Do incentives for change exist? Some scholars claim that corporations *cannot* change and that wholly new types of organizations will have to be created before women will receive equitable treatment—types that eschew hierarchy, a division of labor based on expertise, and bureaucracy itself (e.g., Ferguson, 1984; Rothschild & Whitt, 1986). Others say that corporations will inevitably improve in their treatment of women as women's numbers and demands—such as for more flexibility or supports for their familial duties—increase (Naisbitt & Aburdene, 1990). Still others claim that recruiting and advancing entire cohorts of women into management, instead of one or only a few, will help women succeed (Kanter, 1977).

I believe that corporations will change only if feminists organize, take political action, and force them to (see Acker, 1990; Martin & Chernesky, 1989). Along with others, I doubt that corporations will improve simply because many women work there. I also believe that men who benefit from current arrangements will not relinquish them without a struggle (Bergmann, 1986; Cohn, 1985; Martin & Chernesky, 1989; Reskin, 1988; Reskin & Roos, 1987, 1991).

For lasting change to occur, Acker (1990) concludes that women's and men's duties in the realms of paid and unpaid work—the corporation and the home—will have to change (also see Hochschild, 1989). Why is this so? If male managers prioritize job over children, marriage, home, and even self, and if men chosen by other men for advancement are the ones who do so, women who want to succeed in management will have to do so too. But, in complying with a male-normative conception of management, women's costs—of time, effort, and emotion—will be greater than men's because women will almost certainly not have husbands who will take care of child care and home-related duties for them. Women will have to forgo family life or do the double duty of paid and unpaid work, without substantial help. Even when help is purchased in the marketplace, women typically arrange for and supervise the helper(s), thus remaining responsible (Hochschild, 1989). It is mostly women who stay home with a sick or out-of-school child. Demands on women managers who have children but no husband are even heavier.

Men who are married to women managers are expected to put their own jobs first and, in most corporations, are punished if they do not (Finch, 1983; Kanter, 1977; Margolis, 1979). Men disapprove of other men who volunteer for extra family duties. This probably explains why only a handful of men used AT&T's parental leave benefits during the program's first five years of operation (Conference Board, 1985). Other men disapproved of the men who used parental leave and saw them as unqualified for further advancement. A man who prioritizes home and family over job risks a loss of respect from other men and a loss of opportunity to advance. Men judge each other by their income, status, and paid work success, thus few are likely to prioritize family over job unless fundamental change occurs (Connell, 1987).

Men can benefit from changes in the balance of paid and home/family work, however. Eliminating the norm that paid work is more important than home and family would allow men to invest more in their personal lives. Given more freedom, men might become less competitive and less concerned with proving their superiority and dominance. If men assumed more responsibility for children and home, work loads for women would lessen and women would have more freedom, time, and opportunity to gain parity at home and on the job (see Hardesty & Jacobs, 1986). I return to the benefits issue at the chapter's end.

THE GENDERED CORPORATION

A great deal of sociological research documents the pervasiveness of gender beliefs, constructions, and practices in corporations (Baron, Davis-Blake, & Bielby, 1986; Bielby & Baron, 1986; Boyd et al., 1990; Cockburn, 1988; Cohn, 1985; Hearn & Parkin, 1988; Hearn et al., 1989; Martin, 1991; Reskin & Hartmann, 1986; Reskin & Roos, 1991). This research shows that corporations are not sets of empty, gender-neutral positions that are filled in accord with the dictates of rationality or efficiency, based on applicants' objective qualifications irrespective of gender (see Chase & Bell, 1990; Zimmer, 1988). Rather, it shows that practically all jobs—and job ladders (see Baron et al., 1986)—are gender specific and practically all job searches are gender searches. Women are sought for women's jobs; men are sought for men's jobs (Acker, 1990; Williams, 1989). Women and men rarely hold identical jobs or, if they do, their titles, locations, work groups—and compensation rates—almost always differ (Bielby & Baron, 1986). Women are rarely hired to manage men whereas many men manage women (Reskin & Ross, 1990).

The gendering of jobs, positions, groups, tasks, and locations varies across organizations, and over time, but, in any particular organization at a given time, the vast majority of workers are segregated horizontally and vertically by gender (Bielby & Baron, 1986, 1987; Cohn, 1985). If gender were irrelevant to the conception and filling of jobs—as gender blind organizational theory claims—such conditions would be exceptional and rare. Research findings show otherwise.

Bielby and Baron (1986), in a study of occupational sex segregation in 393 California establishments (over a 20-year period, 1959 to 1979) found the mean sex-segregation score (the percentage of jobs that contained only women or only men) was 93.4%. All jobs in 232 (or 59%) of the establishments were completely sex segregated. Of 61,000 employees covered by the study, only 8.5% were employed in establishments with segregation scores lower than 90. In firms with less sex segregation, men and women with the same job titles were usually separated by physical location; for example, they were apartment complex managers who lived at separate complexes. In a five-year follow-up of 75 organizations to see if sex segregation of jobs decreased over time, 11 establishments had become substantially less segregated, 7 had become substantially more segregated, and the rest remained more or less the same. (Also see Bielby & Baron, 1987; Reskin & Roos, 1987.)

Research by Glenn and Tolbert (1987) asked if women experience success equal to men's in the new computer industry. They reasoned that women may fare better in a new field than in one that historically favored men. The data failed to support this view. Women in the computer industry are crowded into the lowest-level, most repetitive and routine, least flexible, and least-well-compensated jobs, such as data entry or computer equipment operator (also see Strober & Arnold, 1987): 32% of all women but only 3% of all men hold these jobs. Of the white men in computer work, 60% hold the highest-level jobs (computer scientist or programmer), which are well-paid, allow freedom and creativity, and provide opportunities for advancement. Only 23% of computer industry women, white and minority, hold such jobs. Glenn and Tolbert's results are replicated in research by Baran (1985) on the insurance industry. Baran found that computer technology both deskilled and reengendered the job of claims adjustor. As it became routinized through computerization, claims adjustor work lost its high status, high pay, flexibility (e.g., going to a site to examine damage, making judgments about claims), and male members. As claims adjustor work lost its status and pay advantages, men abandoned it and women were recruited and allowed in (see Reskin & Roos, 1987, 1991).

Sociological research substantiates the ubiquity of gendered arrangements, practices, and expectations in the corporation (see Martin, 1991). As noted, gender is used to make decisions about job content and activities, salaries and perks, and the selection and advancement of employees, individually and collectively (Acker, 1990; Baron & Newman, 1990; Cockburn, 1988). Perhaps most important, managers are *active gendering agents*. Because of their authority and control over resources, the gendering that managers do is particularly consequential. Armed with a feminist vision, they can initiate change. In practice, feminist managers can refuse "to gender" in ways that harm women or minority men and that privilege majority men.

FEMINIST MANAGEMENT

Although feminism has many goals and takes many forms, it consistently tries to change the sociopolitical, economic, and cultural contexts that bring about systematic harm or disadvantage to women (see Bartlett, 1990; Olsen, 1989). Feminism values an end to the oppression of women and other disadvantaged groups (Taylor, 1983). It values mutuality and interdependence, inclusion and cooperation, nurturance and support, participation and self-determination, empowerment, and personal and collective transformation (Ferguson, 1984; Martin, 1990a). *Feminist practice* is the employment of feminist methods and tactics to improve women's (and other excluded groups') social, economic, and symbolic rewards (Martin, 1990a; Taylor, 1983) and to promote values like those in the foregoing list. Feminist practice is what feminists *do and how they do it* in pursuit of feminist goals and aims (Acker, 1989; Eisenstein, 1985; McCormack, Thorne, & Milkman, 1990).

Feminist management is discussed here in terms of a range of feminist practices. These practices, consistent with feminist values and goals, are different than the practices that prevail in most corporations (see Jackall, 1988; Smith, 1990). According to my view, feminist practice emphasizes connective*ness*, cooperation, and mutuality over separative*ness*, competition, and individual success (England, 1989) and aims to produce conditions that benefit women and other out-group members. It can also help majority men. Benefits and costs to various groups are discussed at the chapter's end.

Feminist Management Practices

I begin with Bartlett's (1990) three methods for use by feminist attorneys in the practice of law and apply them to feminist management in the corporation. These methods are followed by a list of additional practices that reflect an aspect of feminist philosophy and values as it might be applied to the practice of feminist management. Several practices are similar to those espoused by grass-roots cooperatives (Rothschild & Whitt, 1986), employee-owned corporations (Greenberg, 1986), and management approaches that emphasize employees' development and growth, such as McGregor's Theory Y (1960), Ouchi's Theory Z (1981), and Naisbitt and Aburdene's shared vision and alignment (1985). The current discussion differs from all of these, however, in placing the interests of women at the focus of its orientation and concern.

(1) Asking the "woman question" consists of "identifying and challenging those elements of existing . . . [corporate] doctrine that leave out or disadvantage women and members of other excluded groups" (Bartlett, 1990, p. 831). Asking the woman question can, according to Bartlett, expose gender bias in ostensibly gender-neutral norms, practices, rules, and values. The woman question simultaneously poses the "man question" (Kalantzis, 1990, p. 41). Thus the woman question challenges claims that male-normative values and practices are necessary or correct. It can be used also to challenge assumptions that good managers must prioritize paid work over family obligations. A feminist challenge of norms and expectations that favor masculinity and men in management positions can increase awareness of the ways women managers are devalued in and excluded from many management jobs (see Hearn & Parkin, 1988).

(2) Using feminist practical reasoning is "reasoning from an ideal in which . . . [corporate] resolutions are pragmatic responses to concrete dilemmas rather than static choices between opposing, often mismatched perspectives" (Bartlett, 1990, p. 831). Feminist practical reasoning can be used to challenge the legitimacy of the norms of those who claim to speak, through rules, for the supposedly (monolithic) community (Bartlett, 1990, pp. 850-851, 855). Feminist practical reasoning directs attention to the existence of multiple communities and the diverse circumstances in which different people live. It challenges claims that so-called universal rules apply to everyone in the same way—women as well as men, unmarried as well as married, black as well as white. It *contextualizes* issues so that greater understanding and exposure of injustice can occur (Bartlett, 1990, p. 863). Feminist practical reasoning can be used by feminist managers to introduce alternative conceptions of paid work, corporate purpose, and managerial tasks and effectiveness and to offer new ways of dealing with problems and dilemmas, ways that affirm the concerns of women and members of other out-groups.

(3) Consciousness-raising is the search for "insights and enhanced perspectives through collaborative and interactive engagements with others based upon personal experience and narrative" (Bartlett, 1990, p. 831). Consciousness-raising relates personal experience to general principle and general principle to personal experience through an ongoing, open-ended dialogue. Feminists have long used consciousness-raising methods to validate their personal experiences and relate them to the experiences of others in similar or parallel conditions. Consciousness-

raising can help affirm the legitimacy of women's experiences an
views. It can show women (and men) that their circumstances are ne
unique and it can facilitate the collaborative resolution of problem
(Bartlett, 1990, p. 865). Consciousness-raising is a feminist practic
that promotes collaboration through exposing the multiple realities c
organizational participants and undermining claims that a single solu
tion or view is necessary or correct.

(4) Promoting community and cooperation. Feminism values commu
nity, cooperation, inclusion, interdependence, and group identificatio
(England, 1989; Taylor, 1983). It rejects extreme individualism, compet
tion, and interpersonal dominance (Leidner, 1991). Hegemonic masculin
ity in the form of a male-normative model of management—that emphasize
for example, constant competing and beating out the next guy—encou:
ages practices that feminist management rejects (see Jackall, 1988).

A focus on cooperation does not mean an absence of difference
conflict, competition, or hierarchy. Rather, it means a *deemphasis c*
winning and losing (and winners and losers), status differences, an
invidious comparisons. Employees are encouraged to do their person:
best, to pursue excellence rather than compete to prove superiority ove
others. Cooperative management views winning as a multiple-sum go:
and encourages entire work units and firms, rather than individuals, t
compete. The benefits of community-oriented management are con
firmed in research on leadership by nuns who direct Catholic parishe
via a *collaborative leadership* strategy (Wallace, 1991) and by wome
executives who employ *collaborative negotiation* strategies to resolv
organizational conflicts (Helgesen, 1990).

Francis Hesselbein, executive director of Girls Scouts U.S.A., pro
vides an example of cooperative, community-oriented managemei
(Helgesen, 1990, chap. 4). Hesselbein views herself as at the heart of
circle or web of relationships rather than the head of a hierarchy «
authority. A web of concentric circles around the director gives emplo:
ees a sense of connectedness without the negative feelings associate
with comparative hierarchical standing and worth. When a persc
changes jobs, she or he simply moves to a different place within a circ
or to another circle—avoiding the sense of being elevated or lowere
in relation to others.

Though Helgesen does not say this, employees probably know whe
a personnel change is a promotion, lateral move, or demotion. Neve

theless, Hesselbein's deemphasis of hierarchy and affirmation of functional change probably discourage employees from making invidious comparisons or being overly concerned with superiority and dominance. The utility—indeed possible necessity—of hierarchy for communication, coordination, and productivity in large-scale organizations is not in dispute (see Martin, 1987; Perrow, 1986). My point is that an emphasis on hierarchy encourages a focus on power as control over people (as described in Jackall, 1988) whereas an emphasis on community encourages a focus on power as a means to produce and get work done (French, 1985; Kanter, 1977, 1989).

(5) Promoting democracy and participation. Democracy is, in a classic sense, the participation of people in their own governance. Rules are made with the involvement and consent of the governed rather than by others, such as dictators or totalitarian regimes. Also, democracy means the right to dissent, to disagree with the status quo or powers that be, without being punished or retaliated against. A third aspect of democracy is freedom—of speech, action, and choice. Democracy guarantees freedoms (Siriani, 1988). Some scholars argue that the bureaucratic organization is democracy's enemy (Ferguson, 1984) but others say that bureaucracy enhances democracy through assuring fairness in procedures and rules (Cafferata, 1982), making duties and obligations explicit (Perrow, 1986), and increasing discretionary time, which is necessary for innovation, creativity, and autonomy (Czarniawska-Joerges & Joerges, 1990).

The right to self-determination and control over one's life—including one's body—are tenets of feminist thought that honor the right to express dissent and oppose the silencing of oppressed groups (Leidner, 1991). In a study of voluntary associations, Knoke (1990) found that women's political associations—which were feminist—were run more democratically than associations of any other type. Feminism can enhance managers' and employees' effectiveness and satisfaction with their jobs through promoting democratic participation, open discussion, and the benefits of discretion and choice (see Helgesen, 1990). Encouraging employee participation does not mean that "everyone is equal" or that bosses lack authority. Rather, feminist managers exercise authority carefully and they share rather than hoard information, resources, and opportunities. As the next section suggests, a feminist perspective on authority views it as an obligation as well as a privilege.

(6) Promoting subordinate empowerment: Power as obligation. Feminism values the empowerment of women, and members of other excluded groups, and allocates responsibility for this to managers and the entire corporation. Feminists are concerned also with how power is used. Is power used to force, control, and exploit or to affirm, encourage, and empower? Are subordinates encouraged to grow, learn, and expand or to follow orders and submit? Feminism views managers as obliged to help subordinates grow and do their best. Managers are obliged to empower, not exploit, subordinates for personal or corporate ends. (See Heilbrun, 1988, for a note on feminists' discomfort and frequent refusal to deal with power issues.)

This perspective turns the table on accepted views of hierarchy and authority. A traditional, hierarchical-down focus views the subordinate as obliged to please the boss and the boss as deserving to be pleased; that is, authority obligates the subordinate to the superordinate (Jackall, 1988; Smith, 1990). Feminism encourages inverting the equation to a hierarchical-up focus, where superiors are judged by how well they use authority—power or clout—to direct, support, and facilitate the work of their subordinates. The core work of a corporation is performed by workers at the lowest rungs of the hierarchy. Managers who use authority to empower employees—to help them grow, learn, and develop through their work—can help the corporation also by fostering higher production, cooperation, and good work quality.

(7) Promoting nurturance and caring. Nurturance is affectionate caring; caring is a concern for something. Feminist practice as nurturance and caring requires corporate managers to view personnel as women and men with spouses and dependent children, with obligations and lives that extend beyond their jobs. Feminist managers affirm the multiple obligations and demands that employees have on their affections, energy, and time. They support the provision of benefits and policies to help them with child care and family obligations, such as day care on site, benefit packages to cover day-care costs, leave policies that take children's activities and health into account, adequate health insurance, and so on (Martin et al., 1988).

Feminist managers nurture employees by assuring good health and safety practices, reasonable pay and benefits, and a share of corporate profits and success. Feminist management rewards risk taking and hard work and avoids demeaning or embarrassing employees who make mistakes (see Jackall, 1988). Feminist management protects employees from layoffs during hardship times.

(8) Striving for transformational outcomes. Feminist transformational outcomes are changes that result from participation in feminist activities, groups, or organizations (Martin, 1990a). According to feminist theory, such outcomes include feminist consciousness and political awareness, high self-esteem, and a commitment to work for change in the conditions and status of women and minority men (Acker, 1990; Eisenstein, 1990; Martin & Chernesky, 1989). Feminist transformation produces new understandings of women and their place in society relative to institutions and to men (Cassell, 1990). Feminist transformation makes a person more politically aware, less tolerant of oppression, more motivated to work for change, and more identified with women who, compared with many men, are everywhere oppressed (Ryan, 1989).

Feminist management can be transformative in four realms.

(a) Individual women. Individual women—managers and employees—can be transformed by feminist management. Participation in feminist management can foster the learning of new knowledge and skills, new understanding of women's place and treatment in society, and greater awareness of the necessity for political action to produce changes that will end the devaluation of women (and minority men) in the corporation.

(b) Women collectively. A male manager told Hardesty and Jacobs (1986) that women can improve the corporation only if women secretaries, middle managers, and senior officials work together for change. Women collectively can be transformed by participating in activities that increase awareness of their common interests, conditions, and goals. Understanding that the success of individual women leaves intact the structures and practices that oppress most women can heighten the commitment to identify, organize, and act collectively for change (Acker, 1990; Hardesty & Jacobs, 1986; Reskin, 1988). Organization and political action inside and beyond the corporation will likely be required (Acker, 1990; Martin, 1980, 1990b; Martin & Chernesky, 1989; Martin, Montgomery, & DiNitto, 1983).

(c) Men. Male managers and employees can be transformed by feminist management also. They can benefit from a paid work climate that values cooperation, participation, nurturance, and empowerment and that ap-

preciates the participation and contributions of women and minority men. With a better balance of family and paid work obligations, men's enjoyment of work and home and family life can increase. Their treatment of women, and of other men, will improve. Feminist management has costs for some corporate men, however. These are noted and compared with its benefits below.

(d) The corporation. Feminist management can transform the corporation. A corporation run by feminist principles would oppose the exploitation of employees and the environment. A value on community welfare—and the collective—would foster concern with making the corporation a more habitable, hospitable, and equitable work environment (Martin, 1990a; Taylor, 1983). Feminist management would protect workers' health, safety, and well-being. It would protect the physical environment through recycling, cleaning up, or detoxifying industrial wastes, complying with regulations and rules that protect workers and the ecosystem, and using biodegradable materials. It would promote the public interest and return profits to workers and the community (in addition to officials and shareholders). Feminist managers would resist closing factories as tax write-offs or moving them to Third World countries, where cheaper labor is found. Feminist managers would cooperate with and improve, rather than dominate and degrade, the community and environment.

The feminist challenge to management is the creation of a corporation that values and includes women—and members of other excluded groups—in ways that give them dignity, treat them fairly, and improve their status and opportunities in an enduring fashion. In doing this, feminist management can enhance the experience of paid work and family life for majority men as well.

WILL THE CORPORATION SUPPORT FEMINIST MANAGEMENT?

If feminist management benefits women and out-group men, and is oriented to improving their treatment and status, why should majority men and the corporation support it? The case for feminist management must take two issues into account: (a) its impact on the corporation and (b) its impact on men.

(1) Corporations. In a market economy such as ours, corporations value profits, sometimes to the exclusion of all else (see Fligstein, 1990; Jackall, 1988; Lewis, 1989; Smith, 1990). If feminist management can increase profits, senior managers and shareholders might favor it, although research by Cockburn (1988) and Cohn (1985), among others, questions this view. If feminism *costs* money or *lowers* profits, it may be rejected out of hand. Because feminist management is not committed to profits at any cost, what conditions might persuade corporations to support it? I suggest two: (a) the need to tap the full range of human resources available to corporations and (b) the possibility that corporations led by feminist management are more effective, productive, efficient, and rewarding than those with a male-normative approach (see Bologh, 1990).

(a) By the year 2,000, more than two thirds of U.S. workers are predicted to be women or minority men (Morrison & Von Glinow, 1990). If corporations continue to segregate women and minority men into less desirable and low status jobs, their commitment to corporations will continue to decline. Like nurses who quit nursing work over poor pay, autonomy, and working conditions, many women managers also quit the corporation in the 1980s when they realized that a glass ceiling kept them from rising, their presence was not valued, and their conceptions of corporate values, purpose, and practice were not consistent with those that held sway (Hardesty & Jacobs, 1986; Morrison & Von Glinow, 1990).

The intelligence, talent, commitment, and skill that women bring to managerial work may be withdrawn if corporations fail to appreciate and value them. Feminist management can foster a rewarding, hospitable climate for women and men in the managerial and subordinate ranks. If they are to remain competitive with corporations in Germany, Japan, and other developed nations, U.S. corporations cannot afford to exclude from full participation the talented, intelligent women and minority men who will constitute the primary work force in coming decades (Edwards, 1990).

(b) Male-normative management that claims to maximize profits, effectiveness, efficiency, and productivity but that in practice often maximizes individual self-interest, duplicity, cheating, lying, and covering up may be more costly to corporations than the kind of feminist management that is outlined here (see Jackall, 1988; Lewis, 1989;

Smith, 1990). It is possible that feminist management will produce more benefits to the corporation because it treats workers well, appreciates varied talents, and affirms a range of experiences and contributions. In its emphasis on inclusion, participation, and diversity, feminist management may succeed where male-normative management fails—in recruiting and retaining a wide mix of human talent and in creating an environment that promotes cooperation, merit, and hard work while also fostering personal growth and fulfillment.

(2) Men. If corporations start to accept women and minority men on the basis solely of talent and ability, the pool of qualified applicants for top management jobs will increase. Majority men will be less assured of the privileges of rank, compensation, control, and decision making that they now enjoy and they will no doubt experience this as a loss. Non-managerial men will find women's fuller incorporation threatening also (Martin, 1991). Majority men at lower ranks derive benefits and satisfactions from having their own kind in positions of leadership and control (Bergmann, 1986; Reskin, 1988). Cohn (1985) found, for example, that (white male) managers protected clerical jobs for (white) male workers in the British railway industry for 80 years after the British post office began to employ women to do clerical work. Jobs were scarce in the capital-intensive railway industry, thus managers protected the clerical jobs for male employees, even though they could have hired women to perform the work for considerably less pay.

Majority men's knowledge that women are paid less for work comparable to theirs also prompts them to resist women's entry (Acker, 1989; Bergmann, 1986). Women's entry indeed poses a threat to some men's job status, pay, and access rights. Why should men support women's rights to hold men's jobs when women's entry may spell men's loss—perhaps of a job and, more likely, of earnings or pay? Why should majority men support feminist management? While some men will lose status and benefits if women become equal participants at work and at home, many will benefit over the long haul. In time, when women are compensated commensurately to men, women's presence will not threaten men's pay rates or job security. Women will bring home larger paychecks to contribute to the family resource pool. Feminist managers will support men as well as women at work, although not at women's expense.

Feminist managers will discourage extreme competition, rivalry, and concerns with dominance and control (Jackall, 1988). They will oppose unbridled games of power and one-upmanship (see Lewis, 1989). They will create opportunities to cooperate, participate in decisions, and gain skills and self-esteem. Finally, they will promote a better balance of paid work and home/family priorities. Women's higher pay will lighten men's burden of economically providing for their families and will free men from having to prove their masculinity through their earnings and jobs (Bergmann, 1986). Men who invest more in home and family will find that relations with their children and wives are more fulfilling. Their spouses will be grateful because men's greater involvement will reduce the double burden that wives who work for pay currently bear.

CONCLUSIONS

Many questions are raised, while few are answered, in this consideration of feminism and management. Yet, avenues for positive change are identified. A feminist vision of management fosters ways of seeing and doing that are fair, inclusive, and affirming of women and of minority men. As Bartlett (1990) notes, reliance on the "same old practices" reinforces the values, structures, and dynamics that devalue and exclude women. Use of new feminist practices will raise new questions and offer new ways of thinking, seeing, resolving problems, and relating to others.

The means by which feminist management can be instituted remain unspecified. This analysis only alludes to the collective organization and politics that will be required. Feminists will have to identify goals, recruit supporters, and organize to work for change (Acker, 1989; Martin, 1990b; Watson, 1990). Resourcefulness and courage will be required in a context that is almost certain to be hostile to feminism, particularly at first. Organizations do change, however, and feminism can prevail (Flammang, 1987; Mueller, 1984).

This analysis is unable, within its space constraints, to address issues of race/ethnicity and social class, as they condition the odds of corporate change and the benefits of feminist management. All women are not the same. They differ by race/ethnicity, social class, age, marital status, sexual preference, geographic region, education and experience, and in many other ways. The material, positional, and attitudinal barriers that divide them will have to be resolved if feminism is to benefit all corporate women rather than only a select few (see Acker, 1989; Blum, 1987; Glenn & Tolbert, 1987; Klein, 1980; Morrison & Von Glinow, 1990).

Many women are searching for meaningful identities, roles, and positions in today's corporations (Hardesty & Jacobs, 1986; Helgesen 1990). I believe feminist management can help them as well as stem the tide of women managers' exodus. While it is understandable for women who are blocked by a "glass ceiling" or poor treatment to quit, their departure leaves the status quo—the rule of hegemonic masculinity and of men—intact. Armed with feminist vision, tactics, and a sense of purpose, feminist managers can teach a corporation the way it should go and create a more responsive and responsible workplace—for women minority men, and majority men alike.

REFERENCES

Acker, J. (1989). *Doing comparable worth: Gender, class, and pay equity.* Philadelphia Temple University Press.

Acker, J. (1990). Hierarchies, jobs, and bodies: A theory of gendered organization *Gender & Society, 4*, 139-158.

Baran, B. (1985). Office automation and women's work: The technological transformation of the insurance industry. In M. Castells (Ed.), *High technology, space, and society* (pp. 143-171). Beverly Hills, CA: Sage.

Baron, J. N., Davis-Blake, A., & Bielby, W. T. (1986). The structure of opportunity: How promotion ladders vary within and among organizations. *Administrative Science Quarterly, 31*, 248-273.

Baron, J. N., & Newman, A. E. (1990). For what it's worth: Organizations, occupation and the value of work done by women and nonwhites. *American Sociological Review 55*, 155-175.

Bartlett, K. T. (1990). Feminist legal methods. *Harvard Law Review, 103*, 829-888.

Bergmann, B. R. (1986). *The economic emergence of women.* New York: Basic Books.

Bielby, W. T., & Baron, J. N. (1986). Men and women at work: Sex segregation and statistical discrimination. *American Journal of Sociology, 91*, 759-799.

Bielby, W. T., & Baron, J. N. (1987). Undoing discrimination: Job integration and comparable worth. In C. Bose & G. Spitze (Eds.), *Ingredients for women's employment policy* (pp. 211-229). Albany: State University of New York Press.

Blum, L. (1987). Priorities and limits of the comparable worth movement. *Gender Society, 1*, 380-399.

Blum, L., & Smith, V. (1988). Women's mobility in the corporation: A critique of the politics of optimism. *Signs, 13*, 528-545.

Bologh, R. W. (1990). *Love or greatness: Max Weber and masculine thinking—a feminist inquiry.* London: Unwin Hyman.

Boyd, M., Mulvihill, M., & Myles, J. (1990). *Patriarchy and postindustrialism: Women and power in the service economy* (Departmental Working Paper 90-1). Ottawa Canada: Carleton University, Department of Sociology and Anthropology.

Brenner, O. C., Tomkiewicz, J., & Schein, V. E. (1989). The relationship between sex role stereotypes and requisite management characteristics revisited. *Academy of Management Journal, 32*, 662-669.

Brown, L. K. (1988). Female managers in the United States and in Europe: Corporate boards, M.B.A. credentials, and the image/illusion of progress. In N. J. Adler & D. N. Izraeli (Eds.), *Women in management worldwide.* London: M. E. Sharpe.

Cafferata, G. (1982). The building of democratic organizations: An embryological metaphor. *Administrative Science Quarterly, 27,* 280-303.

Cassell, J. (1990). *A group called women: Sisterhood and symbolism in the feminist movement.* Prospect Heights, IL: Waveland.

Chase, S. E., & Bell, C. S. (1990). Ideology, discourse, and gender: How gatekeepers talk about women in a male-dominated occupation. *Social Problems, 37,* 163-177.

Cockburn, C. (1988). *Machinery of dominance: Women, men, and technical know-how.* Boston: Northeastern University Press.

Cohn, S. (1985). *The process of occupational sex-typing: The feminization of clerical labor in Great Britain.* Philadelphia: Temple University Press.

Collinson, D., Knights, D., & Collinson, M. (1990). *Managing to discriminate.* London: Routledge and Kegan Paul.

Conference Board. (1985). *Corporate financial assistance for child care* (Work and Family Information Center Research Bulletin No. 177). New York: Author.

Connell, R. W. (1987). *Gender and power: Society, the person, and sexual politics.* Sydney: Allen & Unwin.

Czarniawska-Joerges, B., & Joerges, B. (1990). *Organizational change as materialization of ideas* (Report No. 37). Stockholm, Sweden: Stockholm School of Economics.

Edwards, H. (1990, November 14). *The black athlete and sports in America.* Lecture in the Distinguished Lecture Series, Florida State University.

Eisenstein, H. (1985). The gender of bureaucracy: Reflections of feminism and the state. In J. Goodnow & C. Pateman (Eds.), *Women, social science, and public policy.* Sydney: Allen & Unwin.

Eisenstein, H. (1990). Femocrats, official feminism, and the uses of power. In S. Watson (Ed.), *Playing the state: Australian feminist interventions.* London: Verso.

England, P. (1989). A feminist critique of rational-choice theories: Implications for sociology. *The American Sociologist, 20,* 14-28.

Ferguson, K. (1984). *The feminist case against bureaucracy.* Philadelphia: Temple University Press.

Finch, J. (1983). *Married to the job: Wives' incorporation in men's work.* London: George Allen & Unwin.

Flammang, J. A. (1987). Women made a difference: Comparable worth in San Jose. In M. F. Katzenstein & C. M. Mueller (Eds.), *The women's movements of the United States and Western Europe.* Philadelphia: Temple University Press.

Fligstein, N. (1990). *The transformation of corporate control.* Cambridge, MA: Harvard University Press.

French, M. (1985). *Beyond power: On women, men, and morals.* New York: Summit.

Gilson, E., & Kane, S. (1987). *Unnecessary choices: The hidden life of the executive woman.* New York: William Morrow.

Glenn, E., & Tolbert, C. (1987). Technology and emerging patterns of stratification for women of color: Race and gender in computer occupations. In B. D. Wright (Ed.), *Women, work, and technology* (pp. 318-331). Ann Arbor: University of Michigan Press.

Greenberg, E. S. (1986). *Workplace democracy: The political effects of participation.* Ithaca: Cornell University Press.

Gutek, B. A. (1985). *Sex and the workplace: Impact of sexual behavior and harassment on women, men, and organizations.* San Francisco: Jossey-Bass.

Gutek, B. (1989). Sexuality in the workplace: Key issues in social research and organizational practice. In J. Hearn, D. L. Sheppard, P. Tancred-Sheriff, & G. Burrell (Eds.), *The sexuality of organization* (pp. 56-70). London: Sage.

Hardesty, S., & Jacobs, N. (1986). *Success and betrayal: The crisis of women in corporate America.* New York: Franklin Watts.

Hearn, J., & Parkin, W. (1988). Women, men, and leadership: A critical review of assumptions, practices, and change in the industrialized nations. In N. J. Adler & D. N. Izraeli (Eds.), *Women in management worldwide.* London: M. E. Sharpe.

Hearn, J., Sheppard, D. L., Tancred-Sheriff, P., & Burrell, G. (1989). *The sexuality of organization.* London: Sage.

Heilbrun, C. G. (1988). *Writing a woman's life.* New York: Ballantine.

Helgesen, S. (1990). *The female advantage: Women's ways of leadership.* New York: Doubleday.

Hochschild, A. (1989). *The second shift: Working parents and the revolution at home.* Viking Penguin.

Jackall, R. (1988). *Moral mazes: The world of corporate managers.* New York: Oxford University Press.

Kalantzis, M. (1990). Ethnicity meets gender meets class in Australia. In S. Watson (Ed.), *Playing the state.* London: Verso.

Kanter, R. M. (1977). *Men and women of the corporation.* New York: Basic Books.

Kanter, R. M. (1989). *When giants learn to dance.* New York: Simon & Schuster/Touchstone.

Klein, G. D. (1980). Beyond OEO and affirmative action: Working on the integration of the workplace. *California Management Review, 22,* 74-81.

Knoke, D. (1990). The mobilization of members in women's associations. In P. Gurin & L. A. Tilly (Eds.), *Women in twentieth century politics.* New York: Russell Sage.

Leidner, R. (1991). Stretching the boundaries of liberalism: Democratic innovation in a feminist organization. *Signs, 16,* 263-289.

Lenz, E., & Myerhoff, B. (1985). *The feminization of America: How women's values are changing our private and public lives.* Los Angeles: Jeremy Tarcher.

Lewis, M. (1989). *Liar's poker: Rising through the wreckage of Wall Street.* New York: Norton.

Loden, M. (1985). *Feminine leadership or how to succeed in business without being one of the boys.* New York: Times Books.

Lorence, J. (1989). *Service sector growth and metropolitan occupational sex segregation.* Houston: University of Houston, Department of Sociology.

Maccoby, M. (1988). *Why work? Leading the new generation.* New York: Simon & Schuster.

Margolis, D. (1979). *The managers: Corporate life in America.* New York: William Morrow.

Martin, P. Y. (1980). Women, labor markets, and employing organizations: A critical analysis. In D. Dunkerley & G. Salaman (Eds.), *International Yearbook of Organization Studies 1980.* London: Routledge.

Martin, P. Y. (1987). A commentary on *The feminist case against bureaucracy* by Kathy Ferguson. *Women's Studies International Forum, 10,* 543-548.

Martin, P. Y. (1990a). Rethinking feminist organizations. *Gender & Society, 4,* 182-206.

Martin, P. Y. (1990b). The moral politics of organizations: Reflections of an unlikely feminist. *Journal of Applied Behavioral Science, 25*, 451-470.

Martin, P. Y. (1991). Gender, interaction, and inequality in organizations. In C. Ridgeway (Ed.), *Gender, interaction, and inequality*. New York: Springer-Verlag.

Martin, P. Y., & Chernesky, R. (1989). Women's prospects for leadership in social welfare organizations: A political economy perspective. *Administration in Social Work, 12*, 117-143.

Martin, P. Y., Montgomery, D., & DiNitto, D. (1983). Advancement for women in hierarchical organizations: A multilevel analysis of problems and prospects. *Journal of Applied Behavioral Science, 19*, 19-33.

Martin, P. Y., Seymour, S., Godbey, K., Courage, M., & Tate, R. (1988). Corporate, union, feminist and profamily leaders' views on work-family relations. *Gender & Society, 2*, 385-400.

McCormack, T., Thorne, B., & Milkman, M. (1990, July). *What happened to praxis?* Paper presented in the session Women's Movements, International Sociological Association World Congress, Madrid, Spain.

McGregor, D. (1960). *The human side of management*. New York: McGraw-Hill.

Morrison, A. M., & Von Glinow, M. (1990). Women and minorities in management. *American Psychologist, 45*, 200-208.

Mueller, C. M. (1984). Women's organizational strategies in state legislatures. In J. A. Flammang (Ed.), *Political women: Current roles in state and local government*. Beverly Hills, CA: Sage.

Naisbitt, J., & Aburdene, P. (1985). *Re-inventing the corporation*. New York: Warner.

Naisbitt, J., & Aburdene, P. (1990). The 1990s: Decade of women in leadership. In J. Naisbitt & P. Aburdene, *Megatrends 2000*. New York: William Morrow.

O'Farrell, B., & Harlan, S. L. (1984). Job integration strategies: Today's programs and tomorrow's needs. In B. Reskin (Ed.), *Sex segregation in the workplace: Trends, explanations, remedies* (pp. 267-291). Washington, DC: National Academy Press.

Olsen, F. (1989). Unraveling compromise. *Harvard Law Review, 103*, 105-135.

Ouchi, W. (1981). *Theory Z: How American business can meet the Japanese challenge*. New York: Avon.

Perrow, C. (1986). *Complex organizations: A critical essay* (3rd ed.). New York: Random House.

Powell, G. N. (1988). *Women and men in management*. Newbury Park, CA: Sage.

Reskin, B. (1988). Bringing the men back in: Sex differentiation and the devaluation of women's work. *Gender & Society, 2*, 58-81.

Reskin, B. F., & Hartmann, H. (1986). *Women's work, men's work: Sex segregation on the job*. Washington, DC: National Academy Press.

Reskin, B. F., & Roos, P. (1987). Status hierarchies and sex segregation. In C. Bose & G. Spitze (Eds.), *Ingredients for women's employment policy* (pp. 3-21). Albany: State University of New York Press.

Reskin, B. F., & Roos, P. (1991). *Job queues, gender queues: Explaining women's inroads into male occupations*. Philadelphia: Temple University Press.

Reskin, B., & Ross, C. R. (1990). *Job segregation, authority, and earnings among women and men managers*. Champagne/Urbana: University of Illinois, Department of Sociology.

Rodgers, W. (1969). *THINK*. New York: Simon & Schuster.

Rothschild, J., & Whitt, J. A. (1986). *The cooperative workplace: Potential and dilemmas of organizational democracy and participation*. New York: Cambridge University Press.

Ryan, B. (1989). Ideological purity and feminism: The U.S. women's movement from 1966 to 1975. *Gender & Society, 3,* 239-257.

Siriani, C. (1988). Self-management of time: A democratic alternative. *Socialist Review 18,* 5-56.

Smith, V. (1990). *Managing in the corporate interest: Control and resistance in an American bank.* Berkeley: University of California Press.

Strober, M., & Arnold, C. (1987). Integrated circuits/segregated labor: Women in three computer-related occupations. In H. Hartmann, R. Kraut, & L. Tilly (Eds.), *Computer chips and paper clips: Technology and women's employment* (Vol. 2). Washington, DC: National Academy of Sciences Press.

Taylor, V. (1983). The future of feminism in the 1980s: A social movement analysis. In L. Richardson & V. Taylor (Eds.), *Feminist frontiers: Rethinking sex, gender, and society.* Reading, MA: Addison-Wesley.

U.S. Department of Labor (1991). *A report on the glass ceiling initiative.* Washington, DC: Government Printing Office.

U.S. Department of Labor. (1993, January). *Employment and earnings.* Washington, DC: Government Printing Office.

Wallace, R. A. (1991). *They call her pastor.* Albany: State University of New York Press.

Watson, S. (1990). The state of play: An introduction. In S. Watson (Ed.), *Playing the state: Australian feminist interventions.* London: Verso.

Williams, C. (1989). *Gender differences at work: Women and men in nontraditional occupations.* Berkeley: University of California Press.

Zimmer, L. (1988). Tokenism and women in the workplace: The limits of gender-neutral theory. *Social Problems, 35,* 64-77.

Commentary

HEIDI HARTMANN

These three chapters (by Martin, Northcraft and Gutek, and Lee) raise important issues for managers, both male and female, scholars, and policymakers. With the exception of the argument made by Northcraft that discrimination against women managers is rapidly declining and has real potential to disappear entirely soon, these authors seem to agree that, at the current time, it is difficult indeed for a woman manager to advance in business without experiencing the burden of her gender.

This message may be difficult for many managers, particularly women managers, to hear, because those who have trained hard to acquire skills that should bring advancement and rewards aplenty do not want to hear that the playing field is not equal. If the playing field is not equal, we who have invested time and energy in the game have been duped.

Yet, women managers should pay attention to the arguments made in these chapters, because overcoming the obstacles to women's advancement identified here will surely require collective action. If some feel betrayed by these revelations, others will welcome confirmation by scholars of what they've always suspected or known. And, whether the knowledge receives welcome or grudging acceptance, the reaction should be the same: In the immortal words of Mother Jones, a long-lived labor rebel whose protests spanned much of the nineteenth and twentieth centuries, "Don't mourn—organize!"

Policymakers, too, have much to learn, because these authors identify areas where public policy can make a difference. And this is true even though some of the authors decline to place much faith in the effectiveness of legislative and legal remedies. Scholars can learn from the ambivalence expressed by their colleagues. Do the barriers and problems we so readily identify really defy solution? Or can we not work harder at identifying and testing potential cures?

But perhaps the group that can learn the most for immediate practical application is male managers. Take notes carefully; you'll find much to implement at your workplace and many reasons you should do so. Remember, you're not losing your privilege, you're gaining a colleague.

Martin's very challenging chapter "Feminist Practice in Organizations: Implications for Management" seeks to harness the insights of feminist theory and practice to the task of improving management for the benefit of all. "Feminism," Martin states, is a "political orientation and practice aimed at improving the status of women." Feminist management practices, Martin argues, can lead to an environment that is more accepting of innovation, experimentation, and new ways of seeing and doing. These ways, which are more inclusive and affirming of women and minority men, will also yield a more productive and responsive corporation and thereby benefit majority men as well. But most provocative for women managers is Martin's claim that women managers today are seeking a more meaningful role in corporations and that learning about and applying feminist management principles can help them find that role, increasing their satisfaction as managers and their longevity in the corporate world.

Martin shares much of her analysis of the causes for women's current position in corporations with Gutek, who argues in her section of the chapter, "Point-Counterpoint: Discrimination Against Women in Management," the "going but never gone" position. Both believe that corporations as they are structured today are normatively male; they depend on the willingness of men to devote themselves to their jobs—men who are able to do so because they have supportive wives at home. It is almost impossible for women to seem as appropriate for management as men, because women simply do not have the support at home to enable them to devote the same effort at similar personal costs. Their personal costs are greater, given the equally, or even more, entrenched norms at home. And even women who forgo marriage to a man and raising children are suspect—they could always change their minds! Gutek notes that, for men, the extra work hours seemingly required from successful managers are accepted as part of their traditional duty to their families—to earn money—while, for women, these hours are seen to conflict with their traditional duty of providing hands-on family care. Men who try to opt out of this unfair system, by sharing family care equally with their wives, may be written off at work, perhaps because they may be thought to have failed as men.

Gutek notes that the powerfulness of gender as an organizing dimension of human life means that the idea of gender difference is constantly reinforced. If we see a woman manager acting in a way thought to be stereotypical of women, we attribute the behavior to her gender (even though there are likely to be other causes, such as low pay or limited advancement opportunities). Women managers are persistently seen as different than male managers, in the face of research that shows they actually are quite similar. Male managers, who have more power, can define this difference in terms favorable to themselves. Men, who control this system, see that it works to limit competition from women and allows them to surround themselves with like-minded men at work. "Managers," writes Martin, "are *active gendering agents*."

Thus, to change the rules, and make the playing field more equal, not only do women need to wield more power in corporations, but gender itself must become less salient in human life. This in turn requires progress on the home front. Progress on the home front, Gutek argues, requires enabling action by government or others, action she deems unlikely. Others, in addition to women, must take on the family care activities women must at least partially relinquish. This is because substantial assistance with child and elder care provided by the public sector would be expensive. And passing legislation to get men to take on a larger share seems both unlikely to occur and unlikely to be effective.

Contributing to this rather negative view of the possibilities of helpful legislation and public policy is Lee's useful overview of a wide range of court actions with respect to equal employment opportunity. Although Lee points to the many past successes in litigation and enforcement of Title VII of the 1964 Civil Rights Act, she also focuses on the ways these gains have been endangered by recent Supreme Court decisions. In *City of Richmond v. J. A. Croson, Wards Cove Packing Co. v. Atonio*, as well as *Lorance v. AT&T Technologies* and *Patterson v. McLean Credit Union*, specifically affirmative contracting programs have been invalidated, disparate impact cases have been made more difficult to win, "late" filed claims have been invalidated, and defense of sexual harassment cases has been made more difficult. As pointed out by Lee, the Civil Rights Act of 1991, had the effect of reversing these decisions. Lee's review suggests to me not that laws and legal action cannot help but that they do help. They have been effective in the past, which is why they are now under attack. Political power is necessary to assure the appointment of judges more favorable to equal opportunity, executives more aggressive in enforcement, and legislators more inclined to expand the reach of law. For example, Lee points to the low rate at which women managers file sex discrimination claims and the dismal results when they do. Aggressive enforcement, with EEOC personnel going out into the business community educating female managers on their right to file and male managers on their legal obligations not to harass women who do file, coupled with new legislation that would increase penalties on employers for noncompliance, would substantially improve the employment opportunities of women and minorities. In my opinion, more resources and new legislation *can* make a difference.

Gregory B. Northcraft, arguing the "going, going, gone" position with respect to discrimination against women managers, is quite a bit more optimistic about the future than Gutek or Lee. He sees the very large increase in the number of women with MBAs contributing to reducing stereotyping and discrimination in the workplace, because the sheer presence of women will provide the contact men (and women) need to learn to undo stereotypes. He also points to changing corporate practices that encourage telecommuting, flextime, and "daddy tracks" (i.e., parenting leave and the like). These, he suggests, will allow women to devote primary attention to a career at the same time that they will be able to enjoy a family life (in much the same way men have traditionally been able to enjoy a family life). He mentions as well women's increased networking and entrepreneurship as practices that can enhance their power in corporations. And, in the final analysis, he points to corporations' need to diversify their work forces, including at the management level, as the total U.S. work force continues to diversify rapidly in terms of race, ethnicity, and gender. Like Martin, he believes that greater diversity means more creativity and adaptability, leading to a more productive corporation. In short, Northcraft sees women fitting in very nicely in the corporation of the future, without extraordinary measures being required, so long as current trends continue.

Martin's view of the potential contributions of feminist management practice, on the other hand, suggests that more change is in store for the corporation—or should be. Feminist management practice, according to Martin, "emphasizes connective*ness*, cooperation, and mutuality over separative*ness*, competition, and individual success" and, because feminist ideals suggest that power be used to empower others, feminist transformation of the corporation would tend to benefit other out-groups as well as women.

Perhaps, as Northcraft and Gutek suggest, the Fagenson model can be used to resolve these differing viewpoints. Fagenson notes that three levels of analysis are important in understanding the prospects for women managers. At the *individual* level, gender is a very salient characteristic, but, as individual women and men change their behavior, women, by increasingly pursuing business school and careers, and men, by increasing their share of family care, the salience of gender can decrease. At the level of the *organization,* change also needs to take place; for the changed behavior of individuals to have the expected impacts, organizations must adapt to new roles for women and men. Both individual and organizational-level change will be more possible if system-level changes occur—if new behaviors become so widespread they affect the expectations and attitudes of a broad sector of the society and if new norms can be codified in law.

In my view, the prospects for change lie very much with women and men themselves. Either we can organize collectively to influence public and private policy, or we can simply accept the rather frustrating status quo.

SECTION V

Challenges

11

Final Commentary

ELLEN A. FAGENSON
JANICE J. JACKSON

> There has been a great diversity of opinion on the subject, but the generally accepted rule is pink [is] for the boy and blue [is] for the girl. The reason [is] that pink being a more decided and stronger color is more suitable for the boy; while blue, which is more delicate and dainty is prettier for the girl. (The Infants Department, 1918, from the "Who wears the pants?" exhibit at the American History Museum of the Smithsonian Institution)

At times, we think and operate as though the current situation is natural and normal, that what currently is has always been and will always be. This approach is exemplified by the above quotation. Most individuals who are reading this chapter were taught that blue is for boys and pink is for girls with pink (not blue) being the more feminine color. Yet, there was a time when the assignment of pink to boys and blue to girls was considered to be an immutable fact.

We also operate this way in our organizations. We act as though organizations are bigger-than-life entities that are beyond our control. Yet, feeling and thinking human beings create organizations and invent their rules of order. Therefore organizations can be restructured, reordered, and re-created in any form that people deem feasible. They are not immutable entities.

Unfortunately, when some individual or group tries to change the status quo, they often meet resistance. Whether good or bad, the status quo represents the familiar and change represents the "feared" unknown. Manifestations of resistance to change include labeling individuals who introduce new concepts, make different assumptions, or take new approaches as crazy, radical, or illegitimate, and such labeling serves to discredit them and their ideas. For example, in 1932, Aldous Huxley, in his book *Brave New World,* envisioned a society without art, religion, individualism, and humanitarianism. The *New York Herald Tribune*'s review of his work referred to it as "a lugubrious and heavy handed piece of propaganda" (Henderson, 1987, p. 50). Ironically, Huxley's "unorthodox" views of a futuristic society included widespread use of hallucinogenic drugs, alternative and disintegrating family relationships, and scientific mass production of the human race in the form of test tube babies and genetic engineering. Now, contemporary analyses of Huxley's work focus on his insightfulness and prophetic brilliance.

In the field of management, men represent the status quo while women are the modern-day Aldous Huxleys who are rewriting a "brave new world" of their own. Women managers have entered a world that was not designed by them or for them, yet, somehow they must fit in to them. Throughout this book, we have seen how the presence of women managers in corporations has resulted in basic organizational assumptions being questioned, new ideas being offered, and previously untried approaches adopted. Their lives and the lives of those who live and work with them have been substantially altered.

This final chapter is a commentary. As such, our goal is to draw the readers' attention to and expand upon some intriguing issues presented in the previous chapters. We will explore unquestioned assumptions, separate myths from facts, and highlight common themes across chapters. Future directions for individuals, organizations, and society will be suggested. We begin this endeavor with an examination of a long-held assumption regarding women's and men's "places" in society.

HISTORICAL PATTERNS

For much of U.S. history, the colonial toast, "Our land free, our men honest and our women fruitful," has applied (Abigail Adams).[1] As Alpern points out in her chapter, "In the Beginning: A History of Women in Management," the idealogy of separate spheres for the sexes held hat women's primary function was to manage the home and volunteer n the community while men's role was to work outside the home in the public business sphere. Yet, women historically—whether working in paid employment, at home, or volunteering in local civic organizations—have continually contributed their fair share to support the household and the community. In doing so, these women have honed management skills that could be transferred to the business domain. Unfortunately, many employers and women seeking positions in the labor force have failed to recognize the value of their "nonpaid" work experience, considering homemaking and community work to be of little practical worth. As a consequence, many women omit this valuable expertise from their resumes, echoing and confirming the views of employers.

Must this devaluation of women's contribution to their families and communities prevail? No, contend Berthoin Antal and Izraeli in Chapter 3, who report that, in some European countries, the skills required for running a household (e.g., budgeting, organizing, motivating, and mediating) are recognized as managerial skills. Employers such as the British Civil Service now encourage women to include these experiences on job applications; personnel managers are trained to discuss them in job interviews. Moreover, the U.S. federal government has also adopted these types of progressive policies and currently requests uncompensated or volunteer work experiences on application forms and during job interviews (Waelde, 1990). But legislation such as "The Unremunerated Work Act of 1991," proposed by U.S. Representative Barbara Rose Collins, and similar legislation introduced by Britain's member of Parliament, Mildred Gordon, aimed at implementing the 1985 U.N. resolution to include women's unwaged work in the gross national product are examples of legislation that perhaps offer the most promise for valuing the work performed by women.

Alpern's historical record of women's progress in business also reveals that women's marriages/romantic involvements with men negatively affected their work opportunities. In contrast, women's independence, whether temporary or permanent, helped women to establish themselves in the business sector. As pointed out by Alpern, prior to the American Revolution, once free women married, they could not buy or sell properties, sign contracts, or sue for damages. Any wages earned by women belonged to their spouses. When men left home to fight in the American Revolution and subsequent wars, however, many women were legitimately able to take over the businesses owned by their husbands or were hired for jobs that otherwise would have been offered to men.

Alpern reports that women's matrimonial relationships with men also
hindered their ability to work in the U.S. government in the 1930s. At
that time, a policy stating that a husband and wife could not simultaneously work for the government was enforced. As a result of this
policy, many women were dismissed from their jobs. Today, there are
no such federal regulations regarding married employees. Similar restrictions involving romantically involved coworkers, however, still
exist in some corporations. As reported by Mainiero in her chapter on
office romances (Chapter 6), companies typically terminate the woman
rather than the man when a disruptive romantic liaison is suspected.

What lesson should we learn from these historical patterns? Is that
women who want to succeed in the business world should not marry or
be romantically involved with men? If this is the case, then many of
today's women managers have instinctively understood this fact for a
large number have forsaken matrimony for career upward mobility (see
Chapter 7 by Parasuraman & Greenhaus). Historically, matrimony and
childbearing have been associated with women having to interrupt their
employment or significantly slow their career progress. While many of
this book's authors have advocated that women managers' progress
would be bolstered if the traditional male model of management were
discarded, this pattern intimates that women should "discard" the male
instead—a rather disturbing suggestion for many women.

GLOBAL CHALLENGES

In "A Global Comparison of Women in Management: Women Managers in Their Homelands and as Expatriates," authors Berthoin Antal and
Izraeli draw our attention to the many common challenges and problems
women are facing internationally. One problem encountered by women
managers worldwide is that they are not advancing at the same rate as men.
An explanation often cited and considered by these authors as a cause for
women's limited upward mobility is that the image of a successful manager
incorporates characteristics typically associated with men—that is, masculine characteristics—rather than with women—that is, feminine attributes. Yet, the authors cast doubt on this explanation by pointing out that
countries that value feminine characteristics do not have significantly
higher percentages of women managers than countries that do not value
these characteristics. The implication here is that changes in the characteristics associated with a successful manager are not likely to nec

essarily result in a significant increase in the number of managerial women globally. Rather, *concerted* efforts must be made by government, organizations, and individuals to reduce sex discrimination and attract, promote, and retain more female managers.

It also becomes poignantly clear in Chapter 3 that, although Europe, Israel, and the United States demonstrate inequities in their treatment of employed women, Europe and Israel surpass the United States in protecting parental rights in the workplace. This discrepancy has been discussed by scholars, politicians, and the media, but until recently little had been done to change it. And, as Lee observes in Chapter 9, legislation that would help the United States eventually establish more progressive parental rights protection had been consistently vetoed by former President Bush. How can progress be facilitated? Perhaps, as Lee suggests, Americans will have to "vote with their feet," lending their support only to candidates who are strong supporters of parental rights in the workplace. The results of the 1992 presidential election suggests that this may have occured. Bill Clinton, President of the United States, signed a parental rights bill (the Family and Medical Leave Act) into law in his first month on the job.

Berthoin Antal and Izraeli's chapter suggests that one way for women managers worldwide to transcend the barriers that exist within the corporate world is for them to start and manage their own firms. Northcraft and Gutek in Chapter 8 also lend support to this recommendation. Yet, operating a business presents another set of problems—financial risks, long hours, and complex responsibilities. Nonetheless, despite these limitations, business ownership offers women greater independence and flexibility in scheduling work hours and accommodating family needs. The fact that more female entrepreneurs are married than are female managers, as revealed in Chapter 7 by authors Parasuraman and Greenhaus, supports this argument. Furthermore, by accepting the challenge of business ownership, female managers can become organizational leaders and avoid the traditional corporate obstacles that prevent women from obtaining leadership positions. If women-headed firms were structured around norms conducive to women's life priorities, it would not be unreasonable to expect that they would eventually become a dominant force within the global business community as qualified women (and perhaps men) would be attracted to these organizations.

Of course, securing the financial resources needed to start one's own business is difficult for most entrepreneurs and even more so for women who, as a group, earn relatively low wages and have had difficulty securing loans (Hisrich & Brush, 1985; U.S. Department of Labor,

1992). Fortunately, a modicum of recent U.S. government support for female entrepreneurship suggests that this may be changing. The Women's Business Ownership Act of 1988 furnishes financial assistance to private organizations that provide financial, managerial, marketing, and technical assistance to women business owners. The U.S. Small Business Administration sponsors a program that fosters long-term mentoring relationships between successful and fledgling women-owned businesses (U.S. Department of Labor, 1989a, 1989b). Obviously, not all women will possess the desire or ability to become entrepreneurs; most will remain in the labor force working for others. Therefore entrepreneurship can never be the complete solution to the problems faced by women managers in corporations. Organizations need to have policies and programs that address issues such as sex discrimination and family-career conflicts that are faced by women managers.

Sex segregation of the labor force (i.e., women and men clustered in different occupations) is another more subtle form of sex discrimination that needs to be confronted by organizations. Many of the authors in this volume have suggested that women's problems in the workplace stem from this type of segregation. In the Berthoin Antal and Izraeli chapter, a discussion of a very unusual form of sex segregation—foreign job assignment—is presented. The authors reveal that men are selected more often than women for overseas assignments. The ramifications of this discriminatory treatment can be monumental as the authors remind us that international experience is often a prerequisite for promotion to managerial positions. Moreover, Berthoin Antal and Izraeli also indicate that discrimination against women for international assignments is not generally based upon a poor performance record—in fact, women do quite well in foreign positions. Rather, women are passed over for foreign assignments because management *fears* that they will not be accepted by members of the host country.

Ironically, many female employees reveal that the greatest discrimination they face in international assignments is from their American male peers. Thus it cannot be assumed that individuals in host countries will discriminate against expatriate women as these women are viewed as having three identities—as a manager, a foreigner, and a woman. Further, it is not unusual that a woman's status as a foreigner and manager will be more salient than her status as a woman. This status conflict is quite vividly illustrated by the experiences of Pat Burns, a director of a public relations organization who was sent to the Sudan in North Africa (Solomon, 1989). While in the Sudan, she was invited for meal at a businessman's home where, in violation of cultural norms Solomon, 1989, p. C9), he "brought her a cushion, served her food and vashed her arms with rose water"—treatment reserved only for men. Burns questioned the businessman's disregard for Sudan's social order. Oh it's no problem," she recalls being told. "Women do not do business; therefore, you are not a women" (Solomon, 1989, p. C9). In a ootnote to Chapter 3, Izraeli describes her own experience with "con-icting identities" which are quite intriguing.

Do American women managers receive more equitable treatment when they work abroad? If the answer is yes, then perhaps American women should pursue employment outside of the United States so that aey will have the "privilege" of being treated as foreigners instead of s American women! Alternatively (and less facetiously), individuals nd organizations should vigilantly seek out and actively address un-ounded prejudices that hamper the selection of women for interna-onal as well as local assignments.

RACE, PREJUDICE, AND MULTICULTURALISM

In Chapter 4, Bell, Denton, and Nkomo draw our attention to the pecial challenges and problems faced by women of color in manage-ient. One issue addressed by these authors is the prejudice that exists a the academic community toward this topic. Research and discussions f women managers typically analyze the experiences of white women aanagers or white men managers, yet findings are generalized to all omen managers. Of course, this is not just a trend that is evidenced xclusively with respect to research on women managers, it is also a ias that occurs in investigations of male managers (generalizing the xperiences of white male managers to all male managers). In this hapter, Bell et al. pay particular attention to the different perspectives nd unique cultural dilemmas faced by women of color in management ho must function in societies where white males maintain economic ontrol and hold a disproportionately large amount of power.

The unique problems of women of color in management are explored a Ella Bell's theory of multiculturalism. According to Bell, as a result of eing black and female, black women must manage two cultures that can nd often do conflict with the majority group's culture, that is, the culture f white males. Although it may be very difficult, often a choice between ae's "dual cultural identities" must be made. A notable example of this

balancing of cultures and its associated outcomes is illustrated by th
case of Derrick Bell, a black male professor, who, according to Ell
Bell's theory, must balance being black in a white culture. Derrick Be
was one of three black male professors at Harvard Law School who too
an announced, unpaid leave of absence to protest the school's failure to fi
its faculty ranks with women of color. Bell informed Harvard that he woul
resume his appointment when the faculty was more culturally diverse
Bell currently has a position at New York University's School of Law

Derrick Bell was forced to pay a high price to resolve the conflict h
faced. His consciousness as a black person deprived him of one of th
major benefits that his outstanding achievements merited—a positio
at Harvard. It also deprived Harvard law students of access to a highl
principled member of the faculty who is black. In the long run, howeve
if Bell's protest is heeded by Harvard, the school's law students will b
taught by many individuals of color. Even more, because Harvar
serves as a beacon to many colleges and universities, such actions coul
positively influence not only Harvard but other institutions of highe
education to increase the number of women of color on their facultie
At this writing, it appears that Derrick Bell's protest has been somewh;
successful in the area of consciousness-raising. Harvard's recent an
nouncement of new hires "broke with tradition." It not only listed th
number of new women who would be joining their faculty in 1992 b
the total number of women on the faculty at Harvard Law School as we
("Name Dropping," 1992). The press release failed to mention Dr. Bell'
protest, however, which may have inspired Harvard's calculations.

The authors also present the argument that women of color shoul
not be treated as a "monolithic group." Bell et al. suggest that we shoul
either focus on the differences of all peoples, not just limiting ourselve
to the socially constructed racial categories, or, we should focus on th
similarities of all peoples. While the authors' focus in this chapter wa
on women of color, this axiom should also apply, although it rarely doe
to Caucasian women (and men) who possess distinctly different lan
guages, cultures, and religious beliefs. Caucasian women are typicall
seen and referred to as a monolithic group, creating the impression tha
white women are a stronger, more unified group than they actually are

The authors observe that race relations inside organizations are
reflection of race relations outside organizations. While this may b
valid, it could also be argued that individuals who work in culturall
diverse organizations are more likely to involuntarily interact wit
persons of different races, ethnicities, and backgrounds inside rath

than outside organizations. Further, because corporations appoint individuals to positions that require contact with employees whose racial and ethnic backgrounds are diverse, these mandatory interactions can have both positive and negative outcomes. As Gutek warns in Chapter 8, interactions with women and/or ethnic minorities, if negative, can be used to reinforce negative stereotypes and justify discriminatory behavior toward the entire group. Alternatively, Northcraft argues (in Chapter 8) that this proximity and interdependence of persons of different races/sexes will breed familiarity and encourage less prejudiced behavior. Only the continuing trend toward increased employee diversity, which both Gutek and Northcraft argue in favor of, and the passage of time will reveal whether the outcomes predicted by Gutek or Northcraft are supported.

How do white males affect the actions and reactions of female managers of color? This is another interesting question raised by Bell, Denton, and Nkomo. These authors note that the experiences of black women managers are context dependent; conclusions cannot be made about these women without acknowledging that white males have an impact upon them. A study that examines the relationships, actions, and perceptions of black female managers with and without white males (and/or white females and other men and women of color) in their corporate environment should be undertaken. Based upon research by Ely (1990), in which the impact of men on the relationships of white professional women at work were examined, we would predict that corporate life for black women managers would be improved without the presence of white males. More specifically, Ely found that the greater the number of senior-level men in a firm, the more disruptive were the relationships among the women; the more senior-level women there were in the organization, the more positive were women's relationships.

HEALTH MATTERS

Not only do men influence women's relationships with each other, they also have a major impact on the research conducted on their health matters. In Chapter 5, Offermann and Armitage present an impressive compilation and analysis of the health issues affecting women managers. But caution must be exercised when reading their chapter due to an insidious prejudice harbored by medical science. More specifically, male-subject health research findings are typically generalized to the female population (LaFolette, 1990). Further, women are not consistently included as subjects in federally sponsored biomedical research (LaFolette, 1990). The NIH Advisory Committee on Women's Health Issues reported in 1987 that women's health matters constituted only 13% of the total NIH budget (Schroeder, 1990). This has occurred despite the fact that, in 1986, guidelines were adopted (although not implemented until 1989) to encourage women's inclusion in medical investigations (LaFolette, 1990). Moreover, scientific investigators are not mandated to analyze their data by sex (LaFolette, 1990). Such omissions occur even with respect to medical issues that are specific to women or are more prominent among women than men. For example, male subjects have been used exclusively in NIH-supported research on conditions such as breast cancer in women (study conducted at Rockefeller University) and as preliminary subjects in baseline analyses of tissue structures common to men and women in studies investigating cancer of the uterine lining (Jaschik, 1990; LaFolette, 1990; Snowe, 1990). In response to these outlandish studies, Senator Olympia Snowe, in her testimony at the congressional subcommittee hearing on women's health research, declared, "Somehow I find it hard to believe that the male-dominated medical community would tolerate a study of prostate cancer that used only women as research subjects." This reliance on male subjects in medical research on women's health issues, and the paucity of support for research on women's health overall, clearly restricted the type and number of ailments that could be discussed by Offermann and Armitage. But, even more, it may culminate in physicians' disregard for or misdiagnosis of uniquely female health ailments, a practice that could ultimately cost many women their lives. Not only would this be inhumane, it would prove costly to organizations and society at large. Will this relative neglect of women's health change? A bill that would have earmarked significantly more funds for women's health issues was passed by Congress but was vetoed by former President Bush, and Congress failed to override his veto. However, President Clinton appears to be more sensitive to and supportive of women's health issues. Hopefully, this will result in more attention to and support for women's health.

Offermann and Armitage point out that stress is one of the fastest growing threats to the health and well-being of women managers. We were spared an exceedingly long and discouraging discussion of *all* stress-produced ailments engendered by women managers' work environments in this chapter. Instead, the authors focused on sources of stress unique to women managers. Their discussion of these sources

:veals that increased stress and associated ailments may be part of the ievitable cost of women's upward mobility.

The authors discuss the stress-related impact that sex discrimination, :xual harassment, and tokenism have on the health of women in lanagement positions. Yet, a more elusive and indirect cause of women lanagers' stress occurs when women seek legal remedies for discrim- latory treatment or sexual harassment. In many cases, litigation is a)sing proposition for women managers that creates even more stress. 1 Chapter 9, Lee paints a somewhat discouraging picture for female lanagers attempting to exercise their legal rights.

Offermann and Armitage (in Chapter 5) and Parasuraman and 'reenhaus (in Chapter 7) highlight the difficulty women encounter in ttempting to balance their careers with their family lives. Offermann nd Armitage also cite the various health outcomes that stem from this)urce of stress. The reluctance of organizations and government to evise significant and meaningful programs to lessen women's stressful ome and career conflicts are discussed and the authors are comprehen- ve in their enumeration of programs and policies that would help 'omen managers balance career and family concerns. Yet, while the uthors' suggestions may strike some readers as either costly or exten- ve, they need not be. Research suggests that simply providing women ith more satisfying jobs (despite the lack of day care, flextime pro- rams, and so on) has a positive spillover effect into the home (Barnett . Marshall, 1992). Further, child-care programs such as on site day are, day-care referral services, flexible leaves, child-care discounts, ıbsidies, and tax savings have positive outcomes for employers who, s a result of these efforts, experience lower absenteeism and turnover ıd higher employee satisfaction and morale (Burud, Aschbaker, & IcCroskey, 1984; Dawson, Mikel, Lorenz, & King, 1984; Magid, 983; Perry, 1979).

It becomes clear from reading Chapter 5 that the health status and ıreer success of women managers involves an irony. Research has iown that, the more "masculine" characteristics possessed by women, ıe more likely the women are to be perceived as successful managers ıd located in powerful corporate positions (Brenner, Tomkiewicz, & chein, 1989; Fagenson, 1990; Heilman, Block, Martell, & Simon, 989). In line with these findings, books have been written and training rograms designed to help women managers emphasize these traits Iarragan, 1977; Molloy, 1977; Sargent, 1983; Smith et al., 1984). Yet, ıe orientations that women have been socialized to possess, such as

seeking help when in need and being able to express both troubling an
positive emotions, have been found to be buffers of stress. Thus, whi
it may be important for women managers to be "masculine" to succee
in the corporate environment, women also need the health protectio
that their typically devalued "feminine" characteristics provide, esp
cially given the gender-unique sources of stress they will experience
successful "masculine" women managers.

ROMANTIC ALLIANCES

In Chapter 6, "Dangerous Liaisons? A Review of Current Issu
Concerning Male and Female Romantic Relationships in the Wor
place," Mainiero discusses problems that arise when the proverbi
"girl meets boy" scenario occurs in organizational settings. Mainie
reveals that involvement in an office romance is not necessarily
dangerous liaison as the parties involved do not typically experien
adverse career consequences. The position of the individual who is t
object of a woman's romantic interests does, however, appear to affe
how she is perceived and treated by her coworkers. Women involved
relationships with senior-level managers are viewed more negative
than women involved with their peers. These women are perceived
be unfairly advantaged and privy to inside information and promotion
It is both interesting and ironic that the concerns expressed about t
advantages women may accrue from romantic liaisons with powerf
men are similar to those that have been voiced about men's relationshi
in "old boy networks."

Are similar career advantages and disadvantages experienced
women managers who are permanently romantically involved—that
married—to men in their profession? While this topic was not address
in Mainiero's chapter, it is an interesting area for speculation. A husba
and wife who are both managers have much to gain from their relatio
ship. They can learn skills from each other, expand their individu
networks, share knowledge, create opportunities for one another, u
their partner as a resource, and benefit from one another's recogniti
and achievements. Yet, the management literature portrays women as
homogeneous group whose marital relationships with men are not releva
to their career progress. Researchers need to investigate whether marryi
within one's profession advantages some women (or men) over othe

For example, do these women receive higher salaries, promotions, and recognition and have more power and greater opportunities than women of similar backgrounds who are either single, lesbian, or married but not to men in their field? If differences are found between these groups of women, the issue needs to be discussed even though it may be divisive.

Of course, managerial women married to managerial men may also experience negative outcomes. Not being taken seriously or receiving appropriate credit for one's work are major consequences. An historical, though little known example of this treatment involved Mileva Einstein, Albert Einstein's first wife, who, like Albert Einstein, was also a mathematician and scientist (Booth, 1990). Evan Harris Walker, a leading authority on Albert Einstein's work, contends that, at a minimum, Mileva Einstein was a collaborator, if not a great deal more, in the development of Albert Einstein's theories of space and time (Booth, 1990). Scientists and historians have not acknowledged Mileva Einstein's contributions, however—not even a footnote (Booth, 1990).

Romantic liaisons (whether marital or not) with powerful men within a company or occupational field can deprive women of the corporate visibility and recognition that their own contributions merit. But these relationships can also provide them with opportunities for growth, development, and career advancement. This raises the question: Do women romantically or sexually pursue powerful men within the office as a means to advance their careers? Mainiero's chapter provides no evidence to support this conjecture and Gutek (1985) reports that, although women are perceived to be the carriers of sexuality, they do not use their sexuality to attain promotions. Thus the often voiced contention that women are progressing into the board room by way of the bedroom is not supported by research. In fact, sexual experiences in the work setting often result in negative work-related outcomes for females, while similar encounters for men have virtually no effect on their careers. Moreover, men will often experience positive social consequences, such as an image of virility or an enhanced self-concept, the more sexually promiscuous they are (Gutek, 1985). While, however, there seems to be no significant use of sexuality by either men or women to gain work- or career-related advantages over other employees, men appear to use sexuality in the workplace more than women (Gutek, 1985). This is done for social gratification rather than for career enhancement purposes (Gutek, 1985).

CAREER VERSUS FAMILY

"Childseat in the back, carphone in the front," describes the personal lives of many women managers today (Castro, 1989, p. 72). In Chapter 7, Parasuraman and Greenhaus profile what life is like for women managers. It is clear from this chapter that many women managers are having difficulty managing their families and their careers. The problem largely emanates from careers being designed around men's life stages and men's orientations, that is, their priorities, interests, and goals. While male managers marry and have children at significantly higher rates than women managers, women are often faced with a choice between career, marriage, and children. Women also do not enjoy the level of spousal support at home that is experienced by men. While few organizations appear to be concerned about this inequity, it is important to note the steps taken by the few executives who are trying to bring attention to these issues. For example, one male executive asks his managers to consider the following questions (Skrzycki, 1990):

- Would you feel you had not met your affirmative action goals if almost all top women were childless and top men were parents?
- Have you analyzed your management ranks to determine, of those with children, what portion of male managers have nonemployed spouses?

These questions can provoke thought, draw attention to gender-based workplace inequities, and perhaps lead to policies that make a difference. While acknowledging, however, that an increasing number of organizations are trying to establish programs that will help women (and men) to balance their career and family responsibilities, Parasuraman and Greenhaus note that very few individuals in organizations and society are asking these types of questions. Indeed, very few organizations are proactively addressing this issue at all; only approximately 2% are providing on-site child care, for example (Fagenson & Jackson, in press). Furthermore, many U.S. businesses lobbied against parental/family leave regulations and supported former President Bush's veto of such legislation. In contrast, President Clinton signed the Family and Medical Leave Act, 1993.

Parasuraman and Greenhaus also bring our attention to the benefits experienced by the spouses and children of women managers. This is indeed a refreshing perspective, given the media's inordinate amount of attention and tendency to focus primarily on the negative impact working women have on their families' lives. For example, problems attributed to mothers working outside the home include children in unhealthy, poorly run day-care centers, the loneliness and delinquency of latchkey children, and troubled, disintegrating marriages (Faludi, 1991).

Northcraft and Gutek discuss career and family conflicts faced by female managers in Chapter 8, as part of the continuing debate over whether discrimination against women managers will ever disappear. Gutek notes the difficulty women encounter when trying to balance their career and family priorities in a male-dominated environment and the discrimination that is often a consequence. This discrimination could not be more apparent than in the case of Zena Levine, a pregnant chief resident at Stanford University, who, in 1983, was informed by her superior that having a child (Cannon, 1991, p. A3) "was presumptuous and a disservice to one's self and certainly to one's professional colleagues."

Northcraft acknowledges that it is difficult for women to effectively balance their career and family responsibilities, but he expresses more optimism. He argues that it is not necessary for women to perform all home and job tasks to fulfill multiple responsibilities and goals. Rather, Northcraft points out the positive actions that are being taken, such as corporate "daddy tracks," greater father involvement in the home, and organizations that are providing more flexible, innovative work arrangements for both men and women. Gutek contends that, to date, these efforts are relatively small, while a more promising, growing trend is the number of women who are escaping corporate discrimination by running their own businesses (noted previously). While we recognize that not all women can or will be entrepreneurs, women who start their own ventures may have businesses with a competitive edge over traditional organizations. If they provide a woman-friendly work environment, they may have greater success attracting and retaining women managers than traditional organizations. Thus the competitiveness of these women-run businesses may offer an alternative, diminishing Gutek's concern that fully convincing traditional organizations to end sex discrimination and other sources of stress for women managers may be an insurmountable challenge.

DISCRIMINATION'S FUTURE

The essence of the Northcraft-Gutek debate on discrimination against women managers—will it ever end?—addresses the manner in which women are treated and how their behavior is different than that of men in management. In an invited address to the American Psychological Association in 1990, Carol Travis (1990, p. 33) spoke of three approaches to gender differences: (a) "women are the opposite of men and inferior"; (b) "women are the opposite of men and superior"; and (c) "women are just like men." She noted that these perspectives are inherently discriminatory because they accept men as the human norm with women "in orbit around" them. She warns that, when such a perspective is adopted, biased conclusions are automatically drawn. In business circles, the male norm of management is widely accepted and both Northcraft and Gutek acknowledge that stereotypes about the characteristics of successful managers favor men. This conclusion has also been reached with respect to leadership styles—with men's being considered superior to women's—until recently.

Researchers such as Dobbins and Platz (1986) indicate that gender has no significant influence on organizational leadership style in terms of initiating structure, consideration, and satisfied subordinates. More recent research and analysis, however, suggests that women tend to adopt a more democratic, participative, or transformational style of leadership while men are more likely to employ a more autocratic or directive approach (Eagly & Johnson, 1990; Rosener, 1990). Some scholars suggest that women's styles of leadership are more effective and perhaps should be the norm to which men are compared (Bass, 1991; Peters, 1990; Rosener, 1990). If this new approach is embraced and women's style is viewed as the norm, many men will lack the proper socialization necessary for being organizational leaders and may, applying Carol Travis's framework, be the targets of subtle discriminatory practices. It could be argued, however, that a more likely scenario may be that not only will women's style not be valued but instead women will be expected to be warm and nurturant and asked to resolve the problems of others, which will not be helpful to them personally or professionally.[2]

Marcell LaFolette (1990, p. A56), in her discussion of women in science, expresses an intriguing perspective that takes the position argued by Gutek one step further: "The problem is not so much in the presence of overt discrimination as in the lack of vigilance against it." A similar statement is appropriate in describing the situation of women managers. While there are numerous instances of overt discrimination against female managers, the more insidious problem lies in individuals' apathy and silent disapproval of such behaviors. This attitude is understandable in the workplace because it follows the path of least resistance and involves the least amount of personal risk. Yet, women and men who pursue this course of inactivity not only fail to lend support to individual advocates of and proposals for positive organizational change but are often perceived as condoning or accepting—and therefore reinforcing—sexist and discriminatory behaviors toward women.

Given such apathy and negative attitudes, we should not be surprised at the treatment of women managers in organizations where these dispositions or orientations are often compounded by deeply entrenched attitudes, resulting from prior conditioning to view women unfavorably. This negative conditioning toward females begins considerably before women enter the management ranks. For example, a review of the research on teachers' treatment of students by the American Association of University Women shows that teachers provide more and higher quality attention to boys than to girls (Sadker & Sadker, 1991). Boys receive very directed feedback and are asked more questions. In later life, this is likely to translate into boys having high career aspirations and a firm belief in their ability to realize these aspirations; girls, in contrast, might feel that they are "not smart enough" or "not good enough" to achieve their career goals. With such systemic discrimination, negativity, and inferiority encouraged in and toward girls (and observed by boys) from such early ages, can women managers ever hope to avoid gender discrimination and reverse its long-term negative effects?

Northcraft persuasively argues that increased contact between women managers and other organizational members may result in more positive feelings and less discrimination against women. Gutek argues that, if gender salience were reduced, discrimination would lessen and women would be seen as managers rather than as women managers. Gutek contends, however, that it is very difficult to make women managers' gender less salient because very few of them are in higher organizational ranks. Although Gutek pragmatically warns of potential problems associated with increased male-female interaction, Northcraft and Gutek both acknowledge that the mere presence of significant numbers of women in organizations can positively influence their behavior and treatment. Increasing contact with women by hiring and promoting more of them will reduce not only their visibility but, we hope, the level of discrimination against them and the need for legal remedies.

LEGAL REALITIES

In Chapter 9, Barbara Lee reveals various legal and political realities that women managers must face. Lee enumerates the numerous monetary, professional, and personal costs involved in legally confronting sex discrimination or harassment in the workplace. More specifically, Lee indicates that judges tend to favor the corporation, deferring to corporate judgment when a sex discrimination claim is filed by a woman; women lose discrimination cases more often than they win them; and cases typically involve years of litigation before a decision is reached. During this process, women incur substantial legal costs, and the legal action places a strain on women's personal relationships. When women do "win," they may receive some back pay and some punitive damages that are limited by a legal cap on the amount awardable. Moreover, women may be subjected to retaliation for the legal action taken if they are reinstated in their former jobs. Legal action may also halt a woman's career if she is labeled a troublemaker or, in the case of sexual harassment, if she is blamed for being victimized. Given the increased level of stress women managers face when they attempt to use the legal system, we cannot advocate strongly enough that women should seek work, if at all possible, in organizations that have impressive track records hiring and promoting women and avoid firms whose policies are weak with respect to the treatment of women and issues important to them.

Given the extreme difficulty female employees encounter when attempting to exercise their legal rights, one has to question for whom the laws are designed—the powerful or the powerless—a philosophical debate that is too complex and lengthy to be resolved in this chapter. As noted by Lee, however, the underlying message to organizations is quite clear: While discrimination is illegal, it has few serious legal consequences. What will prevent an organization from allowing its employees to engage in such behavior? Protective legislation and policies (i.e., for combat, working with hazardous materials, and so on) often have been offered as a means to protect women from harm.

Unfortunately, protective legislation has often been damaging to women workers, promoting discrimination against them. Based on the assumption that women are biologically different than men, these types of laws inhibit the ability of women to build careers that can culminate in interesting work, a sense of achievement, prestigious positions, a respectable salary, or power. Whether it is protecting women from hazardous materials or engaging in combat, the intentions may be worthwhile, but often the outcome is not. Instead of requesting that organizations accommodate differences between men and women, legislators have chosen to write protective laws that exclude women. For example, women in the military are allowed to provide combat support but are "protected" by being prohibited from directly engaging in combat. Yet, the primary route to many top military positions is gained through combat experience. Fortunately, much early protective legislation was repealed by the 1964 Civil Rights Act and subsequent administrative orders.

Lee does not express much hope for women managers in view of the recent conservative political climate and the "backlash" many women are experiencing in the courts. The passage of the 1991 Civil Rights Act, however, which supersedes many recent conservative court rulings, should help strengthen the cases of women who need to seek legal redress. Nonetheless, Lee concludes that, until the political climate clearly changes and establishes itself as one that is supportive of women, women should look beyond the legal and political systems for solutions.

FEMINIST MANAGEMENT

In the final chapter, by Martin, "Feminist Practice in Organizations: Implications for Management," an alternative view to traditional management theory and practice is presented. Martin refutes the untested axiom that women adopt a feminist approach to management when they achieve positions of managerial power. While there are numerous documented cases of women supporting one another, Martin warns the reader that the assumption that women (and not men) are feminists is unfounded, discriminatory, and could prove costly if women unquestioningly invest their futures in other women. Feminism is no more synonymous with the female gender than sexism is with the male gender.

Internal organizational change demands concurrent change in societal norms and behaviors. Stigmatizing men who take time from their careers to devote to their families is a practice that needs to change. Unpaid family work needs to be valued on the same scale as paid work, and all workers should realize the positive impact of women in the work force. The proliferation of female workers has resulted in significant improvements in family-oriented policies, practices, and programs that benefit everyone—women, men, and their families. In general, both men and women should recognize the need and accept the challenge to contribute equitably to their families and communities. If they do, they can share in the rewards of well-balanced lives in which they achieve their career and family goals.

Martin goes even further to question the criteria by which individuals are selected for jobs. Although it is considered an axiom that employee selection is based on rationality, objectivity, and merit, Martin argues that this is far from what actually occurs. Rather, women are hired to manage women; women are put into jobs separate from men; and men are hired for men's jobs and women for women's jobs. Until this type of practice ends and individuals are hired on the basis of merit, many very competent, deserving women managers will be passed over unless a "woman's position" is vacant.

The alternative management philosophy—feminist management—recommended by Martin may seem threatening to those who are currently in powerful positions in organizations because it represents a change in the status quo. Using this new philosophy as a guide, Martin suggests that all current norms, formal rules, and policies that exclude women should be challenged. Diversity—whether in gender, ethnic, sexual orientation, or "other"—would be acknowledged, accepted, and valued. People would be made aware of all the inequities that exist in organizations so that action could be taken to rectify them. The organizational hierarchy would be dismantled and a web of relationships that foster community feeling, democracy, participation, and empowerment would be adopted. Employees would be viewed as whole people with relationships that extended beyond corporate walls.

The critical, strategic question is how to convince organizations of the monetary and nonmonetary benefits of adopting this alternative system. Martin tackles this dilemma by suggesting that current management practices, which include lies, back stabbing, coverups, and blind self-interest, are not in the best interest of the organization, managers, or employees. Fair, equitable treatment of men and women improves the organization and society for all. Of course, Martin recognizes that organizations will not accept such an alternative if managers believe that it will negatively affect the bottom line.

Social responsibility need not be synonymous with red ink, however. As reported by Ballen (1992), many of the "most admired companies" in the United States are also the most socially responsible—internally and externally. In the long term, their intense commitment to philosophies such as the well-being of all their workers has produced family-friendly, low stress workplaces that have engendered increased trust from industry leaders, employees, customers, and suppliers and have paved the way for increased efficiency, productivity, sales, and profits.

CONCLUSIONS AND RECOMMENDATIONS

This chapter has highlighted several themes and problems faced by female managers, and it has refuted the popular view of women managers as a privileged, protected, or preferred group. While women are joining the managerial ranks in increasing numbers, few women within the United States or abroad are managing to reach middle-level management or above (U.S. Department of Labor, 1991). Women of color are faring even worse in the field of management as they are underrepresented, faced with both sexual and racial discrimination, and forced to deal with conflicts emanating from multiculturalism.

The problems of women managers are grounded in historical traditions, which include the socialization of women in the home, the devaluation of women's work, and the employment of women in traditionally undervalued female positions and occupations. Women managers also confront discriminatory organizational policies and job assignments as well as protective laws that have excluded women from the workplace and limited their access to positions of power. The legal process, which is designed to redress sexual/racial discrimination and harassment and alleviate stress is, ironically, and unfortunately, often both stressful and professionally devastating.

Women managers are not homogeneous, contend many of this book's authors, but our analyses typically ignore their differences. Not only is little attention paid to their different cultural, racial, and ethnic backgrounds, but their varying relationships with men are often ignored, an important area for future research. Yet, interestingly enough, despite these differences, women managers worldwide have many problems in common, with prejudice being prominent among them. This is very evident, and frighteningly so, among researchers who, for example, generalize research on white males to all people, generalize research on white females to women of color, and employ men as subjects in studies of women's health issues.

It also becomes clear from reading this book that women managers arouse fear, can be sacrificed, and are not valued as much as men. For example, organizations fear the reaction of host countries if a woman rather than a male manager is sent abroad. Men fear that women managers will advantage themselves by using their sexuality when competing for promotions. Women's health, equity in education, and chance to succeed in the corporate world based upon merit are not guaranteed. Reading between the lines of this book, we think it has become particularly clear that women in general are not considered as important as men, and this devaluation of women is carried over into the management sector. For example, competent women managers lose their jobs or are stalled in their careers simply because of their gender and/or refusal to be victimized. Most women managers do not have enough support to be mothers, wives, and powerful, successful career women, because society, organizations, and spouses are not willing to provide what it will take to make this a reality. Women and not men are typically asked to leave if a romantic relationship considered to be disruptive is suspected in the workplace. Our norms, assumptions, ideas, values, and approaches need to change if women managers are to have improved personal and professional lives. A "brave new corporate world" that is proactive on issues important to women managers must emerge.

What would this new world look like? In this book and final chapter, we have suggested several ways in which organizations, society, and individual men and women can improve the situation of women managers. These include the following elements:

- increased satisfaction in, recognition of, and valuing of women's paid and unpaid work
- increased valuing and pay for jobs held by women and an end to "women's job's/men's jobs"
- promotions/assignments based on individual merit and qualifications rather than personal associations
- proactive organizational policies and practices that disparage all discriminatory/harassing behavior and foster equal opportunity and support for all employees
- increased efforts to decrease organizational sources of stress and organizational support of family needs that affect the job
- legal reforms to more fairly and rapidly correct discriminatory practices and protect the rights of all parents in the workplace
- equitable redistribution of labor in the homes and communities of dual-earner and career families

- increased numbers of women entrepreneurs and greater assistance and support for women establishing their own businesses
- equitable treatment of males and females from childhood
- careers in organizations structured around both men's and women's life stages
- women's (in particular) employment in organizations that have women-friendly policies and practices
- greater attention to the differences among women managers
- increased numbers of women included in research involving women's health issues
- increased sensitivity to managers from racially, culturally, and ethnically diverse backgrounds
- an action orientation, with conscious, concerted efforts, challenges to, and vigilance against discriminatory treatment of women managers and women in general
- the shattering of the "glass ceiling" as more women join the ranks of top management
- increased studies of behaviors, interactions, and problems distinctly associated with managers who are women of color
- more research on the effect women managers' relationships with men have on their careers

While changes are occurring, they seem to be in small steps primarily because, as noted by many authors in this book, we continue to use the male model as the generic model. When we do this, women try to fit in and become "male" women. If, instead, we view women's personal lives as positive contributions, we change paradigms. As noted by Bell, Denton, and Nkomo, we are currently operating on a patriarchal axiom that people at work exist apart from other aspects of their lives. If we are to learn anything from history, we must realize that all too often women simply fit themselves into the jobs men have designated for them; too many women are not the determiners of their own fates. As Harvard University professor Claudia Goldin says, "Our best hope for the future are women who don't see the ceiling but the sky" (Fierman, 1990, p. 62). Self-empowerment—not blindly accepting the traditional model—appears to be the answer for women, whether they remain inside corporate America or strike out on their own entrepreneurial endeavors.

NOTES

1. From "Who wears the pants" exhibit at the American History Museum of the Smithsonian Institution.

2. Correspondence from Barbara Gutek.

REFERENCES

Ballen, K. (1992, February 10). America's most admired corporations. *Fortune*, pp. 40-72.

Barnett, R., & Marshall, N. (1992). Worker and mother role, spillover effects and psychological distress. *Women's Health, 18*, 9-40.

Bass, B. (1990, January-February). Debate. *Harvard Business Review*, p. 151.

Booth, W. (1990, March 8). The relative theory of Albert Einstein: Was the genius's first wife the real brains in the family? *The Washington Post*, p. C1.

Brenner, O., Tomkiewicz, J., & Schein, V. (1989). The relationship between sex role stereotypes and requisite management characteristics revisited. *Academy of Management Journal, 32*, 662-669.

Burud, S. L., Aschbaker, P. R., & McCroskey, J. (1984). *Employer-supported child care: Investing in human resources*. Boston: Auburn House.

Cannon, L. (1991, June 23). Surgeon's sexism charge hits nerve in profession. *The Washington Post*, p. A3.

Castro, J. (1989, March 27). Rolling along the mommy track. *Time*, p. 72.

The corporate woman officer. (1986). Chicago: Heidrick and Struggles.

Dawson, A. G., Mikel, C. S., Lorenz, C. S., & King, J. (1984). *An experimental study of the effects of employer-sponsored child care services on selected employee behaviors.* Chicago: CRS, Inc.

Dobbins, G. H., & Platz, S. J. (1986). Sex differences in leadership: How real are they? *Academy of Management Review, 11*, 118-127.

Eagly, A. H., & Johnson, B. T. (1990). Gender and leadership style: A meta-analysis. *Psychological Bulletin, 108*, 233-256.

Ely, R. (1990). *The role of men in relationships among professional women at work.* Paper presented at the Academy of Management Conference, Miami.

Fagenson, E. A. (1990). Perceived masculine and feminine attributes examined as a function of individuals' sex and level in the organizational power hierarchy: A test of four theoretical perspectives. *Journal of Applied Psychology, 75*, 204-211.

Fagenson, E. A., & Jackson, J. J. (in press). The status of women managers in the United States. In N. Adler & D. Izraeli (Eds.), *Competitive frontiers: Women managers in a global economy*. Boston: Basil Blackwell.

Faludi, S. (1991). *Backlash: The undeclared war against American women*. New York: Crown.

Fierman, J. (1990, July 30). Why women still don't hit the top. *Fortune*, pp. 40-62.

Gutek, B. (1985). *Sex in the workplace: Impact of sexual behavior and harassment on women, men and organizations*. San Francisco: Jossey-Bass.

Harragan, B. (1977). *Games mother never taught you: Corporate gamesmanship for women*. New York: Warner.

Heilman, M., Block, C., Martell, R., & Simon, M. (1989). Has anything changed? Current characterizations of men, women and managers. *Journal of Applied Psychology, 74,* 935-942.

Henderson, B. (1987). *Rotten reviews: A literary comparison.* New York: Penguin.

Hisrich, R., & Brush, C. (1985). *The woman entrepreneur: Starting, financing, and managing a successful new business.* Lexington, MA: Lexington.

Jaschik, S. (1990, June 27). Report says NIH ignores own rules on including women in its research. *The Chronicle of Higher Education, 37,* A27.

LaFolette, M. (1990, October 3). Point of view. *The Chronicle of Higher Education, 37,* A56.

Magid, R. (1983). *Child care initiatives for working parents: Why employers get involved.* New York: American Management Association.

Molloy, J. T. (1977). *The woman's dress for success book.* New York: Warner.

Name dropping. (1992, April 15). *The Chronicle of Higher Education, 39,* A49.

Perry, K. (1979). Survey and analysis of employer-sponsored day care in the United States. (Doctoral dissertation, University of Wisconsin-Milwaukee, 1978). *Dissertation Abstracts International, 39,* 5305A.

Peters, T. (1990, September). The best new managers will listen, motivate, support. Isn't that just like a woman? *Working Woman,* pp. 142-217.

Rosener, J. (1990, November-December). Ways women lead. *Harvard Business Review,* pp. 119-125.

Sadker, M., & Sadker, D. (1991). *Shortchanging girls, shortchanging America: Summary.* Washington, DC: American Association of University Women.

Sargent, A. (1983). *The androgynous manager.* New York: AMACOM.

Schroeder, P. (1990, June 18). [Testimony of Representative Patricia Schroeder, Subcommittee on Health and the Environment, Hearings on National Institutes of Health reauthorization]. Washington, DC: Congressional Caucus for Women's Issues.

Skrzycki, C. (1990, March 25). Stand up for affirmative action. *The Washington Post,* p. H3.

Smith, M., Wood, E., Langrish, S., Smith, K., Davidson, L., & Mogridge, C. (1984). *A development program for women in management.* Brookfield, VT: Gower.

Snowe, O. (1990, June 18). [Testimony on women's health research, Subcommittee on Health and the Environment]. Washington, DC: Congressional Caucus for Women's Issues.

Solomon, J. (1989, June 6). Women, minorities and foreign postings. *The Wall Street Journal,* p. C9.

Travis, C. (1990, October). Mismeasure of woman: Paradoxes and perspectives in the study of gender. *APA Monitor,* p. 33.

U.S. Department of Labor. (1989a, December). *Women business owners: Facts on working women* (No. 89-5). Washington, DC: Government Printing Office.

U.S. Department of Labor. (1989b, December). *Women in management: Facts on working women* (No. 89-4). Washington, DC: Government Printing Office.

U.S. Department of Labor. (1991). *A report on the glass ceiling initiative.* Washington, DC: Government Printing Office.

U.S. Department of Labor. (1992). *Employment and earnings.* Washington, DC: Government Printing Office.

Waelde, D. E. (1990). *How to get a federal job.* Washington, DC: Fedhelp Publications.

Index

About the Authors

Sara Alpern received her Ph.D. from the University of Maryland at College Park. Associate Professor of History, she teaches the history of American women at Texas A&M University. Her book, *Freda Kirchwey: A Woman of The Nation* (Harvard University Press, 1987), is a biography of Kirchwey (1893-1976), editor, owner, and publisher of the political journal *The Nation*. She is also a contributor and coeditor of *The Challenge of Feminist Biography: Writing the Lives of Modern American Women* (University of Illinois Press, 1992). She has written on a number of topics in women's history including the effects of woman suffrage, the history of eating disorders among women, and women in banking. She is currently at work on a book-length manuscript on the history of women in business.

Michele A. Armitage is a doctoral student of Industrial/Organizational Psychology at George Washington University. She is a researcher for the Center for Management Excellence in the Department of Health and Human Services, Office of the Assistant Secretary for Personnel. She is currently evaluating a Federal Management Internship program designed to fast-track high potential employees to senior management positions. Her research interests include leadership and management, career development, stress and interventions, and gender and minority issues.

Ella L. Bell is Visiting Associate Professor at the Sloan School of Management at the Massachusetts Institute of Technology. Her research investigates the bicultural life structure of black professional women. During the last 12 years, she has been an organizational consultant to both industry and public sector organizations with a special focus on management of race, gender, and culture in organizational life. She has been an American Sociological Association Fellow and was selected Outstanding Educator in Connecticut by the Coalition of 100 Black Women. She is a current board member of the Organizational Behavior Teaching Society. She recently edited a special edition of the *Journal of Organizational Behavior* focusing on the "Career and Life Process of Black Professionals" (1990), in which her article "The Bicultural Life Experience of Career Oriented Black Women" appeared.

Ariane Berthoin Antal is Director of the International Institute for Organizational Change (IOC-Ashridge) in Archamps, France. She obtained an M.A. in international relations from Boston University and a Ph.D in sociology from the Technical University in Berlin. Before joining IOC, she was Senior Fellow at the Wissenschaftszentrum Berlin für Sozialforschung. Her research and consulting are international and focus on innovation in organizations and promoting individual and organizational learning. Her publications include *Comparative Policy Research: Learning from Experience* (edited with M. Dierkes and H. Weiler; Gower), *Making Ends Meet: Corporate Responses to Youth Unemployment in Britain and Germany* (Pinter and the Anglo-German Foundation), and *Corporate Social Performance: Rediscovering Actors in Their Organizational Contexts* (Campus Verlag and Westview). In addition, she has published many articles in English and German on women in management, organizational culture, and social innovation processes. She is Consultative Member of the Board of the European Women's Management Development Network (EWMD), of which she was previously president.

Toni C. Denton is Assistant Professor in the Career and Interdisciplinary Studies Department at SUNY-Binghamton in Binghamton, New York. Her background includes an M.A. in counseling and several years as a family, marriage, and individual therapist. She currently consults with a number of organizations to facilitate their support of diversity through understanding race and gender dynamics. Her research explores patterns of social support and bonding relationships among professional women. Her dissertation, *Bonding Relationships Among Black Professional Women: Rituals of Restoration,* resulted in an article published in a special edition of the *Journal of Organizational Behavior* (1990). She currently serves as a board member for the Organizational Behavior Teaching Society and the Institute for Women and Organizations.

Mary Anne Devanna is Adjunct Professor and Associate Dean of Executive Education at Columbia Business School. She is coauthor of *The Transformational Leader* and coeditor of *The Portable MBA* and of *Strategic Human Resource Management.* She has done extensive research on human resource management and women managers in American corporations. She is currently a Senior Consultant for "Workout," a major change effort at General Electric. Earlier in her career, she was director of advertising at Longines.

Ellen A. Fagenson is Assistant Professor of Management at George Mason University. She received her Ph.D. from Princeton University and was a Post Doctoral Fellow at Columbia University. She has published several articles in the *Journal of Applied Psychology, Journal of Applied Behavioral Science, Journal of Organizational Behavior, Journal of Vocational Behavior, Journal of Business Venturing, Journal of Business Ethics, Group and Organization Studies, Entrepreneurship: Theory and Practice*, among others. Her research has been covered in the news media by *The New York Times, USA Today*, the Associated Press and United Press International. Her research interests and consulting activities are in the areas of organization development, mentoring, power, women managers, and entrepreneurs. She serves as a reviewer for several journals in the fields of management and psychology and is on the Editorial Review Board of *The Executive.* She is the former Chair of the Women in Management Division of the Academy of Management.

Jennie Farley, Professor of Industrial and Labor Relations at Cornell University, has written two and edited three books on women workers, among them *The Woman in Management* and *Women Workers in Fifteen Countries* and contributed a chapter on American women professors to *Storming the Tower: Women in the Academic World* (London: Kogan Page, 1991).

Jeffrey H. Greenhaus, Professor of Management at Drexel University, received his Ph.D. in industrial-organizational psychology from New York University. He is a member of the Academy of Management and the American Psychological Society and has served on the editorial review boards of the *Journal of Vocational Behavior, Journal of Applied Psychology, Lifestyle: Family and the Economy,* and *International Journal of Career Management.* Author of *Career Management* (Dryden, 1987), his current research interests include career management and decision making, the career experiences of women and minorities, and career-family linkages.

Barbara A. Gutek is Professor, Department of Management and Policy, University of Arizona. She has written or edited seven books and numerous articles on women and work and served as Chair of the Women in Management Division, Academy of Management, 1990-1991. Other research interests are the impacts of computers and contacts at work.

Heidi Hartmann is currently director of the Washington-based Institute for Women's Policy Research, a scientific research organization on policy issues of importance to women. She has co-authored several reports at IWPR including *Unnecessary Losses: Costs to Americans of the Lack of Family and Medical Leave, Increasing Working Mothers' Earnings,* and *A Chart Book on Part-Time and Temporary Employment.* She has delivered Congressional testimony and participated in briefings on numerous issues including comparable worth, family and medical leave, child care, and health care policy. She also lectures on public policy, feminist theory, and the political economy of gender to women's organizations, labor unions, community and business groups, and at universities.

Dafna N. Izraeli is Professor, Department of Sociology and Anthropology at Bar-Ilan University. She is author or editor of six books and numerous articles on women in Israel and in cross-cultural perspectives. Her most recent volumes include *Dual Earner Families: International Perspectives* (with S. Lewis and H. Hootsmans, Sage, 1992), *Women in Israel* (with Y. Azmon, Transaction Press, 1993), and *Competitive Frontiers: Women Managers in the Global Economy* (with N. J. Adler, Basil Blackwell, in press). Her current research focus is on public policy, work, and gender in Israel.

Janice J. Jackson is Chairperson of the Management and Marketing Department at Virginia State University. Beginning her teaching career working with emotionally disturbed preschoolers, she taught English and mathematics at the elementary, junior high, and senior high school levels before entering academia. She has taught graduate and undergraduate courses. Her research interests and publications have focused on managerial communication, women in management, minorities in business, and equity issues.

Barbara A. Lee is Associate Professor at the Institute of Management and Labor Relations, Rutgers University. She directs the master's program in human resource management and teaches courses in employment law and labor law. She has published in the areas of sex and disability discrimination, faculty personnel processes, and has published a book, *Academics in Court* (with George LaNoue) that analyzes several sex discrimination lawsuits by women faculty members. She is currently completing the third edition (with William Kaplin) of *The Law of Higher Education.*

Lisa A. Mainiero (Ph.D.) is currently Associate Professor of Management at the School of Business, Fairfield University. Her research interests include the careers of executive women, power and political strategies, office romance, career development for technical professionals, and designing corporate career development programs. She has published in journals such as *Administrative Science Quarterly, the Academy of Management Review, Journal of Management, Personnel, Personnel Journal,* and the *Training and Development Journal.* She also is the coauthor (with Cheryl L. Tromley) of *Developing Managerial Skills: Readings, Cases and Exercises in Organizational Behavior* (Prentice-Hall, 1989). She received an A.B. degree in psychology from Smith College, an M.A. and M. Phil. in administrative sciences from Yale University, and a Ph.D. in organizational behavior from Yale University.

Patricia Yancey Martin is Daisy Parker Flory Alumni Professor, Department of Sociology, Florida State University, Tallahassee. She specializes in gender and organizations. She has contributed to recent publications on feminist organizations, feminism and organizational politics, fraternities and rape, and gender inequality and interaction at